CONSUMER PRODUCT SAFETY

Dedication

With love to Elizabeth, Laura and Bethan

Consumer Product Safety

GERAINT HOWELLS

Ashgate

DARTMOUTH

Aldershot • Brookfield USA • Singapore • Sydney

Published by
Dartmouth Publishing Company Limited
Ashgate Publishing Limited
Gower House
Croft Road
Aldershot
Hants GU11 3HR
England

Ashgate Publishing Company
Old Post Road
Brookfield
Vermont 05036
USA

British Library Cataloguing in Publication Data
Howells, Geraint G.
    Consumer product safety
    1.Product safety - Law and legislation - Great Britain
    I.Title
    344.4'1'047

Library of Congress Cataloging-in-Publication Data
Howells, Geraint G.
    Consumer product safety / Geraint Howells.
        p.   cm.
    ISBN 1-85521-474-1 (hardbound).
    1. Product safety–Law and legislation. I. Title.
    K3663.H69   1998
    344'.042–dc21   98-20165
                                                                         CIP

ISBN 1 85521 474 1

Printed and bound in Great Britain by Nuffield Press Ltd., 21 Nuffield Way, Abingdon, Oxon OX14 1RL

Contents

Preface   *vii*

1. Consumer Product Safety Regulation   1
   Introduction   1
   Data Collection   13
   Pre–Market Controls   15
   Post–Market Controls   46
   Export Controls   54

2. Product Safety – The European Dimension   61
   Why is Product Safety a Matter of Concern to Europe?   61
   Technical Barriers to Trade   62
   Technical Standards Directive   70
   Positive Harmonisation   75
   Relationship Between Essential Safety Requirements and
   Standards   85
   Standardisation   87
   Conformity Assessment   100
   EHLASS   117
   General Product Safety Directive   119
   Fortress Europe?   155
   Conclusions   156

3. International Product Safety   159
   Introduction   159
   WTO   160
   ISO   177
   OECD   187
   UN   189
   Conclusions   194

4. United States   195
   Introduction   195
   Consumer Product Safety Commission   198
   Voluntary Standardisation   240
   Conclusions   249

5. United Kingdom   251
   Introduction   251

Accident Data Collection 251
Legal Regulation 253
Standardisation 286
Consumer Movement 293
Conclusions 294

6. France 299
Introduction 299
History 300
Institutions 301
Law of 1 August 1905 308
Law of 21 July 1983 313
General Criminal Law 323
Reform 323
Standards 324
Conclusions 328

7. Germany 331
Introduction 331
Data Collection 333
Institutions 336
Gerätesicherheitsgesetz (GSG) 341
Implementation of the EC General Product Safety Directive 352
Standardisation 358
Conclusions 363

8. Conclusions 365
Internationalisation of Consumer Product Safety 365
Role of the Regions 366
Deregulation – Standards and Beyond 367
Consumer Input 367
Regulators 369
Exports 370
Final Hopes 371

Index 373

Preface

I often find writing the preface a rather irrelevant irritation at the end of the long process of producing the manuscript. In this case, however, I feel a genuine need to explain to the reader a little of the history and motivations for writing this book.

When I read Richard Lawson's review of my previous book *Comparative Product Liability* I was heartened to read his comment that '...it is to be hoped that the author can be prevailed on in the near future to write a similar book on the forthcoming implementation of the EC Product Safety Directive'. I had agreed with my publisher to write just such a book and so it was encouraging that at least someone else thought this a worthwhile venture.

However, *Consumer Product Safety* is somewhat different from my earlier book. *Comparative Product Liability* had involved the study of numerous legal systems within Europe, N. America and Australasia. From the outset it was clear that this book would concentrate on fewer countries. This was not only due to reduced energy and a dampened enthusiasm for international travel with the arrival of my children (not subdued sufficiently according to my wife!). It was also because the present book had slightly different objectives from the first. One important aspect of the first book had been to consider the extent to which the Product Liability Directive had harmonised laws in the member states; this required both a knowledge of the pre–existing laws of the states, which remained applicable, and consideration of how the Directive had been implemented particularly in the light of the options which it had contained. This harmonisation dimension is not considered in the same way in the present book. Certainly the move towards harmonised standards and approaches is a central theme of the work, but I have been less concerned with the minutiae of how one particular Directive was implemented and have preferred to concentrate on the broader picture.

In fact a rather limited number of countries were chosen for detailed analysis. Within Europe, the United Kingdom, France and Germany were selected not only because they are the three most significant member states, but also because inevitably their national policy has heavily influenced, in different ways, European policy. The United States was also selected because, in the seventies, it was the standard bearer for what many consumerists believed a product safety regime should be. There is no doubt that the study would have been enhanced by more detailed consideration of those countries with well developed systems of product safety regulation – countries such as Australia, Canada, the Netherlands and the Scandinavian states. Although passing references are made to these countries I have tried for the most part to favour in depth analysis of a limited number of countries and to resist temptations to stray too far into other jurisdictions. It may also have been salutary to look at some countries with less developed legal regimes. In countries with well developed systems the problem of product safety can sometimes be marginalised and looking at countries without any adequate controls can serve as a reminder of the benefits of regulation. Also the General Product Safety Directive has had only a modest impact in the European countries that are studied in detail. If time had permitted a study of the Southern European countries one would notice greater benefits being derived from it. However, the book is already of more than sufficient length.

The need to restrict the national reports was in part due to the lengthy treatment of European and international regulation. This was in turn due to a realisation that a study of product safety regulation would be far from complete if it simply concentrated on the type of provisions contained in the General Product Safety Directive. These are mainly post–market controls, although the general safety requirement certainly tries to influence pre–marketing behaviour of producers. Such controls are often directed at the most blatantly dangerous products or product safety emergencies. In making these assessments the regulatory rules and self–regulatory standards are often important starting points. Moreover the actual level of safety enjoyed by consumers is largely determined by these pre–market controls. Therefore I found myself inescapably drawn into the web of the standardisation world. Like Alice I found myself in a magical (or at least fascinating world) which I could never have imagined existed and in which few lawyers had previously feared to tread. It is a world full of acronyms and scientific jargon. I realised it was important for me to shed light on these activities and to show how best they could be integrated into the legal structure in a way which guaranteed certain minimum safety standards and consumer participation in the decision–making process.

This work has been the culmination of five years' research. It has benefited from generous grants from the British Academy and the Nuffield Foundation. Some of the early research was carried out with the assistance of three Liverpool University students, Gillian Ackerman, Clare Birro and Rachel Chapman. We have since lost touch, but hopefully they will come across this work and make contact. I have also enjoyed the co–operation of many lawyers, standardisers, regulators and consumer advocates who gave of their time freely and put up with my numerous requests for materials. I hope they feel I have produced a balanced assessment of the current regime. I was universally impressed by the genuine commitment of those involved in product safety regulation to ensure consumer safety. Obviously there are differences of approaches and also institutional and economic and political limitations as to how far results can be achieved by particular individuals or organisations. I hope my work will encourage consideration of how best consumers can be protected in a climate which favours free trade, deregulation and light enforcement.

Particular thanks should go to Peter Cartwright and Hans Micklitz who (were) volunteered to read the draft text. One of my most difficult decisions was to know whether to abandon the vertical country/regional approach in favour of a horizontal issue by issue approach. A natural person to turn to for advice was Hans who has written several texts in this area. With typical Germanic rigour he suggested I do both. That is why the first chapter resembles a mixture of an introduction, synopsis and conclusion. I think the format works, but if it does not appeal to the reader I should take the blame for imperfect implementation of Hans's sound advice.

I have tried to state the law as of 1 July 1997. However, one of the dangers of comparative studies is that developments happen of which one is unaware. If there are some omissions (or even some minor inaccuracies) I hope they are forgiven and that they do not detract from the more important aspect of comparative research which is to help shed new light on the best method of dealing with legal regulation.

Naturally I would like to thank John Irwin, my publisher, for having faith in the project and for being tolerant of delays. His production team have as usual produced a high quality product. Special thanks must go to Julie Prescott who once again converted my text from disc to camera–ready copy with skill and alacrity and was patient with my requests for last minute alterations.

Finally mention should be made of my wife Elizabeth who continues to carry the burden of family life whilst I am away enjoying myself on research trips. Thankfully, my daughters, Laura and Bethan, show signs of missing me when these trips become too extended, but the presents compensate somewhat. Hopefully, the final product justifies these intrusions on family life.

1   Consumer Product Safety Regulation

1.   INTRODUCTION

A.   Consumer Products

Consumer safety should be the first objective of any consumer protection policy.[1] Even governments which adopt laissez–faire economic policies accept that a pre–condition for free market transactions is the existence of guarantees about the safety of consumer products circulating in their economy.[2]

Some products present easily recognisable dangers to consumers. Drugs are of course inherently dangerous and there have been numerous major incidents concerning drugs and medical devices (Thalidomide, Opren, human growth hormones, breast implants etc.). Recent health scares concerning, *inter alia*, BSE, E–coli and listeria, have emphasised the dangers consumers face from food products. Motor vehicles also pose obvious safety concerns and even safety features such as air bags have been subject to debate as to whether they create their own dangers. However, this book is not about these types of consumer products. Many of the general issues raised could apply to these products, but they tend to be subjected to tailor–made regulatory regimes administered by specialist agencies, and so a detailed sector by sector analysis would need to be undertaken before any sound conclusions could be reached.

Instead, this book is about the residual class of general consumer products. Many of these products are familiar to us in our everyday life and because they are commonplace we often fail to appreciate their dangers. The boundaries of this category are not definite. The way in which such products

---

[1]   Micklitz goes so far as to call for the recognition of the human right of consumers to safety: see H.–W. Micklitz, 'Consumer Rights' in *Human Rights and the European Community: the Substantive Law, Volume III European Union – The Human Rights Challenge*, A. Cassese, A. Clapham and J. Weiler (eds) and *Internationeles Produktsicherheitsrecht*, (Nomos, 1995).

[2]   The same principle ought to apply to consumer services, but this is often a more neglected topic, cf G. Howells and T. Wilhelmsson, *EC Consumer Law*, (Dartmouth, 1997) at Chapter 2, section 2. We shall concentrate on products, but it should be borne in mind that similar principles can be applied to the regulation of services.

are regulated tends to depend upon the extent to which special regimes/agencies exist for food, drugs, motor vehicles and whether a clear distinction is drawn between consumer and workplace safety. A sense of our subject matter can perhaps best be gained by looking at some examples. Of central importance in debates on consumer safety is child safety. The safety of toys and nursery equipment are typically priorities for consumer safety officials.[3] Electrical equipment creates an obvious source of danger to consumers and is also usually closely regulated.[4] Garden equipment (lawn–mowers, chain saws etc.) is another significant source of product related accidents. Sports equipment also creates dangers and there is much research into how protective equipment (eg helmets) can best protect product users. Ladders are another important source of product–relate injuries. In fact our subject–matter can extend to almost any household item, including furniture, white goods, cooking utensils and clothing.

Many of these products appear to be relatively low risk products (perhaps with the exception of the need for special protection for the young, old and disabled). However, home and leisure accidents account for a significant number of deaths and personal injuries (see, for instance, the figures produced by the National Commission on Product Safety in the United States, Chapter 4, section 1). Some of these accidents may be caused by poor quality manufacture, eg a ladder which breaks when someone stands upon it because a rung was inadequately secured. Others may be related to the product design. As products have become more complex it is harder for consumers to judge for themselves whether or not a product poses dangers. Indeed the risk of long term health risks due to exposure to toxic and carcinogenic substances is something which consumers are particularly poorly placed to judge. Other products may be unacceptably dangerous, because consumers have not been sufficiently well informed of a risk, which otherwise is an acceptable characteristic of the product. Equally the risk may derive from the consumer being inadequately instructed in the use of the product.

Of course not all accidents involving a product are caused by the product. Each incident has to be looked at to assess whether the product caused the injury, was merely part of the setting for a genuine accident, or if the injury was induced by the consumer's behaviour. However, one should not rush to blame consumer behaviour for an incident without first

---

3   This often extends to playground equipment.

4   However, as standards for electrical equipment are usually made by different bodies from other consumer products we will not look at the specifics of standardisation in that sector, but in general it parallels the development of standards making for other consumer products.

considering whether or not the consumer's behaviour was foreseeable and whether any steps could have been taken to prevent harm occurring.

Dealing with such a wide range of heterogeneous products causes a number of problems for the regulators of consumer products. Each product sector requires its own technical knowledge and gives rise to its particular design and ergonomic problems. Producers and trade associations have plenty of relevant expertise and have carefully developed positions on the crucial topics. Consumer product regulators have to spread their limited resources over a wide range of products. They therefore have either to spread their resources thinly and accept an imbalance in knowledge between themselves and the regulated industry or else prioritise areas and leave some consumer products hardly regulated. Consumer organisations typically face even more difficulties in stretching their meagre resources to cover a wide range of products.

The regulators of consumer products have to deal with numerous manufacturers. This places them at a disadvantage when compared with specialist agencies (dealing with, say, drugs and motor vehicles[5]) which have opportunities to build up close working relations with a limited number of manufacturers. Although such close relationships pose the danger of 'agency capture' by the industry which is being regulated, in reality a lot of regulation, both at the stage of setting standards and when imposing post–market controls, relies upon negotiations between regulator and regulated. This can be most effectively undertaken when the regulatory officials know whom to contact in the businesses concerned and have established a working relationship so that the regulated know the powers which can be used against them and have some respect for the officials' ability to utilise those powers. This knowledge will then speed up procedures and prevent the regulators having to use up vital resources by invoking formal procedures.

B. Regulatory Strategy

(i) Private or Public Law

This is not the place for a detailed analysis of the ability (or otherwise) of the private law, in particular product liability rules, to protect consumers.[6] Some brief comments are, however, in order to permit the reader an insight into the perspective from which the book is approached.

---

5 The argument applies with less force to the food sector where there are also numerous manufacturers.

6 For an earlier study of product liability rules by the present author see G. Howells, *Comparative Product Liability*, (Dartmouth, 1993).

One rationale for product liability rules is to create incentives for producers to manufacture safer products. This is most evident in the United States where ease of access to justice in personal injury cases combines with high damage awards (including punitive damages) to make manufacturers fear product liability suits. In theory civil liability rules should ensure manufacturers make the most efficient cost:benefit analysis to produce products with the optimum degree of safety. Debate centres on whether this is best achieved by negligence or strict liability standards. Advocates of the negligence standard argue that it forces manufacturers to make the most rational decision possible given the information available to them at the time of production. They argue that strict liability will lead to inefficient choices being made since producers will have to be defensive in their decision-making in order to protect themselves against development risks, ie those risks which are only detected after marketing. Advocates of strict liability plead that manufacturers are better able to bear and spread the cost of damages resulting from such risks and that strict liability causes producers to give safety a higher priority.

Private law has not produced a perfect solution. Whether or not strict liability is adopted, the rules on causation and difficulties of access to justice prevent producers feeling the full force of private law rules. Where strict liability has been adopted there has been a tendency to soften it by accepting state of the art/development risks defences.[7] This seems to result from a failure to carry through the compensation objectives of strict liability in the face of responsible behaviour by producers. However, there is a more deep rooted problem, which results from using the same legal principle both to provide compensation and to set design and production standards.[8] The result is that neither is necessarily satisfactorily addressed.

The private law continues to be a lottery, which requires an injured party to be able to recognise a legal claim and have the resources to prosecute it, as well as the good fortune to find a solvent accessible defendant and the evidence to link him to his injury. It also typically insists that compensation should move between two individuals who are causally linked to the damage. Broader based compensation schemes which impose responsibility on industry sectors or society (in the form of the Government) are hardly

---

7   See, N. Terry, 'State of the Art Evidence: From Logical Construct to Judicial Retrenchment' (1991) 20 *Anglo–Am. L. Rev.* 285.

8   This has been neatly labelled as the 'two questions/one answer' approach: see A. Hutchinson and S. Hodgson, 'Who's Zoomin' who? Comments on Liability for Pharmaceutical Products in Canada' in G. Howells (ed.) *Product Liability, Insurance and the Pharmaceutical Industry*, (Manchester U.P., 1991).

developed.[9] The private law places victims of product induced accidents in a privileged position compared to many other accident victims, and certainly to those who suffer the same symptoms from natural disease. In doing so it uses up a great deal of resources in meeting legal and expert witness fees and paying insurance company rake–offs. This money could be better devoted to meeting the needs of the injured.

A cheaper, fairer system of compensating accident victims would be a social insurance scheme. The New Zealand scheme is the prime example of such a social insurance model.[10] However, political reality dictates that such schemes are unlikely to be established elsewhere and are even presently being rolled back in New Zealand. Private law rules are therefore the only feasible means of ensuing that product victims receive compensation.

However, this does not mean that standard setting should be left to the private law. We have already noted reasons why producers do not feel the full impact of product liability rules – causation requirements, evidential problems and access to justice barriers all favour producers. Therefore producers may provide safety at a less than optimum level, even if one accepts that private law rules are capable in theory of producing the desired result. Most producers do, however, have a more genuine concern for their consumers. These responsible producers could benefit from regulation as some risks are complex to assess and a regulator can draw on more experience than a single firm. Equally defining an appropriate safety level is not a precise science. It should result from a complex balancing of different interest and values and once again a regulator would seem better placed to find a consensus than an individual firm, no matter what incentives the private law provides for efficient decision–making. Equally public regulation is justified as consumers should not have to trust to private decisions to guarantee the safety of the market place. If a firm miscalculates the risks it may suffer financially, but it is the injured consumer who suffers the physical harm

It is generally assumed that public regulation would be stricter than the private law.[11] In other words the private law removes X products from the market and the public regulations also remove Y products (ie those products – or, probably more accurately, product designs – which producers still find it efficient to produce despite product liability rules, but which are deemed

---

[9]   There are some examples in the drugs area: see G. Howells, 'Drug Product Liability in West Germany and Sweden' in Howells (ed.), *op. cit.*

[10]   Howells, *op. cit.*, at Chapter 16.

[11]   Of course there may be an impact on the private law through enhanced public regulation. Sometimes a private law action might be based on a breach of a public regulation, but also regulations (and standards) can be used as an objective measure to judge the behaviour of producers.

by the regulators to be unacceptable). This is probably a true reflection of the present position where product liability rules are based on negligence or a weak form of strict liability which permits development risk and system damage.[12] However, this is not the inevitable, or even desirable, outcome.

Product regulation does not mean the development of risk free products. Rather it is about ensuring that products only pose acceptable risks. Acceptability needs to be judged against the utility of the product and the possibility of developing safer alternatives or using substitutes. Equally product regulation cannot be expected to regulate for risks which were unknowable at the time of marketing. Product regulation will certainly lead to products being marketed which will pose dangers to consumers. Consumers are likely to be injured by the acceptable risks inherent in lawfully marketed products. One could therefore imagine a legal regime which permitted products to be marketed with acceptable (and of course unknowable) risks, but which also provided compensation to those who were injured by them.

It must be possible for producers to factor into their price an amount to cover the cost of liability for acceptable/unknowable damage without forcing them to withdraw from the market completely (for then a socially useful product would be lost). The cost of acceptable risks ought to be relatively moderate as by definition they are proportionate to the utility of the product. Development risks pose more serious problems to actuaries, but generally insurance has been available for these risks.[13]

Any price increase ought, according to economic theory, to lead to a reduction in consumption of the goods. Supporters of the free market would suggest that this is a good thing as it means that only the economically efficient amount of the product will be produced. However, this rationing ought not to be necessary as regulation should have ensured only acceptable products are marketed. Of course a distinction could be drawn between the permission to market goods and the amount which it is desirable for society to consume. In a market economy price will inevitably be the tool for determining consumption patterns. This can lead to inequities in so far as low income consumers do not have the same access to goods as wealthier citizens. However, this issue is part of a broader debate about social justice. For present purposes it is important to note that it is legitimate to market products which pose dangers so long as the risk is acceptable/unknowable. It

---

12   'System damage' is the inevitable damage inherent in a product which it is nevertheless considered justifiable to market: the phrase was coined by B. Dahl, see, 'Product Liability in Scandinavian Law' (1975) 19 *Scan. Stud. in Law* 59 at 84.

13   I. Vegas, 'The Defence of Development Risks in Spanish Law' [1997] *Consum. L.J* 144.

must also be accepted that a democratic society should be free to require compensation for those injured by these risks.

Many free marketeers and consumer activists would probably agree that in an ideal world it would be inappropriate to impose the burden of meeting this compensation obligation on producers directly. Free marketeers object to reasonable manufacturers having to bear the cost of political decisions to compensate individuals and consumers object to the fact that access to a socially useful product is rationed on the basis of the increased price, which the manufacturer has to charge to cover this extended liability. The circle can only be squared by the Government stepping in to meet the costs of the political decision to provide compensation to the victims of acceptable/unknowable risks. But that seems unrealistic in the present economic and political climate. The choice therefore becomes one of leaving these victims uncompensated or marginally restricting the choice of poorer consumers through price increases.[14] However, this compensation question perhaps takes us beyond the scope of the current book, which is to consider how products can best be regulated through regulation.

(ii) Models of Public Regulation

In the previous section we contrasted product regulation through private law product liability rules with public regulation. Yet there are various forms of public regulation, including delegation of the responsibility for setting standards to private standards bodies.

The strongest form of direct intervention is for public authorities to control the supply of products by requiring producers to obtain a license before marketing them. However, this is an extremely burdensome requirement which can only be justified where there are strong grounds to believe that products may pose unacceptable risks. Therefore such regimes tend to be restricted to sectors such as pharmaceuticals and do not normally apply to general consumer products.

Without going too deeply into specifics at this stage, two general patterns of regulation can be mapped out. These are perhaps best described as the old and the new approaches (to borrow terminology from the EC, see Chapter 2, section 4).

The old approach assumed that technical experts could carefully balance risk and benefits and produce detailed regulations containing design specifications which producers should follow. This approach had the drawback that it restricted the scope for innovation by producers. Moreover the process of drawing up detailed regulations was over complex and too

---

14   It is unlikely that such liability will lead to significant price increases.

drawn out. It also lacked democratic legitimacy for it placed the *de facto* power to make these decisions in the hands of public officials with only limited duties to consult interested parties and with only negligible political control and accountability.

The new approach limits the role of statutory regulations. In the United States they are only permitted where voluntary solutions are inappropriate (Chapter 4, section 2D). Europe has attempted to achieve an enterprising combination of regulation and voluntary standards. The essential consumer safety principles are set out in regulations, whilst voluntary standards provide one concrete way of satisfying those objectives (Chapter 2, section 4C). In both the United States and Europe the emphasis has been placed on the role of voluntary standardisation. This represents a shift in the role of law from being a means to prescribe outcomes to being a facilitator of debates between interested parties so that a consensus can be achieved. Of course there are dangers for consumers from this process. Under the United States model, the Consumer Product Safety Commission (CPSC) may not be able to resist the preference for voluntary standards even when it is not certain that the voluntary approach will assure consumer safety. Equally in Europe it seems clear that voluntary standards are not merely technical standards giving effect to politically agreed norms, but also go a long way to determining the actual level of safety enjoyed by consumers. The standards making process is therefore crucial in both systems. Consumers suffer from structural weaknesses when trying to make their voice heard in a standardisation process dominated by industry concerns. These problems need to be alleviated by ensuring that the standardisation process operates within a legal framework which addresses consumer safety concerns and by improving consumer representation within standardisation.

There has also been another deregulatory tendency, of perhaps even more practical significance. This concerns conformity assessment procedures. Third party conformity assessment of products is expensive. It is therefore tempting only to require it for those products which have a serious potential to cause harm and even then sometimes to permit assessment on the basis of sampling. For many products the manufacturer's own declaration of conformity is now the norm, although this is sometimes combined with third party certification of quality assurance systems to ISO 9000. One might wonder whether conformity assessment procedures have not become too lax. A balance needs to be struck. Although one does not want to impose unnecessary costs, third party certification is in fact a very practical way of promoting consumer safety. There seems to be too great an emphasis on manufacturer's self–declaration. This is particularly worrying in Europe, where manufacturers can use self–declaration as the basis for attaching the CE marking, which in the consumer's mind might suggest that the product has been approved by a third party (see Chapter 2, section 7D).

This new approach to product safety offers consumers the hope of greater choice by encouraging innovation and reducing costs. However, it also creates uncertainties. These concerns are increased because of the growth of regional free trade zones and developments within GATT/WTO aimed at reducing barriers to trade. This has led to moves to harmonise standards on a regional (eg CEN at the European level) and international level (eg ISO). This of course raises concerns – not entirely unfounded – about standards being reduced, if not to the lowest common denominator, then at least to a lower level than that enjoyed in countries with the most protective regimes.

Likewise the growth in mutual recognition of both conformity assessment schemes and programmes to accredit assessors is in principle a worthy objective; after all it is consumers who pay indirectly if unnecessary tests and examinations are carried out. However, mutual recognition should only occur after confidence has been built up between the assessors and accreditors. There must be confidence that they actually are working to equivalent standards. The difficulty of establishing this equivalence – along with the natural self–interest of assessment and accreditation bodies to maintain fee income – has meant that voluntary mutual recognition agreements have been slow to develop (Chapter 2, section 7C(ii) and Chapter 3, section 2C(iii)). However, within the scope of products covered by the new approach directives, the CE marking gives access to all EC markets. Where third party conformity assessment is required before the CE marking can be attached then approval from a notified body in any member state will suffice (Chapter 2, section 7C(i)). This provides manufacturers with incentives to search out favourable assessment bodies. To the extent that competition is based on price and efficiency such competition is healthy. However, there must be a suspicion that some companies will be attracted to assessment bodies which are known to apply standards in a laxer manner. Even if these bodies do not fall below the minimum standards required for the CE marking, nevertheless disincentives are placed on other assessment bodies from testing to standards higher than the minimum, perhaps by making a holistic assessment of the product as well as judging it against the specific criteria laid down in the standards.

The new approach grants the producer greater autonomy. One would have imagined that this ought to be compensated for by increased market surveillance, so that authorities can check if the freedom is being abused and react accordingly. This trend is certainly seen to some extent in the United States where the CPSC now makes greater use of its powers to recall and take other action against hazardous products (Chapter 4, section 2F). In Europe, however, the whole philosophy of the new and global approaches is to relax the supervision of products bearing the CE marking. Moreover, these changes are taking place against a background of reduced resources for enforcement authorities, whereas the changed market conditions would actually justify more resources going into enforcement. The modern state seems unable to ensure that some of the gains to business from the new approach are transferred to the public authorities to assure consumer safety. This would require tax transfers which are unpopular in a climate which favours private over public wealth.

The need for market surveillance because of the new approach also conflicts with the trend towards regionalisation and internationalism. Too much interference by national authorities will undermine efforts to promote trade by producing harmonised standards and establishing mutual recognition agreements. In Europe this hands–off enforcement philosophy is clearly seen by the fact that goods bearing the CE marking should be presumed to conform to the directives. The European Court of Justice is also vigilant to ensure that the actions of national authorities are proportionate to legitimate goals of protecting the consumer and are not disguised barriers to trade (Chapter 2, section 2). The new approach embraces a hands off theory of enforcement, which involves a preference for reacting to reported dangers rather than closely monitoring the market to detect dangerous products.

Another counterbalance to the increased producer autonomy within the new approach is the need for a general safety obligation (in more detail see section 3E(iv)). This general standard will apply wherever there are gaps in the legal regime. It can serve both as a plimsoll safety line which all products should reach and also as a trigger for enforcement action against dangerous products. Of course this safety net can only be invoked once dangers have been detected and this links back to concerns about the increasingly passive role of enforcement agencies.

C.   General Issues

(i)   Pre– or Post–Market Controls

A distinction in the literature on product safety regulation is drawn between pre– and post–market controls. Pre–market controls certainly include licensing requirements and rules which determine standards, whether in statutory regulations or voluntary standards. They are generally directed at the producer in order to influence the manner in which products are manufactured and marketed.

A general safety obligation is also best viewed as in part a pre–market control, for although it may impose no specific controls it attempts to influence the producer when he addresses safety issues. This is most clearly the case where breach of the safety obligation is an offence in its own right, but the same effect should in theory occur even if breach of the general safety duty is simply a trigger for consequential measures. However, there must be a danger that producer behaviour is not very strongly influenced by such a general safety obligation (see section 3E(iv)). Producers may be ignorant of its application to their products or feel that it gives them little practical guidance.

Post–market controls are concerned with monitoring products in the market place and ensuring that action can be taken once dangers are apprehended. These rules are directed at both producers and enforcement authorities.

Ideally the law should help create a climate in which producers take responsibility themselves for monitoring their products and reacting to dangers. The law can play a role by imposing requirements on producers to create procedures to detect and react to concerns about their products. In Europe, for instance, the General Product Safety Directive imposes post–marketing monitoring obligations on producers and distributors (Chapter 2, section 9G and H) and in the United States there are significant obligations to notify potential dangers to the CPSC (Chapter 4, section 2E).

As a back up to this form of self–regulation, enforcement authorities need to have powers to detect and seize dangerous products. Such products should then either be destroyed or disposed of in a manner which does not harm the consumer interest, eg they could be modified, sold as scrap or in some circumstances exported. Products which have reached final consumers need to be subject to the publication of warning notices and potential recall.

(ii) Regulating Different Types of Safety Risks

Legal rules need to cover a wide variety of potential safety risks. Some risks are blatantly unacceptable. The acceptability of other risks is more debatable. The acceptability of a risk might be based on the fact that it is doubted whether an admitted risk is likely to cause consumers much harm. Efforts to reduce noise levels on lawn–mowers are typically challenged on this basis. We could describe these as 'evident but questionable' risks. The task of the law is to find a balance between countervailing viewpoints.

However, the more contentious situation arises when the acceptability of a risk turns on differences of opinion as to whether any risk actually exists. This allegation might relate to (a) an entire category of products (for example, it might be disputed whether a product exposes consumers to the danger of contracting cancer in the long term), or (b) simply a particular product or batch of products (if, for example, it is suggested that they have become contaminated or are subject to a production flaw). Here the problem lies in the fact that the existence of the risk itself is not evident. If the risk is found to exist it is likely radically to affect the way a particular product category is regulated or to determine how a particular product or product batch is disposed of.

The above categories of risk do not necessarily call for different rules, although the manner in which the law is applied will vary depending upon whether the safety risk is blatantly unacceptable, 'evident but questionable' or not evident, but potentially unacceptable if established.

Modified procedures are, however, needed when emergencies arise. In emergencies standards need to be adopted without the usual consultation period and enforcement authorities need to react quickly on the basis of suspicion rather than proof. Where the danger is obvious the use of emergency powers tends to be relatively unproblematic. Equally where the risk is evident, but there is debate as to whether as risk is acceptable there is normally no call for emergency procedures as the risk is usually not a serious one, or at least does not require an immediate decision (cf France where emergency powers seem possible for either serious or immediate dangers. Chapter 6, section 5D).

The difficult decision is to determine what emergency powers should be available when a danger is suspected, but has not yet been established. Most legal regimes provide powers for emergency action to be taken in such situations so that further investigation can be undertaken. Where the uncertainty affects a category of products temporary regulations can usually be enacted so that a more in depth study of the issues can take place. Where the uncertainty relates to specific products or product batches enforcement officials are usually permitted to seize suspect goods for further examination. However, this study was unable to gain a complete picture of how these powers are used in practice. Whilst one would favour the borrowing of the 'precautionary principle' from environmental law, one gains the impression that concern to protect commercial interests restrains authorities from reacting without strong and convincing evidence that products pose a danger. Regulators and enforcement officers are no doubt influenced by the current deregulatory climate to be slow to use their emergency powers to the full. In many cases enforcement authorities have an added incentive to be slow to take action because of the knowledge that they can be subject to compensation claims if their fears prove to be unfounded (section 4B(iii)).

(iii) Who Should be Responsible for Product Safety?

We have tended to refer to the producer/manufacturer as the party primarily responsible for the safety of products. As they manufacture the product this is an obvious first principle. Where a retailer represents themselves as the producer by selling goods under their own brand, or someone attaches their brand name to goods, then there is an increasing trend to also treat them as the producer. This is justified not only because of the impression created to consumers that they are in fact responsible for producing the goods, but also because very often these parties will indeed have had a good deal of influence over the production of the product.

However, in order to ensure that safety concerns are addressed from the design table to the point of consumption it is also necessary to involve other intermediaries, in particular the supplier of the goods to the final consumer. They have to play their part in post–market surveillance of the product and to assist in complying with any orders made by the supervisory authorities or the courts. Although most legal systems do extend controls to distributors and retailers, we shall see that in Germany some problems were created by the law's attempts to insulate, to a large extent, the mere supplier from responsibility (see Chapter 7, section 4E).

In an age of increasing cross–border trade there is a further incentive to place responsibility on the supplier, as he is often the party most easily accessible to the enforcement authorities in the consumer's home state. This also explains why importers are typically equated to producers in product safety regimes.

2. DATA COLLECTION

In the next section we will look at pre–market controls, before considering post–market controls in the subsequent section. However, first systems for collecting information on product related accidents are considered as they should inform policy in relation to both pre– and post–market controls. The potential value of such systems will be explained, before outlining the ways in which they operate and assessing their practical benefits.

Data on product related accidents is important for several reasons.[15] Resources to promote consumer safety are scarce. Funds need to be directed to where they can produce the greatest benefits. This includes directing regulatory, standardisation and enforcement activity to priority areas. It should also be used to focus educational, information and publicity campaigns undertaken by regulatory authorities, accident prevention and consumer organisations. Although not considered in detail in this work, these non–legal techniques of promoting safety have a considerable practical impact.

One of the positive aspects of the current deregulatory climate has been to force regulators to consider carefully the need for regulation. Accident

---

[15] See OECD reports on *Data Collection Systems Related to Injuries Involving Consumer Products*, (OECD, 1978) at 6–8 and *Severity Weighting of Data on Accidents Involving Consumer Products*, (OECD, 1979) at 7–8.

data can be useful evidence to justify the need for intervention. However, the limits on the use to which data can be put need to be respected, especially given resource constraints and the complicated interrelationship between product, user and the environment. Thus data on product accidents cannot be the sole determinant of whether regulation is needed (or indeed of whether regulation has been effective). Particularly in the United States one suspects that the demands for concrete data to justify the activities of the CPSC are sometimes too excessive (Chapter 4, section 2D(iii)).

It must be conceded that the raw data is of only marginal value. A criticism often made of such data is that it records the number of injuries but not the probability of injury since it does not relate the number of injuries to the intensity of use of a particular product.[16] Equally the nature of the injury needs to be weighted to reflect its severity. The United States is the only country to have attempted this in a systematic manner (Chapter 4, section 2C(i)). Such attempts to weight injuries are of course open to easy jibes at the subjectivity of the process by which weightings are attached to injuries,[17] but can be of practical value.[18] Criticisms tend to come from those who have too high expectations of what the data can achieve. Policy in this area is too complex to be based on simplistic number crunching. Data can provide guidance, but should not be treated as a litmus test for regulatory conduct.

Once the decision to regulate or create a standard has been addressed, accident data can assist the decision–making process. It can be used to identify problem areas and to suggest solutions. For instance, if a product is involved in a particular type of accident, but only with respect to a certain section of the population, eg the elderly, then a desirable solution could address the particular needs of that group.

The most effective way of collecting data on product related accidents appears to be through recording admissions to a representative sample of hospital accident and emergency rooms. The first and still most extensive system of this kind is the United States' NEISS (Chapter 4, section 2C). The United States also has the most effective complementary systems for collecting data on those injuries which miss the hospital emergency room, ie minor injuries which do not require medical treatment and deaths which go

---

16   K. Viscusi, *Regulating Consumer Product Safety*, (American Enterprise Institute, 1984) at 49–50.

17   Asch cites commentators who have described the severity weighting scale as being 'wholly arbitrary' and 'without any rational foundation': see P. Asch, *Consumer Safety Regulation*, (Oxford UP, 1988) at 134 citing S. Kelman, 'Regulation by Numbers: A Report on the Consumer Product Safety Commission' (1974) 37 *The Public Interest* 83 and N. Cornell, R. Noll and B. Weingast in H. Owen and C. Schultze (eds), *Setting National Priorities: The Next Ten Years*, (Brookings, 1976).

18   OECD (1979), *op. cit.*

straight to the hospital mortuary. Within Europe a scheme modelled on the NEISS was first established in the United Kingdom (Chapter 5, section 2) and has gradually spread across Europe under the influence of the EC's EHLASS scheme (Chapter 2, section 8). Some member states remain resistant to such a method of data collection (notably Germany, see Chapter 7, section 2) and are allowed to provide data based on questionnaire surveys. However, that technique is more susceptible to errors being introduced due to the poor memory of interviewees. The Germans have also been criticised for being too willing to allocate blame to the way the consumer used the product, rather than any risk related to the product itself (Chapter 7, section 2). In part this might be related to the more subjective manner in which their data has been collected.

However, critics of the EHLASS system have some justification. Data collection is something which either needs to be done well or not at all. Sufficient data must be generated for the results to be meaningful. None of the national systems within the EC compare in scale to the United States' NEISS system. Until recently there has been no attempt to collate the national reports to produce a European wide report which may add value to the sum of the individual reports. It is understood that the EC is attempting such a development, although the exact contours of the new system have still to be elaborated (Chapter 2, section 8). Although technical hurdles need to be overcome this objective is surely correct. Whilst national conditions do affect accident incidence to some extent, it must surely be useful to see if national trends are reflected in the European figures, even if only to seek explanations for any differences. Equally it would be advantageous if the EC and United States data was comparable. In this respect the WHO efforts to create a common system for classifying injury data is to be supported. However one problem with such efforts is to find a way of moving to common classification systems without destroying the possibility of comparing data within individual countries over time.

3. PRE–MARKET CONTROLS

A. Rationales for Intervention

Pre–market controls such as regulations or standards which prescribe minimum product standards are an obvious form of intervention in the market to promote consumer safety. The same effect is achieved by the conditions imposed by licensing authorities. General safety obligations represent a similar if less specific form of intervention. Equally, although the context sometimes makes the matter less obvious, it should be remembered that the rules and policy adopted with respect to post–market controls also represent a form of intervention which restricts producer freedom. An order recalling or seizing and destroying goods already in circulation is as much a judgment of the optimum safety level as a rule prohibiting the marketing of those products (this is most clearly seen in the United States where the CPSC increased the use of its post–market controls in response to reductions in its ability to regulate product standards, Chapter 4, section 2F). All these instances of intervention need to be justified.

The case for some form of public authority intervention to ensure safety is relatively uncontroversial. Protection of life and health is too important to simply be left to the market. Where consumer economic interests are at stake it may be sufficient to establish legal rules which remedy market failures by subsequent transfers of wealth through the litigation system. However, where life and limb are at stake the consumer understandably favours prevention to reparation. The topic becomes more controversial when one goes on to discuss the extent of any intervention.

(i)   In Defence of Paternalism

Views differ as to whether public regulation should simply try to remedy market failures or if its role is to impose a different – impliedly superior – conception of the optimum safety regime to that which may commonly be held by the general public. It will become evident that the writer favours the latter approach. In doing so one is open to criticism that one is attempting to use the law as a means of social engineering, based on patronising paternalistic attitude. However, accepting the charge of paternalism, if by that one means ensuring that the true interests of others are promoted (even if they are not aware of what their true interests are), does not involve admitting the charge of self–righteousness. Indeed implicit in my vision of a product safety regime is a desire to promote more informed choices than can be made by any one individual, including the present writer.

What is being argued for is a system which permits an objective assessment of the safety policy alternatives. In making this assessment it is assumed that individuals cannot at present adequately reach a satisfactory judgment about what is in their best interest. This starting point is relatively uncontroversial. Differences emerge over the extent to which the individual can be assisted to overcome his difficulties so that he can be trusted to protect himself. Some argue that this can be largely achieved through providing the consumer with more information on safety risks. Although there is certainly some room for consumers to be protected by warnings, many advocates of this approach are unrealistically optimistic about its potential. Consumers come into contact with a wide range of products and have only limited resources in terms of time and knowledge to resolve the complex issues involved.

Those who accept the limits of the information based approach, but still favour regulation reflecting individuals' preferences often favour a second–best approach under which regulators see their task as being to determine what consumers would have decided if they had the relevant knowledge. Leaving aside the obvious point that subjectivity is now being introduced, one should note the more fundamental objections to a regulatory policy which premises itself on the ability of consumers accurately to assess the risks they expose themselves to. The basis of these objections will be considered below, for now it is sufficient to note that these weaknesses are not to be found in a particular group of consumers which need special protection. Rather they affect most, if not all consumers, who under (or over) value safety because of their inability to assess risks.

What is being argued for is a certain humility about one's own abilities to look after one's own interests in an increasingly complicated environment. Critics of intervention argue that the technical experts cannot produce the optimum balance between risk and safety. This may be true. But their efforts are likely to be better than those of the average consumer.

Those who prefer individual choice as the determinant of safety policy display a kind of machoism. They view promoting autonomy as a prime objective and consider the best way to achieve this is to rely on the natural instinct of man to preserve himself and his interests through his own efforts. This view of human behaviour may have been true in simple primeval society. It is no longer appropriate for today's complex society, in which man cannot control all the elements which affect his life and the solutions to problems he attempts may have unexpected ripple and side effects. Accepting that it is natural for man to want to protect his self interest, the best way to do this in the modern world is often to delegate the task of representing one's interests to institutions which one trusts (see section 3B). Strength may lie in admitting that sometimes one needs to rely on the experience and wisdom of others. The meaning of autonomy may have changed. Instead of a right to decide one now has the right to influence and control the decisions of those to whom decision–making power has been entrusted. This does not mean that any one group in society is claiming to have a monopoly on wisdom, for those who advocate the need for technical assistance to help determine appropriate safety levels, must concede that they themselves are in as much need of this assistance as others. Of course much depends upon the decision–makers having the confidence of the public. This would in turn seem to require that they permit public participation and are accountable.

The above argument has not sought to justify interfering with individual preferences on the basis of the third party effects of individual decisions. This externalities argument is usually a less controversial basis for overriding individual choices. It points to the detrimental effects individual actions can have on other individuals (eg bystanders injured by defective products) or to the collective, which has to carry all or part of the costs of the injuries (eg medical, social security costs etc.). Frequently, externality arguments are put forward as a 'false' justification for policies which are really based on a desire to alter safety expectations. This may be politically astute, but is intellectually dishonest. Although undoubtedly the externalities issue has to be factored into the policy–making process.

(ii)   The Role of Social Science Research

There is a wealth of economics and psychological literature which seeks to find the best ways of regulating for product safety and critiquing (and usually condemning) the actions taken by the regulators of consumer products.[19] It is easy to criticise consumer product regulators. The costs they impose are obvious – higher priced consumer products, reduced choice or irritating safety features which inconvenience the user. The benefits of their labours are less easily identifiable. It can never be proven how many lives have been saved or how many accidents avoided. Indeed the 'would have been victims' of the unregulated product are oblivious to their good fortune.

Economic models and consumer behaviour experiments to test the desirability or effectiveness of product safety regulation are unlikely to be able to produce firm conclusions. The subject matter – involving consumer, product and the environment – is too complex to yield simple results. There are also policy choices and value judgments to be factored into the decision-making process. For instance, should regulation pay particular attention to the needs of groups like children, the aged or disabled; how should the needs of the poor – who desire access to products – be balanced against the interests of the rich in having safety features built in to products; to what extent can consumers be left to choose between levels of safety and when should their liberty to choose be restricted?

This does not mean that regulators should not take account of social science research. There is probably broad agreement with the view of a former chairman of the Federal Trade Commission in the United States that:

> 'We have learned that we must be accountable for the costs and burdens of regulation. But we will not concede that the economist's useful, but

---

19   Two of the most accessible introductions to these issues are Asch, *op. cit.*, and M.W. Jones–Lee, *The Economics of Safety and Physical Risk*, (Basil Blackwell, 1989), especially Chapter 1.

imperfect, tool of cost–benefit analysis dictates policy judgments on what is right or wrong.'[20]

Economics provides some basic lessons which regulators would do well to heed. For instance, it underlines the fact that safety is not a priceless commodity. Safety must be paid for. Indeed many dangers inherent in products are necessary if society is to have the range of products which permit it to function efficiently. This lesson is usually well understood by consumer activists. For instance, Susan King, a former Chairman of the CPSC has noted that a 'risk–free society is not attainable'.[21] One sometimes cringes when one hears calls for the complete eradication of all risks. Often this follows a tragedy and there are many examples of over–regulation resulting from regulators responding to public outcries when disaster strikes. What is needed are not *ad hoc* responses, but a rational system for analysing risks and setting safety standards which provides society's best guess at where the optimum safety level should be fixed.

However, industry often cries wolf about the costs regulation will impose. For instance, in the early 1960s the American car industry warned about the costs of mandatory seat belts and then priced them at only around $10 per vehicle.[22]

Equally safety decisions can only be taken when the potential victims are anonymous. Once an individual is identified as being at risk then human sympathy and generosity require action at almost any cost. This explains why large amounts of money are expended to save an around the world yachtsman in distress, despite the fact that the money could save more lives if used on, say, product safety regulation.

Research into consumer behaviour also has some lessons for regulators. One interesting theory is that consumers may have a certain tolerance to risk so that as products become safer they react by consuming more of the product or using it in a more dangerous manner. Thus as cars become safer, drivers may tend to drive faster and closer to the car in front.[23] The lesson from this should not be never to regulate, but rather to see how the rules can be formulated to prevent this effect or how they need to be combined with measures to change consumers' attitudes, perhaps through education or enforcement policy.

---

[20] M. Pertschuk, *Revolt Against Regulation*, (University of California Press, 1982) at 138.

[21] *New York Times*, 25 February, 1979, cited in Viscusi, *op. cit.*, at 43.

[22] R. Nader, *Unsafe at Any Speed*, (Grossman, 1965) at 121 and 128.

[23] See Asch, *op. cit.*, at 127–133; see S. Peltzman, 'The Effects of Automobile Safety Regulation' (1975) 83 *J. of Pol. Econ.* 677.

Consumer agencies need to make two types of policy decision. First, they need to prioritise their efforts. This is, of course, a major reason why data collection systems are established (see section 2). Naturally, in addition to identifying products which cause injuries, one also has to consider the extent to which regulation can improve safety. It is not perhaps surprising that toys, ladders etc. continue to produce a significant number of accidents even though they are often well regulated; the question is whether any further regulation would improve the situation significantly. Such decisions are based on judgments of cost–effectiveness, and differ from the cost–benefit analysis which needs to be undertaken when agencies take their second type of decision about the desirability of a specific rule.[24]

There are several different ways in which cost–benefit analysis can be undertaken.[25] Sparing ourselves the majority of the debate which has raged amongst economists on this topic, it is probably sufficient to outline two of the principle ways in which cost:benefit analysis can be undertaken. The first way is relatively familiar to lawyers. It involves a balance sheet with costs on one side and benefits on the other. If the benefits of regulation outweigh the cost then regulation would seem to be desirable. The problem with this approach – even if policy is not left solely to mathematical equations– is that it is hard to identify with certainty the costs and benefits and to link them to the proposed regulation. Whereas lawyers are happy to put a price on everything, economists prefer to question whether it is possible to put a price on life (or limb or pain and suffering).

Economists tend to answer their own rhetorical question by suggesting that one should ask a different question. Instead of asking how much an injury is worth, one should ask how much individuals would be willing to pay to avoid the risk of such injury. Different versions of this 'willingness to pay' approach exist, but they share common features which make them susceptible to challenge as an authoritative guide to regulatory conduct. For instance, it may disadvantage poorer sections of society, for their reluctance to pay for safety features may be disregarded if the more affluent majority agree to the extra costs. It also smacks of majoritareanism. If the majority of the population is willing to accept a risk then the minority (who would prefer to pay for added protection) do not have their interests protected. Equally if the majority favour protection this could lead to restrictions on the freedom of those who would choose to accept risks. Of course in a democracy the minority has sometimes to accept restrictions placed on it by the majority, but it would be unfair automatically to apply the majority preference, when

---

24   Cf Jones–Lee, *op. cit.*, at 8.
25   *Ibid.*, at 9–26.

there is a good deal of evidence that these expressed preferences may be irrational.[26]

Consumers may not attain their preferred balance of risk, because their decisions are frequently based on misconceptions about risk. Often these lead to a willingness to accept too many risks or the wrong kind of risks. In part this results from the inability of the human mind to grasp the complexity of the problems posed by product safety regulation. As Herbert Simon has noted a human has to construct 'a simplified model of the real situation in order to deal with it. He behaves rationally with respect to this model, and such behaviour is not even approximately optimal with respect to the real world'.[27] Although most economists reject this broad interpretation, which after all would shatter the very image of the rational agent theory which is at the heart of most economic models,[28] there are more concrete examples of the limit of human's ability to process information and arrive at rational decisions which are harder to refute.

Psychological research gives some insights into the problems individuals have when assessing risk.[29] For instance, it has been shown that individuals do not behave rationally – in the economic sense of exercising consistent preferences. Depending upon how options are framed they may have inconsistent preferences between available options.[30] Possibly there is a tendency to settle for a more certain outcome, rather than an option which is more likely to optimise benefits but includes a greater risk.[31] Equally, there is evidence that whilst consumers prefer bets with a high probability of winning, they actually pay more for bets with higher prizes but less chance

---

[26]   Here I use rationality in the lay sense which relates to the reasonableness of arguments based on logical reasoning. Economists treat behaviour as rational so long as it is internally consistent regardless of the quality of the choices. Thus to an economist it could be rational to prefer to live in Liverpool rather than Manchester, and Manchester rather than Bolton so long as you did not prefer to live in Bolton rather than Liverpool. Strange people these economists!

[27]   H. Simon, *Models of Man: Social and Rational*, (Wiley, 1957) at 199.

[28]   Asch, *op. cit.*, at 55.

[29]   Asch, *op. cit.*, at 70–79. The following text draws upon the clear explanations provided by Asch and the references to which he refers.

[30]   This is known as the Allais paradox: see M. Allais, 'Le comportement de l'homme rationel devant le risque: critique des postulats et axiomes de l'école Americaine' (1953) 21 *Econometrica* 503.

[31]   D. Kahneman and A. Tverski, 'Prospect Theory: An Analysis of Decision Under Risk' (1979) 47 *Econometrica* 263.

of winning.[32] Consumers' decisions seem to be highly influenced by the way in which questions are posed.[33]

The above, are just some of the findings which suggest that individuals do not in practice always behave in the way economists assume. With regard to consumer safety there are some particular factors which affect consumer judgment. For instance, people tend to believe they can control chance events.[34] This perhaps explains why people feel safer behind a car wheel than on an aeroplane seat, although the statistics might suggest otherwise.[35] This is connected to an optimistic tendency to assume that accidents are more likely to happen to others. Equally our decisions on safety are likely to overemphasise large remote risks (eg that a plane will explode) and to underrate common smaller risks. One might also wish to question the assertions of those who express a willingness to expose themselves to high levels of risk, for it is easier to accept a risk than to accept the consequences once the risk has materialised.

This brief excursion into economics and psychology seems to highlight two elements. First, the economics' debates highlight the need for a trade off to be struck between safety and risk. Second, the psychological literature illustrates the problems individuals face when having to make those difficult decisions. In an age in which products are becoming increasingly complex and the trade off between risk and utility ever more difficult to judge, it is therefore sensible for consumers to delegate the task of weighing the options to experts. Experts may not strike the perfect balance, but they are likely to reach their conclusion from a more informed position. Equally the inherent problems consumers have in calculating risk highlights the limitations of a strategy which premises regulation on either (a) solely information provisions, or (b) attempting to second guess how consumers would respond to exposure to risk.

In the area of product liability the American Law Institute has proposed a Restatement (Third) on Torts which suggests that design defects should

---

32   See S. Lichenstein and P. Slovic, 'Reversals of Preference Between Bids and Choices in Gambling Decisions' (1971) 89 *Journal of Experimental Psychology* 46 and D. Grether and C. Plott, 'Economic Theory of Choice and the Preference Reversal Phenomenon' (1979) 69 *Am. Econ. Rev.* 623.

33   A. Traversky and D. Kahneman, 'Rational Choice and the Framing of Decisions' (1986) 59 *J. of Business* S251.

34   L. Strickland, R. Lewicki and A. Katz, 'Temporal Orientation and Perceived Control as Determinants of Risk–Taking' (1966) 2 *J. of Experimental Social Psychology* 143.

35   After all most of us consider ourselves to be better than average drivers: see O. Svenson, 'Are We Less Risky and More Skilful Than Our Fellow Drivers? (1981) 47 *Acta Psychologica* 143.

require the plaintiff to prove a reasonable alternative design.[36] This rule can be criticised in a liability regime designed to compensate product related accident victims, but this approach makes more sense in a regulatory regime. Product safety regulators are in practice far more likely to have to make concrete choices between different designs, rather than having to enter into complicated economic analysis.

Obviously political values remain part of the regulator's decision–making process, both about the level of safety and the means to achieve it. One can agree with Broome when he argues that the politicians (or more likely technocrats) who make these decisions have to be responsible for the choices they make:

> 'Why on earth should *economics* be expected to deliver a neat answer to morally agonising questions about what ends justify the sacrifice of some number of lives? No doubt it will ease a politician's mind to be given a sophisticated calculation of the precise weight to be put on the loss of a life. But surely the difficulty with these questions is that there is no answer that can straightforwardly be called the right one. Politicians ought not to expect the ease of mind that comes from knowing they did the only thing that was right. I think it is better to force them to appreciate the difficulty of their decisions than to give them easy answers.'[37]

Nevertheless it is useful if that decision is made bearing in mind the need for a sensible trade off to be made between risk and safety, the limits of individual preferences as a guide as to where to strike that balance and an awareness of the factors which should influence the choice of means to promote the optimum safety of products.

Of course even given perfect information and decision–making ability there will always be some people who are risk takers and others who are risk avoiders. Regulation should not seek to deny these individual characteristics, but rather seek to find an appropriate accommodation of the different attitudes. Consumer education is important both to reduce the gap between public perceptions of risk and the results of regulation and also to assist consumers in exercising the discretion which many regulations will continue to permit consumers to exercise concerning their own particular exposure to risk.

---

36 *Restatement of the Law, Torts: Product Liability* (Proposed Final Draft, 1 April 1997), (American Law Institute, 1997). This has now been adopted with some minor amendments.

37 J. Broome, 'Trying to Value a Life: A Reply' (1978) 9 *J. of Pub. Econ.* 259 at 261–2.

B. Who Should Intervene?

If individuals are to leave decisions affecting their safety to others, they need confidence in that decision–making body. This requires that it both be independent of business interests (and sympathetic to consumer concerns), as well as being technically competent. In the consumer safety field the choice seems to be between regulation by government or by interest groups through standardisation bodies. The possibilities offered by each model will be considered in order to suggest the best way of combining the strengths and mitigating the weakness of both models.

(i) Government

Government intervention is the traditional method of setting product standards. Its weaknesses have often been associated with procedural matters, such as the slow pace of enacting legislation, because of the need to consult and seek parliamentary approval of the rules and any amendments. Also the rules have traditionally been drafted in terms which followed legislative drafting traditions, rather than being written in a manner which was user friendly to industry. The sanctions were also traditionally rather unimaginative. If they included criminal penalties this often affected the way the rules were formulated, because of the need for certainty when creating penal offences.

These procedural criticisms are no longer the main objections to Government intervention. It has come to be appreciated that rule–making in the standardisation process can also be as long and drawn out as legislating. The drafting points have been ameliorated through a greater willingness to provide for general obligations, although this has of course gone hand in hand with the integration of the standardisation process into the legal regime. The nature of sanctions still remain problematic, although there have been improvements in the range of post–market controls (see section 4C).

The use of criminal sanctions remains problematic in some jurisdictions. The criminal law's procedural requirements relating to evidence and the burden of proof seems inappropriate for legal rules which seek to change behaviour more than punish to abuse. The general criminal law (eg manslaughter) could be left to deal with truly culpable behaviour, with a different form of regulatory law applying in most of this area. This is especially so given that producers are typically protected by the procedural constraints of the criminal law and invariably escape without any significant criminal penalties being imposed. The United States does have civil penalties for breach of the Consumer Product Safety Act, although even then there is still the requirement that the act have been committed knowingly (although this is given an extended definition, see Chapter 4, section 2H).

Modern criticisms of Government intervention focus on its lack of technical knowledge and its tendency to be more responsive to industry than consumer concerns. It will be argued that both can be mitigated by the establishment of consumer product safety agencies. Such agencies would also have other advantages in terms of providing a focal point around which a coherent consumer safety policy could be developed.

The idea that Government officials can provide the technical expertise to establish product standards is no longer (if it ever was) tenable. Establishing a consumer safety agency would not necessarily increase the pool of Government expertise, but it would concentrate them in one place and provide a clear focal point to bring together experts in other Government departments, non–governmental organisations and the business community. We have already noted that one of the problems with regulating consumer products is the sheer number of different types of products concerned (section 1A). Creating an agency at least provides some framework within which attempts can be made to monitor relevant developments. Such an agency should probably concentrate on co–ordinating technical expertise in line with broad policies, rather than dealing with specifics.

Within agencies a distinction needs to be drawn between its technical work and its political control and orientation. The last paragraph was essentially concerned with the work of the agency's technical staff. It might be objected that their good work could be undermined by poor political leadership. The risk of this is to some extent reduced given that the role of such agencies will increasingly be less to develop their own rules than to monitor the activities of the standards bodies, but of course political direction remains important.

In this book we will study two existing consumer product safety agencies, the CPSC in the United States and the French Consumer Safety Commission (Chapter 4, section 2 and Chapter 6, section 3A). The American agency is more powerful than the French. In part this is because it has more powers, but also the independent commission has a greater tradition and political status within the United States' system of Government.[38]

This is probably an area which is best not treated as a political football. There is a danger that the goal of promoting consumer safety becomes confused with more short term political trends and objectives. For instance, there are signs that the CPSC suffered because some of its politically appointed commissioners adopted with zeal the budget cuts and deregulatory

---

38   S. Breyer and R. Stewart, *Administrative Law and Regulatory Policy* (2 ed.), (Little, Brown and Co, 1985) and M. Bernstein, *Regulating Business by Independent Commission*, (Princeton U.P., 1955).

philosophy of the Reagan years.[39] Of course consumer product safety policy cannot and should not be insulated from changes in modern regulatory policy. Indeed, the move towards general regulatory standards backed up by standardisation reflects modern political philosophy. However, the establishment a consumer product safety agency is/would be a recognition that these new approaches also generate concerns for consumers. The agency should act as a buffer for consumers and this would not be possible if it is subjected to the same direct political forces as the legislator.

Deregulation, in so far as it is linked to the need to make industry more competitive, also brings into question the neutrality of Government as an arbiter between producer and consumer interests. Government naturally has concerns for the safety of its consumer–citizens, but these concerns may be 'softer' than the need to promote its industry by cutting red tape and allowing businesses to operate in a less regulated environment.

In the United Kingdom, at the moment, the ability of one government department to protect both producers and consumers is being questioned. After BSE and other food scares, the role of the Ministry of Agriculture, Fisheries and Food (MAFF) as both a promoter of the farming and protector of the consumer interests is being called into question. Calls have been made for the establishment of an independent food agency to ensure food safety. There is indeed much to be said for an agency which is expressly directed to make safety a priority and works to that goal. The same arguments could be used to question whether the Department of Trade and Industry is best placed to protect the consumer.

However, some care is needed for an agency can also be highly influenced by industry lobbyists. Sometimes industry may support the establishment of an agency because it then knows whom it has to tame. This is less likely to be the case with a consumer product safety agency, as there is not one distinct industry which will be regulated. However, there are dangers that agencies forget their original objective and lose their youthful zeal. They establish working relations with those they regulate, come to compromises and seek to perpetuate and justify the status quo they have established. Bernstein has painted a picture of the life cycle of regulatory commissions which involves a long gestation period, a youthful stage during which it defines its role, which then gives way to a mature stage in which controversy subsides and the agency takes on the role of resolving conflicting interests within established procedures, before finally old age, debility and decline set in as the agency loses vitality.[40] This pattern is not universal and is not inevitable, but it is worth remembering this image so that the implicit dangers can be guarded against.

---

[39]   D. Bollier and J. Claybrook, *Freedom From Harm*, (Public Citizen, 1986) at 173.
[40]   *Op. cit.*, Chapter 3.

(ii) Standardisers

Standardisation bodies benefit from being able to draw upon a wide variety of technical expertise from the ranks of its membership. However, there is no disguising the fact that the bulk of these experts are drawn from industry and that industry dominates the standardisation process. The task for the standardisation bodies is to ensure that they have open democratic procedures which ensure that the consumer's voice is heard and that where consumers are not adequately represented they themselves ensure consumer issues are addressed. The important topic of consumer input is expanded upon below (see section 3D).

There is much appeal in the concept of a self–regulatory structure which permits interested parties to participate in discussions aimed at reaching a consensus. However, it is not realistic to rely upon this process alone to protect the consumer interest. Given the structural weaknesses of the consumer movement there is no chance of consumers having as great an influence as producers, unless there are some external controls. Therefore the task is to determine the proper role of the voluntary standards in a product safety regime.

Standards are technically competent documents written in a way which is comprehensible to the technicians who have to use them. They should be utilised because of these valuable characteristics. This can best be achieved by placing them within a legal framework where the broad safety principles have first been established in legislation (as under the EC's new approach see Chapter 2, section 4C). Such a regime also has the advantage of removing the voluntarism from self regulation, as all traders will have to satisfy the legal regime, regardless of whether they choose to adopt the standards.

It should be recognised that even in a standardisation regime underpinned by legal regulation, important safety decisions will still be made by the standardisers. This may not be a bad thing. Some of the trade offs between safety and utility involve a careful balancing of interests which cannot always be undertaken within the legislative process and the resulting choices may need to be reviewed on a frequent basis. Provided there are appropriate structures for consumer participation and that legislation sets the parameters for debate and fixes the basic principles of safety policy, then standardisation may be an appropriate vehicle to fine tune safety policy in the face of concrete problems. At several points the EC's new approach will be favourably contrasted with the position in the United States where voluntary standards have come to replace rather than supplement legislative rules (Chapter 4, section 2D). Although the CPSC retains some supervisory and fall back powers, the United States seems to have thrown the baby out with the bath water when they reacted to flaws in the regulatory–making scheme by preferring stand–alone voluntary standards rather than trying to create a partnership between regulation and standardisation.

C. Geographic Scope

Just as ideally every individual would be able to have products which provide optimum safety for their particular circumstances and preferences, so ideally each political unit should have safety laws which matched its values and traditions. We have already seen that individuals have to accept safety standards which are accommodations between different interests. Equally some safety rules are the result of compromises between different jurisdictions. This may be the result of experts from different countries working together to produce better quality rules and standards. Primarily, however, these harmonised norms result from the desire to promote international trade and the need to adopt harmonised technical standards to reduce barriers to trade.

Safety standards can be set at the local, national, regional or international level. Local rules are, however, becoming less and less sustainable. Local laws only really exist in a large federal country like the United States and even there the CPSC is given broad powers of pre–emption. Most product regulations and standards take the form of national laws and standards. The important question is the extent to which these should be influenced by regional and international developments. Only within Europe is there a compulsion to adopt regional laws and standards as national rules. Members of the EC must implement EC directives and national standards bodies must adopt European standards (Chapter 2, section 6E). The influence of regional and international developments is, however, *de facto* significant elsewhere and systems for notifying national rules and standards and allowing other countries to comment on them play an important role in preventing new technical barriers to trade (Chapter 2, section 3 and Chapter 3, section 2C).

From the consumer perspective there are obvious threats to consumer protection if the resulting harmonised standards reflect a low common denominator. More generally there is a danger that national values and traditions are sacrificed to free trade. Of course, some national rules represent disguised barriers to trade, rather than genuine attempts to meet national concerns. Equally, one should always be willing to consider changing one's values and traditions if a coherent argument can be made out for doing so; either because previous rules can be shown to be no longer relevant or because the benefits of promoting trade make some compromises worthwhile. Nevertheless one must be sure that the new regional or international rules meet legitimate consumer concerns.

It is normally easier to reach agreement on regional rules to replace national rules than it is to come to international agreements. States within regional trading zones tend to share relatively homogenous values and to have similar socio–economic conditions. At the international level one comes up against widely different expectations and interests between the different regions of the world and between developed and developing nations.

One therefore has a dichotomy between international agreements which are desirable to promote free trade and local/national rules which are more likely to reflect conditions on the ground and presumably are closer to consumer expectations in their area of application. Market integration is a powerful objective. Ricardo economics suggests that there are large welfare gains to be made from free trade between nations with each country specialising in the products and services which it produces most efficiently. This theory of comparative advantage retains an important influence on the trade policy of most countries. Consumers should benefit from a free trade policy which removes unnecessary barriers to trade and thereby increases choice and promotes competition. Consumers should be prepared to make some concessions for these benefits. They should be willing to re–evaluate rules to see if they still reflect the level of protection they desire or whether the required safety level can be delivered by different means. However, they should not be expected to forgo their right to a level of safety commensurate with their legitimate expectations.

Consumers should have confidence in regional and international rules and standards. This requires that they can participate in and effectively influence the decision–making processes which produce the regional and international norms. Industry should not forget that it is the major beneficiary of free trade agreements and so should be prepared to support consumer participation in the processes which bring it about. After all consumer confidence is needed if increased cross border trade is to flourish. Of course most governments are today also keen on free trade and are perhaps better placed than industry to provide the financial support which consumer groups need to help them organise on the international stage. The advantage of government rather than industry support is that it poses less threat to the independence of consumer groups. It also spreads the burden fairly on society as a whole, rather than imposing it on only those companies who accept their responsibilities to involve consumers.

D. Consumer Input

Regardless of whether the decision to intervene to assure minimum safety standards is made by Government, a state agency or standardisation bodies, it is important that account is taken of the consumer viewpoint. One reason for preferring that at least the main principles of intervention are set out in legislation is to guarantee that there is some degree of consultation with consumers. In some countries this is assured by formal due process requirements. In the United States, for instance, formal due process requirements apply to rule–making by the CPSC (Chapter 4, section 2D(i)). In the United Kingdom regulation making powers expressly impose a consultation duty (Chapter 5, section 3D). In most countries it is standard practice to consult widely before enacting regulations. This will almost certainly include listening to the main consumer organisations. Of course consultation does not guarantee that the consumer gets a good deal. The powerful lobbying power of industry is likely to be better able to manipulate both formal and informal means of influencing regulators and legislators than their under–resourced counterparts in the consumer movement.

Regulation, however, at least assures that consumers are able to influence decisions through democratic procedures. Self–regulation in theory offers consumers no such safeguards. However, within Europe, more or less formal agreements between the EC and Governments have been struck with European and national standards organisations. These have granted standardisation a special status, which almost amounts to making the standards bodies private legislators (at least within areas governed by the new approach). In return the standards bodies have agreed to adopt transparent procedures, to work for the public interest and to provide for the representation of a wide spectrum of opinions, including in particular consumer representation. At the international level, and in other countries where standardisation is less directly interwoven into the regulatory structures of the state, there is still nevertheless a developing consensus that the consumer voice should be heard in the standardisation process.

Given the central role which standardisation currently plays in establishing safety standards it is important to consider how best consumers can influence this process. The important questions relate to the forums within which the representation should take place and who should represent the consumer.[41]

(i)   Forums for Influence

It is important to differentiate between two levels (or stages) at which consumers should be able to influence the standardisation process. At the policy level, the standards organisations should give consumer safety a high

---

[41]   See, G. Howells, 'Consumer Safety and Standardisation – Protection Through Representation' in *Law and Diffuse Interests in the European Legal Order*, L. Krämer, H.–W. Micklitz and K. Tonner (eds), (*Nomos*, 1997).

priority. This means both that topics of interest to consumers are included in standardisation work programmes and that there are policies for ensuring that safety aspects are properly covered in standards. In the most developed standards bodies, this political input typically comes from a Consumer Council within the standards organisation, which will sometimes have representation on other organs of that body. This political input is certainly necessary. However, of more practical importance is the ability of consumers to influence the work of the technical committees which draft the standards. The political and practical representation may not necessarily be undertaken by the same persons.

(ii) Consumer Representatives

There are various possible candidates to represent the consumer interest. In considering their respective claims it is important to consider whether they wish to represent consumers at the policy or the technical level. It should also be remembered that there is not such a large army of consumer advocates (especially with technical knowledge) that one can afford to be too choosy about who speaks for consumers.

Being a consumer advocate on a standardisation technical committee can be a lonely affair and any support from whatever quarter is most certainly welcome. Moreover, ideally standardisation should bring together technical experts who work together for the best consensus solution. Although one may be critical about the interpretation of consumer needs put forward by some industry members of standardisation committees, most committee members do genuinely view consumer safety as important and it is necessary to build upon this starting point. Nevertheless when it comes to the use of public funds one can legitimately be more selective about how this is used to subsidise consumer representation. Here there should be a presumption that consumers or their representatives are better placed than industry representatives or bureaucrats to represent their views. However, this should be balanced by an appreciation that in some countries the consumer movement is too underdeveloped and lacks sufficient technical expertise adequately to address the issues raised by standardisation.

(a) Industry

Industry often claims that it can be trusted to take the consumer interest into account. It argues that it is in its own interest to ensure that standards afford consumers the appropriate amount of safety. Indeed in the United States ANSI uses this self interest as a reason for encouraging industry to participate in its Consumer Interest Council (see Chapter 4, section 3(ii)).

It is certainly true that many of the industry representatives who are active in standardisation come from companies which seek to adopt responsible safety policies; this may even be for more altruistic reasons rather than simply because they are seeking to squeeze out competitors who work to lower standards. Many of the individuals who devote their time to standardisation work probably view their input as having a wider value than simply promoting the interests of their employer. Indeed in recessionary times this non–income generating work probably does themselves little good in career terms. However, although the efforts made by industry representatives to promote consumer safety standards are to be welcomed, it is not enough to trust to the benevolence of manufacturers. Industry representatives will also have their own agenda, which may at times conflict with the consumer interest.

A slightly different point is raised in relation to organisations responsible for purchasing goods for sale on to consumers. They sometimes claim that they have experience which can benefit consumers and that they share the same interests as consumers. Thus the British Retail Consortium has used this argument to obtain a seat on BSI's Consumer Council (Chapter 5, section 4D). Whilst it is heartening that such bodies wish to lobby for effective consumer standards, there is a problem about their having a seat on a body which is supposed to represent the consumer interest. It seems appropriate that individual consumers should have a forum in which to develop their own policy on standardisation and that business interests of any kind have no place there, however, well intentioned they may be.

(b) Government

Government clearly has an interest in ensuring standards adequately protect the consumer's safety. Even in the present deregulatory climate Government retains some residual responsibility for assuring consumer products are produced to standards which secure the consumer's safety. For instance, in the United States the CPSC must be assured that voluntary standards adequately protect consumers (Chapter 4, section 2D(i)). Within Europe, adequate safety ought to be assured through the essential safety requirements set out in the new approach directives (Chapter 2, section 4C).

Government typically has technical experts – something which the consumer movement typically lacks – and can be expected to view consumer safety as an important factor. Therefore it is useful if its technical experts can participate at the technical level. However, this should not be a substitute for direct consumer representation, for Government has to balance the consumer interest against other competing demands of trade policy and therefore it may not always come up with the same answers as the consumer movement.

The need for government to balance other interests than simply the concerns of consumers also augurs against permitting government an input into the political structures for consumer participation. However a distinction might be drawn between government departments, such as the Consumer Safety Unit within the United Kingdom's Department of Trade and Industry (Chapter 5, section 3B), and more independent government agencies which have the express objective of promoting consumer safety, such as the CPSC in the United States (Chapter 4, section 2). Government bodies may of course be usefully granted associate/observer status within consumer councils so that their experience and support can be drawn upon when desirable.

(c) Independent Test Houses

The role of independent test houses can be equated in many respects to that of government. They have a lot of technical expertise and typically share many of the concerns of consumers. Therefore their participation at the technical level is to be welcomed. However, this should be in addition to direct consumer representation and should not extend to direct political input, because they may also have their own agendas which do not necessarily coincide in all respects with the consumer movement. There is also a problem of legitimating any claim they might make to be the representative of consumers. A distinction might be made for test houses which are established by the consumer movement and also undertake comparative testing (eg Stiftung Warentest in Germany, see Chapter 7, section 3F). These may be well placed to participate in both the political and technical representation of consumers.

(d) Standards Officers

Consumer Council secretariats within the standards organisations usually have a degree of autonomy. Their officers tend to be sympathetic to the consumer interest. This is even the case where, as in AFNOR, the secretariat's role is to facilitate the involvement of the consumer movement rather than voicing consumer concerns itself (Chapter 6, section 9E). This neutral role is, however, probably not the best means of ensuring effective consumer representation. The consumer movement has a relatively weak infrastructure in many countries. Pro–active consumer advocates within the standards organisations can help to galvanise the efforts of the consumer movement. The consumer movement itself has relatively few technical experts, but it has also, until recently, neglected the political side of standardisation.[42] Consumer organisations adopted the traditional view of standardisation as being a purely technical subject and failed to appreciate the increased significance of standardisation. The role of the Consumer Council can be to sensitise the consumer movement to the politics of standardisation.

The BSI Consumer Council is a good example of a secretariat which associates itself with the political aspirations of consumers (Chapter 5, section 4D). Officials can exert a significant influence over the direction of consumer policy, but this can be seen as a healthy support to the consumer movement so long as the officials are truly autonomous from the values of the standards body. Of course, even with the best intentions this may not be wholly possible as the officials are bound to be affected by the climate within which they work. It is therefore essential that the officials are clearly accountable to a council dominated by consumers and their representatives. Where the consumer movement is well developed and sensitive to the issues in standardisation it can be expected to need little direction from the secretariat, but officials can provide a useful safety net where consumer representation is less well developed.

In Germany the DIN Consumer Council goes one stage further and provides technical staff to represent the consumer position in technical committees as well as organising the political input of consumers (Chapter 7, section 6D). It is difficult to evaluate the policy of providing in–house technical experts. It is clearly an attempt to address the need for more pro– consumer technical experts to participate in the work of the technical committees. The DIN experts do seem to have independence and be able to represent consumers effectively. Although the German solution seems to work for them there are reasons for favouring public funds (the government meets 80% of the cost of the DIN Consumer Council) being paid directly to consumer groups to employ their own technical experts. Although there are problems with claiming that consumer organisations truly reflect consumer opinion, at least some legitimation is possible. However much standards officials consult consumer groups or undertake consumer opinion research, in the final analysis they have to make a personal judgment, which at least to some extent must be constrained by their position as an employee of the standards organisation. It is also possible that the funds could be used more

---

42   One suspects the American consumer organisations still do not participate fully enough in standards work, whereas in Europe the profile of standardisation has increased because of its central role in the new approach and consumers have accordingly shown more interest in the subject.

effectively by the consumer organisations, as they may be able to combine it with their own limited resources.

(e) Consumers

Direct consumer input is of course essential. However this can take several forms. One distinction is between those consumer representatives with technical knowledge and those without. The only way consumers can really influence the technical committees is for their representatives to be respected for their technical knowledge by the other members who will all have a technical background. Thus in the European countries studied consumer representation seemed most effective in the United Kingdom (where the Consumers' Association has a number of technical experts) and in Germany (because of the DIN officials and Stiftung Warentest).

The consumer movement also has a political side made up of activists who lobby for improved consumer protection. These activists are usually found in consumer organisations. Within consumer organisations a distinction must be drawn between their employees and the political officers of the association. Although the employees are typically very committed to the consumer cause, it is the political officers, who (assuming they are democratically elected) have the best claim to sit as consumer representatives on the Consumer Council and other organs of the standards–writing bodies.

There is, of course, a complex debate about who is entitled to represent consumers. Consumers are not a section of society with homogenous interests and values, rather all members of society are consumers. Obviously some products will have their own specific consumer organisations (eg the motoring organisations), but even with respect to these products there are complex balances to be struck. For all products there is a need to balance safety concerns against other issues, such as price, availability, choice etc. It is difficult for an organisation to represent all the diffuse interests of consumers, but unless one accepts the exclusion of the consumer voice one has to take account of those consumers who have organised themselves along open democratic lines. This is acceptable because the consumer groups will not be determining what policy should be adopted, but will merely be able to inform and influence the debate. However, it also places an onus on the consumer organisations to become more professional in the ways they operate. In many countries consumer groups remain largely semi–professional bodies and this is next to useless if they are really going to influence policy and technical debates.

The involvement of 'professional' consumerists – be they technical experts employed by consumer organisations or consumer activists – needs to be tempered by other means of involving the wider public. This is necessary both to try to gauge whether the views of the consumer movement are in line with general public opinion and because lay participation can bring a new perspective. Technical experts and political activists may overlook the practical needs of consumers. Consumers, who actually use the products, are often best placed to appreciate the problems which standards have to address. They are also able to comment on the proposed solutions, because they know how the product is used in practice and this may differ from the way indicated in the manufacturer's instructions.

Of the countries studied in detail, the BSI in the United Kingdom has perhaps gone furthest down the route by recruiting lay members to sit on technical committees (Chapter 5, section 4D). Although a welcome recognition of the need to involve lay consumers, this is not perhaps the best way of using consumer volunteers as they may not be able to follow or influence the technical debates. Canada may provide an interesting model for consumer participation.[43] Canada adopted and developed the idea, originally introduced in the United States, of Consumer Sounding Boards. These involve lay members of the public who review draft standards and participate in seminars and meetings held by the standards–writing bodies. The Canadian Standards Association established Consumer Advisory Panels in Toronto, Vancouver, Montreal, Winnipeg and Halifax. These have now been disbanded, apart from the one in Winnipeg board which continues to specialise in health and safety at work matters. The members of the disbanded boards have been merged into a Consumer Network which will be consulted on a more *ad hoc* basis. The motivation for this move was largely finance driven. It was considered to be more effective to use resources to send experts to sit on committees. There also seems to have been a feeling that the system needed to be reinvigorated as the Consumer Advisory Board meetings, which were usually held in the evening in hotels, had evolved into pleasant social events at which members were educated about consumer problems, but did not necessarily provide sufficiently useful feedback to justify the cost of the sessions.

Nevertheless, the idea of sounding boards or consumer networks warrants further consideration, for in principle they seem to be a useful model for involving lay consumers in the review of draft standards without having to place them on technical committees, where the detail may go over their heads. It may be more appropriate for lay consumers to undertake this broad review rather than for them to become entangled in technical debates. It is, however, important that they are involved at an early stage and not simply left to respond to drafts. A liaison between the technical consumer experts and these lay advisers could take place and one could envisage delegates from amongst the lay advisers sitting on the Consumer Councils to

---

43   See *Standards and the Consumer*, (Standards Council of Canada, 1993).

counterbalance the political representation from the formal consumer movement. Of course even these lay members may not necessarily be representative of the public at large. By their action in coming forward and being willing to participate they have marked themselves out as distinctive. Therefore consumer groups, government departments and agencies and the standards bodies should complement this by consumer opinion research. The objective should be to establish as accurate as possible a picture of consumer needs and demands. Of course it follows from our previous discussion that the role of regulators/standardisers is not necessarily to mimic public opinion, but it should surely be an important starting point for debates.

(iii) Structures for Consumer Representation

Those organisations which claim to represent consumers need to come together to develop co–ordinated strategies. At the national level the only effective forum may be within the Consumer Council structures established by the standards organisations. In the Netherlands there had been an attempt to organise the consumer representation on the Consumer Council of the Dutch Standards Institute (the COCON of the NNI) within an independent Dutch Platform for Standardisation (NCN) made up of the standards work co–ordinators of consumer–oriented organisations.[44] However, this has now been abandoned with consumer groups seeing their efforts better directed at co–ordinating at the European level within the ANEC structure (Chapter 2, section 6D).

At the regional (at least in Europe and N. America)[45] and international level consumer groups may be better able to organise themselves outside the standards bodies. At this level there should be enough consumer organisations to create an independent structure and it is more desirable that the representation comes from the consumer movement than the consumer wing of the standards bodies, for it is not always clear how representative some Consumer Councils are of the consumer interest. In some countries there is even no Consumer Council and merely a member of staff responsible for consumer affairs. Thus it will be obvious that the structure in Europe of ANEC co–ordinating consumer representation by consumer groups within the CEN structure (Chapter 2, section 6D) is to be preferred to the ISO–COPOLCO solution based on consumer representation from within national standardisation bodies (Chapter 3, section 3C). However, ISO contrasts favourable with the IEC (International Electrotechnical Commission) which

---

44   ANEC, *Consumer Participation in Standardisation*, (ANEC, 1996) at 33–34.

45   Although in the United States many consumer organisations display a surprising and disturbing lack of commitment to participation in the standardisation process.

believes that consumers can be adequately represented within national delegations.

The general pros and cons of regionalisation and internationalisation of standards making have already been mentioned (section 3C). It causes particular problems with respect to consumer representation. Where this has been established at the national level, the national consumer organisations find that they now have to fight for a place within national delegations to regional or international committees, where they have to represent the national position even if this contradicts in some respects their view of the consumer interest. There are also the added costs of having to co–ordinate the approach of consumers in different countries, which may have different priorities or values. Within a relatively homogenous group of nations, such as the members of the EC, these problems can largely be overcome by funding co–ordinating bodies such as ANEC. It even offers opportunities to pool resources for effective representation at the regional level, rather than having to fight on several different fronts.

However, at the international level the position is different. In the developing world there is very little consumer representation and it is appropriate that there is an organisation such as Consumers International (CI) which prioritises protecting the interests of third world consumers. However, it is wrong that CI – particularly because it has this open bias – should be the only consumer organisation permitted direct access to ISO negotiations (Chapter 3, section 3C). CI should have direct rights of representation, but so too should regional consumer groups. Often consumers have the same concerns globally; but sometimes the needs of first and third world consumers conflict. If the standardisation process really wants to have a well developed consensus ISO should be more open to these regional groups and not hide behind formal constitutional matters to argue that its membership is only open to international bodies.

(iv)   *Role of Consumers Within Standards Organisations*

Within standards bodies consumers need to be able to influence decision–making. They therefore need to be represented on committees, boards, assemblies etc. which deal with general policy or matters of particular interest to consumers. It is obviously better if they have full status within the standards body and full voting rights on any organs they serve on, but as consumers are unlikely to be able to out vote the other members – their main weapon being moral suasion – observer status is not too much of a handicap.

Influence at the political level is important to ensure that the standards body appreciates the need for consumer input, but in reality it is far less important than being able to influence the decisions of technical committees.

Here consumer organisations ought to be represented in their own right and ought not to need the sponsorship by any internal organ of a standardisation body, such as a Consumer Council. Funding must of course respect this principle with resources being directed to independent consumer organisations.

Standards committees work on the consensus principle and it is important that this means that the consumer voice cannot be ignored. Just as the opposition of an important industry concern might block a proposed standard so should consumer resistance. Consideration should also be given to making a consumer representative the chairman – with appropriate financial backing – whenever a committee is dealing directly with a consumer concern (this has occurred at the European level, Chapter 2, section 6D). A chairman of a committee heavily influences the direction of discussions and there can be no better guarantee of the quality of the resulting standard from the consumer's perspective than to have its development overseen by consumer experts. Industry has a lot to gain from the harmonisation of standards and the internationalisation of trade. It is important that consumers also gain and are protected from its dangers. In this process consumers should be given a central role in influencing the standard–making process and should not be simply left at the margins. Whilst the US experience suggests it is too much for consumer groups to be entrusted to develop a wide range of standards by themselves (Chapter 4, section 2D), the chairing of relevant committees provided it is backed up with resources, should allow consumers to have confidence in the resulting standards.

E. Forms of Intervention

In this section we will look at some of the issues surrounding the form which rules and standards should adopt. Some of these clearly go to the heart of regulatory policy. Others may appear more technical in nature, but are also significant in ensuring that the norms combine flexibility with the need to provide effective consumer protection.

(i) Information vs Product Specification

Those who fear excessive regulation will erode individual autonomy, frequently argue that the main purpose of regulations and standards should be to provide consumers with information on product risk so that they can make informed decisions for themselves. Certainly information warning about product risks is important for those risks which are acceptable characteristics of the product. Warnings can provide the means for consumers to take steps to avoid potential dangers or to decide whether to expose themselves to a potential risk by using the product. Warnings therefore can serve either as a means of removing the danger or as a method for communicating information about the danger. However, there are limits to the effectiveness with which warnings can perform these functions.

For some groups such as the young, old or disabled it may be difficult or impossible for them to appreciate the warning and/or to make use of the warning to protect themselves. Some members of these groups will also have difficulty in using the warning to make an informed decision whether or not to risk exposure to a potential risk. These categories have particular vulnerabilities which require regulators to consider whether the special risks they face justify regulation over and above that required to protect the general public.

However, warnings are not an unproblematic form of protection even for the 'average' consumer. Returning to the theme of the need to acknowledge that individuals are not always equipped to protect themselves, one needs to understand that this also extends to their ability to understand and make use of warnings. Warnings may be written in too technical language; consumers may be unable satisfactorily to undertake the precautions needed to avoid the danger or to weigh up the risks involved.

There are some circumstances in which it is desirable to permit consumers a discretion to decide whether to expose themselves to a risk. This may be because the scientific evidence is indecisive or the risk may lie within the tolerable range where reasonable people can come to different conclusions as to the desirability of incurring the risk. Equally some products may have exceptional utility to particular consumers. However, where risks are unacceptable and warnings cannot be relied upon to remove them, then, regulations simply imposing warning obligations can be inappropriate and amount to little more than sham protection.

A distinction should also be drawn between warnings and instructions. Many products are unsafe unless operated properly. Therefore consumers must be given sensible comprehensible instructions. Equally consumers can sometimes only be persuaded to follow instructions if they are warned of the consequences of failing to do so.[46] Therefore appropriate rules on instructions for use are a legitimate part of any regulatory regime. There have indeed been calls for regulators to develop the use of this type of information provision.[47] It is probably fair to suggest that this approach will

---

[46]　Cf H.C. Dillard and H. Hart, 'Product Liability: Directions for Use and Failure to Warn' (1955) 41 *Virginia L.R.* 145.

[47]　See, R. Petty, 'Regulating Product Safety: the Informational Role of the US Federal Trade Commission' (1995) 18 *J.C.P.* 387.

have a greater impact on consumer behaviour than pre–purchase information, which often goes over the heads of many consumers more interested in the benefits than the risks of products. However, it would be unfortunate if a strategy promoting the improvement of user instructions was used to give succour to the argument that the problem of product safety is more a problem of consumer (mis)behaviour than product design.[48] Although it is true than there are many accidents involving products where the product is merely incidental to the injury, there are other situations where what looks like an injury induced by the consumer's behaviour could have been avoided by designers taking account of foreseeable misuse or where aspects of the product or its marketing encouraged misuse.

(ii) Performance vs Design

There is a clear trend to favour product standards framed in terms of performance objectives rather than design specifications. In the United States this goes so far as prohibiting the use of design specifications in regulations (Chapter 4, section 2D(i)(a)).This is due to an understandable desire to permit manufacturers as much scope for innovation and product differentiation (which increases consumer choice) as is consistent with consumer safety.

However, it is sometimes difficulty to maintain a clear divide between performance and design standards. Some performance standards may be so specific that in practice the choice of design is severely limited. Equally design standards may still be appropriate where a particular design solution is known to be superior to alternatives or where potential risks are so severe that the producer's discretion should be curtailed. The United States therefore seems to have gone too far by totally prohibiting the CPSC from using design standards.

Where standards do leave producers a large margin of discretion as to how they meet performance goals this has implications for the systems of market surveillance. This relates back to the criticism that the trend to rely on harmonised voluntary standards and to ease conformity assessment procedures have unfortunately gone hand in hand with a more hands off approach to enforcement (section 1B). Under the new approach producers are given the freedom to decide whether they comply with essential safety requirements by complying with standards or by other means. If a producer chooses to rely on his own judgment, rather than follow the standards, then third party conformity assessment is usually required (Chapter 2, section 4C). However, standards can themselves contain a broad discretion as to

---

[48]   *Ibid.*, at 388.

how to meet general performance requirements and often third party approval is not required to confirm that the performance standards have been satisfied. This would seem to suggest that a regime which includes flexible performance standards requires increased post–market supervision of the design choices of producers.

(iii) Vertical vs Horizontal

Traditionally regulations and standards have been product related. They have attempted to cover a number of risks associated with the product by providing solutions tailored to the particular subject matter being regulated. Recently the idea has been proposed of regulating generic risks in horizontal norms.[49] This approach recognises that many risks are common to a wide variety of products and that it is sensible to develop a framework policy for responding to these generic risks.

The solutions adopted in the resulting horizontal norms can of course be developed and adapted to the specific needs of certain products through vertical norms. However, the horizontal norms can not only be used as an informed starting point for the development of vertical norms, but they also provide principles to guide producers in product sectors where norms covering these safety aspects have not yet been developed.

To date the standardisation bodies have only made tentative moves towards embracing horizontal norms (Chapter 2, section 6C). This may be partly explained by the preference of producers to have the certainty which comes from knowing that all their obligations are found in standards which specifically relate to their products.

(iv) General Safety Obligations

There is also an increased tendency to rely on general clauses. This occurs in two types of situation. General clauses requiring that products do not endanger consumer safety are sometimes found in product specific regulations. New approach directives contain such clauses (Chapter 2, section 4C). Here the objective is to ensure that all product *risks* are covered. However, the general law can also contain general safety obligations not to market unsafe products; as in the General Product Safety Directive (Chapter 2, section 9). Here the objective is to ensure that all *products* are covered.

---

[49]   W. van Weperen, 'A Hazard–Oriented Approach to Product Safety Criteria' [1992] *Product Safety and Liability Reporter* 359.

The General Product Safety Directive imposes a substantive obligation that all products placed on the market must be safe. This is clearly a form of pre–market control which attempts to influence producer behaviour (although France has no sanction for breach of its general safety obligation, see Chapter 6, section 5A). However, post–market controls can also be triggered by breach of this substantive standard. Although the United States has no positive obligation to market safe products, its powers to act against imminently hazardous products and substantial product hazards can be seen as a post–market control based on a general safety obligation (Chapter 4, sections 9D and E).

If general safety obligations are a form of pre–market control they should attempt to regulate the behaviour of the producer, whereas if they are post–market controls they should be are directed to enforcement officials and judges. Of course general safety obligations will frequently have both pre– and post–market functions. Producer behaviour will be influenced by both the wording of the standard and the interpretations given to it by both enforcement officials and the courts.

General safety obligations probably have their most powerful effects when used as a means of post–market control. It is hard to influence producer decision–making by simply exhorting them to make a safe product; most producers would claim that this was their natural intention. Producers respond better to more specific rules directing particular steps be taken. On the other hand enforcement officials and, sometimes, courts find general clauses useful as a catch all provision to prevent any dangerous products from slipping through the regulatory net.

By definition a general safety clause is abstract. Some commentators have argued that the concept of the legitimate expectation of consumers is a useful concept to assist in concretising this norm.[50] The 'legitimate expectations' concept is a useful heuristic tool and of practical relevance when dealing with the protection of consumers' economic interests where expectations can be founded in negotiations, contracts and advertising. In the safety context, products must of course satisfy the reasonable expectations of consumers, but in fact the legitimate expectations concept masks disagreements about what consumers should expect – should the product be safe or only as safe as a reasonable producer could have been expected to make it? Equally safety regulation should establish responsible safety norms rather than merely reflect individual preferences which may not be very demanding in terms of the level of safety expected (section 3A(i)). Perhaps,

---

[50]   H.–W. Micklitz, 'Principles of Justice in Private Law Within the European Union' in *Principles of Justice and the Law at the European Union*, E. Paasivirta and K. Rissanen (eds), (Institute of International Economic Law, University of Helsinki, 1995) at 284–286.

the best one can do is to have a general safety requirement that products pose no or only minimal risk and structure the assessment of that risk by requiring certain factors to be taken into account (for the factors relevant under the General Product Safety Directive, see Chapter 2, section 9D).

One matter which the general clause can address is whether safety should be judged only according to the uses prescribed by the producer or whether the producer should have to take into account the possibility of the product being misused. The solution most commonly adopted is to require the producer to guard against the consequences of foreseeable misuse, but not wholly unreasonable uses.[51] This seems to strike a sensible balance between giving the producer the freedom to place unrealistic restrictions on the uses to which the product can be put and making him responsible for the results of consumer misconduct.

The general safety obligations found in new approach directives are supplemented by the essential safety requirements. Where the law contains a general safety obligation this is usually structured in such a way as to give the producer some confidence that if certain rules, standards or common practices are followed then he will not have committed an offence by marketing the product (for the General Product Safety Directive, see Chapter 2, section 9D). The principle behind this is that breach of an abstract standard alone is too uncertain a basis for criminal liability to be imposed on a producer. However, under the General Product Safety Directive this standard could still be invoked to justify exercising post–market controls.

Where the law contains a general safety obligation the relationship between this and the rules and procedures laid down in specific product safety regulations needs to be worked out. An appealing solution would be for the two sets of rules to have concurrent application. One might express a preference for the application of the specific regulation, but the general law would always be available to fill gaps. However, there has been resistance to this approach, mainly by industry which prefers the comfort of knowing that it has to deal only with those rules and procedures which specifically apply to its sector. These are often administered by its traditional regulator with whom it would normally have established a working relationship. If the general safety obligation is administered by a different agency from the specific regulations, industry may be concerned that the equilibrium it has established with its regulators will be disturbed. One might consider this a good thing, but legislation has tended to accept the principle of the general safety obligation being subsidiary to specific laws (for the position under the General Product Safety Directive see Chapter 2, section 9C; for the extreme

---

51   C. Joerges, J. Falke, H.–W. Micklitz and G. Brüggemeier, *Die Sicherheit von Konsumgütern und die Entwicklung der Europäischen Gemeinscaft*, (*Nomos*, 1988) at 43.

position taken in Germany see Chapter 7, section 5A and for the more flexible approach in the United Kingdom see Chapter 5, section 3L). However, there is a general acceptance that even where products continue to be governed solely by specific legislation so far as fixing the standards demanded of the goods is concerned, nevertheless there should be the possibility of post–market controls based on breach of the general safety obligation.

(v) Conformity Assessment[52]

Conformity assessment is becoming a key element of product production and marketing. Commercial buyers are increasingly looking for evidence that products conform to standards and that businesses operate accredited quality assurance programmes. This is happening on a voluntary basis. The EC's new and global approaches places this on a regulatory basis (Chapter 2, section 4). However, to the extent that there is a preference for manufacturer's self–declaration of conformity over third party assessment there may be some concern that the system is in reality based on 'affirmation' of conformity rather than 'assessment' of conformity.

Information on conformity assessment is usually communicated by a mark. Within Europe the CE marking has gained a certain amount of familiarity with the general public, as well as within the business and enforcement communities. However, the CE marking signifies no more than that the product conforms to EC new approach directives. It does not necessarily signify that the product has been tested by third parties, nor is it an explicit safety mark comparable to the German GS mark (Chapter 7, section 4D). From the consumer's perspective it is probably more important to promote a safety mark which is backed up by third party approval, than a mark which signifies conformity to directives whose content is unknown to most consumers and which can be awarded by a manufacturer to himself. There is of course a danger that the number of marks proliferates so that the aim of informing the consumer is lost amongst the resulting confusion. The aim therefore should be to promote meaningful regional and international marks which consumers can have confidence in so that national marks can become obsolete.

Assessments of the value of signals about conformity will depend upon to whom the message of conformity is addressed. The CE marking is not primarily directed at consumers, but rather at enforcement authorities in order to indicate that the product should be permitted free circulation within

---

52   See generally *Certification – Principles and Practice*, (ISO, 1980) and R. Wankling, *Quality Assurance*, (Institute of Trading Standards Administration, 1985).

the community with minimal regulatory supervision. Equally in the United States the requirement on manufacturers to produce a certificate indicating compliance with standards is for the benefit of distributors and retailers. The problem is that consumers are using the CE marking and probably unfortunately drawing incorrect inferences from it about the product's safety.

There is a certain irony in the fact that as a conformity mark, such as the CE marking, becomes more widely recognised by consumers and plays a more decisive role in their purchasing decisions, so does the temptation for producers to use the marking even when it is not warranted. Within the European context there is a further temptation to do this because of the light enforcement policy for products which bear the CE marking. This is a further example of how a deregulatory policy needs to be supported by effective market surveillance and supervision.

4.   POST–MARKET CONTROLS

A.   Institutions

(i)   Need for Local Presence

With respect to the pre–market control function of establishing safety standards we saw that it was important that this was at least undertaken by an agency at the national level and that wherever possible this should co–ordinate activities with regional and international bodies (section 3C). With respect to post–market control functions different criteria apply.

Ideally there should be a strong presence at the local level so that enforcement officers can detect dangerous goods in circulation and develop working relations with traders. The United Kingdom's system of trading standards officers in each local authority is perhaps the best example of a locally organised enforcement service (Chapter 5, section 3B), although Germany also has a decentralised system based on its Länder (Chapter 7, section 3B). The United States has a more centralised system with the CPSC having to rely upon three regional offices and relatively few field officers (Chapter 4, section 2A). France lies somewhere in between with a central authority in Paris having a number of regional offices (Chapter 6, section 3B).

However, localised enforcement gives rise to its own problems. Difficulties may be created for businesses which trade on a national basis if the law is interpreted differently by individual local enforcement authorities. There are at least two responses to this potential problem: the French resolve it by the regional offices referring policy questions back to Paris, whereas the United Kingdom has developed the home authority principle so that ideally one authority will handle all policy questions affecting a particular business. Businesses sometimes question the quality of local decision–making – they fear the loose cannon which can cause businesses unnecessary trouble. Certainly one would want to see local enforcement officials working to common national guidelines.

If the unit of enforcement is too localised this can create its own problems for enforcement officials. In the United Kingdom there are difficulties providing consumer protection services in very small local authorities. This is particularly so given the general squeeze on resources within trading standards departments. This may mean that some local authorities do not have the infrastructure to handle large product safety problems. The solution may be for smaller authorities to co–operate with one another and/or their larger neighbours.

There is much to be said in favour of there being a national authority co–ordinating consumer safety policy. The lack of such a structure is a major criticism of the German system. Of course national traditions differ as to the extent to which national authorities become involved in enforcement and integrate this role with their data collection and standard setting functions. The United States' CPSC represents the best example of an integrated approach, whereas the Consumer Safety Unit of the United Kingdom's Department of Trade and Industry tries to avoid becoming involved in enforcement. In France a distinction is drawn between the enforcement function carried out by the DGCCRF and the educative and informational role of the Consumer Safety Commission. Although the strong national traditions render it pointless to lay down any blueprint, an ideal model might be one which combined the integrated approach of the United States' CPSC with the local enforcement of the British trading standards officers.

(ii) International Co–operation

Within regional trading zones, such as the EC, a strong argument can be advanced for the establishment of a European Safety Agency. This could have the role of ensuring that pre– and post–market controls are exercised in a co–ordinated and consistent manner by the member states and also pool research and act as the co–ordinator for information exchanges.

The scale of international trade in consumer products means that enforcement can no longer be a purely national matter. Customs officials need to be integrated into the system to ensure that dangerous products do not enter markets. For free trade zones there is the challenge of ensuring that their external border checks are effective so that goods can with confidence be permitted to circulate freely once they have entered the trading area.

There has also been an increasing recognition that consumers in different countries may face dangers from similar products. This problem is most acute in free trade zones, but in fact applies equally to most trading nations as dangerous products are likely to appear on several national markets. Enforcement authorities have recognised the need for information exchange systems. Of course international information exchange systems would not be concerned with matters of purely local concern, although nowadays most products are likely to have international dimensions as many products can be switched with ease from one market to another.

The EC's RAPEX system is the most developed international information exchange, but suffers from bureaucratic structures and rigid rules (Chapter 2, section 9J(b)). The OECD's voluntary system is in danger of becoming moribund as European authorities direct their efforts into the RAPEX system, but in principle provides a more flexible mechanism for exchanging information between a wider group of nations (Chapter 3, section 4). Equally informal exchanges between enforcement officers can be useful, but cannot be relied upon to secure consumer safety. What is needed is a network of regional information exchange systems which could be based around a series of central co–ordinating points in each of the regional free trade zones. Information could then be disseminated both within the regional network and when appropriate passed on to other regional centres. A possible model for such international exchanges might be the suggested exchange of information between the EC RAPEX system and a system which is being proposed for the PHARE countries of Central and Eastern Europe (Chapter 2, section 9J(b)).

Of course care would have to be taken to ensure confidentiality and the question of whom should have access to the information would have to be considered. Probably such an international exchange system would have to be restricted to national authorities, although they could have discretion to disseminate the information responsibly within their territories. This need not preclude national or regional information systems having closer links with other groups, such as consumer organisations who may benefit from information on product safety risks.

B.   Enforcement Issues

(i)   Obtaining Information on Dangerous Products

It is important that national authorities have information of risks present within their territory, both so that they can take action themselves and also so that information can be passed on to other countries. The United States has an interesting technique for obtaining such information, by placing the responsibility on producers and traders to notify the CPSC of risks (Chapter 4, section 2E). This approach is appealing in times of reduced resources, although it should be stressed that market surveillance by enforcement officials should not be done away with altogether. If self–reporting is to be relied upon there must be effective sanctions to ensure that traders take their reporting obligations seriously. In the United States it may be significant that the risk of punitive damages in product liability suits may encourage traders to comply with their obligations.

(ii) Enforcement Powers

Whichever authority is given the task of enforcing consumer safety, it is imperative that they have adequate powers to track down and act against dangerous goods. This requires them to have access to all levels of the production and distribution chain. They should have the power to take and test samples and to require the production of relevant documents. It is also important that they have the right to act against suspect as well as obviously dangerous products.

(iii) Compensation for Traders

An inhibiting factor preventing effective post–market control can be the exposure of enforcement authorities to compensation claims. A balance needs to be struck between protecting (a) the trader whose products may be falsely accused of being dangerous and who incurs losses as a result and (b) the need to protect consumers by ensuring enforcement officials can use their powers effectively.

The problem is not as acute for many consumer products as it is for food which is perishable, but some compensation claims can be potentially large. Although it may be possible for authorities to insure against such risks, many public authorities are likely to act as self insurers.

In any event officials are unlikely to act precipitively against suspect goods because of the political backlash they are likely to suffer if they get such decisions wrong. Traders can also be protected by providing them with rights of appeal and requiring the courts to sanction the actions of officials. Given these controls the decision to impose compensation obligations should be carefully considered.

If compensation is considered appropriate, attention should be given to whether it should extend to loss of profits or only cover deterioration in the goods. In principle it would also seem fairer to restrict the compensation obligation to situations where the enforcement authority did not have reasonable grounds for taking the steps they took. A claim ought not be possible simply because after a more detailed examination it was discovered that the relevant provision was not in fact breached. Unfortunately the legal regimes do not seem to be so lenient to enforcement officials.

C. Types of Control

(i)   Introduction

The distinction between pre– and post–market controls is not always clear cut. Indeed the main tools of pre–market control (regulations, standards, general safety obligations etc.) only bite when post–market action is taken for their breach. We have also already seen that the criminal character of many of these sanctions impose the burdens of criminal procedure on enforcement authorities. This is perhaps unnecessarily onerous since infringements of this sort are not generally regarded as being 'truly' criminal and certainly the punishments do not usually reflect any serious moral turpitude.

Distinct from these powers to act against breaches of pre–market controls are the specific powers to take action to prohibit goods which are already in circulation from being marketed. The aim of these powers is to prevent dangerous goods from reaching consumers by restricting their further sale. However, the distinction between post– and pre–market controls remains elusive, for whilst some countries, such as Germany, achieve this by using a prohibition order (Untersagung) (Chapter 7, section 4E), others use the mechanism of emergency regulation–making powers (see, United Kingdom, Chapter 5, section 3E and France, Chapter 6, section 5D). Indeed the United Kingdom did at one time have a prohibition order, but the need for this was removed when the emergency regulation–making procedure was introduced. In both the United Kingdom and France a distinction is drawn between generic problems which are now addressed through emergency regulations and risks associated with particular products and/or specific traders for which special rules apply (prohibition notices in the United Kingdom, Chapter 5, section 3F and for the French equivalent see Chapter 6, section 5E).

These post–market controls often need to be invoked with urgency. The law seems to recognise the difficulty enforcement authorities face when having to react at speed to developing situations in which there is uncertainty about the extent and real nature of the danger, if any, posed by the product.[53]

---

[53]   H.–W. Micklitz and T. Roethe, 'Federalism in Progress' in H.–W. Micklitz, T. Roethe and S. Weatherill (eds), *Federalism and Responsibility*, (Graham & Trotman, 1994).

Consumer safety is usually given priority; thus rights of consultation and to appeal are typically postponed until after the emergency measures have come into effect.

(ii) Seizure, Detention and Destruction

If dangerous goods are on the market place it may not be sufficient simply to prohibit their use. Unscrupulous traders may try to dispose of them to unwitting consumers or they could pass into the hands of traders who do not appreciate their dangers. Therefore enforcement authorities need powers to seize and detain suspect goods; although for practical reasons the goods will normally be left in the trader's possession (unless the trader cannot be trusted). Most legal systems give authorities the power to seize and detain goods in this way, although the final decision on the fate of the product is usually left to the courts. Often this power will be available where goods are merely suspected of breaching safety rules: it is in these situations that the rules exposing authorities to compensation claims usually have their greatest impact.

Normally dangerous goods will be destroyed. This is often the sensible approach to ensure that they do not find their way back into the distribution chain. The destruction should be carried out in a manner which does not endanger the environment. Often it will be undertaken by the public authority, although at the expense of the person responsible for the goods. Occasionally it may be possible for the goods to be rendered safe by modification or for dangerous goods to be used as scrap and some legal systems provide for these possibilities. Naturally there must be confidence that, if goods are released for these purposes, the person to whom they are entrusted will in fact use them only for permitted purposes. Some jurisdictions permit dangerous goods to be exported in some circumstances. This raises complex moral questions which are considered below (see section 5).

(iii) Warnings, Recalls and Corrective Action

The measures considered above are post–market controls which are directed at traders who have potentially dangerous goods which they intend to market. However, some of the most serious risks to consumers arise from dangerous products which have already found their way into the possession of consumers. The powers to counter these risks will now be considered.

The United States' CPSC has one of the most extensive regimes for providing corrective action (Chapter 4, section 2F). This extends to requiring notification to consumers, the repair or replacement of products or the refund of the purchase price. The EC's General Product Safety Directive seems to require authorities to have the power to recall dangerous products (Chapter 2, section 9I). This power was already established in France (Chapter 6, section 5D) and Germany adopted this principle in 1992 and has consolidated it in its 1997 implementing law (Chapter 7, sections 4E and 5E).

The United Kingdom has failed to introduce a recall power. It believes that its power to issue warning notices,[54] when combined with its other supervisory powers, is sufficient. It clearly sees the Directive's obligation to have powers to require the withdrawal of dangerous products on the market as only extending to goods which are not yet in the possession of consumers. Whether this breaches the letter or spirit of the Directive is considered elsewhere (Chapter 2, section 9I and Chapter 5, section 3L). However, it certainly seems to be a gap in consumer protection.

Simply relying on warning notices will not in many instances be sufficient to ensure consumers are informed of product risks. Clearly the nature of the corrective action programme should depend upon the nature and severity of the risk, the type of product involved, the character of consumers likely to purchase and use the product, how easy they are to trace and what means are available to track them down (see the categorisation of hazards and responses adopted in the United States, Chapter 4, section 2F). However, the authorities need to have broad powers to ensure that appropriate action is taken. The reluctance to provide these powers (or sometimes to use those powers which are available) seems based on a hesitation to become involved in the internal affairs of companies. Although it is desirable to allow businesses to put their own house in order wherever possible, it is not too extreme to suggest that the state should have back up powers to protect consumers when they are in very real danger from unsafe goods in their possession.

The effectiveness of corrective action programmes varies greatly depending upon the techniques used and the skill with which the corrective action programmes are put into place.[55] Consumer associations can have a role in monitoring the effectiveness of recall campaigns. Their ability to control producer behaviour is, however, inevitably limited by the meagre resources available to them and by the extent to which producers are sensitive to the moral pressure and publicity which consumer associations can generate. Public safety should not be left to private initiative and public

---

54   Even though procedural requirements make them impracticable to use (Chapter 5, section 3G).

55   For practical advice on product recalls see C. Hodges, M. Tyler and H. Abbott, *Product Safety*, (Sweet & Maxwell, 1996) Ch. 10.

authorities should supervise producer and trader reaction to risks discovered subsequent to the product being marketed. They should have the ability to intervene where traders are not acting appropriately.

As regard the giving of warnings a distinction should be drawn between the ability of public authorities to issue press releases about product dangers and the power of the authorities or courts to require traders to issue warnings. The former power may exist even where there is no specific authority in product safety statutes. This may be a useful means of alerting consumers to potential dangers given the interest of the media in such stories. However it will be of limited practical use if the authorities are subject to strict rules offering traders the possibility to sue for compensation if the authorities cannot fully support their claim (cf German *Birkel* case, see Chapter 7, section 4E).

Where there is a product recall a number of secondary issues arise which affect consumers. They should of course be entitled to compensation or a replacement safe product and also recovery of any expenses incurred in pursuing their remedies. These matters are most comprehensively provided for in the United States law.[56] The French law provides for the possibility of confiscating the supplier's profits from the sale of the dangerous products, but presumably leaves compensation of the consumer to the private law. This is unfortunate for the law should facilitate consumer redress. Of course if the private law gave consumers full refunds there would be no profit to confiscate. The German law is also silent on these supplementary remedies, which are therefore also presumably subject to the private law, as is the position in the United Kingdom.

(iv) Enforcement by Negotiation

The provisions described above provide a wide panoply of powers to enforcement authorities to assist them in detecting and acting against dangerous products. Many of these rights were pioneered in the United States and have now been established in Europe following the implementation of the General Product Safety Directive. However, the market is awash with numerous consumer products of a bewildering variety. Enforcement authorities cannot hope to monitor all products. Above all the law needs to inculcate into producers a concern to ensure that their products are safe. Ironically therefore the objective of regulation is to promote self–regulation.

---

[56] Australia also has rather extensive recall powers which also go into this level of detail, see D. Harland, 'Post Market Control of Technical Consumer Goods in Australia' in H.–W. Micklitz (ed.), *Post Market Control of Consumer Goods*, (*Nomos*, 1990).

However, to do this effectively enforcement authorities need to have clear rules, which provide them with the possibility to take strong action so that industry has to take its responsibilities seriously. Where industry's response has been found to be inadequate it must appreciate the need to negotiate in earnest with the regulatory authorities so that matters can be put right.

Lack of resources and the risk of suits for compensation of course inhibit strong enforcement practice. Certainly the former problem is unlikely to be resolved in the foreseeable future, but the law can ensure that authorities are able to use their limited resources to the full by providing them with a flexible arsenal of effective sanctions with which to persuade industry to take responsible action to protect consumer safety.

D.   Consumer Organisations

The above has concentrated on the role of public authorities, however, consumer organisations also play an important role in the post–market control of consumer products. Their testing programmes often reveal dangers which they either refer to the public authorities or else they lobby producers directly themselves for remedial action. In many respects producers may fear adverse publicity from consumer associations more than the sanctions available to enforcement authorities. Consumer groups can also use their publications and media contacts to assist producers undertaking recall and corrective action programmes. The ability of consumer groups to monitor the market place would be enhanced if they could take action themselves before the courts where they suspected goods were dangerous. Not only would this provide further incentives for traders to take the concerns of consumer groups seriously, but also such action would be a useful reserve power where public authorities were proving ineffective in protecting the public interest. A limited right of this nature exists in France (Chapter 6, section 3D).

5.   EXPORT CONTROLS

Much of the previous discussion has been concerned with how national law and practice can ensure that consumers are not exposed to dangerous products. International trade has been discussed in the context of the need to ensure that increased free trade is permitted in a manner which does not threaten the physical security of consumers. However, not all countries are able to protect their own citizens. In particular many developing countries do not have the facilities to assess the safety of products. Many may also be afraid to impose too strict conditions on products for fear of sending out the 'wrong' signals about their regulatory policy and thereby driving away foreign investment. For these countries international trade may mean the dumping of sub–standard products on to their markets. This in turn imposes a moral obligation on developed countries to control the quality of their exports.

Developed countries also have a self interest in controlling the export of harmful products. It is sometimes suggested that they will wish to preserve the reputation of goods originating in their country. Whilst there may be some truth in this, one suspects that a small number of potentially harmful products being exported will do little to tarnish the image of the major trading nations such as the United States, Japan and the members of the EC. Their self interest is more likely to lie in wishing to prevent the harmful products from being re–imported to threaten their consumers. This is clearly a major factor influencing United States' controls over exports of banned consumer products (Chapter 4, section 2L). This could easily happen in relation to pesticides where a residue can be found in the resulting produce. However, even harmful consumer products which have been exported may also find themselves illegally re–imported. This may be a particular concern for the EC as a trader may try to find a weaker link in the union's external borders if refused entry by one state (Chapter 2, section 10). Strict controls on the export of dangerous products can also create incentives for improved domestic production, for if producers are aware that they will not be able to export sub–standard products they will seek to ensure product quality is right in the first place.

There have clearly been some blatant examples of dumping. Three classic incidents in the 1970's which helped to highlight this problem were (i) the exportation from the United States of children's nightwear containing the banned carcinogenic fire–retardent chemical TRIS; (ii) the sale of the pesticide Velsico to developing countries, although it had never been registered in the United States, and its continued marketing despite causing major suffering to farmers and water buffalo in Egypt; and (iii) the over the counter sales of Lomotil to treat diarrhoea and stomach disorders in third world countries (in the United States this is a prescription drug because of the slight difference between the recommended and fatal dose).[57]

On the other hand there are circumstances in which countries would welcome products despite their having been banned in another country. This may be because countries have different interpretations of the available scientific data relating to risks. For instance, the EC bans American beef because it contains hormones, but this does not mean that every country should follow the same reasoning.[58] However, in order to make such

57 D. Bryan, 'Consumer Safety Abroad: Dumping of Dangerous American Products Overseas' (1981) 12 *Texas Tech. Law. Rev.* 435 at 435–437.

58 See, D. Vogel, *Trading Up*, (Harvard University Press, 1995) at 154 *et seq.*

assessments countries need to have research facilities and expertise at a level which developing countries do not usually have.

It might be possible to argue in rare cases that the danger did not exist in the importing country. This may be because of environmental factors, such as the danger only materialising at certain temperatures which are never reached in the importing country or because of different cultural traditions. For instance, some countries would prohibit baby feeding seats without a harness as it is customary to leave the children in such seats without close attention; in other countries where the seats are only used at meal times and under close supervision such harnesses may be viewed as unnecessary and a positive hindrance to the child's social development.

However, the typical justification for exporting banned products to developing countries is that the social conditions in these countries justify the increased risks. A good example of the type of issue at stake is illustrated by the case of the injectable contraceptive Depo–provera. Although banned in the United States because of its side effects, does the need of some developing countries to control their populations by means of this easily administered long lasting contraceptive override the concerns of the affluent United States' user?[59] In an ideal world this judgment should be made by the importing state, rather than have the values of the developed world imposed upon them. Such a judgment must, however, be made with full knowledge of the risks involved. The problem is that even if the information is available many developing countries do not have the expertise to process it so that a proper balancing of the risks and benefits for their country is achieved. The dilemma for developing nations is well captured by Francine Schulberg who describes how they:

> 'vacillate between claiming that they do not want their countries to be used as a dumping ground for products that cannot be sold in the country of manufacture and claiming that they want to retain the right to decide which products should be permitted for sale within their borders.'[60]

However, arguments based on the special utility to developing nations of products are less likely to be persuasive for consumer goods than for products such as drugs or pesticides. Few consumer products are vital to a nation and there will almost always be an alternative consumer product which does not have the same risk associated with it. Indeed harmful consumer products are almost always exported after being banned in the

---

59   See D. Harland, 'Legal Aspects of the Export of Hazardous Products' (1985) 8 *J.C.P.* 209 at 226.

60   'United States Export of Products Banned for Domestic Use' (1979) 20 *Harv. Int. Law. J.* 331 at 337.

domestic market; whereas some drugs and pesticides may be made specially for the overseas conditions without ever being intended for domestic markets.[61]

This last matter leads on to the important practical question of deciding which products should be subject to export controls. Certainly products which have been banned ought to be subject to some controls, but clearly if products have never been marketed domestically they are unlikely to have been banned and testing and authorisation rules may not apply to goods intended solely for export. Equally it is increasingly unlikely to find that products have actually been banned (or found to breach safety standards).[62] Current enforcement practice favours negotiated solutions being found and reliance on optional voluntary standards will make it more difficult to label products as having been found to be harmful by the legal system. The problem becomes still more complex in relation to products which are subject to restrictions. For instance, they may be permitted but only with certain warnings, or only if supplied through professionals or so long as they are not supplied to certain groups, eg children. Clearly there is a need to decide how onerous the restriction has to be before export controls are imposed. For instance, many toys are restricted to children over three years, but it would be unrealistic to impose export controls on such toys; whereas one might wish to control the supply of drugs which can be fatal to children. Most commentators and legal regimes suggest that export controls should only apply to products which have been severely restricted in the sense of virtually all uses having been prohibited and it only being allowed in specified conditions.[63] However, in the few instances where export controls are imposed there is no agreement and sometimes a certain degree of ambiguity as to when they should apply.

There are various regulatory models which might be adopted with regard to the export of dangerous products.[64] At one extreme safety rules may not apply to exports (although exports may be subject to labelling rules). For instance, the EC general product safety obligation and new approach directives would not seem to be applicable to exports; although member states should interpret their implementing legislation so as to protect exports from their country to other member states. The EC would no doubt justify its lack of regulation of exports on the basis that this topic lies within the competence of the member states. However, none of the member states we

---

61   *Ibid.*, at 358.

62   Which Harland convincingly argues should be equated with a ban: Harland, *op. cit.*, at 230.

63   See, H.–W. Micklitz (1995), *op. cit.*, at 37–39 who discusses the definitions in various international codes and guidelines.

64   Cf Harland, *op. cit.*, at 220–221.

study – the United Kingdom, France and Germany – have well developed policies relating to the export of dangerous products.

At the other extreme a principled stance could be taken so that goods banned at home can also not be exported. Few countries adopt such a stance either because of economic self–interest or out of respect for the sovereignty of other states to decide whether to allow the marketing of such products. It is arguable that this was the position in Australia under s. 62 of the original Trade Practices Act 1974. However, this ambiguity seemed to be due to a failure to address the question of exports and a 1975 amendment provided a blanket exemption for exports.[65] However, this was viewed as going too far in the other direction and now exports of banned products need ministerial approval.[66]

In fact most serious attempts to develop an export policy for potentially harmful products do permit their exportation, but either only under specified conditions or subject to notification conditions. Such schemes may differentiate between banned products and products whose marketing is merely severely restricted. For instance, the United States requires notification to be given to the CPSC of exports of banned products or products which breach safety standards; the CPSC then informs the recipient government. This notification regime does not apply to severely restricted products. President Carter had made an order which would have covered severely restricted products and have required an export licence, but this never came into effect (Chapter 4, section 2L).

Express approval of exports is a preferred policy to one based on notification, because notification shares many of the weaknesses associated with a protection policy based on informing consumers of risks. Although theoretically appealing, in terms of increasing the autonomy of nation states, notification rules can all too easily be merely of cosmetic value if the recipient nation is unable to assess the risks itself or is forced to discount long term risks because of pressing immediate needs.

The United Nations favours a two tiered solution. Banned products can only be exported where they are expressly requested by or permitted in the importing country; severely restricted products are subject to notification and labelling agreements (Chapter 3, section 5). However, if severely restricted products are construed narrowly so as only to include products which are permitted to be sold in very specific limited circumstances then one would have thought that closer control by the importing nation would be appropriate. Equally in the case of banned products control by the exporting

---

65   *Ibid.*, at 210–213.

66   J. Goldring, L. Maher, J. McKeough, *Consumer Protection Law*, (4th. ed.) (Federation Press, 1993) at 154.

nation should be needed, as well as a request by the importing state, in order to permit the exporting nation to protect its own interests and to maintain an ethical trade policy where it can detect that the importing nation is unable to assess the risks accurately.

2 Product Safety – The European Dimension

1. WHY IS PRODUCT SAFETY A MATTER OF CONCERN TO EUROPE?

Concern for the safety of products has long been a concern of the Community. The first two of the Community consumer protection and information programmes[1] and the Commission's internal communication to the Council in 1986 on *A New Impetus for Consumer Protection Policy* emphasised the importance of product safety. By 1990, when the Commission published its first three year action plan,[2] the direction on Community consumer policy was clear. Priority areas would be covered by vertical directives, which since 1985 were drafted in accordance with the new approach to technical harmonisation. This would be complemented by national authorities having general powers to ensure only safe consumer products are placed on the market and to ensure the withdrawal of any unsafe products. The Community would have exceptional powers to act in emergencies, but otherwise would act as a co–ordinating point to enhance communication and co–operation between national authorities especially in emergency situations. It would also have a role collecting data on home and leisure accidents.

Although consumer protection was not expressly written into the original Treaty of Rome as an objective of the Community, product safety was one area which could not be ignored because national rules on product specifications and testing could act as barriers to trade and the creation of a single internal market for European products.[3] The free movement of goods provisions, arts 30–36 of the Treaty and the surrounding jurisprudence of the European Court of Justice (hereafter ECJ), are a potential threat to consumer

---

1 See OJ 1975 C 92/1 and OJ 1981 C 133/1.

2 COM(90) 98: less prominence was given to the matter in the second (Com (93) 378) and third (Com (95) 519) three year action plans largely because the elements of Community action were already in place.

3 Indeed the Community went further and created a consumer protection programme covering a wide range of matters without there being much basis in the Treaty for such broad ranging activity prior to the Maastricht amendments: see now, arts 3f and 129a of the Maastricht. See, generally, G. Howells and T. Wilhelmsson, *EC Consumer Law*, (Dartmouth, 1997).

protection as they emphasise the need to remove technical barriers to trade and the promotion of mutual recognition. However, this has always been limited both by the exceptions to the principle of free movement found in art. 36 and by the 'mandatory requirements' exception developed by the case law.

Both the Commission and the ECJ appreciated that there were limits to the extent that the internal market could be created simply by deregulating. Perhaps the most fundamental barrier was the need to protect the health and safety of consumers. This arose out of both humanitarian concerns and the need to create a single market in which consumers would have confidence. Thus whilst the free movement provisions might be useful in removing unnecessary regulations which were antiquated, quirky or disguised protectionism, there were also legitimate safety concerns which had to be addressed. National rules safeguarding these interests could not be dismantled without positive Community rules being put in place to protect consumers. The rules which seek to establish the internal market through positive integration – technical harmonisation standards and the General Product Safety Directive – will be the focus of our attention. First, however, the rules in arts 30–36 governing negative harmonisation will be summarised because they set the limits for national rules in relation to products which have not been harmonised and may still play a similar role where harmonised legislation exists if it does not totally pre–empt national laws.

2.   TECHNICAL BARRIERS TO TRADE

A.   Arts 30–36[4]

Art. 30 not only prohibits quantitative restrictions on imports, but also 'all measures having equivalent effects'. This was given a broad interpretation in *Procureur du Roi v Dassonville*[5] to cover 'all trading rules enacted by member states which are capable of hindering, actually or potentially, intra–Community trade'. This clearly covers pre–marketing product safety regulations, for producers will be deterred from exporting if they have to adapt the design and construction for each market or be subject to different testing and certification procedures. The same result could arise even if they are merely forced to the trouble and expense of undertaking in a member

---

4   See, generally, N. Green, T. Hartley, J. Usher, *The Legal Foundations of the Single European Market*, (OUP, 1991) Chs 5–7; J. Steiner and L. Woods, *EC Law*, (Blackstone, 1994) Chs 8–9; S. Weatherill, *Law and Integration in the European Union*, (Clarendon, 1995) Chs 5, 7–8.

5   Case 8/74 [1974] ECR 837 at para. 5.

state testing and certification procedures which have already been gone through elsewhere within the Community.

The *Dassonville* formula was, however, interpreted very broadly and so even differing post–market controls might fall within its compass if there was the mere chance that a producer would be discouraged from importing into a member state because he did not wish to risk exposure to onerous post–market controls. Recently there has been some drawing back. In *Bernard Keck and Daniel Mithouard* the ECJ expressly moved away from its previous case law and held:

> 'the application to products from other Member Stares of national provisions restricting or prohibiting certain selling arrangements is not such as to hinder, directly or indirectly, actually or potentially, trade between member states within the meaning of the *Dassonville* judgment, so long as those provisions apply to all relevant traders operating within the national territory and so long as they affect in the same manner, in law and in fact, the marketing of domestic products and those from other member states.'[6]

The aim was to restrict the application of art. 30 to measures which prevent access to the market and not to encompass measures affecting the product once in reaches the market, albeit that they may have the affect of deflating the number of sales of imports (as well as usually also domestic production). The *Keck* refinement might be thought to be limited to 'selling arrangements' and thus not cover the matters we are interested in, but it is likely that the ECJ would be more interested in the principle of leaving member states free to regulate where measures do not affect imports any more than domestic production.

The majority of pre–marketing product safety regulations are likely to still be caught by art. 30 even post–*Keck* as their practical affect would be to favour domestic production. However, there is the possibility that some pre–marketing controls, for instance obligations placed on retailers to keep certain records, or post–marketing controls would be exempt from art. 30 as they affect all products equally irrespective of their origin. The practical significance of this possibility will depend upon whether the General Product Safety Directive is held to be a minimal directive giving member states the freedom to impose more protective laws within the confines of the Treaty.

It is important to remember that the thrust of arts 30–36 is to promote economic integration between member states. In the landmark *Cassis de*

---

6   Joined cases C–267/91 and C–268/91 [1993] ECR I–6097 at para. 16.

Dijon[7] case the ECJ refused to accept a German prohibition on the marketing of a French liqueur on the grounds that consumer health was threatened by its low alcohol content! It stated what has become a fundamental tenet of Community policy, namely the principle of mutual recognition whereby products lawfully produced and marketed in one member state should have access to the entire single market. Mutual recognition was approved by the Commission in its White Paper on *Completing the Internal Market* in 1985.[8] It noted that as the objectives of national legislation are more often than not identical, then although the rules and controls developed to achieve those objectives may take different forms, they essentially come down to the same thing and so should normally be recognised in all member states. Thus where harmonisation was not essential imports ought not to be prohibited simply because they were manufactured to different specification from those of the importing state, nor should the importer be required to comply with additional technical tests or certification procedures. Art. 100b gives the Council the power to decide that provisions in force in a member state must be recognised as being equivalent to those applied by another member state; but this power has not been invoked to my knowledge.

Exceptions to the mutual recognition principle are to be found in (i) art. 36 which, *inter alia*, protects prohibitions and restrictions justified on the grounds of protection of health and life of humans, animals or plants in so far as they do not constitute a means of arbitrary discrimination or a disguised restriction on trade between member states; and (ii) the *Cassis de Dijon* judgment itself which conceded that :

> 'Obstacles to movement within the Community resulting from disparities between the national laws relating to the marketing of the products in question must be accepted in so far as those provisions may be recognized as being necessary in order to satisfy mandatory requirements relating in particular to the effectiveness of fiscal supervision, the protection of public health, the fairness of commercial transactions and the defence of the consumer.'[9]

Technically there is a distinction between art. 36, which operates once art. 30 has been found to be breached, and the 'mandatory requirements' which preclude a finding that art. 30 was breached. Art. 36 is available for both distinctly and indistinctly applicable measures, but the mandatory

---

7   *Rewe–Zentrale v Bundesmonopolverwaltung für Branntwein*, Case 120/78 [1979] ECR 649.

8   COM(85) 310 at 22.

9   *Op. cit.*, at para. 8.

requirements are only available for indistinctly applicable measures, ie measures which affect imported and domestic goods alike.

Consumer safety measures will be covered by both art. 36 and the mandatory requirements.[10] In theory therefore the courts need not invoke art. 36 as art. 30 would not be breached, but as the two tests are effectively interchangeable the courts may prefer to assess it in the light of art. 36. Reich has noted that the ECJ has tended to only speak of 'consumer protection' and 'fair trading' as mandatory requirements, leaving health protection to be exclusively regulated by art. 36.[11]

The mandatory requirements and art. 36 justifications share two further conditions which must be satisfied before a national measure is exempt from challenge. The objective which is being sought must be a valid one; and the means must be proportionate to the objective.

In the absence of harmonised Community rules member states are in principle free to decide for themselves what degree of protection of human life and health they wish to assure.[12] They must, however, when setting the standard take into account international scientific research[13] and bear in mind the requirements of free movement of goods within the Community. The ECJ has been astute to discover cases where national standards are used as a front for protectionism, but has been prepared to allow member states freedom to protect their citizens against legitimate fears, even where this has been based only on a serious doubt as where the scientific evidence is inconclusive.[14] This approach is well illustrated by the different reactions of the ECJ to restrictions placed on the import of poultry following the outbreak of the highly infectious Newcastle disease. The British measures were struck down by the ECJ as it was convinced they were a response to pressure from poultry producers who wanted to protect the Christmas market for turkeys from French imports.[15] Similar measures introduced in the Irish Republic were upheld as the Irish had exceptionally high standards not matched by the British flocks.[16]

---

10   Cf. measures protecting the consumer's economic interest which are not covered by art. 36 and can therefore only be justified if indistinctly applicable: see *Commission v Ireland*, Case 113/80 [1981] ECR 1625.

11   See N. Reich, *Internal Market and Diffuse Interests*, (Story Scienta, 1990) at 62, citing *Industrie Diensten v Beele Handelsmaatschappij*, Case 6/81, (1982) ECR 707 (although of course that case did not raise health and safety issues).

12   *Officier van Justitie v Sandos BV*, Case 174/82 [1983] ECR 2445.

13   *Commission v Germany (Re Beer Purity Laws)*, Case 174/84 [1987] ECR 1227.

14   *Officier van Justitie v Kaasfabriek Eyssen*, Case 53/80 [1981] ECR 409.

15   *Commission v UK (Re Imports of Poultry Meat)*, Case 40/82 [1982] ECR 2793.

16   *Commission v Ireland (Re Protection of Animal Health)*, Case 74/82 [1984] ECR 317.

The majority of cases on this point relate to foodstuffs, but the same principle can be seen applied in the leading case on goods.[17] This involved a clash between philosophies of how best to protect the users of woodworking machines. French legislation required the machines to be designed to prevent the users harming themselves should they make a mistake. Other countries, notably Germany, favoured requiring workers to be trained to respond correctly if a machine malfunctioned. The ECJ rejected the Commission's argument that France should be forced to accept goods produced according to the alternative philosophy. It did so because it could not be shown that the machines provided the same level of protection. Indeed this claim had not been made by the manufacturers who had complained to the Commission; moreover it is hard to see how such machines could offer the same level of safety to French users who would not have been trained to avoid risks which they expected the product design to eliminate.

Even if the protective objective of member states' legislation is legitimate this must be achieved by means which are reasonable and proportionate. A prohibition of a product will not be allowed unless the objection is to the nature of the product itself (eg a dangerous type of knife, such as flick–knives) or the presence of a substance (eg blue asbestos or a carcinogenic substance). Usually, it will be sufficient to rely on labelling to warn the consumers of the presence of substances they may wish to avoid.[18] Equally requiring products to be licensed or handled by approved agents in the importing state will usually be excessive if a declaration by the importer, accompanied where necessary by certification, would be adequate.[19]

Inspections only carried out on imported goods would normally breach the requirement that national measures should be non–discriminatory, but might be justified if alternative measures were put in place to control domestic production.[20] Inspections of imported products should not normally be necessary where another member state had carried out inspection on exportation.[21] If inspections are necessary then any sampling of imported products should not be disproportionate.[22] Importing states should usually rely on test results and data carried out in other member states[23] and should not require information to be duplicated if similar products were already on

---

[17] *Commission v France*, Case 188/84 [1986] ECR 419.

[18] *Commission v Germany (Re Beer Purity Laws)*, *op. cit.*, at para. 35.

[19] *Commission v United Kingdom*, Case 132/80 [1981] ECR 995.

[20] *Rewe–Zentralfinanz v Landwirtschaftskammer Bonn*, Case 4/75 [1975] ECR 843.

[21] *Denkavit Futtermittel v Minister für Ernährung, Landwirtschaft und Forsten des Landes Nordrhein–Westfalen*, Case 251/78 [1979] ECR 3369.

[22] *Commission v France*, Case 42/82 [1983] ECR 1013.

[23] *Frans–Nederlandse voor Biologosche Producten*, Case 272/80 [1981] ECR 3277.

the market.[24] It is hoped that this sample of the case law gives an indication of how the ECJ seeks a solution which protects national consumer interests in a manner which causes the least impact on the free movement of goods.

B. Products Covered by EC Harmonising Legislation

We have seen that in the absence of Community harmonising measures member states are free to put in place measures to protect the safety of consumers to the extent that these are compatible with the Treaty, in particular arts 30–36. Where harmonisation legislation exists the position is more complex.[25] As a general principle it can be asserted that where the Community has established common standards it can be said to have moved into the area in a pre–emptive manner, prohibiting national initiatives, however well intended. However, such bold assertions are too simplistic to give an accurate statement of the limits of member states' powers.

The ECJ has decided on many occasions that directives have established harmonised regimes with which domestic regulatory activity was incompatible.[26] However, this was on the basis that the measures were of the total harmonisation type; if the directives only intended to deal with certain aspects the member states would retain their competence to legislate for the other aspects.[27] Thus each measure must be examined to define the outer limits of its scope.

Most 'new approach' technical harmonisation directives are likely to be held to be total harmonisation directives (see section 4C). This would seem to be supported not only by the case law of the ECJ, but also by the preamble to General Product Safety Directive which disapplies its controls to the marketing for products covered by 'specific rules of Community law of the total harmonisation type' (recital 7). However, it can be argued that no measure can be categorically labelled a total harmonisation measure for all time, since it is always possible that new categories of risk not thought of at the time the Directive was adopted become associated with the product. In any event new approach directives contain safeguard clauses allowing

---

24   *De Peijper*, Case 104/75 [1976] ECR 613.
25   Weatherill, *op. cit.*, Chapter 5 is particularly useful on this point.
26   *Oberkreisdirektor des Kreises Borken v Handelsonderneming Moormann*, Case 190/87 [1988] ECR 4689; *Firma Eau de Cologne & Parfumerie – Fabrik Glockengasse v Provide*, C–150/88 [1989] ECR 3891 and *Commission v United Kingdom*, Case 60/86 [1988] ECR 3921.
27   See, *Van Bennekom*, Case 227/82 [1983] ECR 3883; *Commission v Germany*, Case 205/84 [1986] ECR 3755.

member states to take action if a product endangers safety and there is provision for the revision of inadequate standards.

The problem of determining the limit of a member state's autonomy to continue to protect its citizens is most acute in relation to its ability to continue checks on imported goods, where there is a Community procedure in place. In principle the existence of a Community procedure should remove the need for all but occasional health inspections carried out at the state of destination.[28] Sometimes, however, the Community measures can be viewed as supplementary to national measures and thus permit the national authorities to continue with their own controls.[29] These must of course be proportionate and in accordance with the general principles of arts 30–36 discussed above. Whether the General Product Safety Directive (see section 9) pre–empts more restrictive national measures, is best considered in the context of whether or not it is a minimal harmonisation measure.

There is a general tendency for directives to be less prescriptive in tone. The new approach directives are indicative of this as they set down essential safety requirements, but leave the method of compliance in the hands of the producer who can either comply with standards or obtain type–approval for their chosen design. Directives framed in such a way are flexible, but still compel conformity to the fixed European rules. Some directives go further and expressly include options. The Product Liability Directive is a good example of this as it allows member states to decide if primary agricultural products and game are included, whether the development risks defence applies and if there should be a limit on personal injury damages. Neither the technical harmonisation directives nor the General Product Safety Directive contain options of this nature.

Recently it has become fashionable, in the interests of subsidiarity, for directives to be treated as minimal harmonisation directives. Such directives form a floor of harmonised protective rights with the ceiling of national measures being controlled by arts 30–36. Neither the new approach technical harmonisation directives nor the General Product Safety Directive expressly state that they are minimal in character. Although some directives do contain such clauses, the absence of them should not be crucial.[30] It can, however,

---

28   *Oberkreisdirektor v Moormann*, Case 190/87 [1988] ECR 4689.

29   *Rewe–Zentralfinanz Gmbh v Landwirtschaftskammer*, Case 4/75 [1975] ECR 843.

30   Many commentators believe that the Product Liability Directive is a maximalist directive. This seems to be on the basis that as it has allowed some options to member states others must be ruled out and because the express preservation of national laws existing at the time of enactment must rule out future divergences. I disagree that the Directive has to be read in that way, partly, on the basis that most pre–existing product liability laws were common law or codified laws which have evolved quite dramatically in recent times. As the Directive could not hope to restrict

be fairly safely assumed that technical harmonisation directive would not be treated as minimal harmonisation measures. Their purpose is to provide a level playing field and additional national requirements would be contrary to this goal. However, we have already noted that the outer limits of the Directive need to be ascertained to see if it truly was intended to cover all risks. Moreover art. 100a(4) now clearly foresees that, even in areas covered by harmonised legislation, member states may deem it necessary to apply national provisions on the basis of art. 36.

The General Product Safety Directive does not require any specific measures to be taken by producers, but rather creates a regulatory framework in which producers must ensure products are safe and member states must have authorities to ensure that duty is complied with. Member states might seek to go beyond the provisions of the Directive, by, for instance, having a stricter definition of safety, extending the range of parties with responsibilities or making distributors (as well as producers) strictly liable. Such measures may indirectly have an effect on inter state trade and in this respect would of course be subject to scrutiny under arts 30–36.

Whether the General Product Safety Directive is a minimal directive has not been settled, and indeed there seems to be some internal disagreement within the Commission on this question. The Directive gives very few clues as to whether it is intended to be minimalist or maximalist. It is true that many of the express obligations placed on producers, distributors and member states are drafted as simply examples of how a broader duty should be satisfied. This leaves member states some latitude during the implementation process but does not really address the question of whether they can go beyond the limits set by the Directive. All that can be said is that the references in the Directive to the need to comply with arts 30–36 and international obligations might suggest that those principles rather than any inherent restriction with the Directive should represent the limit of national competence.

It should also be remembered that this Directive was adopted under art. 100a. Art. 100a was introduced by the Single European Act to make it easier to enact legislation establishing the internal market, since it only required a qualified majority rather than the unanimity needed under art. 100. However, as a safeguard for those member states that feared such legislation might force lower levels of protection on to them, art. 100a(3) requires that proposals concerning health, safety, environmental and consumer protection

their future interpretation by the courts it would be illogical to prevent other legal developments. However, the important point for present purposes is that this discussion turns on a construction of the Directive and the absence of an express minimal harmonisation clause need not be fatal.

should take as their base a high level of protection. As some member states' existing legislation was more extensive than the Directive it could be seen as contrary to the principle of a high level of protection that they be asked to repeal such laws.[31] Certainly there has been no suggestion from the Commission that they should do so – and if existing laws were compatible with the Directive then there should be no objection to subsequent rules which went beyond the Directive so long as they complied with arts 30–36. Indeed in the post–Maastricht era there is now specific competence in art. 129a(1)(b) for the Community to legislate on consumer protection matters irrespective of any internal market justifications; art. 129(3) expressly provides that such measures shall not prevent any member state from maintaining or introducing more stringent protective measures so long as they are compatible with the Treaty. This may suggest a preference for minimal harmonisation which the ECJ may well take into account if it is ever called upon to determine whether the Directive is minimal in character.

3.   TECHNICAL STANDARDS DIRECTIVE[32]

A.   Introduction

We have seen that where there is no harmonising legislation, and even in some cases where there is, member states retain the freedom to introduce safety rules, even if they amount to technical barriers to trade, so long as they comply with the Treaty. The EC's General Programme for the Elimination of Technical Barriers to Trade Caused by Disparities Among National Legislation of May 1969 contained a 'gentleman's agreement' not to legislate at the national level where EC legislation was planned. However, this was of little value and new national regulations could be passed in areas

---

31   There is no equivalent to art. 13 of the Product Liability Directive, which expressly preserves pre–existing laws.

32   Council Directive 83/189/EEC on laying down a procedure for the provision of information in the field of technical standards and regulations: OJ 1983 L 109/8 (as amended by Directive 88/182/EEC: OJ 1988 L 81/75 and Directive 94/10/EEC OJ 1994 L 100/30: hereafter Technical Standards Directive. For reports on the operation of the directive see *Report on the Operation of Directive 83/189/EEC, Laying Down a Procedure for the Provision of Information in the Field of Technical Standards and Regulations 1984–1987*, COM(88) 722, *Report on the Operation of Directive 83/189/EEC in 1988 and 1989*, COM(91) 108, *Report on the Operation of Directive 83/189/EEC in 1990 and 1991*, COM(92) 565, *National Regulations Affecting Products in the Internal Market – A Cause for Concern – Experience Gained in the Application of Directive 83/189/EEC 1992–4*, DOC 16/96–EN.

not covered by that programme. Even in areas covered by the Programme member states were not very good at providing the Commission with information on new national measures. Thus, the Technical Standards Directive introduced procedures to monitor national activity in order to ensure that so far as possible differences between national rules are reduced and new national initiatives do not create additional barriers to trade. However, it should be noted that a recent commission report has commented that the volume and complexity of national regulatory activity still poses a threat to the functioning of the internal market.[33]

B. Regulations

The Directive requires member states to communicate immediately any draft technical regulation[34] to the Commission (art. 8(1)).[35] The reason why the regulation is necessary should be made clear either in the draft or in an accompanying brief statement and any legislative or regulatory texts needed

---

[33] Doc 16/96–EN, *op. cit.*

[34] A technical regulation refers to technical specifications and other requirements, including relevant administrative provisions, which are compulsory, *de jure* or *de facto*, in the marketing or use of a product in a member state or major part thereof, as well as laws, regulation and administrative provisions of member states prohibiting the manufacture, importation, marketing or use of a product (art. 1(9)). *De facto* technical regulations are said to include situations where a law etc. refers to a technical specification or code of practice compliance with which provides a presumption of conformity, voluntary agreements (other than public procurement tender specifications) to which a public authority is a contracting party and where compliance with technical specifications is encouraged by fiscal and financial measures (but not those linked to social security systems). Technical specification is in turn defined as a specification contained in a document which lays down the characteristics required of a product such as levels of quality, performance, safety or dimensions, including requirements regarding the name under which the product is sold, terminology, symbols, testing and test methods, packaging, marking or labelling and conformity assessment procedures. The production methods and procedures for agricultural products, products intended for human and animal consumption, medicinal products and other products where these have an effect on their characteristics (art. 1(2)).

[35] Where it merely transposes the full text of an international or European standard reference to the relevant standard will suffice. Indeed where the member state is, *inter alia*, simply complying with Community acts or obligations arising out of international agreements which result in the adoption of common technical specifications in the Community there is no notification duty (art. 10).

to assess the implications of the regulation should also be supplied. The draft should be communicated again if any changes are made to it. The Commission gives notification of the draft to other member states and may refer the matter to a Standing Committee established under the Directive and, if appropriate, to any other Committee responsible for that field. Member states or the Commission can make comments on the draft which should as far as possible be taken on board in the preparation of the final text (art. 8(2)). Member states shall communicate the definitive text to the Commission without delay (art. 8(3)). As a result of its monitoring work the Commission found 121 cases between 1992–4 where member states had failed to notify at the draft stage and these led to nine cases being submitted to the ECJ.[36]

There is at least a three month standstill during which regulations should not be adopted whilst member states and the Commission are given the opportunity to object to the proposed regulation (art. 9(1)). Comments made to the member state do not block progress of the national regulation, but if within this time a member state or the Commission delivers a detailed opinion to the effect that the measure should be amended to eliminate or reduce any barriers it might create to the free movement of goods the measure should be postponed for six months from its notification (art. 9(2)).[37] Member states seem to comment on draft regulations in about a third of all cases (29% in 1988 and 36% in 1989) and to issue detailed comments, which invoke the standstill procedure in a few more cases (33% in 1988 and 39% in 1989).[38] Between 1992–94 the Commission commented on 46% of notification and gave detailed opinions in 31% of cases.[39] The main criticism seems to be that the draft regulations failed to incorporate the principle of mutual recognition.

This standstill period is extended to 12 months if within three months the Commission gives notice of its intention of proposing or adopting a Directive on the subject (art. 9(3)) or if the Commission informs the member state that the subject matter is covered by a proposed directive or regulation (art. 9(4)). If the Council adopts a Common Position during this standstill period the period is extended to 18 months (art. 9(5)). The standstill obligation lapses if the Commission no longer proposes a binding act or withdraws a draft or an

---

[36]   Doc. 16/95 – EN, *op. cit.*, at 19.

[37]   The period is four months for technical regulations in the form of voluntary agreements to which a public body is a contracting party.

[38]   COM(91)108, *op. cit.*

[39]   Doc 16/96–EN, *op. cit.*, at 18. This was in fact a considerable reduction from the level of 43.5% in 1990, see COM(92) 565, *op. cit.*, at para. 58.

act has been adopted (art. 9(6)). Between 1992–94 community proposals for legislation gave rise to extended standstill periods in 62 cases.[40]

In any event, these standstill provisions do not apply where, for urgent reasons, occasioned by serious and unforeseeable circumstances, relating to the protection of health and life of animals or plants, a member state is obliged to prepare technical regulations in a very short space of time in order to enact and introduce them immediately without any consultations being possible (art. 9(7)). However, when the member state notifies the (draft) regulation it should state the reasons for the urgency of the measures taken. Member states invoked this procedure in 5–6% of cases between 1988–91.[41] The Commission is required to take appropriate action where improper use of this procedure is made; in fact the Commission found this procedure was only justified in a third of the cases.

The notification and standstill provisions in arts 8–9 do not apply where member states are simply seeking to comply with international agreements or binding Community acts, or are making use of safeguard clauses in such acts, implementing a decision of the ECJ, amending a technical regulation at the Commission's request in order to remove an obstacle to trade or taking emergency measures which must be notified under art. 8(1) of the General Product Safety Directive (art. 10(1)).

The standstill procedures in art. 9 do not apply to prohibitions on manufacture which do not impede free movement of products (art. 10(2)) or where the measures are classed as *de facto* because they are linked to fiscal and financial measures (art. 10(4)). *De facto* regulations resulting from voluntary agreements to which a public authority is a contracting party are not subject to the extended twelve month plus standstill period (art. 10(3)).

C. Standards

The preamble to the original Technical Standards Directive noted that in practice national technical standards may have the same effect on the free movement of goods as technical regulations (recital 10). National standards remain particularly important in the construction and foodstuffs sectors.[42] Accordingly similar procedures are put in place for the notification of national standardisation activity.[43]

---

[40] Doc 16/96–EN, *op. cit.*, at 19. But this has fallen rapidly with the completion of the Internal Market programme.

[41] COM(92) 565, *op. cit.*, at para. 39.

[42] *Report on the Progress of European Standardisation*, SEC(95) 2104 at II.2.

[43] A standard is deemed to be a technical specification approved by a recognised standardisation body for repeated and continuous application with which compliance

National standardisation institutes should inform standardisation bodies in other member states, the European standardisation bodies and the Commission of new standards which are being prepared or amended, unless they are merely the identical or equivalent transposition of an international or European standard (art. 2(1)).[44] The information provided should in particular indicate whether the proposed standards will transpose an international standard without being the equivalent or will be a new national standard or an amendment to an existing national standard (art. 2(2)). After consulting the Standing Committee the Commission draws up rules for the consolidated presentation of this information. There have been persistent criticisms of the quality of the notifications from member states. Also insufficient dissemination of the draft standards notified seems to take place within the member states.

On request the Commission and standardisation bodies shall be sent draft standards and be kept informed of any action taken on any comments made relating to the drafts (art. 3). Art. 4 requires member states to ensure that their standardisation bodies communicate the necessary information, publish draft standards so that comments can be obtained from parties in other member states, grant standardisation bodies in other member states the right to be involved passively or actively (by sending an observer) in their planned activities and do not object to their work being discussed at the European level. However, in practice the number of comments made is small and there are only a minimal number of requests to be involved in standardisation work in other states.[45]

Member states should not recognise, approve or refer to standards adopted in breach of the procedures laid down in the Technical Standards Directive.

The Standing Committee (established by art. 5) meets with representatives of the standards institutions twice a year (art. 6(1)). The Commission provides the Committee with a report on the above procedures relating to standards and its proposals for eliminating existing or foreseeable barriers to trade (art. 6(2)). In expressing its opinion the Committee may propose that the Commission request the European standards institutions to draw up a European standard within a given time (art. 6 (3) first indent). Member states must then take all appropriate measures to ensure that their standards institutions do not prejudice this intended harmonisation, in particular by publishing new or revised standards which are not completely

---

is not compulsory and which is adopted by an international, European or national standardisation body and made available to the public (art. 1(4)).

[44] The names of European standardisation bodies are listed in annex 1 of the Directive and the names of national standardisation bodies in annex 2.

[45] COM(92) 565, *op. cit.*, at para. 15.

in line with an existing European standard (art. 7(1)). This obligation does not apply if the work of the standards institution is being undertaken at the request of the public authorities in order to draw up technical specifications or a standard for the purpose of enacting a technical regulation for such products (art. 7(2)). Such measures should be referred to the Commission as draft technical regulations, under the procedures outlined above.

Instead of referring the matter to a European Standardisation body the Standing Committee may decide that initially the Commission should ask member states to decide amongst themselves on appropriate measures, where these are necessary to avoid the risk of barriers to trade (art. 6(3) second indent). It can also ask the Commission to take all appropriate measures (art. 6(3) third indent) and identify areas where harmonisation appears necessary and, should the case arise, undertake appropriate harmonisation in a given sector (art. 6(3) fourth indent).

The provisions on standards are generally recognised to be less effective than those for regulations. However, this may be because the European standardisation bodies have their own procedures to deal with conflicts between national and European standards. For instance, both CEN and CENELEC have a standstill agreement under which national standards boards do not launch new national projects whilst work on a European standard is underway. Indeed the possibility under the directive for standardisation bodies to request the opportunity to be involved in the work of other standardisation bodies is modelled on CENELEC's 'Villamora' agreement which provides for a limited standstill so that partner standardisation bodies in other states can request to be so involved.

4. POSITIVE HARMONISATION

A. Introduction

To the extent that different national rules do not represent barriers to trade or threaten consumer health and safety, one might suggest that there is no need for the European legislator to intervene. The European consumer through the market mechanism can choose which standards he prefers when he makes his marketing decisions.[46] There are several good reasons for not accepting this

---

[46] Such a vision, as set out by the Economic Advisory Council to the German Federal Ministry of Economic Affairs is described in Ch. Joerges, 'The New Approach to Technical Harmonisation and the Interests of Consumers: Reflections on the Requirements and Difficulties of a Europeanisation of Product Safety Policy' in Bieber, Dehousse, Pinder, Weiler (eds), *One European Market? A Critical Analysis of the Commission's Internal Market Strategy*, (Nomos, 1988) at 199. Falke points

approach. First some rules upheld by the ECJ do impede trade but are accepted as necessary by the ECJ. These could not be subject to this principle. These are the very instances where harmonisation is most urgently needed. Second, the move towards harmonisation is nearly always desirable if it can be achieved. Most such moves would in the long run facilitate cross border trade. Third, and most importantly, this market based approach places too much onus on the capabilities of the consumer. We have noted the difficulty which consumers have in reading signals about product safety (see Chapter 1, section 3A). It is also asking too much for them to have to evaluate the quality of the decisions of national regulators and standardisers. At worst this will lead to decisions based on prejudices against particular countries. So positive harmonisation is necessary. The more difficult question is to find the best way of achieving it.

In 1985 the EC started the process of establishing a new approach to technical harmonisation in its Council Resolution on the *New Approach to Technical Harmonisation and Standards*.[47] This marked a move away from detailed technical rules to broad sectoral directives, which laid down essential safety requirements but left the detail to be fleshed out by European Standards.

A further stage was the development of a global approach to certification and testing. A White Paper in 1989 set out the Commission's thinking in this area.[48] A Council Resolution on a *Global Approach to Conformity Assessment* was adopted in 1989[49] which led to a Council Decision in 1993.[50] This sought to create a harmonised approach to conformity assessment so that member states could have confidence that all products stated to conform to European standards actually did so conform. We shall see that this is one of the biggest practical problems created by the new and global approach to technical harmonisation.

---

out that this is based on the contestable assumption that the provisions governing safety in the member states are generally equivalent: J. Falke, 'Reactions to the New Approach Concerning Technical Harmonisation and Standards in the FRG: The Case of the Proposed Directive on Machines' in *Product Liability and Product Safety in the European Union*, Ch. Joerges (ed.), EUI Working Paper no. 89/404 (European University Institute, 1989) at 90.

[47]   OJ 1985 C 136/1.

[48]   *A Global Approach to Certification and Testing: Quality Measures for Industrial Products*: OJ 1989 C 267/3.

[49]   OJ 1990 C 10/1.

[50]   Council Decision concerning the modules for the various phases of the conformity assessment procedures and the rules for the affixing and use of the CE marking, which are intended to be used in the technical harmonisation directives: OJ 1993 L 220/23 (hereafter Conformity Assessment and CE Marking Decision).

We shall also see that the linchpin of the system is the standardisation process. This was recognised in 1990 by the publication of a Commission Green Paper on the *Development of European Standardisation: Action for Faster Technological Convergence in Europe*[51] and a follow up document in 1991, *Standardisation in the European Economy*[52] which preceded the Council Resolution on the role of European standardisation in the European economy.[53] In 1995 there was a *Report on the Progress of European Standardisation*[54] and a Commission communication *On the Broader Use of Standardisation in Community Policy*.[55]

Thus the new and global approach has three limbs (i) more flexible legislation, (ii) a prominent role for standardisation, and (iii) reliance on conformity assessment procedures (leading to the award of the CE mark which allows access to the European market).[56] These three elements will be considered in turn, but first the weaknesses of the old approach will be discussed to illustrate why the change was needed.

B.   The Old Approach to Technical Harmonisation[57]

In May 1969 the EC Council adopted a *General Programme for the elimination of technical barriers to trade that result from disparities between the provisions laid down by law, regulation or administrative action in member states*,[58] which was supplemented in 1973 by a second programme dealing with technical barriers in the foodstuffs and industrial products sectors.[59] However, this old approach to technical harmonisation had been over ambitious. It had sought to set out in detail all the performance objectives and design specifications for the products covered. At the time

---

51   OJ 1991 C 20/1.
52   OJ 1992 C 96/2.
53   OJ 1992 C 173/1.
54   SEC(95) 2104.
55   COM(95) 412.
56   Readers may find it useful to know that the European Commission has published a *Guide to the Implementation of Community Harmonisation Directives Based on the New and Global Approach*. This is intended to serve as a manual and also includes the Commission's interpretation of certain key definitions.
57   See S. Farr, *Harmonisation of Technical Standards in the EC*, (Chancery Law, 1992) at 4–6; Centre for European Policy Studies, *The European Community without Technical Barriers*, (CEPS, 1992) at 29–33 and R. Lauwaars, 'The "Model Directive" on Technical Harmonisation' in Bieber, Dehousse, Pinder and Weiler (eds), *op., cit.*
58   OJ 1969 C 76/1.
59   OJ 1973 C 117/1.

such legislation, based on art. 100 of the Treaty, had to be adopted unanimously. This caused some measures to be dropped where consensus could not be reached in the Council of Ministers or adoption of measures was slowed down whilst the horse–trading went on. It also encouraged making the directives optional with member states being permitted to maintain diverging national regulations and manufacturers having the option as to which rules to comply with.

The detailed nature of the legislation meant that a lot of preparatory work by experts was needed. Therefore only a limited number of proposals could be handled at any one time. For instance, whilst the Commission had envisaged 124 directives would be adopted in the 18 months leading up to the end of 1970 in fact only one measure was adopted by that deadline.[60] Also because the legislation was rather technical it did not attract a great deal of political interest.

Although legislative activity improved afterwards,[61] the old approach also had flaws in the style and content of the resulting legislation. Its detailed total harmonisation objective was too inflexible. It neither allowed for regional considerations to be adequately taken into account, nor did it encourage product innovations.

We have already noted that national initiatives continued apace creating potential barriers to trade. Also whilst various European standards bodies were producing European specifications, this work was not integrated into the EC programme. Although the old approach directives might encourage mutual recognition of testing and certification procedures carried out in other member states this was not required and did not occur in practice. Finally the interests of third country producers were not taken into account, a position which is no longer viable in today's global economy.

C.   The New Approach to Technical Harmonisation

By the mid 1980s the EC sought a new way of removing technical barriers. Their 'new approach' was intended to be both more flexible, leaving a lot of the detailed work to the European standardisation bodies, and at the same time more complete by attempting total harmonisation of safety aspects in order to reassure member states that they could safely permit free circulation of conforming products. Although old style technical harmonisation continued after the introduction of this new approach the thrust of EC policy is to promote new approach total harmonisation directives.

---

[60]   Farr, *op. cit.*, at 6.

[61]   Lauwaars, *op cit.*, at 154–5 calculated that 159 directives on the removal of technical obstacles to trade were adopted between 1962 and 1984.

The basic principles of the new approach to technical harmonisation are set out in the 1985 Resolution as being:

* harmonising legislation should be limited to adopting 'essential safety requirements' to which products should conform and which if they do so conform should be their passport to free movement throughout the Community;
* standardisation organisations should be entrusted with the task of drawing up the technical specifications needed for the production and placing on the market of products conforming to the essential requirements;
* these specification should be voluntary;
* national authorities are obliged to recognise that products conforming to the harmonised standards are presumed to conform to the essential requirements. Manufacturers should have the choice of not manufacturing in conformity with the standard, but in this case they are obliged to prove that their products conform to the essential requirements (and third party conformity assessment is usually required).

The presumption of conformity is of course merely a presumption. Its purpose is to prevent the routine testing of products or requirements that documentation be produced once the product has been found to conform to the Directive. We shall see that this is typically signified by the CE mark, which is the effective passport for products to circulate within Europe. However, the new approach directives also have safeguard clauses and the 1985 Resolution makes it clear that where all the essential requirements are not covered then action under art. 36 (and presumably also under the mandatory requirements proviso) remains possible.

The 1985 Resolution justifies the new approach technical harmonisation on the basis of the need to harmonise safety legislation without lowering existing and justified levels of protection. Directives should specify their sphere of application according to the type of hazard involved (safety, health, environmental, consumer protection) and if need be the relevant circumstances (at home, at work, under road traffic conditions, during leisure activities etc.).

In its criteria for choosing priority areas to which the new approach applies it is noted that the 'general reference to standards' approach is only possible where it is genuinely possible to distinguish between 'essential requirements' and 'manufacturing specifications'. Where a large number of manufacturing specifications would have to be included in the essential requirements then there is said to be little sense in adopting the new approach. It suggests that safety matters ought to be given priority over health matters.

Furthermore existing regulations must in practice genuinely impede the free movement of goods.[62] However, this requirement is likely to be broadly interpreted for the 1985 Resolution provides that harmonisation may be necessary to protect an essential public interest even if the grounds are not obvious. Nevertheless there has been some criticism of some of the measures chosen for the new approach; for instance, the Construction Products Directive has been described as being 'ill conceived' as it is argued that intra–community trade in construction products is more influenced by structural factors such as high transportation costs, and preferences by workmen for local products than technical barriers.[63]

Annex II of the 1985 Resolution contains guidelines listing the main elements that new approach directives should contain – this is sometimes referred to as the 'model directive'. These are worth studying both for what they tell us about new approach directives and also because they contain a guide to the structure and contents of new approach directives. They also establish a Standing Committee, chaired by a representative of the Commission and comprising representatives of the member states who can seek the assistance of experts and advisers. We shall note that it has various tasks entrusted to it and furthermore any question regarding the implementation of a new approach technical harmonisation directive can be referred to it. This is the same Standing Committee as operates under the Technical Standards Directive.

The model directive covers the following points:

---

62   See, N. Burrows, 'Harmonisation of technical standards: reculer pour mieux sauter' (1990) 55 *M.L.R.* 597 at 600 who believes 'harmonisation is necessary only in the area of mandatory requirements since in other areas the Court has recognised the principle of equivalence'. With hindsight this might at first glance be considered prescient of the later jurisprudence surrounding the *Keck* decision (see section 2A). However, a distinction should be drawn between national rules which may not be found to infringe arts 30–36 and those rules which the Community might nevertheless wish to harmonise in order to promote the establishment and functioning of the internal market. This interpretation is supported by the increased competence of the EC in areas such as consumer protection independent of internal market justifications (see art. 129a(1)(b)).

63   Centre for European Policy Studies, *op. cit.*, at 48.

(i) Scope

The directives will list the range of products covered and the nature of hazards it is intended to avert. They should normally cover a broad category so as to avoid the proliferation of directives on specific products; although the possibility of a directive using the general reference to standards formula and covering a single product is not ruled out in appropriate cases. It is also possible that the same product is covered by more than one directive in respect of different hazards. The example is given of a machine whose mechanical safety is covered by one directive and the pollution it generates is covered by another.

(ii) General Clause

The products covered by the directive may only be placed on the market if they do not endanger the safety of persons, domestic animals or goods when properly installed and maintained and used for the purposes for which they are intended. However, particularly in the case of worker or consumer protection this can be strengthened to include foreseeable as well as intended use.

As a rule the directives will provide for total harmonisation, although the possibility of optional harmonisation is allowed for. The general rule is to allow traders the choice of means of attestation of conformity. Thus member states should not, unless it is expressly provided for in the directives, set up pre–marketing controls. However, it is recognised that post–marketing spot checks will be necessary if national authorities are to carry out their obligation to ensure that only safe products are marketed.

(iii) Essential Safety Requirements

Whether the general safety requirement is satisfied will be assessed by applying the essential safety requirements. These essential requirements should be worded precisely enough so that when implemented in national legislation they create legally binding obligations which can be enforced. Certification bodies ought also to be able to certify straightaway that products are in conformity.

(iv) Means of Attestation of Conformity

The means of attestation which a trader may use are:

(a)   certificates and marks of conformity issued by a third party;
(b)   results of tests carried out by a third party;
(c)   declaration of conformity issued by the manufacturer or his agent based in the Community, possibly coupled with the requirement for a surveillance system;
(d)   or such other means as specified in the directives.

Specific directives establish the appropriate means of attestation and in so doing may limit or restrict the above range of options. Third party certification will be needed where there are no standards or the manufacturer chooses not to observe the standards. Where a manufacturer's declaration is relied upon national authorities, if they have good grounds for believing that a product does not offer the safety required in all respects, have the right to ask manufacturers or importers for the data from the safety tests on which they rely. If this is not forthcoming then there is sufficient reason to doubt the presumption of conformity. Only through the use of one of the specified means of attestation can the product benefit from the presumption of conformity. However, the trader remains free to use any means he sees fit to establish that his product complies with the general safety obligation and the essential requirements.

Member states will notify the Commission and other member states of national bodies authorised to issue marks or certificates of conformity (hereafter 'notified bodies'). These bodies must operate within recognised international practices and principles, especially in accordance with ISO guidelines, and responsibility for their operation rests with member states.

(v)   *Free Movement Clause*

Member states are obliged to accept goods which conform to the general safety obligation and the essential requirements. Member states cannot as a general rule require prior verification of compliance with the essential requirements, nor should it lead to the sectoral directives systematically requiring third party certification. Action under art. 36 remains possible in exceptional circumstances.

Proof of conformity – in effect the products passport to free movement within the Community – can be assured by one of the means of attestation referred to above declaring that the product is in conformity with a European harmonised standard, or as a transitional measure national standards.[64]

---

64   Member states must inform the Commission of those national standards which conform to the Directive. These are forwarded by the Commission to member states.

Where no standard is applied proof of conformity with the essential requirements must be established by attestation by a third party.

(vi) Safeguard Clause

Even if a product is accompanied by a means of attestation, a member state must take all appropriate measures to withdraw or prohibit the placing on the market of the product in question or to restrict its free movement, where it finds that it might compromise the safety of individuals, domestic animals or property. If the product was accompanied by a means of attestation of conformity with the relevant directive, the member state must inform the Commission of such measures indicating the reason for its decision and indicating whether the non–conformity resulted from (i) in the case where the product did not claim to conform to a standard, non–compliance with the general safety or the essential safety requirement, or (ii) in other cases an incorrect application of the relevant standard or a shortcoming in the actual standard.

If a member state intends to keep such a measure in place the Commission will refer the matter to the Standing Committee. If the measure is found to be justified the Commission will inform the member state in question and point out to the other states that (all else being equal) they should also prevent the product in question being marketed. If the failure of the product results from shortcomings in a harmonised or national standard then the matter is referred to the Standing Committee. We have already noted that Committee's role in assessing whether national standards, should, as a transitional measure, enjoy the presumption of conformity. It performs a similar function when a harmonised standard is questioned either when it is the reason why a member state has invoked the safeguard clause or where a member state or the Commission simply consider a harmonised standard or draft standard does not fully satisfy the directive's requirements. In such a case the Committee should give its opinion as a matter of urgency. In the light of the Committee's opinion the Commission will notify the member

---

After consulting the Standing Committee, the Commission informs member states whether a national standard should enjoy the presumption of conformity. Referral to the Committee is more to provide a forum for the discussion of objections than for a systematic examination of the entire contents to be carried out. If subsequently the Commission or a member state consider that a national standard no longer fulfils the conditions for presumption of conformity, the Commission shall in the light of the Committee's opinion notify member states whether or not it should continue to benefit from the presumption. Member states must publish references to conforming standards and the Commission must publish them in the Official Journal.

states as to whether or not the standard needs to be withdrawn. Harmonised standards must be published in the Official Journal of the European Communities and member states should publish references to these standards.

Where the non–conforming product was accompanied by a means of attestation the competent member state should take appropriate action against the author of the attestation and inform the Commission and the other member states. Action of this nature will presumably be required where the problem arose because of the incorrect application of the standards.

New approach directives with their emphasis on reference to standardisation work are clearly influenced by the German tradition (see Chapter 7). It should not be thought that it burst on to the European scene unheralded in 1985. As far back as 1973 the Low Voltage Directive contained many of the elements associated with the new approach.[65] Whilst some traditional style directives relating to products continue to be enacted or proposed, since 1985 the main body of product related directives have followed the new approach. Those which affect product safety include directives on:

- simple pressure vessels,[66]
- toy safety,[67]
- construction products,[68]
- machinery,[69]
- personal protective equipment,[70]
- implantable medical devices,[71]

---

65   Council Directive 73/23/EEC on the harmonisation of the laws of member states relating to electrical equipment designed for use within certain voltage limits: OJ 1973 L 77/29.

66   Council Directive 87/404/EEC on the harmonisation of the laws of the member states relating to simple pressure vessels: OJ 1987 L 220/48.

67   Council Directive 88/378/EEC on the approximation of the laws of the member states concerning the safety of toys: OJ 1988 L 187/1.

68   Council Directive 89/106/EEC on the approximation of laws, regulations and administrative provisions of the member states relating to construction products: OJ 1989 L 40/12.

69   Council Directive 89/392/EEC on the approximation of the laws of the member states relating to machinery: OJ 1989 L 198/16; amended by Directive 91/368/EEC to cover mobile machinery and light equipment: OJ 1991 L 198/16.

70   Council Directive 89/686/EEC on the approximation of the laws of the member states relating to personal protective equipment: OJ 1989 L 399/18.

71   Council Directive 90/385/EEC on the approximation of the laws of the member states relating to active implantable medical devices: OJ 1990 L 189/17.

- gas burning appliances,[72]
- medical devices.[73]

5. RELATIONSHIP BETWEEN ESSENTIAL SAFETY REQUIREMENTS AND STANDARDS

The relationship between the essential safety requirements and standards is central to the new approach. In theory in provides the means to ensure safety in a manner which is compatible with economic development. The safety objectives are set out by the politicians in the directives, whilst the technocrats from industry take part in the standardisation process to ensure the means to achieve those goals are acceptable to industry. However, inevitably, the distinction between the standard setting and implementation is not always clear cut.[74] Indeed there is an inherent conflict between the requirement that the essential safety requirements should be sufficiently precise so as to give rise to binding obligations and the other goals of limiting legislative intervention and delegating responsibility to the standardisation bodies.[75]

A perusal of the essential safety requirements in the annexes to the new approach directives shows that the rules they contain vary in character. Some rules are very clear and precise. Thus, for instance, the Toy Safety Directive lays down maximum levels of exposure to eight substances. The Machinery Directive clearly requires that it must be possible to start machinery only by voluntary actuation of a control provided for the purpose and that in so far as their purposes allows, accessible parts of the machinery must have no sharp edges, no sharp angles and no rough surfaces likely to cause injury. Sometimes the directives also require specific warnings; for example, the Toy Safety Directive requires a warning on all toys not suitable for children under 3 years.

Many of the essential safety requirements, however, set down vague objectives and refer, for instance to the need to *minimise* risks or reduce them *as far as possible* or to ensure temperatures do not cause burning (leaving it for experts to decide what temperatures are appropriate). Requirements phrased in this way leave a great deal of room for debate as to how far risks can be minimised or reduced or what the maximum temperature should be. The clear danger is that the directives can produce the symbolism of safety,

---

72 Council Directive 90/396/EEC on the approximation of the laws of the member states relating to appliances burning gaseous fuels: OJ 1990 L 196/15.

73 Council Directive 93/42/EEC concerning medical devices: OJ 1993 L 169/1.

74 In similar vein see Joerges (ed.), *op. cit.*, at 209–211.

75 See, Falke, *op. cit.*, at 92.

but the standards fail to back up this up by providing concrete safety. It also blurs the distinction between safety policy and its technical implementation. Indeed the Commission had to produce interpretation documents to assist the standardisation bodies in understanding the essential requirements in the Construction Products Directive[76] and now regularly gives directions to the standardisation bodies through the mandates it issues when contracting for the work.

As a general rule the standards do not even themselves prescribe the means by which safety should be assured. They are generally framed in terms of performance rather than means, with the belief being that:

> 'only people of the trade can be responsible for choosing the necessary and sufficient technical solutions to obtain the performances defined by the standards so as to meet the essential requirements specified by the directive and intended to guarantee user safety.'[77]

Thus product safety is governed by four layers of controls – the general safety clause in the body of the directive, the essential requirements to be found in its annex, harmonised standards and the means chosen by manufacturers to achieve those standards. Clearly the content of the standards is pivotal as these will be the basis for manufacturers' design and production decisions and also will provide the measure against which products will usually be judged in order to obtain the CE marking and thereby access to free movement within the EC. It is also clear that this process is more than just a technical process. Standards do not just provide the technical details to supplement the safety standards laid down in the essential requirements. More precisely the essential requirements tend to set down the need for various safety concerns to be addressed, whilst the standards give meaning to those exhortations. To put it more bluntly, the directives say that products should be safe, the standards tell us what safe means.

---

[76]   Centre for European Policy Studies, *op. cit.*, at 36.
[77]   See comment by Jeanne Milhaïlov in CEN, *The New Approach*, (CEN, 1994) at 198.

6. STANDARDISATION

A. European Standards Organisations

There are three European standards organisations CEN (European Committee for Standardisation), CENELEC (European Committee for Electrotechnical Standardisation) and ETSI (European Telecommunications Standards Institute). The EC has entered into an agreement with these bodies for them to be responsible for the development of the European standards needed by the EC.[78] We shall concentrate on CEN which deals with the majority of standards work for non–electrical consumer products.

One of the criticisms of CEN and European standardisation in general is that it lacks a rigorous structure. The Commission had suggested that European standardisation be re–organised.[79] It proposed there be a European Standardisation Council responsible for the strategic direction of European standardisation. This would have had an executive body, the European Standardisation Board, responsible for co–ordinating the work of the European standardisation bodies. It was envisaged that in the future other sectors than just the telecommunications sector (which has ETSI) may wish to develop their own European standardisation bodies. The Commission wished to encourage this in the hope that industry would then become more involved in and committed to standardisation, but saw its European Standardisation Council as a means of retaining coherency in the system.

There was opposition to the Commission's proposals which were seen as adding a needless bureaucratic layer,[80] but it did cause the three European Standardisation Bodies to appreciate the need to work more closely together.

---

[78] General Guidelines for co–operation between the Commission of the European Communities (CEC) and the European Free Trade Association (EFTA) and the European standards organisations, CEN/CENELEC Memorandum No. 4. Lauwaars, *op. cit.*, at 165–7 suggests that this amounts to the delegation of the Council's power and that even if this is of a permitted nature, ie a 'clearly defined executive power', nevertheless it breaches the Treaty because there is not the same judicial control of the standardisation bodies as there is of the Council. In fact the basic principles of the new approach are supported by all member states and there has not been, and is not likely to be, a challenge of this nature. If there were, one suspects the ECJ would argue that there had been no delegation of legal power as the standards were voluntary and in the final analysis producers could rely on the essential safety requirements established by the Directive and enforcement authorities could also act against products which failed to conform to those requirements.

[79] See, *Commission Communication on the Development of European Standardisation*: OJ 1991 C 20/1.

[80] See, COM (91) 521 at 4.

There is now a Joint Presidents Groups which includes the Presidents and Chief Executives of the three organisation and acts as a forum to reach understandings on strategic issues. A Joint Co–ordination Group monitors co–operation between technical bodies of the three organisations in areas of common interest and also acts as a court of last resort in the event of conflicts not resolved through normal processes.[81] They also came together to form an Information Technology Steering Committee (ITSTC), which has now developed into the ICT Standards Board.

We shall note several criticisms of the way in which CEN has operated. These involve suggestions that its procedures are too slow, that it fails to promote the European dimension to standardisation and that it does not fully integrate social partners, such as consumers into its structures and working methods. It has been suggested that criticisms of CEN were part of a shouting match between the Commission and CEN with each trying to pass the buck for problems in implementing the new approach.[82] In truth there were probably unrealistic expectations about the ease with which standards could be created as well as some inefficient procedures. With the push to complete the internal market strains in the system appeared, but these seem to have diminished and CEN and the Commission appear to work more harmoniously at the present time.

Although many of these criticisms made of CEN were valid, it is worthwhile setting them in the context of both the origins of CEN and the changed role it has been called upon to play. When CEN was established in 1961 its role was not so much to harmonise standards, but rather to ensure the more effective implementation of international standards by national standardisation bodies in Europe. Between 1961 and 1982 CEN only adopted 96 standards. By 1995 1,700 European standards were in existence with a further 8,300 projected.[83] As of 30 June 1996 the number of standards had risen to 2,700.[84] Not only the new approach directives, but other moves towards European integration, for instance in the public procurement sphere, have placed increased workloads on to CEN. Thus in 1992 CEN produced 307 new standards, this had risen to 408 in 1993[85] and increased further to a staggering 710 in 1995.[86] Even with this increase in activity there is a large backlog of projected proposals. The Toy Safety

---

81   These arrangements are explained in the pamphlet *European Standardisation* published by CEN, CENELEC and ETSI.

82   J. Pelkmans and M. Egan, *Fixing European Standards: Moving Beyond the Green Paper*, (CEPS, 1992) at 14–15.

83   CEN, *Standards for Access to the European Market*, 2ed, (CEN, 1995) at 13.

84   CEN, *Annual Report 1995/1996*, at 10.

85   CEN, *Annual Report 1993/1994*, at 36.

86   CEN, *Annual Report 1995/1996*, at 10.

Directive is frequently cited as a new approach Directive whose application was hampered by the slowness with which standards were developed. The Commission itself admits there are problems in relation to machinery, where industry has been slow to react, and construction products where there is a discrepancy between what the authorities express through mandates and what can be obtained through the voluntary process.[87] The simple truth is that whilst standards bodies may be more competent to decide technical matters than bureaucrats they face the same problems of having to resolve conflicting interests and this inevitably involves a lengthy process.

Thus CEN is trying to perform a task – harmonisation – which it was not originally established to achieve and the size of the harmonisation task has grown exponentially in recent years. Its basic constitution as a body representing and comprising national standards bodies causes some problems. Industry does not feel it 'owns' CEN and therefore does not see why it should fund it.[88] Equally, national standardisation bodies are themselves industry oriented and so other social partners feel excluded. The need to reach consensus between national interests and traditions may both water down proposals and cause them to be delayed. To make these points clearer the structure of CEN will be outlined before consideration is given to its decision–making procedures.

B. Structure of CEN

General oversight of CEN is carried out by its General Assembly. This comprises representatives of national standardisation bodies from EC and EFTA states. These members have the right to vote. There is also an affiliate status which is given to non–EC and EFTA European States, ie the PHARE countries of Central and Eastern Europe. Their involvement in the European standardisation process is encouraged, but CEN wants to restrict membership to EC and EFTA countries. Presumably as these states join the EC they will also be admitted to CEN, but for the present a process of gradual integration is preferred.

European social and economic organisations can be given associate status within the General Assembly, but again this carries no voting rights. Associate Membership is currently enjoyed by ECMA (European Computer Manufacturers Association), FIEC (European Construction Industry Federation), CEFIC (European Chemical Industry Council), TUTB (European Trade Union Technical Bureau for Health and Safety) and ANEC

---

87   SEC(95) 2104, *op. cit.*, at 8.

88   Cf. ETSI where individual companies are members.

(European Association for the Co–ordination of Consumer Representation in Standardisation).

The General Assembly is represented by an Administrative Board which directs and co–ordinates all the action of CEN bodies. The General Assembly appoints a President and Secretary General.

At a practical level the Technical Board ultimately controls the standards programme and is responsible for all matters concerning the organisation, working procedures, co–ordination and planning of standards work. In 1991/2 Technical Sector Boards were established to improve co–ordination of work programmes and to increase involvement of CEN's industrial and social partners. They have delegated authority from the Technical Board to define and control the standards programme in their sector. There are Technical Sector Boards for building and civil engineering, mechanical engineering, healthcare, health and safety at the workplace, heating, cooling and ventilation, transport and packaging and information technology. For other sectors (gas, food, transport, water cycle, environment, post and rail) there are Programming Committees who advise the Technical Board and co–ordinate and plan standardisation in their field of activity. The institutions discussed so far are serviced by CEN's central secretariat.

The actual standardisation work is carried on by Technical Committees. These are chaired and serviced by national members. The Commission has raised the question of whether there is not a limit to the size of technical structure which CEN can support.[89] The problem is that as new Technical Committees are being created, those which have completed their work are not wound up because of the need for a reference point to deal with future queries.

Instead of establishing a technical committee of its own the Technical Board may contract with one of its Associated Bodies to prepare drafts in accordance with CEN principles. Currently there are four such bodies, AECMSA (Association Européene des Constructeurs de Matériel Aérospatial), ECISS (European Committee for Iron and Steel standardisation), EWOS (European Workshop for Open Systems), WE/EB (Western European EDIFACT Board). There are several benefits of this farming–out approach. It reduces the pressure on CEN itself and allows some of the backlog of standards waiting to be produced to be moved. It also goes some way to meet the EC Commission's desire that industrial sectors be more closely involved in the standardisation process. However, it does make the process more openly controlled by industry. To the extent that the measures are largely internal industry concerns, this may be unobjectionable, but one suspects that users and consumers have an interest in many such matters. Certainly one would be wary if safety issues were to be delegated

---

89   SEC(95) 2104 at I.4.

outside the normal CEN procedures and placed under the supervision of industry bodies.

CEN is funded by annual membership contributions from its national member bodies. However, in 1991 the EC Commission contributed 70% of its annual budget in the form of mandates to harmonise standards in connection with EC legislation. Of course there were other costs associated with standardisation, namely the time of experts and their travel expenses which are funded by industry, whilst some of the secretariat support for technical committees is provided by national bodies. Nevertheless the European standardisation bodies were perhaps unhealthily dependent on EC funding. Whilst prepared to continue to commit public funds for the foreseeable future to standardisation, the EC was rightly alarmed at this imbalance between public and private funding.[90] It suggested national contributions be placed on a long term commitment basis, but also that new sources of funding be developed. One proposal was that part of the revenue from the sale of European standards be channelled directly to the European standardisation body. Presently all European standards are sold as national standards by national bodies who derive a considerable amount of income from sales of standards created out of the CEN process. However, the result of this proposal would simply ensure CEN obtained a certain amount of income in its own right: but as this would result in reduced income for the national standardisation bodies one could expect their annual contributions to CEN to fall. In fact CEN has decided to reduce its dependency on official sources of funding to 25% of its total budget.[91]

Another suggestion was that industry participants in CEN should pay a membership fee. The Commission has rued the lack of commitment by industry to the standardisation process. As they have been hesitant even to support the standardisation process by releasing technical experts to work on standardisation committees, one suspects that there would be little mileage in this proposal. Indeed industry fails to see why it rather than Governments should meet the increased costs of standardisation.[92] No doubt this is short sighted of industry which has and will continue to benefit greatly from the

---

90   *Commission Communication on the Development of European Standsardisation*: OJ 1991 C 20/1 at 20.

91   SEC(95) 2104 at I.6. However, there seems to be some ambiguity as to whether the percentage contributed by the Commission refers simply to the costs of the CEN secretariat or the costs of the CEN and national secretariats servicing CEN committees for it comments lower down that official support is directed not at the European Central Secretariats, but at the national bodies which administer the European work. This caveat did not seem apparent when as already noted the Commission claimed to meet 70% of CEN's annual budget.

92   OJ 1992 C 96/2, *op. cit.*, at para. 7.

development of the internal market. On the other hand it is difficult to justify why those businesses who do involve themselves in the standardisation process, and therefore already commit some resources to the process, should have to pay a membership fee whilst others are effectively free riders. Even levies on trade associations would penalise members over non–members. The truth is that this is a function which should properly be performed by Government – not only is it fairer as between the members of the industry, but it also removes any suggestion that 'he who pays the bill calls the tune'. If industry is helped by the harmonisation of standards then some of the investment can be recouped through higher tax returns. Herein lies the rub, for in the present climate no one is prepared to pay taxes to allow the state to perform the functions it is best placed to undertake for the sake of the general economy. This augurs badly for the prospects of adequate funding of consumer input into the standardisation process.

C.   Standards Making Procedure

Standards implementing the essential requirements found in the new approach directives are adopted on the basis of a mandate from the EC Commission (and sometimes also EFTA). The mandate is a contract between the Commission and CEN for CEN to draft standards.[93] Negotiations between the Commission and CEN on the package of standards should commence from the moment a proposal is made and run in parallel with negotiations on the directive. Problems can arise when CEN is not fully involved in the development of the project. For instance, CEN was annoyed when the Construction Products Directive was adopted whilst discussions were still under way about the financial budget and necessary standards programme. Problems with implementing the programme ensued. The mandate is clearly a crucial document in defining the level of safety. It poses a problem for consumers, for although they may be involved in the subsequent work of the standardisation bodies they are largely excluded from the negotiations over the mandate.[94]

The Commission has introduced the concept of 'open' mandates, which allow the standardisers, and hence the economic interests affected, a broad degree of flexibility in structuring the standards programme. Such mandates state the areas in which standards are needed together with an explanation of legislative and related contexts, but leave the standardisers free to decide which standards are actually needed.

---

[93]   See comments of J. Repussard in CEN (1994), *op. cit.*, at 189.

[94]   H.–W. Micklitz, 'Perspectives on A European Directive on the Safety of Technical Consumer Goods' (1986) *C.M.L.R.* 617 at 633.

The Commission notes, that its preference for 'horizontal' standards covering areas of risk which can be applied to a range of equipment is not shared by industry which prefers 'vertical' standards giving a complete set of requirements for specific types of products.[95] In fact there may not be a clear distinction between horizontal and vertical standards, for horizontal standards will usually be incorporated by reference into vertical standards. However they also serve as a point of guidance for designers without the benefit of vertical standards and have the advantage that they are hazard–oriented, leaving designers more freedom so long as safety concerns are adequately addressed (Chapter 1, section 3E(iii)). CEN has recently developed some horizontal rules for nursery products, but these are not given the status of CEN standards, but rather are merely CEN reports.

Once a draft mandate is agreed upon it is submitted to the Standing Committee set up under the Technical Standards Directive. When approved by that Committee the Commission puts out a tender to CEN. CEN responds with a detailed quotation specifying the number of standards needed, how the work will be distributed between technical committees, how long the standards will take to prepare and the cost of administrative support from the CEN central secretariat, including where needed, any research, testing etc. After financial negotiations a contract is concluded. Requests for standards may also come from CEN national members and European organisations.

When a proposed standard is in the standardisation programme the Technical Board has three options as to how to proceed:

(i) It can be sent to a Technical Committee. This will happen where the matter is a new topic. Once a draft standard (prEN) has been agreed upon it is put out to public enquiry for 6 months.[96] This means it is distributed to CEN members for public comment. The technical committee system, bringing together representatives from 18 countries, has been criticised for being inefficient and the suggestion has been made that it should have smaller 'project teams' developing the proposal so as to make the procedure more efficient.

(ii) Where an existing reference document exists (European trade specification, national standard, ISO standard) there is no need for a technical committee to be established and the questionnaire procedure can be adopted. This replaces the public enquiry procedure, but there is still a six month time limit for replies.

(iii) Under conditions laid down in the 'Vienna Agreement' CEN can transfer work for the execution of European Standards to ISO. There are

95   SEC(95) 2104, *op. cit.*, at IV.1–2.

96   The Commission has recommended that this period be reduced to two months for consensus vote drafts, four months for majority vote drafts.

parallel procedures for CEN/ISO public enquiry and formal vote (see Chapter 3, section 3B).

After the public enquiry the National Members have a formal vote on the final draft. This is done using a weighted voting procedure based on art. 148 of the Treaty of Rome, but adapted to take account of the larger membership of CEN than the EC. However, standardisation has a tradition of working by consensus, because being voluntary measures standards require acceptance by their potential users. This same philosophy applies to standards adopted under new approach mandates, even if the end result is a *de facto* requirement. This consensus approach is another explanation for the lengthy adoption process.

The procedure is largely the same for standards developed as a result of a mandate from the EC under the new approach as it is for any other standard. Although member states may scrutinise new approach standards more closely because of the presumption of conformity which they give rise to.

CEN must send a copy of the standard to the Commission, confirming that it complies with the essential requirements of the Directive and requesting that it be published in the Official Journal and that member states be informed of it. CEN also ensures quality control by appointing consultants to make sure the members of the technical committees understand the Directive and the implications of the essential requirements and that they stay within their mandate. The consultant can comment during the enquiry period and prior to the formal vote must send a report to the Secretary General. On two occasions a committee has had to take its draft back for further action as a result of this procedure.

An important change is likely to take place in the future once the present phase of establishing the internal market is completed. The emphasis will then turn from creating standards to maintaining and updating them. We have already commented that the present structure of retaining technical committees may prove too cumbersome and new streamlined procedures for supervising and amending standards may have to be developed.

D. Consumer Representation in Standardisation

There is general agreement that consumers should be involved in the standards–making process. This has been stated by the Commission on numerous occasions,[97] and is also the position of the European

---

[97]   See, *Second Programme for a Consumer Protection and Information Policy*, OJ 1981 C 133/1, para. 19; Council Resolution on the Integration of Consumer Policy in the

standardisation bodies. Such involvement is necessary if standards are to be acceptable to consumers and to legitimise this form of 'private legislation'.

However, consumer involvement should be more than a few champagne parties for their representatives and pleasant platitudes in annual reports. To be able to operate effectively consumers need to be represented by technical experts.[98] Technical expertise is needed because these consumer representatives will be participating in working groups and technical committees the other members of which will be technical experts from industry. Finding this sort of personnel to represent the consumer is difficult; but consumer political activists are of little use in the technical debates which are involved in the standardisation process. Fortunately there is a scattering of such consumer–oriented technical people in consumer organisations, research institutes and test houses across Europe.

The move from the national to the European level should in theory allow the consumer movement's limited resources to be more focused and permit consumers in those countries which do not have adequate resources for consumer protection to benefit from the input at the European level of consumer experts from those countries where they exist. It should also have the advantage of permitting European consumers to speak with a common European voice, whereas industry involvement may be divided along national lines.[99] However, the Europeanisation of the problem also brings with it the problem of co–ordinating a common consumer position. Legitimate differences in approach can exist between consumer groups, perhaps based upon cultural attitudes to risk or alternative approaches to combating dangers. However, a divided front can, at least if not clearly explained, weaken the impact of the consumer voice. Co–ordination at the European level, however, involves considerable costs.

Moreover, the move to the European level can represent a step backwards for consumers in those countries which had already developed effective means to permit consumers to influence national standardisation procedures. Instead of occupying a place at the national negotiating table, the national consumer voice is represented instead, at best, as a member of

---

other Common Policies: OJ 1987 C 3/1, para. 5; OJ 1991 C 20/1, *op. cit.*, para. 33; OJ 1992 C 96/2, *op. cit.*, paras 32–37 and *Making the Most of the Internal Market*, COM(93) 632 at 37 where it talks of increasing transparency and making the procedures more accessible to 'economic operators' which will presumably also include consumers.

98 As Micklitz graphically puts it: 'Without strengthening the technical equipment there will never be a chance of claiming "a bit more" than the industrial side has offered': Micklitz, *op. cit.*, at 640.

99 H.–W. Micklitz, 'Considerations Shaping Future Consumer Participation in European Product Safety Law' in Joerges (ed.), *op. cit.*, at 201.

a national delegation which is there, primarily, to represent the position of the national standards body. Indeed such representatives are bound to follow the national line even if this is counter to their view of what is in the consumer interest.

At the European level the development of representation through participation in national delegations continues to be an important feature, although there is now also some direct consumer representation on CEN committees through ANEC. Nevertheless, as these participants need technical knowledge even the direct European consumer representative tend to be appointed from those countries with developed consumer technical expertise. In practice this means that Southern European consumers tend to be underrepresented in the standards process.

We shall see that the same debates about the opportunities and dangers for consumers arising out of the move from the national to the European level also occur in the next chapter, which deals with the internationalisation of product safety. In many ways the problems are accentuated when the forum for standards setting switches from the national or European level to the international (Chapter 3, section 3C).

In 1977 CEN published a joint document with CENELEC which stated that there should be 'consultation of consumers in the framing of decisions affecting their interests'.[100] However, the European bodies did not foresee themselves as being responsible for bringing this about, instead encouragement was to be given for the development of consumer representation within national member bodies. However, in 1982 the Commission reached agreement with CEN and CENELEC for consumer representatives to participate in their work. The consumer observers were nominated by the EC's Consumer Consultative Council (EC–CCC) and organisational support was provided by BEUC (Bureau Européen des Union Consommateurs). Soon a more independent structure, although still housed within BEUC, was established – SECO (Secretariat Européen de Co–ordination pour la normalisation). This was to serve as a model for the present structure of consumer representation in European standardisation – ANEC (European Association for the Co–ordination of Consumer Representation in Standardisation).

Prior to the creation of ANEC there was a great deal of debate about the best means of representing the consumer in European standardisation. In fact a body with similar functions to ANEC (representing and co–ordinating the

---

[100]   Joint document No. 2, *Consumer Interests and the Preparation of Standards*, cited in B. Farquhar, 'Consumer Representation in Standardisation' [1995] *Consum. L.J.* 56. This is an excellent analysis of the development of consumer representation in standardisation up to the founding of ANEC, which is heavily relied upon in the following. See also, *Consumer Participation in Standardisation*, (ANEC, 1996).

consumer interest, developing consumer priorities and formulating a consumer safety policy) had been suggested in 1986 in a report to the Commission, by Bosma, a Dutch Consumer Technology and Home Economics Consultant.[101] She had proposed the committee be an advisory committee to the Standing Committee under the Technical Standards Directive. In 1989–90 proposals emerged from within CEN itself for a consumer council based within CEN and whose membership would be derived from the members of CEN; a later proposal tried to meet objections to the proposed composition of the council by adding to its general assembly representation from the EC and EFTA–CCCs. However ANEC is more closely based on the SECO proposal put to the EC–CCC standardisation working group. This suggested a body which would be based outside CEN. This had the advantage of perceived independence and also of being a body which could deal with CENELEC and ETSI as well as CEN. It also had the advantage of drawing its membership from independent consumer organisations, whereas only half of the 18 CEN members had proper consumer councils and their independence was not trusted by all sections of the consumer movement.

ANEC was formed in 1995.[102] Its General Assembly comprises one member of a national consumer organisation in each EC/EFTA member state and four nominees from the EC, and two from the EFTA, CCC. It has carried over the SECO secretariat and structure.

SECO has six working groups – on child safety, electrical appliances, machinery, the environment, gas appliances and traffic safety. These bring together experts to consider particular projects. Their work is overseen in a co–ordination group, which also deals with any issues falling outside the remit of the six working groups and provides a forum for the discussion of horizontal issues and for exchanging information produced at the national level. As the working groups tend to be dominated by technical experts from a limited number of countries, the co–ordination group is important to ensure all countries are involved in the representation of consumers in the standardisation process. This has been said to be particularly important for the Southern European countries and Ireland.[103]

In 1995 750,000 ECU was granted by the EC to support consumer representation in standardisation.[104] An important use of this fund is to pay the expenses on consumer representatives attending CEN working groups. Roughly 50 European committees have an ANEC representative, with

---

101 F. Bosma, *International Standardisation and Consumer Interest 1984–1985*, XI/295/86 – EN.

102 See, ANEC, *Annual Report 1995*.

103 ANEC, *ibid.*, at 18.

104 Farquhar, *op. cit.*, at 68.

consumer representation being assured on another 150 or so committees through national delegations.[105] ANEC is also trying to ensure greater influence can be exerted at the national level by circulating written comments on drafts to national representatives. The use of written comments has increased, with 63 of these written comments being made in 1995 compared to 15 in 1992.[106] Although of some use, one suspects that written communications are unlikely greatly to influence the development of national policy, unless the national consumer representative is able to comprehend and engage in the debate set out in the written comment. Simply reading out a position statement is unlikely to cause industry to take the point seriously.

Successful consumer representation seems to depend upon having technical experts who can engage in debate with and obtain the respect of the industry experts on the standardisation committees. An example of this being achieved can possibly be seen in the appointment of an ANEC representative as convenor of a CEN working group on playground equipment.[107]

Work in the technical committees and working groups of CEN is important, but of course by the time that work is undertaken the main features of safety policy have been formed through the directives and mandates. It is also important that consumers do not merely respond to initiatives, but can force the standardisation process to take on board their concerns. Two developments have taken place which have the potential to help address these concerns.

CEN has opened up its structures to the extent that groups such as ANEC can become associate members. However, it is still unclear what benefits accrue from associate membership and how much ANEC will be able to influence the overall strategy of CEN.

At the end of 1995 a framework mandate was agreed which establishes a mechanism whereby consumer representatives can petition the standing committee under the Technical Standards Directive for a consumer concern to be addressed through standardisation. Implementing mandates could then be issued covering specific products and consumer concerns.[108]

Funding and technical knowledge will be the eventual keys to the success or otherwise of European participation in the standardisation process. In this respect the launch of ANEC has been disappointing, since it was unsuccessful with respect to all 12 research projects for which it sought Commission funding in 1995.[109]

---

[105]   ANEC, *op. cit.*, at 18.

[106]   ANEC, *Annual Report 1995*, at 19.

[107]   *Ibid.*, at 28.

[108]   *Ibid.*, at 9.

[109]   *Ibid.*, at 43.

Co–ordinating consumer involvement in standardisation with a limited budget is bound to be a difficult task. Inevitably ANEC is having to draw upon the knowledge of those countries which already have some expertise and national resources. It is certainly helping to fund some representation at the European level, which otherwise would not be there. However, it is doubtful that European consumer representatives will have as much influence in CEN committees as they do in those countries with developed national systems for consumer representation. It is also still to be seen what influence ANEC can have on the political orientation of EC consumer safety policy in the standardisation context.

E.   The Final Product – European Standards?

European standards (EN) must be implemented at the national level by being given the status of a national standard and by withdrawal of any conflicting national standards. CEN may also publish Harmonisation Documents (HD). These must be implemented at the national level, at least by the public announcement of the HD number and title and by withdrawing any conflicting national standard. However, members can maintain or issue a national standard dealing with a subject within the scope of a HD provided that it is equivalent in technical content. European Pre–standards (ENV) can also be issued. This is a prospective standard which should be made available at national level, but existing conflicting national standards may be kept in force, in parallel to the ENV, until a final decision about the conversion of an ENV into an EN is made.

The key point is that there is no such thing as a European standard. Standards only take effect as national standards. We have already seen that this means all the revenue from standards flow to the national members not CEN. It also means that the harmonisation process is delayed by about six months whilst CEN members adopt their national standards. This might be considered to be rather pointless since in the case of standards adopted as a result of new approach directives the national standards should involve a mere writing out, in their own language, of the CEN standard.[110]

The Commission also believes that reliance on national standards reinforces market segregation. To the extent that this is based on the continued prominence of the national mark, this may be alleviated by the development of the CE marking, but the continued presence of national marks will be a problem for the acceptance of European standards. It is hard to see any logical objection to the direct sale by CEN of EN standards. At

---

110   The CEN standard will be available in its three official languages; English, French and German.

the very least standards should be transposed quickly into national law and their European origin clearly indicated.

However, it is important also to appreciate the position of national standardisation bodies. From a position of quasi–monopoly power within their own territory they are gradually being converted into mere mouthpieces for national interests at European and international standardisation committees. For example in DIN (the German standards organisation) 80% of all projects in 1994 had a European or international origin, ten years earlier 80% had a purely national character. In the French standardisation organisation AFNOR 20% of the projects in 1991 had a European origin, by 1994 this had risen to roughly half.[111] They are losing their power and loss of revenue from sales of standards may be too much for them to bear.

7.   CONFORMITY ASSESSMENT

A.   Introduction

Setting harmonised standards under the new approach is only half the battle to free up trade, because even if products are made to common standards producers still need to provide proof of this. If states differ in the forms of proof they require, or do not recognise test results or certification carried out in other states, then these can provide major practical hurdles to the creation of an internal market. Furthermore problems can arise if different marks are either required to be used, or are permitted, in member states. A Community solution to these problems was necessary. This is necessary not only for products covered by new approach directives, but also those regulated by national regulations which require testing and conformity assessment. Even where there are no regulatory requirements, European co–ordination is needed to promote cross–border trade as firms are increasingly seeking assurances of compliance with standards as part of their attempts to improve quality and limit their liability exposure.

Conformity assessment matters are, however, difficult issues to control on a European wide level. Given the policy of restricting public authority controls to a limited number of products where it is absolutely necessary,[112] states must have confidence that manufacturers, testing and certification

---

111   SEC(95) 2104, *op. cit.*, at II.2

112   See proposal for a Council Decision concerning the modules for the various phases of the conformity assessment procedures which are intended to be used in the technical harmonisation directives: OJ 1989 C 231/3, COM (89) 209. For a critique of this document see H. Micklitz, *Inquiry on EC and current national certification schemes for particular consumer goods*, (SECO, 1990).

bodies in other member states will competently and diligently carry out the necessary procedures to ensure compliance with standards has been satisfactorily achieved. Indeed it is reported that the Commission has itself urged some of the Southern members to improve their track record in testing and certification and has made some funds available to assist them.[113]

The Resolution of 7 May 1985 on technical harmonisation recognised 'that the new approach will have to be accompanied by a policy on the assessment of conformity'. The Commission's response was to develop the *Global Approach to Certification and Testing*[114] which was encouraged by the adoption of a Council Resolution on a Global Approach to Conformity Assessment on 21 December 1989.[115] The concrete outcomes of this global approach have included the Conformity Assessment and CE Marking Decision[116] and the establishment of the European Organisation for Testing and Certification (EOTC).[117]

Resolving the conformity assessment problem requires that (i) the means of assuring conformity are harmonised, (ii) that testing procedures are also harmonised and the competency of those involved in the process is assured, (iii) and that conforming products are awarded a mark which assures them access to the whole of the internal market. The dangers to consumers are that the European rules and practices may be less demanding than those which existed under national law and as conformity can be established in any member state there may be a drift towards undertaking compliance procedures where they are perceived, at least, to be less demanding. This may cause national testing and certification bodies, which had previously applied more stringent criteria, to bring their standards down to the minimum level required by the directives. Further problems relating to the relationship between European certification marks and national marks will be alluded to below.

---

113 Centre for European Policy Studies, *op. cit.*, at 11.

114 OJ 1989 C 267/3.

115 OJ 1990 C 10/1.

116 OJ 1993 L 220/23, *op. cit.* This amended Council Decision 90/683/EEC concerning the modules for the various phases of the conformity assessment procedures which are intended to be used in the technical harmonisation directives: OJ 1990 L 380/13. At the same time Council Directive 93/68/EEC was passed amending various new approach technical harmonisation directives to bring them into line with the Council Decision: see OJ 1993 L 220/1.

117 This was established on 25 April 1990 on the basis of a memorandum of understanding between the Commission, EFTA and CEN and CENELEC.

B.   Conformity Assessment Procedures

The Conformity Assessment and CE Marking Decision[118] states that the essential objective of conformity assurance is to enable public authorities to ensure that products placed on the market conform to directives, particularly with regard to the health and safety of users and consumers. It explains that conformity assessment can be divided into modules relating to both the design and production phases and produces eight modules which, when account is taken of various options, produces 17 possible permutations. However, there are three broad categories of conformity assessment: self–declaration by the manufacturer, third party certification and quality assessment procedures supervised and controlled by a third party.[119]

Normally products must be subject to assessment at both their design and production stages. For each particular product sector the directive will select the appropriate modules taking into account the type of products, the nature of the risks involved, whether third party testing facilities exist etc. However, the emphasis is clearly on reducing the burden on manufacturers. Thus the Decision provides that the directives should leave the manufacturer with as wide a choice of modules as is consistent with meeting the safety requirements and avoid imposing unnecessarily modules which are too onerous relative to the directive's objectives. Notified bodies are also to be encouraged to apply the modules without placing unnecessary burdens on economic operators and the technical documentation required has to be limited to that which is required solely for conformity assessment purposes, with protection being afforded to confidential information.

The Commission, in co–operation with member states, is to ensure close co–operation between the member states to ensure consistent technical application of the modules. This, combined with competition between notified bodies, since approval by any one affords access to the single market, will have a tendency to restrict the freedom of testing bodies to be more demanding than the basic requirements of the directives. Unless the requirements of a particular directive require the application of a certain procedure then the manufacturer should be given the choice whether or not he uses modules based on quality assurance techniques. To the extent that this reduces third party certification, it requires consumers to have a degree of confidence in quality assurance systems and third party surveillance of them, which perhaps does not yet exist and is perhaps not yet justified. Moreover new approach directives usually include an even less demanding option which does not even require a quality assurance system, for example a

---

[118]   The principal guidelines for the use of conformity assessment procedures are found in Annex, IA.

[119]   See, Micklitz, *op. cit.*, at 8.

type examination (module B) in association with a manufacturer's declaration of conformity to type (module C) or it may simply require the manufacturer to declare conformity (module A). As Falke has commented 'conformity declaration of the manufacturer does not really mean *approved* safety, but *affirmed* safety'.[120]

The possible conformity assessment procedures in community legislation are helpfully reproduced in the annex to the Council Decision which is reproduced in table on pages 104 and 105.

Module A (internal production control)
The manufacturer or his authorised representative established within the Community[121] must establish technical documentation to cover the conformity assessment of the design, manufacture and operation of the product; affix the CE marking to each product and draw up a written declaration of conformity. The documentation should be retained for a period, usually ten years, after the product has last been manufactured. If neither the manufacturer or authorised representative is present within the Community the person who placed the product on the Community market has a duty to keep the documentation available.

This module can be supplemented by either:–

(i) a requirement that specific tests be carried out on aspects of the product, either by the manufacturer or on his behalf. These shall be on the responsibility of a notified body whose identification number should be affixed during the manufacturing process, or
(ii) notified bodies can be required to undertake product checks at random intervals. Again the identification number of the notified body should be affixed during the manufacturing process.

---

120 Falke, *op. cit.*, at 92.
121 This phraseology is used in various of the modules. It seems to leave a discretion as to whether the manufacturer or his authorised representative undertakes the function, but the logic of regulating a single market would seem to require the authorised representative to undertake the task if the manufacturer is located outside the EC.

CONFORMITY ASSESSMENT PROCEDURES IN COMMUNITY LEGISLATION

A. (Internal control of production)	B. (type examination)	G. (unit verification)	H. (full quality assurance)
Manufacturer Keeps technical documentation at the disposal of national authorities **D** **E** **S** Aa **I** **G** Intervention of **N** notified body	Manufacturer submits to notified body - Technical documentation - Type Notified body - Ascertains conformity with essential requirements - Carries out tests, if necessary - Issues EC type-examination certificate	Manufacturer - Submits technical documentation	EN 29001 Manufacturer - Operates an approved quality system (QS) for design Notified body - Carries out surveillance of the QS - Verifies conformity of the design[1] - Issues EC design examination certificate[1]

	A / Aa	C (conformity to type)	D (production quality assurance)	E (product quality assurance)	F (product verification)		
P R O D U C T I O N	**A.** Manufacturer - Declares conformity with essential requirements - Affixes the CE marking **Aa** Notified body - Tests on specific aspects of the product[1] - Product checks at random intervals[1]	Manufacturer - Declares conformity with approved type - Affixes the CE marking Notified body - Tests on specific aspects of the product[1] - Product checks at random intervals[1]	EN 29002 Manufacturer - Operates an approved quality system (QS) for production and testing - Declares conformity with approved type Notified body - Approves the QS - Carries out surveillance of the QS	EN 29003 Manufacturer - Operates an approved quality system (QS) for inspection and testing - Declares conformity with approved type, or to essential requirements - Affixes the CE marking Notified body - Approves the QS - Carries out surveillance of the QS	Manufacturer - Declares conformity with approved type, or with essential requirements - Affixes the CE marking Notified body - Verifies conformity - Issues certificate of conformity	Manufacturer - Submits product - Declares conformity - Affixes the CE marking Notified body - Verifies conformity with essential requirements - Issues certificate of conformity	Manufacturer - Operates an approved QS for production and testing - Declares conformity - Affixes the CE marking Notified body - Carries out surveillance of the QS

(1) Supplementary requirements which may be used in specific Directives. Source: OJ 1993 L220/23 at 39.

Module B (EC type–examination)

Under this procedure a manufacturer or authorised representative lodges an application for EC type examination with a notified body. This application includes technical documentation to enable conformity assessment with the design, manufacture and operation of the product. The applicant must also place a specimen 'type' at the disposal of the notified body. The notified body examines the technical documentation to ensure that the 'type' has been manufactured in conformity with it and performs, or must have performed, examinations and tests to check whether if the manufacturer has chosen to apply standards these have been actually applied, or otherwise that the manufacturer's solutions meet the essential safety requirements. If the 'type' meets the provisions of the directive an EC type–examination certificate must be issued; if a certificate is denied reasons must be given and an appeals procedure provided for. Subsequent changes which may affect conformity with the essential requirements or prescribed conditions for use of the product require additional approval. Notified bodies must communicate to other such bodies information of EC type–examination certificates and additions issued and withdrawn. The manufacturer or his authorised representative must keep the technical documentation, EC type–examination and additions available for ten years after the last product has been manufactured. Where they are not established within the Community the person who places the product on the community market must keep the technical documentation available.

Module B is concerned with the design phase and can be used in combination with modules C, D, E and F which concern the production stage. Although, as we shall see modules D, E, and F can be used without B, but then they need a technical specification as set out for module A.

Module C (conformity to type)

Under this procedure the manufacturer or his authorised representative ensures and declares that the product is in conformity with the type as described in the EC type–examination certificate, affixes the CE marking and draws up a written declaration of conformity. He must also ensure that the manufacturing process assures compliance with the type and the requirements of the directives. The manufacturer or his authorised representative must retain the written declaration of conformity for a period, usually ten years, after the product has last been manufactured. If neither the manufacturer or authorised representative is present within the Community the person who placed the product on the Community market has a duty to keep the technical documentation available.

This module can be supplemented by either:

(i)   a requirement that specific tests be carried out on aspects of the product by the manufacturer or on his behalf. These shall be on the responsibility of a notified body whose identification number should be affixed during the manufacturing process, or

(ii)   notified bodies can be required to undertake product checks at random intervals. Once again the identification number of the notified body should be affixed during the manufacturing process.

Module D (product quality assurance)

Under this procedure the manufacturer ensures and declares that the products concerned are in conformity with the type as described in the EC type–examination certificate and satisfy the requirements of the directives which apply to them. He or his authorised representative established within the Community affixes the CE marking (accompanied by the identification symbol of the relevant notified body) and draws up a written declaration of conformity.

The manufacturer must operate an approved quality system for production, final product inspection and testing which is subject to monitoring. The quality system documentation must permit a consistent interpretation of quality programmes, plans, manuals and record and in particular cover:

- the quality objectives and the organisational structure, responsibilities and powers of the management with regard to product quality,
- the manufacturing, quality control and quality assurance techniques, processes and systematic actions that will be used,
- the examinations and tests that will be carried out before, during and after manufacture and the frequency with which they will be carried out,
- quality records,
- means to monitor the achievement of the required quality and effective operation of the quality system.
- Quality systems conforming to EN 29 002 will be presumed to conform to these requirements. The notified bodies must be informed of any modifications.

The quality system must be under the surveillance of a notified body, which shall be able to inspect manufacturing, inspection and testing, and storage locations and be provided with the quality system documentation and quality records. The notified bodies must carry out periodic audits and may pay additional unexpected visits.

The manufacturer must keep the relevant documentation available for ten years after the last product has been manufactured. Notified bodies must provide one another with information concerning quality systems approvals issued and withdrawn.

Module D can be used in conjunction with module B or alone. If used alone then requirements to provide technical documentation as listed in module A apply and of course there is no declaration that the product conforms to the EC type–examination.

Module E (Product quality assurance)

Module E is similar to D except that instead of the quality system covering production, final product inspection and testing, it simply covers final product inspection and testing. The quality systems documentation does not therefore need to make reference to the manufacturing stage. The harmonised standard, compliance with which leads to a presumption of conformity with the requirements in respect of quality systems, is EN 29 003 for this module.

This module can again be used in conjunction with module B, or alone. In the latter instance, the requirements to provide technical documentation as listed in module A apply and of course there is no declaration that the product conforms to the EC type–examination.

Module F (product verification)

The manufacturer or his authorised representative established within the Community checks that the products are in conformity with the type as described in the EC type–examination certificate and satisfy the requirements of relevant directives. The manufacturer shall take measures so that the manufacturing process ensures the product's conformity and he affixes the CE marking and draws up a declaration of conformity which he or his authorised representative must retain for a period of usually ten years after the product was last marketed. The manufacturer then has the option of either:

(a) the notified body individually examining each product and then affixing or causing to be affixed the body's identification symbol to each approved product together with a written certificate of conformity, which the manufacturer or representative must be able to supply on request; or

(b) statistical verification, whereby the producer presents his products in the form of homogenous lots. If accepted, then as under the procedure where products are examined individually, the notified body ensures its identification symbol is attached and draws up a written certificate of conformity. All products from the lot can be marketed, except any from the sample not found to be in conformity. Where a lot is rejected the notified body, or competent authority, must take measures to prevent that lot being put on the market. in the case of frequent rejection of lots the notified body may suspend the statistical verification.

This module can again be used in conjunction with module B, or alone. In the latter instance, the requirements to provide technical documentation as listed in module A apply and of course there is no declaration that the product conforms to the EC type–examination.

Module G (unit verification)

Under this procedure the notified body examines each individual product to ensure its conformity with the relevant directives, affixes or causes to be affixed, its identification number on the approved product and draws up a certificate of conformity. The manufacturer ensures and declares that the product for which a certificate has been issued, conforms to the requirements of the various directives that apply to it. He or his authorised representative established within the community must affix the CE marking and draw up a declaration of conformity. Strangely there is requirement as to how long this declaration and the certificate should be retained.

Module H (full quality assurance)

Whereas the quality assurance system in module E was less extensive than that in module D, that required by module H is more extensive as it covers design, manufacture and final product inspection and testing. The criteria for the product design therefore includes elements to assure the quality of the design phase. For this module, the standard, compliance with which assure a presumption of conformity, is EN 29 001. Other aspects are similar to modules D and E. Hence a manufacturer with an approved quality system declares that the products satisfy the requirements of the directives that apply to them. He or his authorised representative established within the Community affix the CE marking and draw up a written declaration of conformity. The CE marking must be accompanied by the identification symbol of the notified body responsible for approval and surveillance of the quality system.

The requirements for module H can be supplemented by the requirement that the manufacturer lodges with a notified body an application for the examination of the design. The notified body must examine the application and issue an EC design examination certificate if the design meets the provisions of the directive. Modifications need additional approvals from the same body. Notified bodies should inform one another of EC design examination certificates and additions issued and EC design approvals and additional approvals withdrawn.

C.   Testing, Certification and Accreditation Bodies

(i)   In the Regulated Sphere

Wherever possible the approach is to permit manufacturers to undertake as much of the conformity assurance as possible themselves. Although not referred to in the Conformity Assessment and CE Marking Decision, the Community has a policy of promoting quality assurance systems which comply with what is now EN ISO 9 000.[122] However, concern must be expressed about over reliance on manufacturer self–declaration. Self–declaration, even with the advantage of third party surveillance of the manufacturer's quality assurance system, does not provide the consumer with the same degree of confidence as third party certification. This is one reason why consumers will continue to seek the reassurance of national safety marks – which rely on third party certification – like the German GS mark (Chapter 7, section 4D).

The Conformity Assessment and CE Marking Decision requires member states to notify bodies within their jurisdiction which they have approved as being technically competent and complying with the requirements of the directives (annex 1A(k)). Member states must then ensure that these 'notified bodies' retain the requisite qualifications and also keep the competent national authorities informed of their performance. In keeping with the new approach to technical harmonisation, notified bodies which can prove their conformity with harmonised standards (the EN 45 000 series) will be presumed to conform to the requirements of the directives by submitting an accreditation certificate or other documentary evidence. Member states can notify bodies not able to provide this evidence, but then the Commission can ask the member state to provide the documentary evidence on the basis of which notification was carried out. Notified bodies are listed in the Official Journal. The Commission is seeking to develop a co–ordinating role to ensure close co–operation between the notified bodies. In particular this is seen as needed to ensure consistent technical application of the various modules.[123] It is further suggested that the practice of some member states, which require notified bodies to sign a charter defining their tasks and responsibilities, be built upon to produce a common charter containing the

---

122   See Council Resolution of 21 December 1989, *op. cit.*

123   See the paper published by D–G III, *Framework for Co–ordination and Co–operation Between Notified Bodies, Member States and the European Commission under the Community Harmonisation Directives Based on the New Approach and the Global Approach*, CERTIF 94/6 Rev. 4a.

basic rights and duties of notified bodies.[124] Certification by a notified body must be recognised in other member states.

(ii) Non–Regulated Sphere

Outside the regulatory field industry has incentives to encourage the mutual recognition of conformity assessment procedures. The EOTC has a potentially important role to play in developing mutual recognition agreements. EOTC was established in 1990. It has national members from each EC/EFTA national conformity assessment community; European members including bodies organised at the European level and its own sectoral committees; associate members from bodies not falling into either of the above categories and affiliate members from non–EC/EFTA European countries.[125] Counsellors act in a consultative capacity from EC, EFTA, CEN, CENELEC and ETSI.

The work of EOTC is carried on at a practical level by sectoral committees. These should reflect the interests of manufacturers, users (including consumers and workers) and third parties and seek to respond to the perceived market needs for conformity assessment in specific economic sectors. The committee is made up of national delegation, but European economic groupings, including consumer and trade union organisations, have observer status. The main function of such committees is to develop Agreement Groups. Each Agreement Group is also represented on the Sectoral Committee.[126]

An Agreement Group is based on at least three parties (who satisfy EN 45 000) establishing a mutual recognition agreement or certification scheme. The objective is to adopt common understandings on how standards should be interpreted and test methods applied. The scheme must be open to other bodies in EC/EFTA states which meet the same eligibility criteria and are willing to abide by the same rules. By June 1996 15 such Groups had been registered.[127] However, the general feeling is that there is still much work to be done in ensuring mutual recognition of conformity assessment procedures. Many of the existing agreements already existed in some form before being formalised by EOTC. EOTC is a small organisation and whilst it can establish some formal constitutional requirements for the establishment of

---

124   *Ibid.*, at 3.

125   See, *EOTC Directory*, (4th ed.) (EOTC, 1996) This reported that there were no affiliate members.

126   The EOTC Guidelines do not state that this is as an observer, but this must be assumed to be the case.

127   *EOTC Directory*, *op. cit.*, at 72 *et seq.*

agreements it has to leave the technical specifications to the parties concerned. Some of the agreements are also incomplete in that the parties may accept mutual recognition of certain tests, but retain the right to require additional tests and to charge their own fees. One of the problems, from the perspective of the conformity assessors, is that if the logic of mutual recognition is seen through then the income of the conformity assessment bodies is likely to be dramatically reduced.

Absent harmonisation or mutual recognition, the next best thing is knowledge of the relevant procedures and bodies. The EOTC has also produced for the Commission TICQA (Testing, Inspection, Calibration Certification and Quality Assurance) which is a European database of conformity assessment services. This lists conformity assessment operators and shows the services supplied (calibration, testing, inspection, certification of products certification of personnel, certification of quality systems) and the sectors of activity covered. 2031 organisations are listed in total. This illustrates the problem of ensuring such a large number of varied bodies all operate at the same standards and that mutual recognition can be achieved. In fact the number of bodies is probably far higher as it seems there was an under reporting because the questionnaire was originally only sent out in English. Perhaps because of the language factor, the United Kingdom has the most organisations (665). Of the other countries we shall study in detail France has 148 and Germany 137 (although the actual figure is far higher). At the other extreme there are none reported in Iceland and only one in Lichenstein and two in Norway.

Mutual recognition of conformity assessment is only one aspect of the picture. There must also be assurances about the standards adopted by testing laboratories and the competence of the conformity assessment operators. Taking the first issue, there is also a need to develop standardised test methods, inter–laboratory comparisons and mutual audits. Reliance on general principles of testing which cannot be reproduced cannot provide the basis for mutual recognition.[128] One approach adopted in Council Directives 87/18/EEC[129] and 87/19/EEC[130] was to make mandatory the use of the Good Laboratory Practice guidelines, which originated from the OECD. This

---

128   Cf Falke, *op. cit.*, at 101.

129   Council Directive 87/18/EEC on the harmonisation of laws, regulations and administrative provisions relating to the application of the principles of good laboratory practice and the verification of their applications for tests on chemical substances: OJ 1987 L 15/29.

130   Council Directive 87/18/EEC amending Directive 75/318/EEC on the approximation of the laws of the member states relating to analytical, pharmaco–toxicological and clinical standards and protocols in respect of the testing of proprietary medicinal products: OJ 1987 L 15/31.

is, however, exceptional and indeed these directives are likely to be revised to see which aspects can be covered by EN 45 000 standards. Ensuring consistency in how test procedures are' applied remains an area in which much work needs to be carried out.

Within Europe work on achieving the mutual recognition of testing and calibration results produced by accredited bodies is carried on by the European Co–operation for Accreditation (EA). This body was established in 1997 by the merger of the European Co–operation for Accreditation (EAL) with the European Accreditation of Certification (EAC).[131] EAL had itself been established in 1994 as a result of the merger of the Western European Calibration Co–operation (WECC) and Western European Laboratory Accreditation Co–operation (WELAC). It has two multilateral agreements one for testing and the other for calibration to which 12 countries are signatories. On the international level EA liaises with the International Laboratory Accreditation Conference (ILAC). It should be noted that whilst EA includes the validity of test and calibration methods as one aspect of its inspection of laboratories on the whole the emphasis is on the quality of personnel and effectiveness of systems. There will still be problems of tests being applied or results being assessed in different ways where the standards themselves leave room for debate.

There is also an increasing realisation of the need for conformity assessment bodies to be accredited. There was a trend within Europe for such accreditation bodies to be established within the national standards bodies. This was not very satisfactory as often these bodies themselves carried out conformity assessment procedures and, despite the establishment of Chinese walls, there was always the suspicion that they were not completely neutral. These functions are now provided by independent organisations in all European countries, except it is understood Portugal. However, there is also a need to ensure the accreditors are themselves up to scratch. Where does the process of competence checking end one might well ask? This function is in Europe performed by the EA, which took over from EAC which had been established in 1991. EAC's membership had comprised of 17 nationally recognised Western European Accreditation bodies. It had a multilateral agreement for peer evaluation of accreditation bodies and it is understood that by January 1997 10 of its members had satisfied its requirements. As with the EOTC agreements it is likely that national bodies will reserve the right to make some checks themselves before awarding accreditation and some costs will therefore continue to be incurred in each country. EA participates in similar work at the international within the framework of the International Accreditation Forum (IAF).

---

131 See, 'EA Formed', *UKAS Update*, Spring 1998, p. 5.

(iii) Comment

In the regulated sphere the member states take responsibility for the standard of notified bodies. However, one might question whether their reference to EN 45 000 standards when undertaking this function is entirely appropriate. Even accepting the principle of self regulation inherent in the new approach, there are certain reasons for hesitating before applying it in relation to conformity assessment. Standards under the new approach attempt to flesh out the essential safety requirements. The EN 45 000 standards, on the other hand, set standards within no legislative framework. One might suggest that the obligations of member states to supervise their notified bodies are not sufficiently precise. Indeed the system only ensures the competency of the conformity assessment bodies, there is still a need to ensure standards are applied in a consistent manner and that tests are carried out to common standards. The procedures for harmonisation of these matters discussed in the last section remain relevant in the regulated sphere. In fact it is even more important that they are right, for authorities must in principle permit conforming goods bearing the CE marking to be marketed unless they can show that the standard has not been complied with. The CE marking is a short hand indication to consumers that goods conform to standards. The limitations of the CE mark are considered in the next section.

In the non–regulated sphere consumers are faced with an almost impossible task. They have to consider which standards apply, seek assurances of conformity from an accredited conformity assessment organisation and, of course, have confidence in the value of that accreditation. Such a system may be appropriate for commercial purchasers and users, but suggests that all consumer goods should be subject to new approach style regulation.

D. CE Marking

The CE marking is the linchpin of the system as goods bearing it are assured access to European markets, subject to certain safeguard controls.[132] Prior to 1993, community directives had provided for several different Community marks of varying significance.[133] Annex 1, IB of the Conformity Assessment and CE Marking Decision provides the principal guidelines for affixing and use of the CE marking. All products covered by technical harmonisation directives based on the global approach should in principle lead to the

---

132   It is therefore strange to reflect that it was not mentioned in the 1985 Resolution on the new approach.

133   COM (89) 209 Annex 1 at 37.

granting of the CE marking. However, exceptionally, provision is made for certain directives not to provide for administrative procedures for conformity assessment and in these instances there would also be exception from the marking requirement.

The CE marking symbolises conformity to all obligations imposed on manufacturers by virtue of directives which provide for its affixing. This need not be limited to the essential safety requirements, since some directives may impose specific obligations not necessarily forming part of the essential requirements. The person affixing the CE marking verifies that the product conforms to all Community total harmonisation provisions and has been subject to the appropriate conformity evaluation procedures. Where several directives apply to the product each requiring a CE marking then the marking must indicate conformity to all the directives.[134]

The Conformity Assessment and CE Marking Decision specifies the design of the CE marking and that it must not be less than 5mm high, unless particular directives specify otherwise. The notification number of a notified body involved in the production control phase must follow the CE marking. This can be followed by a pictogram or other mark, where it is necessary to lay down conditions for the use of certain products. The marking must be visible, legible and indelible. In principle it should be affixed to the product or its data plate, although if more appropriate it can be affixed to packaging or any accompanying documents. The CE marking must be affixed at the end of the production control stage by the manufacturer or his agent established within the Community, or if exceptionally provided for in directives, the person responsible for placing the product on the Community market. The notified body's identification number should be affixed under its responsibility either by itself or by the manufacturer or agent established within the Community.

It has been suggested that the real benefit of the CE marking is psychological since it forces the manufacturer to act responsibly and to demonstrate that he has done so.[135] However, there is a danger that too much reliance is placed on the CE marking. The CE marking establishes no more and no less than that the product conforms to the directives based on the new approach. There is also the possibility that a manufacturer may be able to affix the CE marking himself without third party certification. One

---

134 Where directives have transitional arrangements the CE marking only indicates compliance with those provisions applied by the manufacturer and particulars of the directives must be given in the documents, notices or instructions accompanying the product or on its data plate.

135 J. Wettig, 'The Development of the Technical Harmonisation Legislation, Conformity Assessment and the CE marking – A Short Overview' unpublished paper by Commission official.

danger is that consumers believe that the CE marking warrants all aspects of the product or that it is a safety mark.

Member states must refrain from introducing other marks to demonstrate compliance with these directives. Member states must also take all possible steps to exclude the possibility of confusion. But products can carry other marks besides the CE marking, for instance marks which indicate conformity to national or European standards or to traditional directives, provided that such marks are not liable to cause confusion with the CE marking. The legibility or visibility of the CE marking must not be reduced by these other marks being affixed to the product, its packaging or the accompanying documentation. In practice other marks, especially national marks, remain important. National safety marks are important marketing tools, in contrast the fact that all products complying with the relevant new approach directives must carry the CE mark reduces its commercial value.

Ironically the importance of the CE marking as a pre–requisite for entry onto the EC market, may also be its Achilles' heal. Unscrupulous producers are likely to be tempted to simply affix a CE marking to goods regardless of whether they have been tested and found to conform to the requirements. Improper affixing of the CE marking is likely to be a significant problem, despite member states having to take all steps to exclude any possibility of abuse of the CE marking. The decision provides that, without prejudice to safeguard clauses in directives, where a member state establishes that the CE marking has been affixed unduly then the person responsible for affixing the CE marking can be obliged to make the product comply and to end the infringement under conditions imposed by the member state. If non–compliance continues the member state must take all appropriate measures to restrict or prohibit the placing of the product on the market or to ensure that it is withdrawn from the market in accordance with the safeguard clauses. However, these worthy objectives are likely to be undermined in practice because of the new enforcement climate brought about by the new and global approaches to technical harmonisation. The policy is to liberalise trade and the presumption of conformity for products carrying the CE marking is an important part of this because it encourages 'light' enforcement. Market surveillance is still permitted, but systematic control of products is discouraged when they bear the CE marking.

Indeed one might suggest that what is needed is a European safety mark, which covers all the relevant safety hazards (these might be included in horizontal or vertical standards) and required third party certification. This would be a marking which addressed itself to the needs of consumers rather than the administrative functions of enforcement authorities. In part this is the aim of the Keymark certification scheme which has been launched by CEN and CENELEC. This demonstrates compliance with European standards which must be confirmed by third party testing and assured through a quality control system.

Although there are some problems with the Keymark – such as how it is applied to obsolete and superseded standards, or to innovative products or to products hardly covered by European standards – consumer groups have generally welcomed it as an improvement over the CE marking.[136] However, doubts about the viability of the new mark have been expressed because of the reluctance of the important household electrical sector to adopt the mark. This sector was looking into the possibility of developing its own ENEC mark.[137] Of course the last thing consumers want is a proliferation of marks. The Keymark is still based upon the principle of compliance with standards and does not seem to permit a holistic assessment of the product's safety to be integrated into the certification process.

8. EHLASS

Accurate information on which products pose the greatest threats to consumer safety is important if resources are to be effectively targeted. It allows regulators and standardisers to prioritise their work and can result in better standards and more successful consumer education campaigns.

Within Europe only the United Kingdom, the Netherlands and Denmark had on their own initiative established national systems for collecting data on home and leisure accidents. The need for such systems in all member states became apparent. Therefore the Community has moved tentatively towards a European system EHLASS (European Home and Leisure Accident Surveillance System). This development has been marked with caution. In 1981 a 30 month pilot experiment was established.[138] In 1986 a demonstration project was set up,[139] which was amended and extended in 1990.[140] Finally a system was introduced in 1993, but for only one year.[141] The current system was established in 1994.[142]

The system is primarily based upon collecting data from 65 hospital casualty departments across the Community concerning persons injured in product related accidents. Germany has opposed this method of collecting

---

[136] See, Annex to ANEC, 96/GA/34.

[137] *Ibid.*

[138] Council Decision 81/623/EEC: OJ 1981 L 229/1.

[139] Council Decision 86/138/EEC: OJ 1986 L 109/23.

[140] Council Decision 90/534/EEC: OJ 1990 L 296/64.

[141] Council Decision 93/683/EEC: OJ 1993 L 319/40.

[142] Council Decision 3092/94/EC: OJ 1994 L 331/1 as amended by Council Decision 95/184/EEC: OJ 1995 L 120/37.

data, so it (and now also Spain and Luxembourg) are allowed to provide equivalent data based on household questionnaires. The Commission meets 80% of the cost of both methods of data collection as well as providing funds for supporting those member states with less developed national infra–structures.

Member states must submit annual reports to the Commission. The Commission role is to make the material available and also to undertake information campaigns if these appear necessary at the European level.

The EHLASS system has certainly been successful in encouraging the development of national systems of accident data collection in some countries where these did not previously exist. It is less obvious that much use is made of the reports from other member states and no attempt is presently made to compile centralised European statistics. One reason for this is the need to take further steps to ensure that data is collected in a consistent manner in the different states. The EHLASS system is still embryonic and the jury must still be out on its effectiveness, but unless the Commission invests more resources in ensuring there are adequate technical personnel to check the quality of data, assimilate the information and interpret it in order to suggest improvements in product safety regulation and information then one can sympathise with those who view the present system as largely a waste of time and resources. However, this would be to miss an opportunity. We shall see that the United States' NEISS system is a very impressive system for collecting product safety data. The scale of such a system could not be replicated by any one member state, but the European Union provides a framework within which member states can collaborate to produce a meaningful system of data collection.

A recent study has suggested various improvements to the EHLASS system.[143] The recommendations include (i) reducing collection costs, by matching the subsidy more closely to the work carried out and altering the collection sites in favour of those countries with low participation rates; (ii) improving data quality by introducing a new coding system, developing a standard programme for data consistency checking and producing recommedations on 'good collection practice'; and (iii) improving data dissemination by various means including establishing a European EHLASS database accessible via the Internet.

---

143   *Evaluation Study of the EHLASS System*, Contract No. AO–2600196/00062 (English Summary).

9. GENERAL PRODUCT SAFETY DIRECTIVE[144]

A. Introduction

The new approach and global approach are intended to create a raft of EC total harmonisation directives which meet the twin objectives of free movement of goods and consumer protection. However, there was felt to be a need to impose a general safety obligation only to market safe products, to encompass products not covered by new approach directives and possibly safety aspects not covered in vertical directives. The General Product Safety Directive also includes important provisions relating to the exchange of information and novel provisions for a Community procedure in emergency situations.

B. Scope

The Directive's definition of 'product' makes it clear that it is only intended to apply to consumer products (art. 2(a)). To fall within the definition the product must be both:

(a) intended for consumers or likely to be used by consumers; and
(b) supplied, whether for consideration or not in the course of a commercial activity.

Thus the product must be both consumer goods and supplied commercially.

The definition is objective in the sense that so long as the product is intended or likely to be used by consumers the powers can be invoked in respect of a product which has actually been supplied to a business. It is also objective in that it does not apply to all products actually used by consumers, if it was not foreseeable as likely that they would be used by them. On the other hand products cannot be excluded simply by producers claiming they were only intended for use by professionals, if it is likely that they would in fact be used by consumers. In determining whether products were likely to be used by consumers the courts will probably be persuaded by evidence of actual use by consumers. Thus although actual use by a consumer does not of itself render the product a consumer product, evidence that it forms part of a wider body of actual use may have that effect. This would seem to be the case even if the producer expressly states the product was not to be used by non–professionals, although in such a case appropriate instructions may render the product safe.

---

144   Council Directive 92/59/EEC on General Product Safety: OJ 1992 L 228/24.

Unlike some other directives the General Product Safety Directive contains no definition of consumer,[145] but whilst one might suggest a broad interpretation of consumer to cover any purchases, even by businesses, it is more likely to be interpreted along the lines of the definition of consumer to be found in other consumer directives and be restricted to products purchased for private consumption.[146] But it is important to remember that the products do not actually have to have been used by consumers, it is sufficient that they are likely to be used by them for the powers to bite.

The goods must be supplied in the course of a commercial activity. There is no definition of commercial and so it may be a moot point if goods sold by charities or other non–profit organisations are covered, but the better view is that the commercial activities of such organisations would be covered. There is no restriction that the product must be of the type normally supplied by the business. Thus one off supplies would be covered and even a drink offered whilst waiting for a service would seem to be caught. As consideration need not be provided the Directive applies to free gifts and promotional offers. Supply is not defined but must be taken to mean any situation where the product passes into the consumer's control. This would seem to be wider than simply situations where consumers obtain ownership of the goods. For instance, although goods must be supplied commercially the Directive does not require that they be supplied to the consumer, merely that they are intended or likely to be used by a consumer. Thus, for instance, producers of ice skates sold exclusively to ice rinks to be hired out to skaters or manufacturers of shampoos which are only supplied to hairdressers, would not avoid regulation by the Directive as the goods were supplied commercially and it was intended that they would be used by consumers.[147]

Of course consumers do use products which form part of the infrastructure of the business, such as escalators in shops or carriages of trains. This is why recital 5 in the preamble to the Directive states that production equipment, capital goods and other products used exclusively in the context of a trade or business are not covered. Distinguishing between

---

145 Cf art. 2(b) of Council Directive 93/13 on unfair terms in consumer contract: OJ 1993 L95/29 which provides that consumer means 'any natural person who ...is acting for purposes which are outside his trade, business or profession'.

146 This could be implied from references in the preamble to 'consumer protection' which is normally understood to refer to the protection of private individuals. The Community consumer protection programmes are not mentioned as such in the preambles, but as noted the General Product Safety Directive was mentioned in those programmes. The ECJ has shown itself reluctant to give a broader definition to consumer than one restricted to private individuals: see Howells and Wilhelmsson, *op. cit.,* Chapter 1, section 1B.

147 Cf the interpretation of the United Kingdom Government: see Chapter 5, section 3L.

products which are exempted and those which are not might be difficult in some instances. One test might be whether consumers have control of the goods so that they can be said to be used by them rather than their being used by the business to provide the service. It should be remembered that recital 5 referred to goods used *exclusively* in the context of a trade or business. Thus in supermarkets one might decide that shopping trolleys were covered as they were used by the consumer, but that the checkout conveyor belt was not as it was under the control of the assistant. Some difficult examples might be thrown up. Take, for example, a simple visit to the hairdresser. The scissors are presumably not covered, as they are used exclusively by the hairdresser. Although the hairdresser applies the shampoo, this ought to be seen as being used by the consumer as it physically passes into her control when on her hair. The fineness of these distinctions is well illustrated by the example of the hooded hair–dryer one finds in hairdressing salons. If the drying is supervised by the hairdresser then presumably this would not be covered, but if the consumer can control it then it ought to be regulated. Thus in practice the sensible distinction between consumer goods and capital goods used to provide services may be difficult to define.

Although the definition of product is restricted to consumer goods, there is surprisingly little help in determining the scope of the word 'product' itself. The first draft of the Directive[148] had usefully spelt out that it included manufactured and agricultural products including raw materials, substances, components and semi–finished products and moveables incorporated into immoveables. Product would still seem to be capable of having such scope, although it is regrettable that this was not spelt out. The present definition does, however, make it clear that the Directive covers new, used and reconditioned products. The only exceptions to this are for (i) second–hand goods supplied as antiques (one can imagine some disputes as to when used goods qualify for the label antique! – presumably the fact that someone simply claimed they were antique and supplied them under that label would not suffice); and (ii) products which need to be repaired or reconditioned prior to use where the supplier clearly informs the buyer of that fact.

C. Relationship With Vertical Regulation

The relationship between the horizontal General Product Safety Directive and vertical directives needs to be considered carefully. One could foresee four possible relationships between the General Product Safety Directive and vertical directives:

---

[148] OJ 1989 C 193/1 art. 2(a).

(i)   both could apply;
(ii) a vertical directive could pre–empt the horizontal directive altogether;
(iii) a vertical directive could pre–empt the horizontal directive with regard to those matters which it covers,
(iv) a vertical directive could pre–empt the horizontal directive with regard to those matters which it covers in an equivalent manner.

The first solution has many attractions. The general safety requirement, notification and exchange of information provisions and Community emergency powers together with the attendant supervisory powers could be viewed as a safety net which could only be improved upon by specific directives. If the objectives of the horizontal directive were achieved by the vertical directive then consumers need not invoke its provisions, but equally nothing would be lost if its powers were invoked. Administrative streamlining could be maintained by there being internal procedures for actions commenced under the general powers to be transferred to product specific procedures. This is, however, not the solution adopted by the Directive, which seems to influenced by the German tradition of preferring specific to general regulation. Thus art. 1(2) in its first indent states that its provisions shall only apply 'in so far as there are no specific provisions in rules of community law governing the safety of the product concerned'. This would seem to point in favour of the second interpretation and indeed recital 7 of the preamble is even more explicit, stating:

> 'when there are specific rules of Community law, of the total harmonisation type, and in particular rules adopted on the basis of the new approach, which lay down obligations regarding product safety, further obligations should not be imposed on economic operators as regards the placing on the market of products covered by such rules.'

However, whilst the goal of new approach directives may be to cover all safety aspects, this is not achieved in practice and it is possible to read the General Product Safety Directive as having some relevance even for products covered by new approach directives. The choice seems to be between the third and fourth options.

The second indent of art. 2(1) seems to qualify the general exclusion in the first indent by stating that when specific rules impose safety requirements then the provisions in arts 2–4 shall not in any event apply. This might imply that the other provisions can apply and this is the approach of some commentators who see the General Product Safety Directive as having a role in relation to new approach directives by supplementing them with notification, information exchange and emergency procedures where these features are absent from the product specific directives.[149] This view is supported by recital 7 which only seeks to prevent further controls concerning *the placing on the market* of products and so would seem to permit post–marketing controls.

However, the question of whether a specific provision ousts the General Product Safety Directive, even if it offers less protection, is open to debate. The second indent of art. 2(1) might suggest it does. The third indent, however, goes on to state:

> 'Where specific rules of community law contain provisions governing only certain aspects of product safety or categories of risks for the product concerned, those are the provisions which shall apply to the products concerned with regard to the relevant safety aspects or risks.'[150]

This seems to qualify indent 2 by stating that where only certain safety aspects are covered by the specific regulations then the other aspects could be dealt with under the general safety requirement. But it would not seem possible to challenge the assessment of safety or risk made in product specific rules even if they seemed to be less rigorous than the general safety requirement – although one would not expect this to be the case. Thus as regards the safety standard the third solution would seem to apply – a specific rule pre–empts the application of the general standard, although it must be underlined that the general safety requirement could still be invoked if it concerned a safety risk not covered by the specific legislation.

The fourth solution – whereby the General Product Safety Directive is a floor of protective rights which other specific directives can only improve on – would seem to apply for the notification and information exchange provisions and the Community emergency powers. Thus we will see that the notification and exchange of information provisions only cease to apply when similar provisions apply in other Community legislation. The Community emergency powers are expressly stated to apply when procedures in specific legislation are not appropriate because of the safety risk involved and the urgency of the case (art. 9(c)).

---

[149] *A fortiori* the General Product Safety Directive would have a role to play with regard to product specific directives enacted before the new approach as they did not seek to deal with all the safety aspects; cf the reference in recital 7 of the Directive to specific rules of 'the total harmonisation type, and in particular rules adopted on the basis of the new approach'.

[150] Cf recital 8 which provides that when specific Community regulations cover only certain aspects of safety the obligations of economic operators in respect of such aspects are determined solely by those provisions.

D.   Safe Product

The central concept around which the Directive is organised is that of the 'safe product' (art. 2(b)).[151] Before commenting on the definition it is perhaps as well to reproduce it in full:

> '*safe product* shall mean any product which, under normal or reasonably foreseeable conditions of use, including duration, does not present any risk or only the minimum risks compatible with the product's use, considered as acceptable and consistent with a high level of protection for the safety and health of persons, taking into account the following points in particular:
>
> –   the characteristics of the product, including its composition, packaging, instructions for assembly and maintenance,
> –   the effect on other products, where it is reasonably foreseeable that it will be used with other products,
> –   the presentation of the product, the labelling, any instructions for its use and disposal and any other indication or information provided by the producer,
> –   the categories of consumers at serious risk when using the product, in particular children.
>
> The feasibility of obtaining higher levels of safety or the availability of other products presenting a lesser degree of risk shall not constitute grounds for considering a product to be "unsafe" or "dangerous".'[152]

From a consumer perspective there are several positive aspects of this definition. It is rather objective assessing the actual risks and in this respect compares favourably with the defectiveness standard in the Product Liability Directive, which refers to the expectations of consumers.[153] The General Product Safety Directive only accepts as safe products which either (i) do not

---

[151]   Sometimes reference is made in the Directive to a *dangerous product*, but this is simply a product which does not meet the definition of a *safe product*: art. 2(c).

[152]   The definition of 'safe' product in the first draft Directive had been more convoluted as it involved reading the definition in tandem with a separate definition of unacceptable risk: see OJ 1989 C 193/1, arts 2(b), (c).

[153]   But note the introduction of consumer expectations in art. 4(2). For a comparison of this definition with the defectiveness standard in the Product Liability Directive see G. Howells, 'Consumer Safety in Europe: in Search of the Proper Standard' in B. Jackson and D. McGoldrick (eds), *Legal Visions of the New Europe*, (Graham & Trotman, 1993).

present any risk, or (ii) only the minimum risks compatible with the product's use. Even these minimum risks must be acceptable. Thus it is not sufficient that a product is the safest design to perform its intended function. The utility of the purpose must be balanced against the minimum inherent risks to judge whether these are acceptable. Although there is room for debate about what is considered acceptable, the Directive indicates that it should be pitched at a high level by stressing that the risks must be compatible with a high level of protection for the safety and health of persons. This is partly a technical/scientific question involving the identification of risk, and partly a social question of determining which risks are acceptable. The function of a safety standard in a regulatory regime is not to remove all risks from the market, but only those not justified by the benefits derived from the product or because safer alternatives exist. Thus the basic definition seems to strike the right balance. However, we shall note that to some extent this rather stringent definition is undermined by the situations in which art. 4 treats products as being safe.

In determining whether a product is safe, the Directive lists factors which should be particularly taken into account. These factors can be separated into those relating to the nature of the product and those concerning the manner of its use:[154]

– Those concerning the nature of product are those relating to its durability, characteristics, presentation, labelling, instructions and the information which is provided, as well as its effect on other products. In particular, the need to look at the durability of goods and their interaction with other products is to be welcomed.
– The product must be judged according to its normal or reasonably foreseeable conditions of use. This is a compromise standard. It does not let the manufacturer arbitrarily restrict the uses to which the product can be put. Equally, the consumer is not to be protected against all misuses. He must, however, be protected against those which are reasonably foreseeable. This would seem to go further than simply preventing the manufacturer from claiming that some typical uses should not be treated as normal uses because they had been stated to be inappropriate uses in the instructions.[155] Conceivably it could require manufacturers to guard against illegitimate uses to which they can reasonably foresee the product might be put. Thus, one might require

---

154 The second draft Directive seemed to have more clearly clustered the factors into these two categories: see OJ 1990 C 156/8, art. 2(b).

155 Note the neat distinction between factors relating to the product and those relating to their use breaks down to some extent as information given may affect the way the product should be used.

toys which imitate adult equipment to make it clear that they cannot be used for that purpose. One can even imagine the need for solvent manufacturers to warn of the dangers of solvent abuse. There must, however, be limits to what is reasonably foreseeable. Thus whilst one suspects that some ladies' tights have been used as an emergency fan belt to repair a broken down car, hosiery manufacturers would not be under an obligation to warn of the dangers of such ad hoc improvisations! It would, however, seem to require that businesses monitor the post–marketing history of their products to determine what uses the product is in fact put to.

It is particularly pleasing that the definition refers to the need to consider the categories of consumers at serious risk when using the product. It states that, in particular, the needs of children should be taken into account; but this should not prevent the interests of other groups, such as the elderly, blind, deaf and disabled being considered. It may have been helpful to cite other at risk groups in the same way as children are specifically mentioned. The danger of the current wording is that the needs of children are viewed as being in some way uniquely important. However, it could be argued that if the list was any longer then exclusion from it might have been more damning and have threatened consideration of the special needs of any at risk group not listed. As it is, at present, the needs of at risk groups for each specific products have to be considered.

Some eyebrows might be raised by that part of the definition of safety which provides that a product should not be considered unsafe or dangerous on the grounds of the feasibility of obtaining higher levels of safety or the availability of other products representing a lesser degree of risk. However, this should be read in a restrictive manner, whereby it merely indicates that those facts alone should not render the product unsafe or dangerous. These safeguards are needed because there are a range of levels of safety risks which are acceptable (compare the differing safety features of various cars). Equally extra safety may be possible, but at a price which is not justified. The feasibility of extra safety and the availability of less dangerous products ought still to be considered when assessing whether a risk posed by a product was acceptable, but by themselves they are not adequate grounds for a determination that the product is unsafe.

The definition of safe product forms the foundation of the general safety requirement in art. 3. This places on producers the obligation to place only safe products on the market and on distributors the duty to take due care to help ensure compliance with that requirement. However, for these purposes the definition of a safe product has to be read in the light of art. 4. This provision lays down a hierarchy of rules and standards against which a product should be judged to determine whether the general safety requirement is satisfied.

Arts 4(1) and (2) provide means whereby compliance with the general safety requirement can be established. However, this is expressly said not to bar the competent authorities from taking appropriate measures to impose restrictions on the placing of the product on the market or to require its withdrawal where there is evidence that despite conformity with the requirement the product is dangerous to the health and safety of consumers. The logic behind this is that the effect of arts 4(1) and (2) may be to deem as safe a product which is dangerous! When we consider these provisions we will see that the theory behind the Directive is that businesses should not be punished if they have not been 'blameworthy'. The argument goes that punishing them would serve little purpose and instead efforts should be concentrated on the recall of dangerous products and the regulation of future behaviour. This is, indeed, what would be the attitude of most enforcement authorities where a business had truly marketed products which they had no reason to have known were dangerous. Nevertheless introducing criteria which tie the hands of authorities when they assess the product needlessly weakens the bargaining power of the enforcement authorities.

Art. 4(1) states that a product shall be *deemed* safe when it conforms to (i) specific Community provisions governing the safety of the products in question, or (ii) failing such provisions specific rules of national law of the member state in whose territory it is circulating which lay down health and safety requirements which the product must satisfy.[156] In fact the article is worded in such a way that only the national rules are expressly stated to be deemed to render the product safe, but it is clear from the superiority of Community provisions that they should have the same effect.

Reference to the product being deemed to be safe is absent from art. 4(2). It simply says that conformity to the general safety requirement shall be assessed having regard to a list of standards. Although art. 4(3) seems to presuppose that conformity with one of these standards would satisfy the general safety requirement, it is possible to argue that this need not be an automatic consequence. The standards although not expressly stated to be hierarchical are listed in such a way that implies the drafters conceived of a hierarchy along the following lines:

(i)   voluntary national standards giving effect to a European standard,
(ii) Community technical specifications,[157]

---

156   Such rules must comply with the Treaty, especially arts 30–36.

157   There is some uncertainty as to what this phrase means. It might simply refer to CEN standards which have not yet been adopted at the national level or it could also refer to other European specifications such as harmonisation documents and European

(iii) standards drawn up in the member states in which the product is in circulation,

(iv) codes of good practice in respect of health and safety in the sector concerned,

(v) the state of the art,

(vi) safety which consumers may reasonably expect.

The inclusion of the last two criteria underlines the dangers created if products which conform to these standards are deemed to satisfy the general safety requirement. An enforcement authority could take a perfectly proper prosecution against an unsafe product only to be met with defences that it complied with the state of the art or that it offered the safety which consumers might reasonably expect. Determining the merits of such defences involves complex technical questions, requiring a great deal of expert evidence and resources which enforcement authorities would probably often not feel they could devote to the prosecution of such cases. Of course the prosecution is largely symbolic, it cannot undo any harm caused, but it is a useful control mechanism which enforcement authorities should be able to invoke to ensure co–operation and to publicise the worst offenders. Wherever aspects of the definition are not precisely defined the practical impact of the regulatory regime is weakened, by increasing the ability of business to challenge the actions of the authorities.[158]

E.   General Safety Requirement

The general safety requirement places different obligations on producers and distributors.[159] In theory the principle obligation to assure safety is placed on producers, with distributors having a supportive role. A starting point should therefore be to determine whom the Directive classifies as a producer and whom as a distributor, but we shall see that in reality this is less important than the precise role they play in relation to the product.

---

pre–norms: see section 6E; cf. the very broad definition of the term in the Technical Standards Directive, see section 3B.

[158] Cf discussion of the due diligence defence in the United Kingdom, Chapter 5, section 3K.

[159] In the first draft directive these obligations had not been placed directly on the producers and distributors, but rather the member states had been placed under a duty to ensure these objective were achieved: see OJ 1989 C 193/1, arts 4 and 6. The Directive's reference to these obligations being those of the producer or distributor may only be symbolic given that member states still have to implement the Directive, but is to be welcomed.

One would anticipate that breach of the general safety requirement ought to give rise to a sanction. However, we shall see that the French authorities are maintaining their existing law, under which the general safety obligation is simply an organisational principle which may trigger other powers but carries no direct sanction for its breach (Chapter 6, section 5A).

F. Producer and Distributor

The Directive gives a broad definition of producer (art. 2(d)). Naturally this includes the manufacturer, but only when he is established in the Community. As we shall see the intention is to impose the obligation on parties within the Community when the manufacturer is based outside. There would, however, seem to be no need to exempt the non–Community based manufacturer. It may be more difficult to force him to comply with the orders of the enforcement authorities, but the option of taking action against a non–Community business should not be excluded. Such action may prompt action from responsible firms and can attract publicity to the dangers posed by the firm's conduct both in the EC and in its home country.

Any person who presents himself as the manufacturer by affixing to the product his name, trademark or other distinctive mark is also treated as a producer. This brings into the definition of producer own–branders and franchisees. However, there may be uncertainty as to whether parties who display such a name or mark can avoid being labelled producers by making it clear on the packaging that they are not the manufacturers. This would seem possible as they would not then be presenting themselves as the manufacturer. This result would be satisfactory if one simply wanted to put the consumer on guard that some other party manufactured the product, but this would not seem adequate where the party using the name or mark failed to reveal the identity of the manufacturer so that action could be taken against them. A person who reconditions a product is also deemed to be its producer.

If the manufacturer is not established within the Community then his representative will be treated as the producer. There may be several representatives in different member states and all would appear to be covered, but clearly national authorities will usually approach the representative in their own state. If neither the manufacturer nor representative are established in the Community then the importer will be treated as the producer.

This apparently comprehensive coverage obscures a potential weakness. If there is no representative in say, the United Kingdom, but there is one in another state, say Finland, then the producer would be the Finnish representative rather than the importer into the United Kingdom. Such an approach derives from a desire to view the single market as a social reality and yet whilst trade has been liberated consumers and regulators still operate largely within national boundaries. Doubtless Europe needs symbolism to bolster the single market, but this should not be at the expense of effective consumer protection. We shall see that this is balanced somewhat by the emphasis being placed on enforcement being focused on the first distributor on the national market.

Also included in the definition of producer are other professionals in the supply chain, in so far as their activities may affect the safety properties of a product placed on the market. The definition of distributor is the mirror image of this, namely those professionals in the supply chain whose activity does not affect the safety properties of the product. Thus the crucial point is to consider whether a party affects the safety properties of the product. Certainly this would cover anyone who affected the design or construction of the product.[160] Thus a party who modifies the product or who helped to assemble or install it might fall within the definition of producer. Those who simply stored, transported or displayed the product may be treated as producers, but only if their activities affected the safety properties of the product. This will not be the case with most products, but the safety of many food products, for instance, might easily be affected by such activities. Thus many parties whom one would colloquially speak of as distributors or retailers, will in fact fall within the definition of producer. Other links in the supply chain are distributors. However, we shall see that the specific obligations of producers correspond to the scope of their activities in relation to the product.

G.   Obligations of the Producer

Art. 3(1) obliges producers to place only safe products on the market. This is an obligation of strict liability, although we shall see that the extent of the specific duties imposed on particular producers depends upon the limits of their respective activities. Art. 3(2) outlines two types of supporting 'information obligations' placed on producers. These involve (i) informing consumers of product risks, and (ii) having systems to keep themselves informed of product risks and to react to them. Although these obligations are framed in a mandatory way, they are not all required of every producer: producers need only undertake them if they could be expected to do so within the limits of their activities. Thus a retailer who is only a producer by dint of activities relating to say, his assembly of the final product or its storage,

---

160   Those who advised the original manufacturer on the design would not be caught as they do not form part of the supply chain.

might not be expected to inform the consumer of risks inherent in the product design or be concerned with generic risks which do not arise out of his particular handling of the goods. These information obligations are simply aspects of the general safety requirement: further precautions will almost certainly be required by producers.

(i) Informing Consumers

We noted that the definition of a safe product provided for products to be marketed containing risks so long as they were the minimum acceptable risks compatible with the product's use. Within the limits of their activities producers must provide consumers with the relevant information to enable them to assess the risks inherent in a product. The information must be such as to enable the consumer to take precautions against those risks. The obligation only arises with respect to risks which are inherent throughout the normal or reasonably foreseeable period of its use. This might be criticised for being too limited, since consumers may face dangers when the product deteriorates beyond a state when it should have continued to be used or from the manner of its disposal. In addition the obligation only arises for risks which are not immediately obvious without adequate warnings. Previous drafts had restricted the obligation to warn to significant risks.[161] On the face of it the Directive requires the consumer to be informed of all risks. This sets a rather high duty of disclosure, although doubtless some *de minimis* waiver rules will be applied and there will be some room for debate as to whether risks have been scientifically/technically established. It is unclear whether this provision would require risks to be disclosed where the risk relates to a cumulative risk posed, for example, by exposure to a substance found in that product and also in other products.

Provision of information warning of inherent risks does not exempt a producer from compliance with the other requirements laid down in the Directive. Thus a product could not be rendered safe by warning of a risk which was not the minimum compatible with its use considered as acceptable and producers would have to comply with other regulatory orders made by national authorities.

(ii) Product Monitoring

Producers must, again within the limits of their activities, adopt measures (a) to enable them to be informed of risks which their products might present,

---

[161]   OJ 1989 C 193/1 art. 4 and OJ 1990 156/8 art. 3 ('not insignificant').

and (b) to take appropriate action to avoid those risks, including, if necessary, withdrawing the product from the market. The list of examples of measures which should be taken include, where appropriate, the marking of products or product batches so that they can be identified, sample testing of marketed products, the investigation of complaints and keeping distributors informed of such monitoring. The nature of these measures suggests that the reference to 'risks which these products might present' was intended to refer to post–marketing risks experience. Of course producers have an ongoing obligation to keep themselves abreast of research and developments in order to forestall risks; that is why it is important to see the specific obligations in art. 3(2) as merely specific manifestations of the general safety requirement.

The product monitoring requirements must be commensurate with the characteristics of the products they supply. This would seem to indicate that higher risk products justify more stringent monitoring procedures. Also whether a single product or a product batch are marked might vary according to the product's individuality. Complex products, such as cars, should be marked individually, but for generic products batch marking might suffice. Some products can easily be tested, even to destruction, whilst others are so rare or expensive that testing to destruction is not viable. The post–marketing monitoring procedures may also be affected by the way the product is supplied. Thus systems would vary depending upon whether goods were supplied direct to the public, through selective distribution networks or via wholesalers to the public.

H. Obligations of the Distributor

The role of distributors is, at least at first glance, subsidiary to that of the producer. They are required to act with due care to help ensure compliance with the general safety requirement. Due care suggests that they will only be liable if they have unreasonably failed to assist in satisfying the general safety requirement. Thus in contrast to the strict liability of producers, distributors' liability is premised on fault. However, due care is usually viewed as an objective standard which would not allow the distributor the defence that he did his incompetent best; rather it judges him against the standard of the reasonably competent person in his position. Albeit that there may be differences of professional opinion and distributors will usually merely have to meet the standard considered adequate by a reasonable body of professional opinion, unless their stance simply does not standard up to external scrutiny.

The objective nature of the duty of due care seems to be underpinned by the Directive, for it states that in particular distributors should not supply products which they know, or should have assumed, do not comply with the general safety requirement. Their constructive knowledge is to be assessed having regard both to information in their possession and as professionals. Reference to 'as professionals' would seem to import to them information which other professionals were aware of even if they themselves did not know of it. It would also require that they processed the information they actually had, or constructively ought to have had, as a professional and came to conclusions about the safety of the product which a reasonable professional would have arrived at.

The duty to act with due care to ensure compliance with the general safety requirement would seem to be placed on all distributors regardless of their activities in relation to the product. However, the due care standard should be sufficiently flexible to expect different standards of different types of distributors. Thus large or specialist retailers should be judged by higher standards than the local small shopkeeper.

Distributors are placed under a particular duty to participate in monitoring the safety of products placed on the market within the limits of their respective activities. In particular, this should involve them in passing on information on product risks and co–operating in the action taken to avoid those risks. This would seem to involve distributors in passing information to producers about consumer complaints and also informing consumers of identified post–marketing risks (by, for example, displaying posters or contacting customers as part of recall procedures).

The distinction between the primary strict obligation of producers only to market safe products and the secondary obligation of distributors to assist in ensuring that the obligation is satisfied is less clear cut that it might appear. This is because although the primary obligation of producers only to market safe products is strict the additional obligations depend upon the limits of the producer's activities. On the other hand the distributor's duty to act with due care will vary according to the nature of his professional involvement and can be quite onerous for large and/or specialist organisations. Thus it is better to see the obligations of producers and distributors in terms of a continuum, with indeed some overlap, for some distributors may be expected to do more than some producers (eg large specialist distributor in comparison to a small retailer who is only a producer because they assemble the final product).

The intention of the specific obligations which expand upon the basic general safety obligation is to encourage business to take more responsibility for ensuring their products are safe, identifying risks and reacting to dangers. Whereas liability laws may have a dual objective of compensation and prevention the rationale of product safety regulation is simply prevention.[162] The extent to which this can be achieved by Government monitoring is limited. The product safety regime needs to inculcate into the business community an ethic of respect for consumer safety. The extent to which the Directive brings about this change in attitude will determine to a large extent its effectiveness.

It is doubtful that the general safety obligation will of itself produce many changes in design. Designers are more likely to be influenced by particular rules and standards than by a general duty to market safe products, which is presumably their intention in any event. Particular elements of the safety definition, such as those which require the effect on other products and the needs of consumers at serious risk to be taken into account, may cause designers to reassess their design, *if* they get to read the legislation. Educating businesses about their responsibilities under the Directive is, however, likely to be a difficult task. The general safety standard may, however, be a practical advantage to enforcement authorities who no longer have to point to a specific law that has been breached by unsafe products.

Recognition of the need to change producers' attitudes towards consumer safety was present from the Directive's inception and in fact was even stronger in previous drafts. The first draft Directive was more specific and demanding in the monitoring arrangements required.[163] As well as product marketing and testing it proposed parties enter into agreements with other suppliers, professional customers and general business organisations in the relevant product sectors to receive and exchange regularly relevant safety information; the systematic assessment and evaluation of complaints or reasons for returns, even when not directly founded on its safety properties; the keeping of adequate records and where necessary the appointment of a person or service especially in charge of organising such functions and supervising their proper functioning. The designation of a particular person or service responsible for product safety together with efficient procedures would be a spur to change internal company attitudes and values in relation to product safety questions. It is perhaps regrettable that the final version of the Directive is not as explicit on the extent of the role envisaged for businesses in taking responsibility for the safety of their products.

---

162 Punishment may be another, but I prefer to see that as a necessary incident of a preventative strategy, rather than a goal in its own right.

163 OJ 1989 C 193/1 art. 6 and annex 1.

I. Enforcement of Duties

Although the ultimate objective should be the creation of a climate in which businesses take on responsibility themselves for producing safer goods, it would be unrealistic to expect this to be achieved simply by enacting legislation. What is needed are both enforcement authorities to enforce the general safety requirement and sanctions for breaching the requirement which are sufficiently serious that businesses are keen not to attract the attention of the authorities.

The role of the enforcement authorities is not just one of prosecutor. The enforcement authorities perform a valuable function in publicising the safety obligations of businesses and educating them as to how these can best be satisfied. The European countries we shall study in detail – France, Germany and the United Kingdom – all have authorities responsible for product safety, albeit that their structures vary and Germany in particular has weak central authorities. These countries, however, needed to do nothing to comply with the obligation in art. 5 to establish or nominate authorities to monitor compliance with the obligation to place only safe products on the market. For some European countries, such as Greece, this, however, involved the creation of institutional structures to control the safety of products. This must be seen as a major development in those countries. The Commission must be notified of the said authorities so that they can pass this information on to the other member states.

The national authorities must be given the necessary powers to fulfil their obligations under the Directive. Art. 6(1) lists a series of objectives which these powers should ensure are achieved.[164] The first three of these powers are concerned with ensuring the authorities have the powers to undertake adequate surveillance of products, whilst the remaining five relate to controls which they should be able to impose on the marketing of products. Enforcement authorities must be able to:

(a) Organise appropriate checks on the safety properties of products. These must be on an adequate scale, involve checks up to the final stage of use or consumption and even involve checks of products after they have been placed on the market as safe.

(b) Require all necessary information from the parties concerned.

(c) Take samples of a product or product line and subject them to safety checks.

(d) Subject product marketing to prior conditions designed to ensure product safety and require suitable warnings to be affixed regarding the

---

164 These are listed below with the same letters as correspond to those used in the article.

risks which the product may present. It is unclear whether reference to marketing is limited to the sales promotional aspects of the product or can extend to the condition of the actual product and its packaging, but a broad interpretation would be preferable.

(e)   Make arrangements to ensure that persons who might be exposed to a risk from a product are informed of it within good time and in a suitable manner. This is said to include the publication of special warnings.

(f)   Prohibit temporarily (whilst checks are being carried out) anyone from supplying, offering to supply or exhibiting a product or product batch, whenever there are precise and consistent indications that they are dangerous. The requirement that the indications be precise and consistent might be thought to be rather demanding, but it should be borne in mind that the Directive is most probably a minimum harmonisation Directive so member states can have laxer requirements.

(g)   Prohibit the placing on the market of a product or product batch which has proved to be dangerous. Accompanying measures to ensure the ban is complied with should also be available. Presumably this refers to the powers to seize and, if necessary, destroy dangerous products.

(h)   Organise the effective and immediate withdrawal of a product or product batch already on the market. If necessary this should involve destruction of products under appropriate conditions. Nothing is said about the issue of compensation of the consumer who has paid for a dangerous product which has been recalled. Of course this would usually be covered by the civil law, but member states would be free to include an express provision in their domestic legislation. The United Kingdom has placed a restricted interpretation on the phrase 'on the market' so that powers are only needed to prevent future supply and not to recall products already in the hands of consumers (Chapter 5, section 3L). This seems an illegitimately narrow interpretation and runs counter to the safety ethos underpinning the Directive.

The enforcement authorities must exercise the powers in accordance with the degree of risk[165] and in accordance with the Treaty, particularly arts 30–36.

Art. 6(2) stipulates the parties against whom appropriate measures can be addressed. Naturally these include both producers and distributors. Regarding distributors, measures should only be addressed to them within the limits of their activities. In particular the distributor responsible for the first stage of distribution on the national market is targeted for enforcement action. This is a welcome recognition of the continued need for controls at

---

[165]   There seems to be a typing error in the English text of the OJ which says 'degree or risk'.

the national as well as European level. However, the responsibilities of distributors are generally less than those of producers and we have already seen that where the manufacturer lies outwith the Community the importer into the Community and not the importer into national markets is deemed to be a producer. However, in addition measures can be addressed to any other person where this is necessary to ensure co–operation with respect to action taken to avoid risks arising from a product.

Art. 5 makes it clear that the powers of the enforcement authorities should include the possibility of imposing suitable penalties. Reference to the word penalties would seem to indicate that there should be some form of regulatory sanction besides civil law penalties. According to national traditions this might take the form of criminal sanctions, administrative fines etc., of course the size of any fine must be adequate and effective.[166] The requirement that the sanctions should be more than those of the civil law is a welcome inclusion and contrast with the absence of such a provision in some other EC consumer law directives.

J. Notification and Exchange of Information

The Sutherland Report on *The internal market after 1992: meeting the challenge* drew attention both to the need to review existing mechanisms for handling urgent and serious consumer problems[167] and for the Commission to have a partnership with member states to ensure the implementation of Community rules and more specifically to ensure the effective handling of urgent problems.[168] The General Product Safety Directive has two procedures under which information must be notified to the Commission. Such procedures have three possible objectives: (i) supervising the appropriateness of the actions of member states; (ii) informing other member states, (iii) taking community action where appropriate.

(a) Art. 7 Notification

Art. 7 is the procedure which is intended to be adopted in non–emergency situations. The duty of the member states to notify arises when they have taken measures restricting the marketing of a product or requiring its withdrawal (as provided for in art. 6(1)(d–h). The Commission must be

---

166 Cf *Marshall v Southampton and South West Hampshire Health Authority (Teaching) (No. 2)*, C 271/91, [1993] 3 CMLR 293.
167 Recommendation 24.
168 Recommendation 33.

notified of the said measures together with an explanation of the reasons for their adoption. The obligation does not apply if such notification is required under another specific Community legislation or 'if the measures relate to an event which is local in effect and in any case limited to the territory of the member state concerned'.

Thus it is clear that the obligation to notify does not apply where the event is confined to one member state, although one might question whether any risk is so confined given the increased ease with which products can be moved across borders. The fact that goods are not presently sold elsewhere does not mean they might not be diverted to other member states once restrictive measures are applied. Equally, similar but not identical products may be in circulation in other member states.

However, the duty to notify also does not apply when the event is local in effect. The Directive is ambiguous as to the meaning of locality. Presumably it does not cover regions like Scandinavia, the Benelux countries or the British Isles as it says it must in any event be limited to the territory of one state. Reference to locality therefore seems somewhat superfluous, unless it is to suggest that where a danger is widespread within a member state and not localised then a notification should be considered.

Once the Commission receives information under art. 7 it enters into consultations with the parties. If it concludes that the measure was justified it immediately informs all member states. Where it believes that it was not justified it immediately informs the member state which initiated the action. We shall note below that notifications under both arts 7 and 8 can form the basis for European emergency measures to be introduced. However, a precondition for the emergency procedure is that the notification revealed 'the existence of a serious and immediate risk from a product to the health and safety of consumers in various member states' (art. 9). The requirement for there to be a 'serious and immediate risk' would indicate that few art. 7 notifications would be the basis of such an action, since notification under art. 8 is the appropriate route by which to notify such risks. Only when a national authority had incorrectly categorised a risk as not serious or immediate could an art. 7 notification lead to Community level action. However, this might easily happen for the concept 'serious and immediate' is vague and national authorities have been pressured to restrict art. 8 notifications to extreme cases.

(b) RAPEX

The system for the rapid exchange of information arising from the use of consumer products (RAPEX) was established in 1984.[169] Its legal basis is now to be found in art. 8 of the General Product Safety Directive together with an annex setting down detailed procedures for the operation of the scheme.[170]

Products covered
The notification obligation arises in relation to all products which fall within the scope of the Directive, unless they are covered by similar procedures in other Community legislation. The annex cites pharmaceuticals,[171] animals,[172] products of animal origin[173] and the system for radiological emergencies[174] as examples of products having equivalent procedures, but the Commission also takes the view that the Directives on active implantable medical devices[175] and medical devices[176] also have comparable procedures.[177]

---

[169] Council Decision 84/133/EEC introducing a Community system for the rapid exchange of information on dangers arising from the use of consumer products: OJ 1984 L 70/16. This entered into force on 7 March 1985. This was subsequently replaced by Decision 89/45/EEC: OJ L 17/51 as amended by Decision 90/352/EEC: OJ L 173/49.

[170] To date there have been four reports on the operation of the scheme: see COM (86) 562 final (interim report), COM 88 121 final, COM (90) 172 final and SEC (92) 618 final. See too the more general survey in *Commission Communication on the handling of urgent situations in the context of implementation of Community rules,* COM (93) 430.

[171] Directive 75/319/EEC: OJ 1975 L 147/1 and Directive 81/851/EEC: OJ 1981 L 317/1.

[172] Directive 82/894/EEC: OJ 1982 L 378/58.

[173] As far as they are covered by Directive 89/662/EEC: OJ 1989 L 347/33.

[174] Decision 87/600/Euratom OJ L 371/76.

[175] Directive 90/385/EEC: OJ 1990 L 189/17.

[176] Directive 93/42/EEC: OJ L169/1.

[177] G. Zahlen, (now former Head of Unit DG XXIV), 'The Community System of Exchange of Information on Dangerous Consumer Products (RAPEX)' in A.-C. Lacoste (ed.), *Rapid Exchange of Information Systems on Dangers Arising From Consumer Products,* (Centre de Droit de la Consommation, 1996) at 32.

The RAPEX system is in fact two systems, one for food products which had been organised by D–G III[178] and the other for non–food products run by D–G XXIV (formally the Consumer Policy Service). Both food and non–food systems operate similarly, but with some minor differences. We will concentrate on the non–food sector RAPEX system.

The subsidiarity of the supervisory controls contained in the General Product Safety Directive to the rules in vertical directives was criticised as unnecessary and leaving open the possibility of loopholes. The same objection does not apply to notification procedures. So long as member states are aware that they must notify the Commission it is desirable that their notification goes to the relevant specialist body. If, however, they mistakenly send it to the wrong body then the Commission is a small enough bureaucracy for the notification to be quickly sent on to the relevant department. National authorities should not, however, be discouraged from notifying more than one Community body if they are unsure of how a danger should be categorised and which procedure applies. It seems that in practice overlap is not a serious problem.[179]

Notification duties of the member states
There is nothing wrong with the basic principle of the RAPEX system nor with the infra–structure put in place to operate it. Once a serious and immediate risk is detected the national authorities should obtain the maximum amount of information about the product and the nature of the danger, by in particular consulting the producer or distributor of the product. This should not compromise the need for quick action. Where because of a serious and immediate risk a member state decides on or adopts measures to prevent, restrict or impose specific conditions on the possible marketing or use of the product within its own territory it *must* inform the Commission forthwith.[180] Member states *may* pass on information about serious and

---

[178]   Prior to the establishment of the RAPEX system there had been an informal system for food safety which worked well and so they decided not to disturb it. Responsibility for food safety has recently been transferred to D–G XXIV.

[179]   COM (90) 172, *op. cit.*, at 6 notes that only two cases had been reported to both D–G III and the Consumer Policy Service (sugar confectionery animals and self–heating containers).

[180]   The duty to notify only arises when measures are taken by the state, there is no duty to notify when measures are taken by a firm voluntarily. Zahlen, *op. cit.*, at 34–35 suggests the duty covers voluntary measures taken following an intervention of the public authorities, but there would seem to be the need for a formal measure causing the firm to act rather than simply informal negotiations. This can be seen as a lacuna as it would be desirable to ensure that similar safeguards are put in place in other

immediate risks even before they decide to adopt a measure. The Directive also introduces the possibility of horizontal contacts being made between national contact points. Where such contacts give rise to information of general interest the member state which initiated the contact should inform the Commission.

There is a standard form for notifications by member states to the Commission (used under both arts 7 and 8 procedures) which asks for details on the product, manufacturer, importer and others in the supply chain, the nature of the danger and measures adopted. The communication should be in writing, usually by fax and accompanied by a photograph of the product; although this can be preceded by a telephone call. It is hoped in the near future that following trials it will be possible for information to be sent, processed and received by computer. The notification will be in the language of the member state making the notification.

Member states can specify that certain information be treated as confidential. However, such a request must be justified bearing in mind that the need to take effective measures to protect consumers normally outweighs confidentiality, especially as the Commission and all members of the network take precautions to void any unnecessary disclosure of information likely to harm the reputation of the product. Although criticised by consumer groups the confidentiality provision is said to be almost never invoked.[181]

Criteria for RAPEX notifications
On receiving a notification the Commission will check that it conforms to the requirements of art. 8. The conditions for an art. 8 reference are very restrictive. The cumulative requirements of seriousness and immediacy mean that consumers in other member states may continue to be exposed to immediate risks which are just below the 'seriousness' threshold and long term serious risks (although the latter are not so problematic as they can perhaps be effectively dealt with under the art. 7 notification procedure). Also the exclusion of the duty when the risks not only cannot, but also do

---

member states, at least on a voluntary basis. Member states would seem to have a discretion to notify such cases, although strictly such a discretion is only prior to adopting a measure and so it could be argued this did not apply where they had decided not to adopt a measure because voluntary measures had been put in place. J. Falke comments that a large number of notifications do in fact relate to measures taken by producers or importers on their own account: see J. Falke, 'The Community System for the Rapid Exchange of Information on Dangers Arising From the Use of Consumer Products in *Federalism and Responsibility*, H.–W. Micklitz, T. Roethe and S. Weatherill (eds), (Graham & Trotman, 1994) at 220.

181 Zahlen, *op. cit.*, at 36.

not, go beyond the territory of one member state gives rise to the possibility of national authorities being too optimistic about the geographic containment of a risk.[182]

The Commission has aggravated the problem by its strict interpretation of these requirements, particularly the serious and immediate condition. The Commission seeks to make a neat distinction between emergency situations when the art. 8 RAPEX system is to be invoked and more long term problems to which art. 7 applies. However, as the annex to the Directive itself notes it is impossible to lay down specific criteria as to what amounts to a serious and immediate risk and the national authorities have to judge each individual case on its merits. It is therefore possible to give a broad or narrow interpretation to the condition. One would have imagined that the Commission would have wanted member states to err on the side of sending too many rather than too few notifications under the RAPEX procedure: after all they could always sift out the ones which needed to be diverted to the art. 7 procedure. Indeed, one would also have expected the Commission to err on the side of consumer protection by being fairly relaxed about the conditions for entry to the RAPEX system. The RAPEX system respects the need for confidentiality and by passing on information on what appears to be a serious and immediate risk the Commission is not expressing an opinion on the appropriateness of the measures taken by the member states. The system is rather innocuous, simply alerting national authorities to potential risks their consumers may be exposed to. Although they should investigate such risks, it leaves the member states free to make their own assessment of the dangers and decide what measures, if any, it is appropriate for them to adopt.

Thus it seems absurd to be strict about the conditions for entry to the RAPEX system. Other notifications systems may be equally efficient, but the RAPEX system is not overloaded and even if it were there are very few extra resources involved in using the RAPEX system than the alternatives. In 1994 there were 9 notification accepted under the RAPEX system (with 12 being refused) and in 1995 (up until October) there were 15 notifications (with 4 being refused).[183] Between 1984–1990 there had only been 90 notifications. At this time the Commission had accepted most notifications unless it was quickly apparent that no danger existed. What marked the Commission's change of policy was the startling increase to 96 notifications in 1991.[184] However, when one investigates that increase one notes that it is largely due to more countries making use of the system (something which should be applauded). Spain made 11 notifications in 1991 compared to none the previous year and Belgium made a staggering jump from zero notifications in

---

182   See criticisms of the similar restriction on the duty to notify under art. 7.

183   Zahlen, *op. cit.*, at 39.

184   SEC (92) 618 final, *op. cit.*, at 5–6.

1990 to 49 in 1991! Whilst it might have been worthwhile having a quiet word with the Belgians to ascertain whether products in their market are really exceptionally dangerous, or to explain to them the scope of the notification requirements, a blanket policy of strictly interpreting the notification conditions is potentially harmful.

The weakness of the system lies in the lack of commitment by national authorities to participate in it. The former Head of the Unit administering the RAPEX system has expressed concern that the participation rate varies between member states and by comparing the number of national measures with the number of RAPEX notifications concluded 'that all national controlling authorities have not yet fully integrated the Internal Market dimension and their corresponding responsibility'.[185] Given that conclusion it seems contradictory to send out signals discouraging RAPEX notifications except in very exceptional circumstances.

Given that 'serious and immediate' is a vague expression it is to be commended that the Commission, through the auspices of the Committee on Product Safety Emergencies (hereafter, the Committee on Emergencies),[186] have started a dialogue with the member states to arrive at 'as homogenous as possible vision of this concept without ...eliminat[ing] the importance of appraisal on a case by case basis'.[187] This venture is to be applauded and indeed some aspects of the discussion, such as the need to be aware of categories of consumers who are particularly sensitive to a particular type of damage are to be welcomed. However, certain other comments, in particular some points made by the Commission give rise to concerns.

The Commission believes the date of notification is important – the inference being that if the report was not forwarded straightaway it could not be said to be an immediate risk. It seems that sometimes national authorities send notifications through in batches. Yet, just because national authorities may be mishandling their notification obligations is no reason to affect the way the Commission treats a situation which genuinely does represent a serious and immediate risk. The Commission also suggests that the content of the measure in question is important, particularly regarding stocks of the product present on the market. The meaning of this is unclear. It is certainly

---

185 Zahlen, *op. cit.*, at 39.

186 This Committee comprises representatives of member states and is chaired by a member of the Commission. There is to be close co–operation between it and committees established by other specific Community rules (eg new approach directives) which deal with health and safety aspects of products.

187 See working document 22 Nov. 1994, *Summary of the Contributions of the Member States and of the EFTA States* in response to working document, *Notion of 'Serious and Immediate Risk'* submitted by Consumer Policy Service to the Committee on Emergencies.

to be hoped that a risk will not be considered as lacking seriousness simply because there are only a few stocks on the market. It seems more likely that it meant to suggest that if national authorities allowed stocks to remain on the market this might be taken to be an indication that there was no serious or immediate risk. But again the criteria for establishing a serious and immediate risk must be kept separate from the considerations as to which measures should be adopted to counter it. The Commission also requires objective evidence of the danger, suspicion is not enough. This requirement would seem more appropriate for a system which handed down judgments rather than for a system like RAPEX which simply aims to alert member states to potential risks. The Commission also takes the view that the notification must concern a product or product batch, with measures aimed at a general category of products being subjected to the emergency procedure under the Technical Standards Directive.[188] Again it is hard to see what harm could be done by using RAPEX to alert national authorities to a general product risk, which after all materialises in defects affecting specific products or batches. They could then consider any emergency measures needed whilst the emergency procedures under the Technical Standards Directive were being undertaken.[189] Whilst the use of the restrictive phrase 'serious and immediate' can be criticised, it seems that those who administer the system have made the position worse by adopting a narrow vision of the purpose of the RAPEX system.

Processing notifications

The notification will be received in DG XXIV by a fax dedicated to the RAPEX system. If the notification is found to conform to art. 8 it will usually be translated within 48 hours into four or five official languages of the EC (English, French, German, Spanish and Italian) with national authorities being asked which language version they want to receive. It is then forwarded to a network of national contacts.[190] These national contacts may be in Economic Affairs, Trade and Industry and Health Ministries or a consumer body attached to a ministry. The circle of contacts can be criticised for being rather limited. Although to some extent one can expect the national

---

188   Zahlen, *op. cit.*, at 35.

189   Indeed in so far as specific products or product batches posed a serious and immediate risk there would seem to be a duty to notify them.

190   A copy is also sent to the permanent representations. The Commission may also contact the member state presumed to be the country of origin of the product for verification. In exceptional circumstances the Commission can institute an investigation of its own motion or convene the Committee on Emergencies.

authority to disseminate the information within its borders,[191] there seems little justification for the Commission sending information to the French enforcement authority (the DGGCRF) but refusing to send notifications direct to the Consumer Safety Commission which is actually responsible for consumer information (Chapter 6, section 3A). A consequence of the RAPEX system of national contacts may well be a centralisation of power. In particular this has caused problems for Germany as enforcement of consumer laws is constitutionally a responsibility of the Länder (Chapter 7, section 3C).

At an early stage in the life of the RAPEX system the suggestion had been made that information should be conveyed to European consumer organisations. The Commission opposed this on the ground that it threatened confidentiality. Whilst the risk of leaks might be serious were the information given to every consumer organisation it may be possible that a co–ordinating body like ANEC (section 6D) could be trusted with the information so as to be able to assess the risk on behalf of consumers and monitor the response of national authorities.

Member states' obligations
On receiving a notification the member states should, wherever possible,[192] inform the Commission without delay as to whether the product has been marketed in its territory and any supplementary information it has including test/analyses results. It must also inform the Commission of any measures taken in respect of the product,[193] or the reason why no measures have been taken, if the product had been found within their territory.

The reaction of the member states is crucial, for the whole point of the system is to prevent accidents by alerting enforcement authorities in other member· states to potentially dangerous products. In turn it is hoped that when surveying the market they may uncover similar dangerous products which could be subject to separate notification procedures.[194] The feedback to the Commission can inform the debate as to whether there needs to be

---

191   The first draft Directive (OJ 1989 C 193/1 at art. 9(1)) had placed an express duty on member states to exchange information rapidly between competent authorities, but this was more concerned with gathering information prior to making a notification. Adequate internal communication between agencies can be taken as implicit in the duty of member states to have adequate and effective enforcement.

192   It is unclear why the proviso 'wherever possible' has been included. Whilst the authorities can never be sure that they have detected all products marketed they can at least say whether they have detected any.

193   This information is then passed on to the network.

194   Zahlen, *op. cit.*, at 38.

Community action because different responses are threatening the internal market.

The statistics on the follow up of notifications are disappointing. The Commission takes the view that member states must systematically react to all notifications, even if only to say that no measures have been taken.[195] Prior to 1994 the average number of member states reacting to notifications was 4. This paltry figure had risen to 9 by October 1995.[196] This may be partly due to the addition of conscientious new members of the Community and also to the introduction of a system of reminders which are sent out after two months and then repeated three times in the year. It may be that national authorities do consider the notifications, but simply do not have the time or systems in place to ensure a response is sent to Brussels. This, however, only serves to underline the reluctance of some national authorities to see their function as having an internal market dimension. This is not true of all authorities. Again, as with the practice of making notifications, there is a great deal of variation between the response rate of the national authorities. Nevertheless there remains a rump of national authorities failing to meet their obligations under the Directive. In most cases this is likely to be because of a lack of infrastructure. This places citizens in those countries at risk from dangerous products which go undetected or uncontrolled. In the internal market this places at risk not only the citizens of those states but also all citizens of the Union. In a minority of cases there is a suspicion that even some well organised national authorities view the EC dimension as an irritating irrelevance to their work and give it low priority. This attitude is dangerous and shows ignorance of the interdependency of member states now the internal market is becoming a reality.

The Commission in the light of the evolution of the case and the information received from member states or a representative of a member state can request the Committee on Emergencies be convened in order to exchange views on results obtained and to evaluate the measures taken. The Committee on Emergencies will also be periodically informed of all notifications received and the follow up in order to allow it to have an overview of the situation.

Assessment

The theory behind the RAPEX system is commendable, but it has some practical limitations. We have seen that its management has been rather bureaucratic and also it is centred upon the national government contact points. Consumer safety officials are themselves aware of the need for

---

195   *Ibid.*
196   Zahlen, *op. cit.*, at 40.

communication across borders. To meet this need the European Consumer Safety Association (ECOSA) was established and this body holds conferences and publishes the *International Journal for Consumer Safety*. Out of this association arose the demand for a less bureaucratic system of information exchange than provided by RAPEX. The Commission, with some hesitation supported this initiative financially, but would not allow ECOSA itself to organise the exchange as it has a broader membership than enforcement officials. Therefore the Product Safety Enforcement Forum for Europe (PROSAFE) was established. This meets twice yearly and also publishes a newsletter *Product Safety Enforcement News* as well as encouraging informal exchanges of information. Its strength as an organisation is that it tends to be made up of officials who are actually responsible for enforcing safety rules, often at the regional or local level. However, it can be seen as something of a 'Northern European club'. The Southern European states can appear to be rather bureaucratic and centralised. Regional officials may not be able to attend PROSAFE by their own means and the central authorities may not be prepared to finance their participation.

A tension clearly exists as to how co–operation should be organised between the EC, its member states and localities. This problem is difficult to address because the different structures within member states may suggest different channels of communication are appropriate for each member state, but such solutions are difficult to organise and legislate for especially as one has to be sensitive to the political sensitivities of different levels of the administration within the member states. The Commission has, for political reasons, normally to channel its communications through the central administration. Complementing this by informal networking along the lines of PROSAFE seems a useful addition, but some mechanism needs to be found for ensuring the participation of all member states. Direct subventions from the Commission would seem to be the best way forward, so that the participation of the Southern European countries can be enhanced. Such a system can complement the RAPEX system, by on some occasions providing a more flexible and speedy means of communicating knowledge of a danger. It can also enhance the understanding of the way the agencies which actually enforce consumer safety laws operate in the other member states.

Phare countries
There is discussion of a parallel RAPEX system being created for the countries of Central and Eastern Europe under the PHARE project.[197]

---

[197]   See, Th. Bourgoignie, 'Summary of Debates and Final Conclusions' in Lacoste (ed.), *op. cit.* It is understood this Phare scheme is now becoming a reality.

Although it is politically inconceivable that the Phare countries would be allowed immediate access to the RAPEX system, in the medium term it is possible to foresee information being exchanged between the EC and the Phare RAPEX systems. The eventual goal being of course full membership of the EC for the Phare countries and hence full integration into the RAPEX system. Apart from funding problems (once EC funding runs out) there are practical problems concerning the creation of such a scheme. Rivalry between Phare countries will make the placing of any central co–ordinating body a sensitive matter (although it is understood that Bratislava has been agreed as its headquarters) and the lack of trust amongst some countries may cause scepticism about the willingness of those countries with struggling economies to damage their reputation by informing their neighbours of dangerous products in circulation originating from their domestic production. Also the supervisory infrastructure varies greatly between the Phare countries so that some countries will simply not be able to detect dangerous products or make use of information provided to them. The Phare countries are a group of countries brought together simply by their common socialist past and their desire to join the EC. Given the lack of a common cultural or trading bond between all the states, the movement of goods between Phare countries may be less extensive than within the EC. For instance a product danger in Albania may seem remote to an Estonian consumer. This may suggest the need for regional information networks in the first instance. A political problem is that the more developed Phare countries. who can realistically expect early accession to full membership of the EC, may be reluctant to be associated with a project which treats them the same as the remaining Phare countries. Indeed some of them are likely to try to negotiate individual membership of RAPEX.

K. Community Emergency Procedures

So far we have seen that the thrust of the General Product Safety Directive has been to ensure that member states have procedures in place to deal with dangerous products. The role of the Commission has been restricted to that of a distributor of urgent messages between member states. We now turn to the potentially more directly interventionist powers of the Commission in relation to emergency situations which are to be found in arts 9–11.[198] However, the Commission's freedom of action remains rather limited and contingent upon the enthusiasm of member states for concerted European action. In fact there have been no occasions to date when the emergency

---

[198] For discussion of Germany's unsuccessful challenge to these powers see Chapter 7, section 5.

procedures have been invoked. When one considers the criteria for activating the emergency procedures this is perhaps understandable. Some commentators think it would be relatively easy to by–pass these restraints.[199] However, whilst an agency inspired with an interventionist zeal might push the limits of its competence, the current philosophy of DG XXIV as evidenced by its limited interpretation of the scope and functioning of the RAPEX system is to restrict Community activity to a minimum in the name of subsidiarity. This does not mean that the powers to be described could not be manipulated to create a more active European response to emergencies, but merely that this is unlikely to materialise in the near future.

(i)   Conditions for Invoking the Emergency Powers

The Community emergency powers can only be activated once the Commission has become aware of the existence of a serious and immediate risk from a product to the health and safety of consumers in various member states. Reference to 'various' member states would seem to indicate that the powers only relate to risks present in more than one state. This policy of restricting Community involvement to problems of an inter–state character can be criticised. The experience of the Commission and the experts on the Committee on Emergencies should be used in a more supportive way to monitor and assist national authorities dealing with serious consumer dangers. This may be particularly helpful for those countries with less developed product safety controls and should promote a more consistent and effective response to emergencies wherever they appear throughout the Community.

As under RAPEX, the conditions 'serious and immediate' are cumulative conditions and one can expect them to be interpreted in the same way.[200] However, the Commission's powers only arise once they are made aware of the risk by member states. In theory information received from consumer groups, injured parties or the media cannot activate the emergency powers. This is one criterion which one can foresee the Commission easily circumventing if such a situation ever arose, by simply enquiring of national authorities whether there was such a risk which they should be notified of. Member states may make the Commission aware by notifying them

---

199   H. Micklitz and T. Roethe, 'Federalism in Process' in Micklitz, Roethe and Weatherill (eds), *op. cit.*, at 58.

200   Previous drafts had required an indeterminate number of persons to be at risk. Why the indeterminacy of those at risk was a relevant factor is unclear, but in any event this condition has been dropped; see OJ 1989 C 193/1 at art. 11(a) and OJ 1990 C 156/8 at art. 8.

of a situation to which the emergency procedures apply or else because the information provided under arts 7–8 indicates that such a situation exists.

The influence of the member states is evidenced not only by fact that the Commission must become aware of the emergency through them, but also because the powers are only activated once one or more member states have adopted measures entailing restrictions on the marketing of the product or requiring its withdrawal from the market.[201] Furthermore the Commission's powers depend upon member states adopting different measures to deal with the risk in question. This would seem to cover situations both where member states adopted different measures and where some adopted a measure and others failed to adopt any measures.

Although the recital justifying the emergency procedure refers to the danger that differences in reaction by member states both 'may entail unacceptable disparities in consumer protection and constitute a barrier to intra–Community trade' (recital 18) the last two criteria for action reveal that free movement is the dominant motive. It is absurd that an emergency procedure should require a member state to have adopted a measure before it can be invoked. Even the duty to inform under RAPEX arises when the decision has been taken to adopt measures (even if they have not yet been adopted) and there is the possibility of notifying at an even early stage. Indeed in some circumstances the decision of an administration to take no measures should be subject to review by the Commission in order that it can check that the decision to take no measures was an appropriate response. This should especially be so where the risk threatens other states. As it stands the Directive reviews measures taken to protect consumers, but is impotent to review decisions to leave consumers unprotected.

Similarly, why should the power of review only arise when states differ in their reactions? The broader perspective of the European regulator may throw a new light on the problem and suggest different solutions than those thought appropriate by national authorities. Certainly where there is a risk of the danger spreading the Commission should be able to protect the interests of citizens in those states whose authorities have not yet had occasion to consider the problem. The need for the Commission to have this broader role need not threaten the member states unduly as in most instances it should simply involve informing states of the situation, co–ordinating information and responses.

There are two further pre–conditions for Community emergency action. The safety issue posed by the product must be such that the risk cannot be

---

201   Art. 9(1)(a) goes on to refer to measures 'such as those provided for in art. 6(1)(d)–(h)' but the phrase 'such as' would indicate that the measures are not limited to those cited.

dealt with in a manner compatible with the urgency of the case, under other procedures laid down by the specific Community legislation applicable to the product or category of products concerned. Thus whatever general conclusion one reaches about the relationship of the General Product Safety Directive to vertical directives it is clear that its emergency powers apply to all situations where equivalent procedures do not exist.

The final pre–condition is that the risk must be one which can only be eliminated effectively by adopting appropriate measures at the Community level. Community action must be needed to ensure the protection of the health and safety of consumers and the proper functioning of the common market. Whilst one can see that different solution could potentially affect the functioning of the common market, it is hard to see how a Community dimension is especially needed to protect consumers. Perhaps some products become dangerous only when used in foreign contexts, perhaps because of changes in climate or because different electricity currents are used. Outside this narrow range of situations what consumers need is protection against risks and this is normally best done by home authorities. This does not mean that the Commission should not have a role in ensuring national authorities take appropriate action, simply that the right of action ought not to be premised on a conceptualisation of a European dimension to the risk which goes beyond the fact that it affects Community citizens. The involvement of the Commission should not be that of a broker negotiating between different responses, but rather that of an advisor or co–ordinator seeking out the best response to emergency situations and ensuring these are adhered to wherever necessary throughout the Community.

Although the need for Community action is a pre–condition to the Commission becoming involved this, surprisingly, does not guarantee that the emergency process will result in a decision. It only gives the Commission the power to consult member states – a process which may lead to a decision, but only if at least one member state so requests. This not only underscores the subsidiary role of the Commission, but further emphasises that internal market philosophy dominates. States will have little incentive to seek a community decision for consumer protection reasons, since they can use domestic law to protect their own citizens. States will, however, be concerned that measures taken by other states do not affect their exports. Thus the most likely use of the emergency procedure is as a means for member states to negotiate down to a lowest common denominator the various responses to emergencies made by national authorities throughout the Community.

(ii)   Role of the Commission

The distinction between the consultation and investigation period and the decision–making role of the Commission had been clearer in earlier versions of the Directive.[202] The second draft Directive had also usefully spelt out the obligations of the member states to support the Commission investigation by, for example, organising checks, taking samples and requesting information from the relevant parties.[203] These might simply be seen as concrete examples of the general power, contained in art. 213 of the Treaty, which permits the Commission to collect information and carry out checks in order to perform its tasks. However, the specific provision had the advantage that national authorities were clearly directed to co–operate and the power to request samples was clearly spelt out. Point 8 of the technical annex dealing with RAPEX does give the Commission the option in exceptional circumstances of instituting its own investigation. Member States are, however, only required to supply the Commission with information requested to the best of their ability. There would seem to be no suggestion of any extra powers to require checks to be made or samples to be taken. In any event these powers only apply to information supplied through RAPEX and of course require there to be exceptional circumstances. If point 8 of the annex is simply a practical manifestation of the Commission's powers under art. 213, it is strange that the 'exceptional circumstances' rider has been added. All in all the failure to spell out the Commission's investigative powers underlines the view of the Commission's emergency powers as 'an instrument of last resort'[204] and of the Commission as predominantly a broker between member states rather than as a protector of the consumer interest. Of course there is scope for the Commission to give a broad interpretation to 'exceptional circumstances', as all serious and immediate risks to consumer health and safety could be so defined.[205]

If requested by a member state, the Commission may after consultation with the member states adopt a decision requiring member states to take temporary measures from those listed in arts 6(1)(d)–(h). It has been said that the 'principles of appropriateness and proportionality' apply so that 'a

---

202   See D. Hoffmann, 'Product Safety in the Internal Market: the Proposed Community Emergency Procedure' in M. Fallon and F. Maniet (eds), *Product Safety and Control Processes in the European Community*, (Story Scienta, 1990) at 73.

203   OJ 1990 C 156/8 at art. 9(3); the first draft had contained an obligation on member states to supply all relevant information at their disposal or which they could obtain, OJ C 193/4 at art 9(4).

204   B. Lorz, 'The Draft General Product Safety Directive: the Core Element of an Integrated Approach to Product Safety' [1991] *E. Consum.L.J.* 129 at 135.

205   Micklitz and Roethe, *op. cit.*, at 57.

Community–wide recall or withdrawal of a product is not necessarily the result of such procedure'.[206]

Measures adopted under this procedure are valid for no longer than three months,[207] but the same procedure can be used to prolong the period. Obviously the temporary measure is intended to provide a breathing space during which more permanent solutions can be adopted, if necessary.

(iii) Procedure for the Adoption of a Decision

The procedure for the adoption of a Decision starts by the Commission submitting a draft measure to the Committee on Product Safety Emergencies. This Committee verifies the conditions for an emergency Community measure are satisfied and then gives an opinion on the draft,[208] within a time–scale set by the Chairman according to the urgency of the situation, but which in any event may not exceed one month. If the Committee agrees with the Commission's proposal it is adopted. If there is disagreement, or the Committee has failed to deliver an opinion, the measure is submitted to Council who can adopt it by qualified majority. If the measure is not adopted within 15 days from submission to Council, the Commission can adopt the proposal, unless a simple majority of the Council has voted against it. Member states shall take all necessary measures to implement the decision within less than 10 days and the competent authorities shall, within one month, give the parties concerned an opportunity to submit their views and inform the Commission accordingly.

The most obvious point to make is that the procedures are fairly cumbersome considering one is responding to serious and immediate risks. The various points of delay are whilst (a) the initial notification is made, (b) the Commission decides whether the conditions for emergency action exist; (c) consultation takes place with the member states; (d) a request for Community action is awaited,[209] (e) the Commission drafts a measure, (f) the Committee on Emergencies verifies the case fits the emergency procedure criteria and considers the proposal and issues its opinion, (g) the Council considers the matter, and finally (h) whilst the measure is implemented by member states. Although some of these stages can be compressed, it might be thought that the Commission could be given exceptional powers in

---

206   Hoffmann, *op. cit.*, at 75.

207   Earlier drafts of the Directive would have allowed the temporary measures to last for six months.

208   Voted on by qualified majority voting.

209   This may of course be made at the time of notification or during consultation, thus not amounting to any further delay.

appropriate cases to issue a decision of immediate effect which could then be subject to review. On the other hand the present procedures could also be faulted for failing to have an explicit mechanism to lift the temporary measure if it becomes unnecessary within its life span.

It is also obvious that the member states retain a great deal of control. A simple majority of states can block an emergency measure and a lesser number can delay its enactment. Furthermore the eventual decision is addressed to member states. Thus the Commission cannot impose any obligations on economic actors. This is the duty of the member states. Although the Commission could invoke art. 169 procedures against a member state which failed to fulfil its obligations under the Decision, any victory would be rather pyrrhic and of only symbolic value in the context of emergency measures.

(iv) Consequences of Adopting an Unjustified Decision

As the member state is the party taking the measure against economic actors in its territory, this has the consequence that the member state and not the Commission would be liable in damages if the measure turned out to be unjustified.[210] However, even leaving aside any general objections to the liability of enforcement authorities, it seems unfair that national authorities should carry the can for a measure they were required to take by the EC.[211] If any damages are to flow from a measure adopted by the collective decision of the Community then the cost of any errors should be borne communally. This might also weaken resistance by national authorities to a more active involvement by the Commission in emergencies. The arguments against such liability are purely pragmatic: namely that the Commission may be reluctant to propose measures if it exposes itself to Community wide liability and as new resources are not likely to be forthcoming any claim can only deplete the limited funds dedicated to consumer protection at the EC level. Of course the rational answer is to limit the circumstances and amounts of damages which can be recovered (Chapter 1, section 4B(iii)).

---

[210] Hoffmann, *op. cit.,* at 75 who cites *Albako v Balm,* Case 249/85, [1987] ECR 2354. In that case, however, the German authorities were permitted to undertake, without liability, conduct which was contrary to national legislation on unfair competition and bonus offers as this was necessary to implement an EC Decision.

[211] Of course if they failed to act and then damaged occurred as a result they would be liable to the injured party under the *Frankovich* principle.

10. FORTRESS EUROPE?

The growth in the economic strength of the European Union trading block has been a cause of some concern to other trading nations, who have in turn responded by establishing their own regional trading blocks (such as NAFTA, MERCOSUR, ASEAN). We shall see in the next chapter that one of the benefits Europe derives from combining the power of its member states is that it is well placed to influence international trade issues, particularly in the context of the international standardisation process.

In part the perception of a Fortress Europe derives from the particular status accorded to European standards within the framework of the new approach directives. Although compliance with European standards is still voluntary in theory, the presumption of conformity with the essential safety requirements which follows from complying with the European standard gives it a *de facto* mandatory character.

On the other hand the EC regulation of product standards could be viewed as providing the opportunity for easier access to the entire internal market for foreign producers. Instead of having to comply with 15 different sets of national controls once the product has been permitted access to the market of one member state then the principle of mutual recognition applies equally to such products as to products produced within the Union.

Of course, this poses potential consumer protection problems if the controls at the Union's external frontiers are not effective.[212] Council Regulation (EEC) No 339/93 on checks for conformity with the rules on product safety in the case of products imported from third countries[213] seeks to address these problems. The principles behind this regulation are that member states should when carrying out controls at external frontiers 'act in accordance with comparable detailed rules' (recital 2) and, in the case of products from third countries, their customs authorities must, 'be closely involved in the market–monitoring and information systems provided for under Community and national rules' (recital 3).

The procedure is for the customs authorities to suspend release of the product and to notify the national authorities responsible for monitoring the

---

212 For this reason some member states argued that an earlier Council Decision laying down provisions on the introduction and implementation of technical regulations and standards: OJ 1980 L 14/36, which sought to apply the same rules to all products irrespective of their origin only applied to direct imports and not to the import of third country products which had already been marketed in another member state: see Lauwaars, *op. cit.*, at 169. There had also been a proposal for a Council Directive on a special Community certification procedure for products originating in third countries: OJ 1980 C 54/5.

213 OJ 1993 L 40/1.

market if a product or batch of products displays characteristics which give rise to a serious doubt as to a serious and immediate risk to health or safety when used under normal and foreseeable conditions and/or it is not accompanied by a document or not marketed in accordance with Community or national rules on product safety (art. 2). The national authorities should then investigate. If the product is found not to be problematic or if the customs authorities are not informed of any action taken by the national authorities within three days then, providing all other formalities and requirements have been met, the product shall be released.

Where the product is found to present a serious and immediate risk its marketing shall be prohibited and the customs authorities should endorse the product's commercial invoice with the words 'Dangerous product – release for free circulation not authorised – Regulation (EEC) No 339/93'. Where the product is not found to conform to Community or national rules the national authorities shall take the necessary action, which may include prohibiting the product and the customs authorities should endorse the product's commercial invoice with the statement 'product not in conformity – release for free circulation not authorised – Regulation (EEC) No 339/93'.

The controls on products at the Union's external frontiers need to be effective because of the free circulation of goods once they are on the internal market. However, the external controls should not represent an unnecessary obstacle to third countries or else the description of a Fortress Europe would be accurate. The Regulation avoids such dangers by requiring that such controls be proportional and in keeping with the requirements of the International Convention on the Harmonisation of Frontier Controls of Goods (recital 11). Furthermore such controls should comply with the Community's obligations under GATT to conduct trade on a non-discriminatory basis and under the GATT Code on Technical Barriers to Trade, according to which standards should not be applied as a means of creating obstacles to international trade (recital 16).

11. CONCLUSIONS

The dominant interest of the EC with respect to product safety regulation has been to create an effective single market by removing national regulations which establish potential technical barriers to trade. However, consumer safety has had to be a feature of EC policy, both because of the concern of member states not to expose their citizens to dangers and because consumer protection has always been a nascent policy of the Community which has been recognised in the Maastricht Treaty.

The new approach to technical harmonisation seeks to take consumer concerns into account by establishing essential safety requirements, whilst preserving a competitive manufacturing environment by leaving manufacturers free to decide how to achieve those objectives but creating a presumption of conformity for products which comply with European standards and bear the CE marking. However, consumers remain vulnerable because of their weak influence on the standardisation process and due to confusion over the significance of the CE marking. There also continue to be problems, both in the regulated and non–regulated spheres, with ensuring that conformity assessment procedures provide adequate protection and that equally rigorous standards are applied consistently throughout the Community.

The General Product Safety Directive provides that all member states should have authorities with adequate powers to ensure that only safe products are marketed and that action is taken when dangerous products are discovered. However, the majority of enforcement work involves market surveillance, education of the business community and negotiation when problems occur. To be effective enforcement authorities need legal powers but also sufficient resources to make use of them. Under–resourcing of consumer protection agencies is universal. The agencies are also hampered by the philosophy of the new approach which favours a light 'reactive' enforcement policy.

Notification procedures seek to produce a co–ordinated response to cross–border problems. However, there is evidence that national authorities do not give their European obligations a high priority. Although the Commission has the theoretical power to impose a decision when cross–border problems emerge the conditions for intervention are restricted and it is unlikely ever to be used.

3 International Product Safety

1. INTRODUCTION

In the last chapter we saw the significant impact EC law has had on consumer product safety regulation throughout the Community. Art. 30 has caused national safety provisions to be scrutinised to see if they create barriers to trade and the process of dismantling them has only been restricted to a limited extent by the member states' right to maintain measures necessary to protect health and safety. In response, in several areas positive regulation at the EC level has occurred, recently, through the development of new approach directives relying on standardisation and a global approach to testing and certification. This approach relies heavily upon there being a high degree of confidence in the actors in other member states and we have seen that especially as regards certification this confidence is not yet fully warranted and has not yet been fully developed. Other EC activities have involved increasing transparency in the standards making process so that new barriers are not created and the development of information exchanges and co–ordination by enforcement authorities to ensure consumer safety is not threatened by the Single Market.

The same tensions between free trade and the need to assure consumer safety are also present in international trade. Indeed we have already noted the interplay between international economic law and EC law, especially in the context of standards making. It is not too much of an exaggeration to claim that those who point to the threat EC law poses for national sovereignty may be missing more significant developments at the international level. In today's global market place and especially after the Uruguay GATT–round one can see international trading laws becoming the dominant influence on safety rules with the role of the EC being to provide the member states with a more influential voice at the international negotiating table than they would have as individual states.

We noted that the members of the EC have yet fully to develop the necessary mutual confidence in one another's safety regulation institutions. This problem is compounded on the world stage, where the nations come from a far wider range of cultural and economic backgrounds. Also the co–ordination of enforcement authorities is more problematic.

In this chapter we first consider the rules of the World Trade Organisation (WTO) to assess what limitations international economic law places on nations' domestic product safety regulation. The function and procedures of the International Standards Organisation (ISO) are then studied. This is particularly important as these often form the basis of CEN and hence national standards. Attention is then paid to the role of the Organisation for Economic Co–operation and development (OECD), particularly in the context of co–ordinating information exchanges and co–ordination between the enforcement authorities. Finally the role of the United Nations (UN) is analysed, particularly in the context of rules to prevent the 'dumping' of dangerous products on developing countries. Many other bodies have some influence upon the international regulation of product safety, some are mentioned *en passant*, but these four bodies seem to be the most significant for our objective of looking at the general features of product safety regulation.

2.   WTO[1]

A.   Background

After the Second World War the need for regulation of international trade and finance was recognised as being important both to bring about the benefits which the fashionable Ricardo–economic theory of comparative advantage predicted would flow from increased trade between nations and to secure peace amongst nations. The resulting set of international agreements are known as the 'Bretton Woods System'. They involved the establishment of the International Monetary Fund (IMF), International Bank for Reconstruction and Development (IBRD – 'World Bank') and significantly for our purposes the General Agreement on Tariffs and Trade (GATT).

It was initially intended that GATT would form part of a broader framework for international trade which would be supervised by an International Trade Organisation (ITO). Although the Havana conference agreed a draft charter for the ITO it was never adopted, because for domestic political reasons it could not be approved by the US congress. Thus the secretariat for GATT became, by default, the body responsible for supervising and monitoring world trade. It was only with the conclusion of the Uruguay Round in 1994 that the WTO was established as the central institution of world trade regulation.

The principle behind GATT was to increase international trade by a policy of encouraging states to use tariff rather than non–tariff barriers (eg

---

1   For a deeper analysis of the law surrounding the WTO see J. Jackson, W. Davey, A. Sykes, *Legal Problems of International Economic Relations*, 3rd ed. (West, 1995) and for a now slightly dated, but very readable, introduction to the issues involved in this area see, J. Jackson, *The World Trading System*, (MIT Press, 1989).

quotas)[2] and then gradually to negotiate for a reduction in the level of tariffs. This policy was supported by two fundamental GATT principles – the *most favoured nation* (MFN) principle which aims at creating equality between imports by requiring that no member[3] be treated less favourably than any other; and the *national treatment* provision which seeks equality between imported and domestic goods by stipulating that once foreign products are accepted on to a national market they should be treated no differently from domestic products.

The process of tariff reductions and other treaty amendments took place through a series of 'rounds' of negotiations. The most significant from our point of view are the Tokyo Round of 1973–79 and the Uruguay Round of 1986–94.

The Tokyo Round saw the adoption of a number of side–agreements and understandings. Although messy, in the sense that their legal status was unclear and their application was restricted to those states which signed up to them, they nevertheless addressed a number of issues which recognised that the fair regulation of international trade was more complex than simply controlling quotas and tariffs. We should note in particular the Agreement on Technical Barriers to Trade (ATBT) and an Understanding regarding notification, consultation, dispute settlement and surveillance.

It was being recognised that technical barriers to trade could be used as indirect means of protecting domestic economies from undesired foreign competition. Indeed one explanation why increased attention was being paid to technical barriers to trade was possibly that the significance of such impediments to trade was becoming more apparent as the more obvious quota and tariff barriers were being removed.

The present focus on technical trade barriers is also making the regulation of international trade more legalistic. There has always been a tension within GATT as to whether it should be a mechanism through which trade disputes between nations could be resolved by negotiation or whether legal rules should be used to settle disputes. This debate largely centres around whether it is possible to persuade nations to accept the application of international law rules which are not favourable to them and whether it is worth doing so as the whole system eventually depends upon goodwill. A legal system could of course be considered fairer since it reduces the ability of the more powerful states to impose solutions by dint of their economic power. Moreover, whilst tariff negotiations raise comparatively few legal questions, apart from technical ones relating to the classification of goods,

---

2   Art XI provides that in principle no prohibitions or restrictions other than duties, taxes or other charges, whether made effective through quotas, import or export licenses or other measures shall be instituted or maintained.

3   Prior to the WTO Charter they had been known as contracting parties.

alleged technical barriers to trade need to be subjected to a fundamental legal analysis to determine whether the disputed rule does in fact act as a barrier to trade.

The process of legalisation has been accentuated by the development of more sophisticated and independent dispute settlement mechanisms. Originally disputes under GATT were taken up at the semi–annual meeting of the Contracting Parties. Next they were brought to an 'inter–sessional committee of the Contracting Parties' and later still to a working party. However, around 1955 the then Director General Eric Wyndham–White brought about a change so that instead of being heard by a working party, made up of nations, disputes were heard by a panel of three to five experts acting in their own capacity and not as representatives of government. This has been seen as marking a shift from a negotiation based system to a legal based system.

The Tokyo Understanding confirmed the move to panels and improved the procedures to some extent, but the system continued to have weaknesses. Another problem was that the various Agreements adopted in the Tokyo Round all had their own dispute resolution mechanisms. The move to a more legal framework for dispute resolution has been confirmed by the establishment of the WTO and its Dispute Settlement Body (DSB), in reality its General Council acting in a specialised role, which deals with all complaints. The Dispute Settlement Understanding (DSU) gives parties to a dispute the right to have a panel convened if negotiations or mediation have failed to resolve a dispute. Importantly the DSB considers the report under a procedure which assumes adoption unless there is a consensus against adoption.[4] A new Appellate Body has now been set up to which a party can appeal and its report is again subject to adoption by reverse consensus. This increased juridification of the dispute settlement procedures, combined with the more frequent raising of technical barrier to trade issues (even in disputes where they are not a central concern[5]) should lead to case law developing which condemns safety measures which are excessive and which discriminate against imports. However, an important difference should be noted between GATT and EC law. Under GATT each nation is permitted to continue to

---

4   Previously there had to be a consensus for adoption of the report which effectively meant that the party aggrieved by the panel's decision could block its adoption. Indeed there has only been one occasion when a party has been authorised to take retaliatory action. In *Netherlands Measures of Suspension of Obligations to the United States*, GATT, BISD 1 Supp. 32 (1953) the Netherlands were authorised to retaliate against US grain when the US imposed a GATT contrary restraint on Dutch dairy products; but the authorisation was never used.

5   This can be explained by the fact that all parties to GATT are now also parties to the ATBT.

decide for itself what level of safety it wishes to provide for and the appropriateness of that choice cannot be questioned. However, the means used to achieve that must be proportionate and non–discriminatory.

Before moving on to consider the actual rules of GATT and the ATBT it may be useful to clarify the structure and legal framework of the WTO following the Uruguay Round. The WTO charter deals with institutional matters, but refers to annexes containing voluminous pages of substantive rules. Annex 1A contains GATT 1994 and Agreements and Understandings on 12 topics including the ATBT, known as the Standards Code. Unlike in the Tokyo Round under which states were free to pick and choose which side agreements they joined, the WTO creates a single package of GATT and related Agreements and Understandings which members accept *in toto*. Annex 1B is the General Agreement on Trade in Services and 1C the Agreement on Trade–related Aspects of Intellectual Property. Annex 2 includes the dispute settlement rules outlined above which are obligatory on all members and apply a unitary dispute settlement to all agreements in annexes 1, 2 and 4. It therefore does not apply to the Trade Policy Review Mechanism (TPRM) established by annex 3. This is not supposed to be a legalistic review of members trade rules and policies. Rather than focusing on consistency with WTO and annex obligations, the TPRM seeks to assess the general impact of trade policies on the country being examined and its trading partners. The TPRM does, however, form a measure of external surveillance and control by the WTO which could raise matters relating to technical barriers to trade if these were seen to be adversely affecting trade with a particular nation. Annex 4 contains four agreements (on government procurement, trade in civil aircraft, bovine meat and dairy products) which breach the single package principle as they are optional.[6]

The institutional structure of WTO is that it has a Ministerial Conference reported to by the General Council, which also functions as the Dispute Settlement Body and the Trade Policy Review Body. Beneath that there are Councils for Trade in Goods, Trade in Services and Trade–related aspects of Intellectual Property Rights. There are twelve committees reporting to the Council for Trade in Goods, the one with which we are most concerned is the Committee Technical Barriers to Trade, but the existence of the Committee Sanitary and Phytosanitary Measures should also be noted.

---

6 They tend to be targeted at a few industrial nations or to be expressed in terms of general goals rather than providing for strict legal rules.

B.   GATT

(i)   Most Favoured Nation (MFN)

Art. 1, para. 1 of GATT contains the cornerstone provision of the whole Treaty, the MFN provision, whereby:

> 'any advantage, favour, privilege or immunity granted by any contracting party to any product originating in or destined for any other country shall be accorded immediately and unconditionally to the like product originating in or destined for the territories of all other contracting parties.'

This is an unconditional MFN provision, by which is meant that it is granted automatically to all contracting parties. This should be contrasted with conditional MFN, where rights granted to one state are extended to others but only after some reciprocal privilege has been extended. After the Tokyo Round when the side agreements were optional, the concept of 'code conditionality' arose where the benefits of the various codes were only extended to other states who were either party to the codes or at least reciprocated with code treatment.[7] Now that GATT and related agreements are treated as a single package the concept of code conditionality would appear to be redundant, save for the exceptional list of optional agreements in annex 4. However, we will return to the question of whether all the provisions of the ATBT give rise to MFN obligations.

Unconditional MFN is an ambitious objective, but the reality of practice and the legal conditions attaching to it mean that the provision is not fully effective; although one should not underestimate the benefits it has produced. Only those exceptions of immediate relevance for our study will be mentioned.

Art. XXIV provides an exception for free trade areas, customs unions and interim agreements leading to one of these within a 'reasonable time'. Some such rule is of course required. We saw in the last chapter that members of the EC are increasingly having to grant access to their markets to fellow members with no or limited formalities. A direct application of the MFN provision would mean that such privileges would have to be automatically extended to all WTO members. However, the concessions to EC members have been granted within a regulated environment which at least attempts to provide safeguards to ensure that equivalent controls should be exercised in the exporting country. Simply extending such rights to all WTO members could not be countenanced if concern for consumer safety is

---

[7]   See Jackson, *op cit.*, at 137.

to be maintained. Nevertheless there is a danger that the GATT concession to free trade areas might give rise to regional cartels. The danger is that free trade zones develop into protectionist bodies – the 'Fortress Europe' mentality – rather than being a staging post *en route* to greater trade liberalisation. In the products standards sphere we shall see that this is one of the reasons why co–operation between CEN and ISO is so important.

Another important set of exceptions are those related to public policy contained in art. XX. We will pay particular attention to the exception governing measures to protect health (see section 2B(iii)).

(ii) National Treatment

The MFN provisions prevent countries favouring one nation over another. A far more significant challenge to safety laws is likely to be based on the national treatment provisions contained in art. III. National treatment imposes a non–discrimination principle between domestic goods and the same imported goods. Art. III, para. 1 states that taxes and regulations 'should not be applied... so as to afford protection to domestic production'. Para. 4 requires national treatment in respect of regulations affecting the sale and use of goods generally. It provides that products imported into the territory of any contracting party 'shall be accorded treatment no less favourable than that accorded to like products of national origin in respect of all laws, regulations and requirements affecting their internal sale, offering for sale, purchase, transportation ...etc'. An interpretative note makes it clear that this extends to measures taken at the time or point of importation.

The reach of art. III, para. 4 has been broadly interpreted by various panels. According to the panel in *Italian Discrimination against Imported Agricultural Machinery*[8] the choice of the word 'affecting' in art. III, para. 4 shows the drafters did not intend to limit control to laws and regulations directly governing the conditions of sale or purchase, but also those which might adversely affect the conditions of competition on the internal market. In that case the panel condemned the provision of subsidised credit facilities which were only available for the purchase of agricultural machinery produced in Italy. Following on from this the panel in *United States – Section 337 of the Tariff Act of 1930*[9] found that art. III, para. 4 applied to enforcement procedures as well as substantive provisions – otherwise discrimination could occur by having formally identical rules for domestic and imported products, but only enforcing them against imported goods.

---

8   GATT, 7th Supp. BISD 60 (1959).
9   GATT, 36th Supp. BISD 345 (1990).

An important difference between art. 30 of the EC Treaty and art. III of GATT is that EC law is more ambitious in seeking to remove all impediments to inter–state trade, whereas GATT only attacks discriminatory rules. Thus it was fairly simple to find that a requirement that sellers of imported eggs have a conspicuous placard stating WE SELL FOREIGN EGGS breached art. III, para. 4.[10] Of course the law would be rather ineffective if it simply challenged overt discrimination. Many technical regulations, however, formally apply equally to domestic and imported products, but in practice they are more onerous on importers either for logistical[11] reasons or because local industry is geared up to comply with local regulations which require adaptation and hence additional costs for importers. If it could be shown that such rules had been introduced so as to afford protection to domestic production then art. III, para. 1 could be invoked. However, this will be difficult to establish because of the practical impossibility of distinguishing protectionist motives from legitimate social policy objectives which are permitted by art. XX. On the other hand the 'no less favourable' treatment standard in art. III, para. 4 was given a vigorous interpretation by the panel in *United States – Section 307 of the Tariff Act of 1930* which said it called for:

> 'effective equality of opportunities for imported products in respect of the application of laws, regulations and requirements affecting the internal sale, offering for sale, purchase, transportation, distribution or use of products.'[12]

This 'effective equality of opportunities' test is a means by which indirectly discriminatory measures can be found to fall foul of art. III. Thus a ban on cigarette advertising in Thailand can be seen to impact more harshly on importers trying to enter a recently liberalised market than on the Government owned domestic industry which until recently had a monopoly.[13] Nevertheless the test remains less severe than that imposed by the ECJ. Measures which are found to breach art. III, can still be justified by, *inter alia*, art. XX.

---

[10] *Hawaii v Ho*, 41 Hawaii 565 (1957).

[11] For instance, the French requirement that VCRs be imported through an inland city where there were limited inspectors, cited in Jackson, *op. cit.*, at 131.

[12] *Op. cit.*, at 5.11.

[13] *Thailand – Restrictions on Importation of and Internal Taxes on Cigarettes*, GATT 37th Supp. BISD, 200 (1991).

(iii) Art. XX

Art. XX is the equivalent of art. 36 in the EC Treaty and the 'mandatory requirement' set out in the *Cassis de Dijon* judgment (Chapter 2, section 2). It provides that, subject to certain conditions, nothing in the Agreement shall be construed as preventing the adoption or enforcement by any contracting party of any of a list of measures. That which is of particular interest to us is item (b) which covers measures necessary to protect human, animal and plant health and life. Art. XX, para. 1 makes it clear that such measures must not be 'applied in a manner which would constitute a means of arbitrary or unjustifiable discrimination between countries where the same conditions prevail, or a disguised restriction on international trade'.

An important limitation on the use of the art. XX exemption power is that the power is contingent upon the measure being necessary. In *United States – Section 337 of the Tariff Act of 1930* a panel decided that a measure could not be necessary if it was inconsistent with another GATT provision when an alternative which did not breach that provision existed. Moreover when a measure which is consistent with other GATT provisions is not available 'a contracting party is bound to use, among the measures reasonably available to it, that which entails the least degree of inconsistency with other GATT provisions'.[14] That decision concerned exception (d) relating to patent laws, but was applied to the health exception (b) in the *Thai Cigarettes* case. It was considered that the objective of preventing more females from taking up smoking could be achieved by means which discriminated less against imports than the advertising ban. There is a parallel here with the jurisprudence of the ECJ, in that there is a clear tendency not to question the objective itself if the measure complained of can be struck down on the basis that it was excessive and disproportionate to the end being sought.[15] A point of difference remains. There is a point beyond which the ECJ will question the policy of a member state and find that the level of protection it requires is excessive. Under the GATT rules there should be no questioning of the policy of individual states. They should remain free to set as high a standard of protection as they wish. All that is required is that they do not positively discriminate against imports and achieve their objectives in the manner which discriminates least against imports.

---

14 *Op. cit.*, at 5.25.
15 L. Kleftodimou, 'Protecting the Consumer under GATT' [1995] *Consum. L.J.* 174.

C.   Agreement on Technical Barriers to Trade (ATBT)[16]

The first ATBT was a result of the Tokyo Round. It was a side agreement and contracting parties were free to choose whether or not to join it. Forty six countries did sign up to it, but now all 121 members are party to the ATBT as it is an integral part of the WTO single package. The main differences between the Tokyo Round ATBT and the new provisions are the inclusion of more extensive provisions on the recognition of conformity assessment and the fact that members are now entitled to request a panel to resolve a dispute.

No panel was actual formed to consider an ATBT issue under the Tokyo agreement, but the Committee Technical Barriers to Trade (which must meet at least once a year, but typically meets at least twice a year) tended to hear three or four complaints at each meeting. Of course many more matters are raised in bilateral discussions between members. Since the Uruguay Agreement six cases had gone to panels up to May 1996. Only one panel decision had been adopted, a second directly concerning ATBT is currently restricted as the parties wish to try to resolve the matter between themselves. In fact of the first 21 cases submitted to the DSB for consultation seven raised ATBT issues.[17] The use of ATBT arguments as additional points to bolster a claim under GATT is likely to increase now that all members are party to the ATBT.

The ATBT provides for the DSB to undertake consultations and settle disputes under arts XXII and XXIII of GATT and the DSU. A technical experts group can be established by the panel to assist with technical questions whether on the panel's own initiative or at the request of a party to the dispute. Annex 2 of the ATBT contains procedures for such technical expert groups, which requires members to be persons of professional standing and experience in the field and provides that they should serve in their own individual capacity. They should not be government officials, nor, save in exceptional circumstances, citizens of a party to the dispute. The panel decides the group's terms of reference and working procedures. Information and advice can be sought from any source. Parties to the dispute shall have access to all non–confidential information provided to the group and a non–confidential summary of any confidential information not authorised for release. A draft report shall be circulated to the parties for comment and the final report given to them when it is submitted to the panel.

---

[16]   Readers should also be aware of the Agreement on the Application of Sanitary and Phytosanitary measures which seeks to encourage the harmonisation of such measures based in international standards so far as practicable and otherwise to increase transparency concerning the procedures adopted.

[17]   Focus (WTO newsletter) 5 December 1995.

The ATBT restates certain GATT principles, such as MFN and national treatment, whilst retaining the right of members to take steps to protect specified national interests. The additional provisions largely involve trying to ensure that technical regulations and standards are developed in accordance with international trends and that where they are not that, this fact is publicised and affected parties are given the opportunity to have consultations. Commenting on the Tokyo Round Jackson had suggested that as the Standards Code – as he calls it – was essentially a set of procedures then it could be argued that the MFN principle did not apply to the mere offer of certain consultation procedures to foreign nations.[18] This was said in the context of discussing a US statute which required countries themselves to apply the code provisions in order to be entitled to code treatment from the US. Now that all members are party to the ATBT this issue should not arise as members need not rely upon the MFN principle, but can rely directly on their rights under the ATBT.

(i) Technical Regulations

Technical regulations are mandatory rules. Art. 2 lays down a series of rules for their preparation, adoption and application by central government bodies, which are similar in objective and method to the EC rules found in the Technical Standards Directive (Chapter 2, section 3). Para. 2.1 includes the MFN and national treatment provisions, namely that central government bodies shall ensure that in respect of technical regulations products imported from any member are treated no less favourably than like products of national origin or like products originating in any other countries. Para. 2.2 states that technical regulations should not be prepared, adopted or applied with a view to creating unnecessary obstacles to international trade. Clearly it implies that some barriers to trade may be necessary and it goes on to list the legitimate objectives which such regulations may address, including the protection of human health or safety and the prevention of deceptive practices. However, such technical regulations should be no more trade–restrictive than necessary to fulfil the legitimate objective taking account of the risks non–fulfilment would create. The preamble makes it clear that a country should be able to protect these objectives 'at the levels it considers appropriate'. Para. 2.3 provides that trade regulations should not be maintained if circumstances or objectives no longer exist or have changed so that they can be addressed in a less trade restrictive manner. So far the ATBT simply restates general GATT principles.

---

18   Jackson, *op. cit.*, at 145.

Para. 2.4 requires that members use existing or nearly completed international standards as the basis for their technical regulations. However, an exception to this principle is made when to do so would be ineffective or inappropriate in order for them to fulfil their legitimate objectives. Fundamental climatic, geographic or technological problems are cited as reasons for departing from international standards.

Members preparing, adopting or applying technical regulations which may have a significant effect on the trade of other members must, when so requested by another member, justify the regulation in the light of the preceding provisions. Regulations aimed at one of the legitimate objectives specifically mentioned in para. 2.2 and which conform to international standards are rebuttably presumed not to create unnecessary obstacles to international trade. International standardisation is further supported by the requirement in para. 2.6 that members, within the limits of their resources, play a full part in the preparation of international standards for products which they have, or expect to adopt, technical regulations.

In an attempt to encourage international trade para. 2.7 requires members to give 'positive consideration' to accepting technical regulations of other members as equivalent, even if they differ from their own so long as they fulfil the objectives of their own regulations. Equally para. 2.8 requires that, wherever appropriate, members specify product requirements in terms of performance, rather than design or descriptive characteristics. This means that products should not be denied access on technical grounds if they meet the required performance standards.

Para. 2.9 provides for some publicity and consultation requirements which arise when a member wishes to create a technical regulation which may have a significant effect on the trade of other members and there is no relevant international standard or the regulation does not accord with such international standards. At an appropriate early stage a notice must be placed in a publication so that interested parties in other members can become acquainted with it. Other members must be informed through the secretariat of the products covered and the regulation's objective and rationale. This notification must be at an early appropriate stage so that comments can be taken into account and amendments introduced. Particulars or copies of the proposed regulation should be supplied upon request to other members and the parts which deviate from international standards should be identified. Members should be allowed a reasonable time to make written comments and if desired have discussions on these matters. These comments and discussions should be taken into account. This right of consultation is said to be available without discrimination, underlining that whatever the position concerning the MFN principle under the Tokyo ATBT, consultation is available as of right to all members. Where urgent problems arise or threaten to arise, concerning *inter alia* health and safety, para. 2.10 allows members to miss out such of the steps, outlined above, as it considers necessary provided that on adoption (a) members are notified through the secretariat (with the nature of the urgent problem being included); (b) copies of the regulation are available on request; and (c) members have the right to comment on and hold discussions about the regulation.

Technical regulations must be published promptly or otherwise made available so that interested parties in other member states can become acquainted with them. Except in urgent cases, a reasonable interval should be allowed between publication and entry into force of the regulation to allow producers in exporting countries to adapt their products or methods of production to the requirements.

Art. 3 covers the situation where technical regulations are the responsibility of local government or non–governmental bodies. Observance of art. 2 remains the responsibility of members and they must take reasonable measures to ensure compliance by such bodies with art. 2. Positive measures and mechanisms should be formulated and implemented to support the observance of art. 2 by bodies other than central government. Certainly members should not take measures which require or encourage such bodies to act inconsistently with art. 2. The notification duties remain the duty of the members[19] and members may require contacts to take place through central government.

(ii) Standards

The policy with regards to non–mandatory standards is to require compliance with the Code of Good Practice for the Preparation, Adoption and Application of Standards which is found in annex 3 of the ATBT. Art. 4 requires that members ensure central government standardising bodies accept and comply with the Code[20] and take reasonable measures to ensure that the Code is also accepted and complied with by their local government and non–governmental standardising bodies (eg BSI, AFNOR, DIN, ANSI) as well as regional standardising bodies (eg CEN) of which they or one or more bodies within their territory are members.

By July 1996 forty four standardising bodies had subscribed to the Code. The Code has many parallel provisions to those outlined above for regulations. Hence standardising bodies shall treat products from other members no less favourably than national products or products from any

---

[19] There is no requirement to notify regulations which are substantially the same as those previously notified by central government.

[20] In some countries standardisation is a government function, but in those we shall study in subsequent chapters it is mainly carried on by non–governmental bodies.

other country. Standards should not create unnecessary obstacles to international trade. International standards should be used unless they would be ineffective or inappropriate because they offer an insufficient level of protection or because of fundamental climatic, geographic or technological problems. Interestingly no guidance is given as to what amounts to an insufficient level of protection. This contrasts with art. 2 which provides, an admittedly non–exhaustive, list of legitimate objectives regulations may seek to secure. Standards should whenever appropriate be based on product requirements framed in terms of performance rather than design or description.

Standardising bodies should within the limits of their resources play a full role in the preparation of relevant international standards, whenever possible by way of one delegation representing all bodies within a territory. Efforts should be made to secure a national consensus on standards. Duplication or overlap of work between national bodies and with the work of regional and international standardising bodies should be avoided. Equally regional bodies should make efforts to ensure there is no such duplication or overlap with international bodies.

The transparency of the standards making process is enhanced by the requirement that at least every six months standardising bodies should publish a work programme. This should list the standards it is currently preparing and those which it has adopted in the preceding period. For each standard there should be indicated, in accordance with ISONET[21] rules, its subject matter classification, stage of development and reference to any international standards taken as a base. A notice of the existence of the work programme should be made in a national or, as the case may be, regional publication of standardisation activities and notice of its existence should also be given to the ISO/IEC Information Centre in Geneva. National ISO/IEC members should become members of ISONET or appoint another member. They should seek the most advanced type of membership possible. Other standardising bodies should associate themselves with the ISONET member.

Usually a period of 60 days should be allowed for comments to be submitted on a draft standard before it is adopted. Before the start of the comment period a notice should be published stating its length and indicating whether the draft standard deviates from international standards. The comment period can be shortened where there are urgent problems of, *inter*

---

21   ISONET is the ISO information network on standards. Members of the network (typically the ISO member) act as specialised enquiry points to disseminate information and to identify sources of information. In most countries the ISONET enquiry point is also the GATT enquiry point, otherwise the two bodies co–operate closely.

alia, safety and health. Comments received during this period shall be taken into account and, if so requested, comments from other standardising bodies complying with the code shall be replied to as promptly as possible and shall include an explanation of why a deviation from the relevant international standard is necessary. The standard should be published promptly once adopted.

Standardising bodies should make available copies of draft standards, standards and work programmes to interested parties in WTO members. Apart from the real cost of delivery, any fees should be the same for foreign and domestic parties.

(iii) Conformity Assessment

Art. 5 seeks to ensure that the procedures for assessing conformity used by central government bodies do not create barriers to trade. Where a positive assurance of conformity with technical regulations or standards is required conformity assessment procedures must be prepared, adopted and applied so as to grant access for suppliers of like products under conditions no less favourable in a comparable situation than those accorded to domestic products or to products from any other country. Suppliers should have the right to an assessment under the procedure, including (when foreseen by that procedure) the right to have conformity assessment activities undertaken at the site of facilities and to receive the mark of the system. Members should also ensure that such procedures are not prepared, adopted or applied with a view to or with the effect of creating unnecessary obstacles to international trade. Therefore they should be no more strict or more strictly applied than is necessary to give the importing member adequate confidence that the product conforms to the applicable technical regulations or standards.

In implementing the above, members must ensure:

- procedures are expeditious and are carried out in an order which does not favour domestic products,
- assessment periods are published or communicated on request,
- applicants are informed of any deficiencies in documentation promptly,
- precise and complete results are transmitted as soon as possible,
- at the applicant's request, even deficient applications are processed as far as possible,
- upon request, applicants are informed of progress with any delay being explained,
- demands for information are limited to what is necessary to assess conformity and determine fees,

- confidentiality is respected in the same manner as for domestic goods and in a manner which protects legitimate commercial interests,
- fees should be equitable compared to those charged for domestic products or those from any other country, but they can take into account costs resulting from the difference between location of the applicant's facilities and the conformity assessment body,
- the siting of facilities or selection of samples should not cause unnecessary inconvenience,
- when specifications of the product change the procedures should be limited to such as are necessary to determine whether adequate confidence exists that the product still meets the technical regulations or standards,
- there is a complaints system and means to take corrective action over justified complaints.

However, the above rules should not prevent members from carrying out reasonable spot checks within their territory.

Wherever there are guides or recommendations issued by international standardising bodies, or their completion is imminent, members should ensure that their central government bodies use them as a basis for their conformity assessment procedures, unless this is inappropriate for reasons of, *inter alia*, protection of human health and safety. Members should play a full part, within the limits of their resources, in the development of such guides and recommendations. Whenever such international guides or recommendations do not exist, or a member proposes a conformity assessment procedure which is not in accordance with such guides or recommendations, then if a conformity assessment procedure may have a significant effect on the trade of other members, a similar procedure as applied to technical regulations must be gone through, eg publication of a notice, notification to the secretariat, provision of copies on request and a willingness to take into account comments and discussions. Again the procedure can be shortened in urgent situations, so long as notification, provision of copies, comment and discussion take place upon adoption.

As with technical regulations, all conformity assessment procedures should be published promptly, or otherwise made available to interested parties. Except in urgent situations, a reasonable time should be left between their publication and entry into force.

In the last chapter we noted that the weak link in EC product safety laws are the rules on mutual recognition of conformity assessment. At the international level this problem was also the last to be addressed – the Tokyo ATBT did not deal with this topic in great detail and the solutions presently proposed are the most tentative. Art. 6, para. 1 provides that members shall, but only whenever possible, ensure that conformity assessment procedures in other members are accepted, even if these differ from their own so long as they offer an equivalent assurance of conformity with applicable technical regulations or standards. However, it is further recognised that prior consultations may be necessary to arrive at mutually satisfactory understandings regarding the adequate and enduring competence of the conformity assessment body in the exporting member so that confidence can exist in the continued reliability of their results (verified compliance, for example by accreditation, with guides and recommendations issued by standardising bodies should be taken into account as indications of adequate competence). It seems that acceptance of conformity assessment results is to be limited to those produced by designated bodies in the exporting member. Members should ensure their conformity assessment procedures permit as far as possible the implementation of these provisions.

Members are also encouraged, when requested by other members, to be willing to enter into negotiations for the conclusion of agreements for the mutual recognition of each other's conformity assessment procedures. There is no obligation to enter into such agreements or even to negotiate towards such agreements, merely an 'encouragement' to do so. In addition members may not only require that such mutual recognition agreements fulfil the criteria of art. 6, para. 1, but also that they give mutual satisfaction regarding their potential for facilitating trade in the products concerned. Clearly there is every excuse for a member not to conclude such agreements, if they desire not to do so.

More ambitious is the provision which encourages members to permit conformity assessment bodies located in the territories of other members to participate in their conformity assessment procedures under conditions which are no less favourable than those accorded to domestic bodies or bodies located in any other country. Again, however, the ATBT only encourages such concessions and does not require them.

Clearly there is a divergence from the MFN principle with regard to conformity assessment procedures. Recognition of other procedures, mutual recognition and acceptance into domestic conformity procedures is undertaken on a case by case basis. The MFN principle is clearly inconsistent with this as once a member had extended such a right to a body in one member, the MFN principle would require it to be automatically granted to conformity assessment bodies in all members.

Art. 7 requires members to take reasonable measures to ensure local government bodies comply with arts 5 and 6 and prohibits them from taking measures which require or encourage them to act in a manner which is inconsistent with arts 5 and 6. Members remain responsible for the observance of arts 5 and 6 and should implement positive measures and mechanisms to support its observance. Notification to the secretariat remains the responsibility of the member and other members can require contacts to be with central government.

Art. 8 imposes similar obligations on members with respect to non–governmental bodies. Central government shall not rely upon conformity assessment procedures of such bodies, unless they comply with arts 5 and 6.

Members are encouraged, by art. 9, to participate in international systems for conformity assessment and to take reasonable measures to ensure that international or regional systems, to which bodies within their territory are members or participants, comply with arts 5 and 6. Central government shall only rely on international or regional conformity assessment systems which do so comply.

D.   Information and Assistance

It has already been commented that the central thrust of the ATBT is transparency. It is all very well to have notification, publication provisions etc., but these will be of little use if members and other interested parties cannot locate such documents. Art. 10 therefore requires members to establish enquiry points to answer reasonable queries and provide documentation at an equitable price. Developed country members must provide translations in English, French or Spanish. These can be summaries in the case of voluminous documents.

There is also an obligation to notify other members, through the secretariat, of bilateral or multilateral agreements relating to technical regulation, standards or conformity assessment procedures which may have a significant effect on trade.

There are also obligations to provide technical assistance to other members on matters covered by the ATBT, especially developing countries (art. 11). Other measures also provide for the special and differential treatment of developing countries (art. 12).

Attached to the ATBT is a Code of Good Practice for the preparation, adoption and application of standards. ISO operates an information service on which bodies have accepted this Code.

3. ISO

A. Structure and Organisation[22]

ISO[23] (International Organisation for Standards) is a non–governmental body founded in 1947.[24] It is the equivalent body at the international level to CEN at the European level. As at the European level there are specialist bodies dealing with standardisation of electrical goods (IEC – International Electrotechnical Commission) and for telecommunications (ITU – International Telecommunication Union). We shall concentrate on the work of ISO. ISO and IEC have detailed procedures for liaising to avoid or eliminate overlapping work and if the liaison procedures do not produce agreement the matter can be referred to the JTPC (Joint Technical Programming Committee).

ISO is governed by a General Assembly. This is comprised of all *member bodies*; these are the national bodies 'most representative of standardisation in [its] country'. Their role is to keep interested parties informed of international standardisation work, present a concerted view of the country's interests during international negotiations, provide secretariats for ISO technical committees and sub–committees in which the country has an interest and pay membership dues to support ISO central operations. Countries which do not yet have as fully developed national standards activities can join as *correspondent members* so that they are kept informed of work of interest to them, but they do not take part in the technical work. If a standard is of very great interest to them, such countries are sometimes known to pay full membership fees for the period for which it is under discussion so that they can take part in the negotiations. A third category of *subscriber members*, permits countries with very small economies to maintain contact with ISO for reduced membership fees. In January 1996 there were 85 member bodies, 24 correspondent members and 9 subscriber members.

---

22 A useful diagram of the organisational structure is provided in ISO, *Annual Report 1995*, at 21. The procedures for the technical work are set out in ISO/IEC, *Directives Part 1*.

23 ISO is preferred to IOS as it is an acronym and because *isos* is the Greek word for equal which is seen as linked to the concept of standards, see ISO, *Compatible Technology Worldwide*, at 3.

24 IEC (International Electrotechnical Commission) was formed in 1906 with work in other fields being undertaken by the International Federation of the National Standardising Associations (ISA). ISA dealt mainly in mechanical engineering matters and its activities ceased in 1942 because of the Second World War.

The daily organisation of ISO is undertaken by its Council, which comprises the principal officers and 18 elected members. Council reports to the General Assembly as do four Policy Development Committees dealing with developing country matters (DEVCO), information systems and services (INFCO), conformity assessment (CASCO) and of particular relevance to our work, consumer policy (COPOLCO). The Council is supported by the Central Secretariat and *ad hoc* advisory groups and also is reported to by the Technical Management Board (TMB) which is responsible for the overall management of the technical work.

We have already noted that members pay subscriptions to support the Central Secretariat. These fees comprise 70% of the Central Secretariat's budget, the other 30% is derived from the sale of standards and other publications.[25] In this respect it will be noted that ISO is different from CEN, which cannot sell standards as the standards it produces are sold as national standards through its member bodies. The Central Secretariat accounts for 20% of expenditure on ISO work; the other 80% being borne by the 34 member bodies holding technical committee and sub–committee secretariats. In 1995 the total annual expenditure was estimated as 150 M Swiss francs.[26]

The TMB is responsible for establishing and dissolving technical committees. It is responsible for the overall management of the technical committee and sub–committee structure, in particular it delineates the scope of the technical committees and deals with co–ordination questions and appeals.

The actual standardisation work is carried out by technical committees, sub–committees and working groups. In 1995 there were 185 technical committees, 611 sub–committees and 2022 working groups.[27] The secretariat for such bodies is provided by national members.

National bodies have to indicate whether they wish to participate in the work of a technical committee or sub–committee. They can participate as P–members, who actively participate in the work and also have an obligation to vote on matters submitted for a formal vote, or as O–members, ie observers who receive committee documents and attend meetings. Working groups comprise a restricted number of individual experts appointed in their personal capacity.

Each technical committee develops a strategic plan for its area. New proposals for work items can be accepted if approved by a simple majority of P–members of the relevant technical committee or subcommittee and a commitment by at least five of them to participate actively in the

25   ISO, *op. cit.*, at 13.

26   *ISO in Figures*, January 1996.

27   ISO (1995), *op. cit.*, at 18.

development of the project. It then goes through a preparatory stage to prepare a working draft and a committee stage when comments from national bodies are taken into consideration. The chairman of the relevant committee or sub–committee is then responsible for deciding whether there is enough support for it to move to the enquiry stage. The definition of consensus in ISO/IEC Guide 2 should be borne in mind when making this decision. This states that consensus means:

> 'General agreement characterised by the absence of sustained opposition to substantial issues by any important part of the concerned interests and by a process that involves seeking to take into account the views of all parties concerned and to reconcile any conflicting arguments.'

It is clear that consensus does not imply unanimity and the ISO/IEC Directives state that within ISO consensus will be based on a two–thirds majority of P–members.

At the enquiry stage the draft is circulated to national bodies to be voted upon within five months. Approval requires a two–thirds majority of P–members and not more than a quarter of the total votes being negative. The same numbers are required when the final draft is circulated at the approval stage, although the voting period is then only two months. Approved standards are to be published within two months.

In 1995 850 new and revised standards were published. By the end of 1995 there were 10, 189 ISO standards and 38 Guides. The average development time was 63.3 months.[28]

The structure of ISO and its way of working are therefore similar to CEN. However, the final product – the ISO standard – does not have to be implemented into national standards and can be modified by national bodies when adopting their own standards. In principle, the ISO standard has to stand its ground in the market place against other national standards, although if the standard is satisfactory there will be a natural impetus towards it being then adopted as the industry norm. As we shall see in the next section there is a co–operation agreement between CEN and ISO and standards adopted under this become European standards and therefore have to be adopted by national members of CEN.

B. Relationship With Regional Bodies

Co–operation between ISO and regional and national bodies is important for business efficiency reasons. In this context, the ISO President has stated that

---

28   *Ibid.*, at 15.

industry has the 'right to expect standardisation bodies to apply the same management principles for achieving efficiency, cost–effectiveness and non–duplication of resources as they have to apply to themselves in order to remain competitive'.[29] However, there is an even more powerful political reason for co–operation, as the ISO President continues:

> 'The challenge for regional markets is to avoid becoming trading blocs, or fortresses, if we are to achieve a global market, where all compete on an equal footing, the present integration we are seeing of national economies must be in the direction of multilateral exchange between the regional trading entities now in formation.'[30]

There are seven regional standards organisations recognised by ISO. In addition to CEN, there are ACCSQ (ASEAN Consultative Committee for Standardisation and Quality Control), AIDMO (Arab Industrial Development and Mining Organisation), ARSO (African Regional Organisation for Standardisation), COPANT (Pan–American Standards Commission), EASC (Euro–Asian Council for Standardisation, Metrology and Certification) and PASC (Pacific Area Standards Congress).

Co–operation between ISO and all the regional bodies should be well developed. Indeed it is one of the themes of this work that, with the drift towards international regulation, regional organisations are becoming increasingly important as a means through which nations can exert influence on the regulatory process. Equally there is a need to ensure that regional blocs do not develop a fortress mentality. Co–operation is most developed between ISO and CEN. CEN is the most integrated of the regional bodies and represents an important trading block which has the potential to develop standards which can be seen as barriers to trade, especially as under the new approach directives they are given a *de facto* regulatory status.

In 1989 CEN and ISO concluded the Lisbon Agreement on the exchange of technical information. This was, however, extended much further by the Vienna Agreement on Technical Co–operation between ISO and CEN of June 1991, with revised guidelines being issued in October 1995. This provides for co–operation by exchanging of information, permitting up to two representatives of each organisation to attend committees and working groups of the other and CEN agreeing to receive comments from ISO members. The most dramatic principle introduced by the Vienna Agreement was for the transfer of work between CEN and ISO. Of the standards produced in this way about 90% are produced by ISO and 10% by CEN. There is a Joint ISO/CEN Co–ordinating Group of the Technical Boards to

---

29   *Ibid.*, at 1.
30   *Ibid.*, at 2.

oversee the co–operation, with day to day matters being handled by the organisation's respective secretariats.

CEN can adopt an international standard under its Primary Questionnaire (PQ) or Unique Acceptance Procedure (UAP). If this leads to some modifications being made then ISO may revise its own standard, leave CEN to put forward its revised standard for ISO to accept under its fast track procedure or accept that the European standard will deviate from the ISO standard. It is also possible for ISO to adopt a European standard, but this is less likely as whereas CEN members will have commented on ISO standards during their preparation, ISO members will not have had the same opportunities to influence CEN standards. Parallel processing is therefore usually the favoured approach of ISO.

Where there is no international standard, CEN can transfer work to ISO so long as five CEN members commit themselves to participate in the ISO work. Equally an ISO committee can leave development of a standard to CEN. In both these cases there will be a procedure for parallel approval by CEN and ISO. In the past one of the problems has been synchronising the work of the two organisations with requests being made for parallel voting when a work item did not exist in one of the organisations. The central secretariats are now to ensure the required steps have been taken well in advance.[31] However in the final analysis it is for CEN and ISO to decide whether they adopt a joint text. This is particularly important in the case of CEN standards being developed under a new approach directive mandate where they have to comply with the Directive's requirements. The fact many European standards fit into this legal framework should assist European negotiators in their debates within international standards committees as they can point out that unless certain features are contained in the standard it simply cannot be accepted by them for legal reasons.

C. Consumer Input

We noted how at the European level it was more difficult for consumers to organise at the regional than at the national level. This problem is accentuated at the international level where not only are co–ordination problems multiplied, but one also encounters the need to resolve conflicts between consumers in different regions and states at different stages of their economic development. The problem is also more acute because there is no

---

31   ISO/CEN, *Guidelines for TC/SC Chairmen and Secretariats for Implementation of the Agreement on Technical Co–operation Between ISO and CEN (Vienna Agreement)*, October 1995 at 7.

international counterpart to the EC, which is prepared to fund consumer representation.

This is not to say that ISO is unsympathetic to the consumer viewpoint. Indeed we shall see that it has a consumer committee (COPOLCO) and has produced many useful guides on matters of concern to consumers. However, it has not developed efficient means for consumers directly to influence international standardisation work and its literature has tended to emphasise the need for national standardisation bodies to embrace the consumer movement so that the international standardisation work can be indirectly influenced thereby.[32] We will, however, concentrate in the following section on the direct means through which consumers can influence the international standardisation process.

(i)   COPOLCO[33]

ISO has recognised for a long time that it is important for consumers to be involved in standardisation work. As far back as 1963 the ISO Council adopted a resolution (48/1964) to promote consumer participation in standards work. In 1977 COPOLCO was established.[34] COPOLCO is the ISO committee on consumer policy, and as we have already noted it reports directly to ISO's General Assembly. Member bodies of ISO can participate as either participating or observer members of COPOLCO, whilst correspondent members can participate as observer members. In 1996 there were 68 members of COPOLCO, with the IEC, International Co–operative Alliance (ICA), Consumers International (CI – formerly IOCU, the International Organisation of Consumers Unions) and the Organisation for Economic Co–operation and Development (OECD) having liaison status. ANEC (the European Association for the co–ordination of consumer representation in standardisation) has been invited to meetings as an observer.

One weakness of COPOLCO as compared to ANEC (Chapter 2, section 6D) is that although the committee is a consumer policy committee its representatives are not drawn from consumer organisations (at least not

---

32   ISO/IEC, *Standards and the Consumer*, (2nd ed., 1986) at 8 where it reproduces recommendations by ISO/IEC to its member bodies for the development of consumer participation in standardisation.

33   See the pamphlet, *Information on COPOLCO*, (ISO, 1996).

34   This arose from the work of the International Standards Steering Committee for Consumer Affairs (ISCA) which suspended its activities following the establishment of COPOLCO: see B. Farquhar 'Consumer Representation in Standardisation' [1995] *Consum.L.J.* 56 at 65.

directly). It is the member bodies of ISO who nominate representatives to attend COPOLCO. Where standards bodies have consumer councils these councils may represent the national body. However, not every country has such a council and even where they exist it is not clear that they all see their the role of actively promoting the consumer cause (cf France, Chapter 6, section 8E). Many independent consumer organisation would challenge their right to speak on behalf of the consumer collective instead of themselves. If there is no consumer council the national body is likely to be represented by an official nominally in charge of consumer affairs, but there is no guarantee that such an official will be sympathetic or in touch with the consumer movement. For example, it was estimated that one COPOLCO meeting was attended by 25 ISO members, with 15 including some form of consumer representative. This does not seem to be very satisfactory.[35]

Again in contrast to ANEC, COPOLCO does not provide for direct representation on ISO technical committees, sub–committees and working groups. We shall see that this right is reserved to CI. When it became obvious that CI were not able to utilise this right fully, COPOLCO had proposed that it be able to send observers to ISO committees. This proposal was rejected by the ISO council.[36] This decision is to be regretted for whilst we shall see that COPOLCO is able to undertake some useful work, the most important element in consumer representation is to have an expert able to present the consumer case during the technical work of developing standards. Although such representation might be found in the national delegations, it should surely be beholden on ISO to ensure there is a mechanism to guarantee the effective participation of consumers in its work. If CI was unable to undertake that role effectively, then sharing that function with COPOLCO – together with some funds to support that work– would have seemed a sensible way forward. It is understood that COPOLCO is sometimes approached to try to ensure that consumers are represented on particular committees, but it has no funds for this purpose and can merely make soundings with likely participants.

COPOLCO's objectives are framed in terms of assisting consumers to benefit from standardisation; improving their participation in national and international standardisation; promoting consumer protection, information and training; providing a forum for the exchange of experiences; liaising with ISO organs and undertaking actions and studies within its areas of competence. It has established criteria for establishing priorities. These are grouped into three categories relating to safety and health, protection of the environment and fitness for purpose. Within each category there are ten or so sub–criteria. From these a list of priorities are established covering products

---

[35]   *Ibid.*

[36]   *Ibid.*

(eg contraceptive devices) or issues (eg air and water quality) or aspects (eg product information symbols) for which COPOLCO tries to ensure that standards work progresses satisfactorily and with adequate consumer interest representation in the relevant technical bodies. This prioritisation approach seems to be the right way forward, although one wonders whether the criteria themselves are not too wide ranging for them to improve decision–making as to the choice of priorities, especially as there is little time for analysis and discussion of the priorities and how they are being progressed.

COPOLCO is essentially a talking shop which meets once a year to prepare an Annual Report to submit to the General Assembly. The annual meeting is preceded by a one day workshop on a matter of interest to consumers. The comments made in the Annual Report and the conclusions of the workshops as well as the resolutions, statements and guides issued by COPOLCO may well have some influence on ISO policy and lead to the inclusion of matters of consumer interest being included in its work programme and some action being taken to address particular consumer grievances. Equally, its twice yearly information bulletin *Consumer Communiqué* may be a useful publication. Nevertheless, consumer representation at the international level through COPOLCO can be criticised both because there are no safeguards to ensure that the participants are part of the consumer movement and also because it does not ensure direct involvement of consumers in the international process, in the same way as ANEC seeks to ensure this occurs at the European level.

(ii) Guides

It is worth dwelling for a while for the various guides which ISO (jointly with IEC) has drawn up. The purpose of these guides is to advise those involved in the technical process of drawing up standards (and also establishing testing and certification schemes). We have already come across the important Guide 2 which sets out *General terms and their definitions concerning standardisation and related activities.* Several others are expressly concerned with consumer safety or are important in this context as well as for other goods and services. It is possible to group these guides into three groups, although obviously some guides overlap or are on the boundaries of these sets.

One group of guides gives guidance as to how the process of standardisation and certification should be planned and developed. Thus Guide 7 provides *Requirements for standards suitable for product certification* and Guide 15 establishes a *Code of principles on 'reference to standards'.* A second group is concerned with the content of standards; these are of particular interest as regards consumer safety. This group includes

Guide 37 on *Instructions for use of products of consumer interest*, Guide 41 on *Standards for packaging – consumer requirements*, Guide 50 on *Child safety and standards – general guidelines* and Guide 51 providing *Guidelines for the inclusion of safety aspects in standards*. The last groups deal with topics related to conformity assessment, testing and certification and include Guide 14 on *Product information for consumers*, Guide 23 on *Methods of indicating conformity with standards for third–party certification systems*, Guide 36 on the *Preparation of standard methods of measuring performance (SMMP) of consumer goods* and Guide 46 on *Comparative testing of consumer products and related services – general principles*.

These guides contain some useful provisions. However, it is doubtful whether the drafter of a standard is likely to able to consider all this guidance when drafting the standard. He is more likely to concentrate on the technical material which is of more obvious immediate relevance to him. The real value of these guides may be that they give consumer representatives a firmer case when they criticise a draft standard if they can point to a principle in a guide which has not been followed.

(iii) Consumers International

Consumers International (CI – formerly IOCU) is the only body with official status to represent consumers on ISO committees, sub–committees and working groups. However, it is unable to satisfy its mandate adequately. We saw in the last chapter the difficulties facing ANEC (Chapter 2, section 6D). ANEC, however has the advantage over CI, that it is co–ordinating consumer representation in a limited geographic region within which consumers share broadly similar expectations and values. Co–ordinating consumer representation on a global scale is a problem of different magnitude. The cost of travel largely prohibits consumer experts coming together to co–ordinate common positions and share experiences. ANEC has rather generous subsidies from the EC, CI has none of this but is expected to operate on the global scale. By their own admission CI has not until recently fully developed its role in standardisation. It is currently reviewing its mission in this area, but is rather sensibly likely to concentrate its efforts on developing consumer representation at the national level in those countries where it is currently weak. This fits in with CI's agenda which is largely biased towards assisting consumers in the developing world. However, at the international level this gives rise to problems of reconciling the sometimes contradictory needs of consumers in different regions of the world.

As CI has no money to subsidise consumer representation at the international level it has to rely upon offers to represent the consumer interest from wherever they come. For instance, ANEC co–operates with CI to ensure that they are represented on those international committees where European projects are being discussed.[37] The Director of CI has commented that in practice two–thirds of CI's representatives are funded by ANEC.[38] The irony of this is that a body which seeks to promote the interests of consumers in developing countries has become largely a conduit for the voice of the relatively well organised European consumer movement. Over–reliance on ANEC is unhealthy as it means that all world consumers will tend to be represented by representatives from the more affluent European countries. Equally, even consumer representatives from these countries may find it difficult to afford to participate at the international level.

ISO seems to take the approach that as it is an international organisation only national member bodies and international organisations can be part of its structure. However, if the only international body which can directly represent consumers is unable through lack of funds to perform this function, then this suggests that the matter needs to be addressed if the organisation is serious about involving consumers. To some extent this principle has been breached since ANEC has been invited to participate as an observer in COPOLCO. One wonders whether regional participation by consumers might not be a more satisfactory way forward. Each of the seven regional standardisation bodies could be made responsible for developing a consumer representation structure similar to ANEC and could perhaps call for financial support from the trading zones and member governments.[39]

This could be a useful mechanism for developing consumer participation in some parts of the world where it is currently less well developed. It would also have the advantage that where consumers in different regions have different concerns there would be more chance of these being voiced. There may be a drawback in that sometimes the consumer position may be confused if consumer representatives from different regions not only say different things, but also say contradictory things. There may be a role here

---

37   ANEC, *Annual Report 1995*, 20–1.

38   Julian Edwards, speaking at the ISO–COPOLCO workshop on *Consumers in Standards*, 12 May 1997, London.

39   If it is too optimistic to expect each region to create a consumer representation body, perhaps the Pacific Area Standards Congress (PASC) could be developed further. This seeks to act as a counterbalance to the European influence on international standardisation. In 1996 it had 21 members from Australia to Canada via Japan, South Africa and the United States. See G. Langmann, *A Review of the National Arrangements for Co–ordinating Consumer Representation in ISO–COPOLCO Member Countries*, background paper to ISO–COPOLCO workshop, *op. cit.*, at 12. Of course the problem of representing consumers in the less developed nations remains.

for a body such as the CI to ensure that any unnecessary misunderstandings are clarified. But if at the end of the day consumers in different parts of the world have different interests it is surely better that these are aired so that a fully informed solution can be arrived at.

A classic example of the different interests consumers might have in the level of standardisation is provided by condoms. The developed world wants very high standard to prevent not only pregnancy, but also the spread of disease. In some countries the main issue is to have affordable contraception so that it becomes common place. If this means lower standards and the occasional mishap then this may be a price worth paying.

In the final analysis international standards are voluntary and there is no obligation to accept them. They are, however, increasingly important and it is proper that all sections of the consumer body are represented in the decision–making process, even if the outcome cannot satisfy all.

4. OECD

The Organisation for Economic Co–operation and Development (OECD) was established in 1961 with the aims, *inter alia*, of contributing to an expansion in world trade, achieving the highest sustainable economic growth and a rising standard of living in member countries. Since 1969 it has had a Committee on Consumer Policy which has been active in the product safety field. In 1972 this Committee established a Working Party of Product Safety (now renamed Consumer Safety). The significance of the OECD activity is that it provides a mechanism for consultation between the members of the EC and other industrial nations. Non–EC members of the OECD include the United States, Canada, Australia, New Zealand and Japan.

The Committee on Consumer Policy has issued several reports on product safety topics, many of which have led to recommendations being made by the OECD Council to member governments. The reports contain useful factual information and the recommendations although having no binding effect have been useful in orienting the debate in favour of setting up systems of product safety regulation.

Some of the earliest reports were directed at safety problems relating to specific problems. For instance there were reports on *Consumer Protection against the Toxicity of Cosmetics and Household Products*,[40] *Safety Requirements for Toys*[41] and *Safety Requirements Concerning the*

---

[40]   (OECD, 1974).

[41]   (OECD, 1975). In 1984 a report was issued, *Measures to Protect Children*, (OECD, 1984).

Flammability of Textile Products.[42] Attention was also paid in the 1970's to how accident data relating to consumer products could be gathered with reports being published on *Data Collection Systems Related to Injuries Involving Consumer Products*[43] and *Severity Weighting of Data on Accidents Involving Consumer Products.*[44]

In the 1980's attention turned to the regulatory framework needed to protect consumers from unsafe products. Reports were issued on the *Safety of Consumer Products*[45] in general and on the particular issue of *Recall Procedures for Unsafe Products Sold to the Public*[46] with a follow up report *Product Safety – Developing and Implementing Measures.*[47] A report on *Risk Management and Cost Benefit Analysis in the Product Safety Field*[48] sought to promote greater uniformity in the management of risks in member countries.

In the 1990s the OECD committee on consumer policy has reflected the increased importance of international trade and standardisation by issuing reports on *Consumers, Product Safety Standards and International Trade*[49] and *Consumer Product Safety Standards and Conformity Assessment.*[50]

As intergovernmental documents the reports tend to be rather bland in the sense that they report rather than criticise the situation in member states. The committee has, however, been supportive of efforts to promote consumer safety by establishing data collection systems, raising standards, monitoring the market and taking action to withdraw unsafe products. In its recent reports on standardisation it has sought to encourage international trade by encouraging the greater use of international standards and mutual recognition. Although there is a recognition of the need for consumers to be involved in this process, by for example adequate representation, one also gains the impression that the committee has bought the idea that the consumer will gain most by breaking down barriers and having increased choice and competition. It notes for instance that manufacturers often view standards as mandatory even if they are formally voluntary and differences between roughly equivalent standards or conformity assessment procedures can impose added costs.[51] Of course one of the themes in the present book is

---

42   (OECD, 1977).
43   (OECD, 1978).
44   (OECD, 1979).
45   (OECD, 1980).
46   (OECD, 1981).
47   (OECD, 1987).
48   (OECD, 1983).
49   (OECD, 1991).
50   (OECD, 1996).
51   *Ibid.*, at 32–33.

that whilst the consumer does have much to gain from the liberalisation of international trade and that disguised barriers to trade should be eradicated, nevertheless care should be taken not to sacrifice consumer safety on the altar of free trade.

The OECD has also undertaken one concrete measure in the product safety field in the form of its notification system.[52] Established in 1973 this provides an early warning system and means to exchange information and to promote discussion of consumer safety issues. The system covers (i) the notification of regulations and similar measures concerning consumer product safety, (ii) notification of measures such as product bans and recalls, and (iii) product safety research. The system deals with consumer goods in a narrow sense, excluding food, drugs, motor vehicles etc., but this exclusion is treated flexibly. The information flows from and to member states through national contact points and the co–ordination is undertaken by the OECD secretariat in Paris. Over 900 notifications have been registered under the system, but there are signs that the system is being less well used now that European members have their own information exchange systems (Chapter 2, section 9J). It would be unfortunate if this informal system was lost, both because it is wider than the European based schemes and its informality could be more attractive to its users than the highly formal RAPEX system. In 1989 the system was reviewed and a report made on *The OECD Notification System on Consumer Safety Measures – Review Analysis, Suggestions for Future Action,*[53] which led to the OECD Council approving a Recommendation and Guiding Principles which set out the tasks and responsibilities of the contact points.[54]

5. UN

Several United Nation's (UN) organisations are involved with product safety matters. For example, the World Health Organisation (WHO) and the Food and Agriculture Organisation (FAO) combine to produce the Codex Alimentarius Commission which governs food standards. The WHO is also trying to establish a common system for classifying injury data so that more comparisons can be made between the various national and regional systems

---

52   See, N. Ringstedt, 'The Importance of the Administrative Co–operation in the Field of Product Safety and the Means to Improve It' in *Rapid Exchange of Information Systems on Dangers Arising from Consumer Products*, A–C Lacoste (ed.) (Centre de Droit de la Consommation, 1996) at 17–21.

53   (OECD, 1989).

54   *The OECD Notification System on Consumer Safety Measures: A User's Manual*, (OECD, 1989).

of injury data collection. The United Nations' Economic Commission for Europe is concerned with safety standards for motor vehicles.[55]

However, the bulk of the product safety work of the international organisations is related to establishing information networks so that developing countries can overcome their information deficit and make informed decisions as to whether products should be permitted to be imported.[56] This work has been most vigorous in relation to drugs with the WHO producing a *Drug Bulletin, Drug Circular* and adopting in 1973 a *Certification Scheme on the Quality of Pharmaceutical Products Moving in International Commerce.*[57] This work has been taken a stage further with the establishment of the *UN Consolidated List.* In this the WHO, FAO and United Nations Environment Program (UNEP) have come together to produce information on the regulatory status of all drugs, chemicals and pesticides. In addition to information on the regulatory status of final products there is also a need for information on the risks associated with products or their constituent elements. For chemicals and pesticides this is contained in the *International Register of Potentially Toxic Chemicals* (IRPTC).

These information systems suffer from weaknesses in that they rely on the co–operation of states and are based only on public information. They also depend upon under–funded international organisations to operate them and assume that the recipient authorities are able to make use of the information provided. From our perspective they can, however, only be viewed as models, for they do not cover consumer goods in the narrow sense with which we are concerned.

ISONET provides an information resource on standards including those for consumer products, but does not concern itself with information on specific dangerous products. Non–governmental organisations have tried to

---

55   See, *Working Party on the Construction of Vehicles – Its Role in the International Perspective,* (United Nations, 1994).

56   See, H.–W. Micklitz, *Internationales Produktsicherheitsrecht,* (Nomos, 1995) at 62–65.

57   This voluntary scheme would require drugs moving in international commerce to be accompanied by a certificate stating that they had been authorised for sale, or if not the reasons why they had not been authorised for domestic sale. The importing state would be permitted to request a batch for analysis. There are several weaknesses in the system including its voluntary nature and its failure to apply to those countries which do not require registration of drugs intended solely for export: see F. Schulberg, 'United States Export of Products Banned for Domestic Use' (1979) *Harv. Int. L. J.* 331. In more detail see U. Wassermann, 'WHO Pharmaceutical Certification Scheme' (1976) 10 *J. World Trade L.* 185.

fill this gap by establishing their own *Consumer Interpol*.[58] This seeks to publicise restrictions which have been imposed on products and also tries to provide additional information on risks to supplement the *Essential Drug List* of the WHO and the IRTPC.

Thus international organisations – with of course the notable exception of the OECD (see section 4) – understandably, tend to focus their efforts on the high risk areas of drugs, chemicals and pesticides. Some soft law rules of international law may, however, be of assistance with respect to consumer goods.

In 1985 the United Nations General Assembly adopted a set of Guidelines for consumer protection.[59] These represent an international consensus on good consumer laws and practices and are aimed primarily at encouraging law reform, particularly in developing countries. Safety features prominently in these guidelines.

Protecting consumers from hazards to their health and safety is the first listed legitimate need which the Guidelines state they are intended to meet. Section IIIA specifically deals with physical safety. It requires that governments adopt or encourage the adoption of appropriate measures to ensure that products are safe for either intended or normally foreseeable use. The possible measures suggested cover a broad category including the legal system, regulations, standards and the maintenance of safety records. Steps should also be taken to ensure that distributors do not render goods unsafe or hazardous through improper handling or storage. Consumers should be instructed in the proper use of goods and be informed of risks involved in their intended or normally foreseeable use. Wherever possible safety information should be conveyed using internally understandable symbols.

Appropriate policies should ensure that if manufacturers or distributors become aware of unforeseen hazards after products are placed on the market, they should inform the authorities and, if appropriate, the public. Governments should also consider ways of informing the public. Where a product is seriously defective and or constitutes a substantial and severe hazard, even when used properly, governments should require manufacturers and/or distributors to recall, replace or modify it or to compensate the consumer if this is not possible within a reasonable period.

---

58   Micklitz, *op. cit.*, at 64 citing Y. Domalski, *Les Interpols des Associations de Consommateurs*, (BEUC, 1984) and IOCU, *The Consumer Interpol Handbook*, (IOCU, 1983).

59   United Nations, *General Assembly – Consumer Protection*, Resolution No. 39/248 (1985). On which see D. Harland, 'Implementing the Principles of the United Nations Guidelines for Consumer Protection' (1991) 33 *J. of the Indian Law Institute* 189, on safety see especially 238–244.

Section IIIC concerning quality and safety standards is also of interest. This requires governments to promote standardisation and to encourage and ensure the availability of facilities to test and certify consumer goods. Interestingly it accepts that local economic conditions may require a local standard to be lower than the generally accepted international standard, but requires that every effort should be taken to raise that standard as soon as possible.

Section IIIF requires that consumer education and information programmes should cover product hazards. Section IIIG, concerns specific areas, notably food, water and medicines, in which safety is clearly a central issue and refers to the work of other international organisations, some of which have been discussed above.

A concrete measure taken by the United Nations was its 1982 Resolution on *Protection against Products Harmful to Health and the Environment*.[60] This imposed a two tier system of restrictions on the export of harmful products. Where products have been banned from domestic consumption and/or sale, because they have been judged to endanger health and the environment, they should only be sold abroad when a request for such goods has been received from an importing country or when the consumption of such products is officially permitted. If products have not been banned, but particular products (in particular pharmaceuticals and pesticides) have either not been approved or severe restrictions have been placed on them with respect to domestic consumption and/or sale, then the country should make available to the importing country full information on these products with a view to safeguarding the health and the environment; this should include labelling in a language acceptable to the importing country.

Thus banned products are subject to a ban on exportation (subject to exemptions); whilst severely restricted products are only subject to notification requirement. An obvious preliminary difficulty is determining which products fall within these controls. The problem of defining when something is seriously restricted may lead to arbitrary determinations. The preamble makes it clear that it is aimed at products which 'although they present a certain usefulness in special cases and/or under certain conditions, have been severely restricted in their consumption and/or sale owing to their toxic effects on health and the environment'; but the difficulty remains of deciding when restrictions are 'severe'. The notification requirement also applies where a country has not approved a product. This was apparently intended to cover new products for which the authorisation procedures had not been completed.[61] It would also cover situations where approval has

---

60   General Assembly Resolution No. 37/137 (1985).

61   This is the presumption of Harland: see D. Harland, 'Legal Aspects of the Export of Hazardous Products' (1985) 8 *J.C.P.* 209 at 231.

been requested and not granted. However, it is unclear as to whether it would apply to situations where no such request was made because the product was only ever intended for export. The stricter rules on banned products will only be effective if they also cover products which fail to comply with a safety standard or general safety obligation as well as products which have been specifically banned.

Regarding the exemptions permitting export of banned products, it might be questioned whether it is appropriate to talk of a request from an importing country. In market economies such requests are more likely to come from private entities rather than the state; Harland therefore suggests that it would be better to refer to 'approval of the importation'.[62] He also points to the ambiguity of the phraseology of the other exemption which is based on the consumption being 'officially permitted in the importing country' and comments that this should be interpreted as requiring compliance with registration provisions or safety standards, for if it meant that the sale merely had to be lawful then the control would be ineffective in those countries with little or no controls on hazardous products.[63]

One might have preferred the system of prohibition, subject to exemption, to be extended to severely restricted and non–approved products to ensure positive agreement on the part of the importing state rather than run the risk of notification being neglected by an overburdened administration. Nevertheless, the Resolution is a serious attempt to help importing countries be able to make informed decisions. However, it is only a soft law measure and therefore depends upon states' voluntary compliance. In this respect it is significant that the United States – despite having some of the most advanced controls on exports (Chapter 4, section 2L)– was the only country to vote against it. The Resolution requires importing countries to have adequate structures to control the import of hazardous products. A 1983 report by the Secretary General of the United Nations was unable to determine whether such structures existed or if they did whether they worked.[64] One can be no more confident today.[65]

---

62   *Ibid.*, at 227.

63   *Ibid.*, at 228

64   *Exchange of Information on Banned Hazardous Chemicals and Unsafe Pharmaceutical Products – Report of the Secretary–General,* (United Nations, 1983) discussed in *United Nations Yearbook 1983* at 778–779.

65   In 1989 the United Nations was still calling for more assistance to be given to developing countries to enable them to make use of the *Consolidated List:* see *General Assembly – Traffic in and Disposal, Control and Transboundary Movements of Toxic and Dangerous Products and Waste,* Resolution 44/226 (1989).

6.   CONCLUSIONS

This chapter has tried to bring together various strands of international activity relating to consumer safety regulation. Undoubtedly the most important aspects relate to the role of the WTO organisation and ISO in attempting to break down trading barriers and promoting harmonised standards. This international activity is likely to become increasingly significant. Few countries will be able to influence these processes individually and regional trading blocks will become vehicles through which influence can be exercised. In this respect the EC has a flying start over other regions as it is far more integrated and has developed a co–ordinated harmonisation and standardisation regime.

As the process of internationalisation becomes deeper, the influence of consumers becomes more difficult to exert on the standardisation process. This is primarily because there are increased costs involved in co–ordinating consumers globally and attending meetings which will be often spread around the globe. However, there are also difficult policy questions involved in reconciling the sometimes conflicting demands of consumers in different regions of the globe.

Within Europe the EC performs a regulatory role, both co–ordinating information exchanges, promoting standards and subsidising consumer participation in that process, as well as having limited powers to require action to be taken against dangerous products. There is no such equivalent body at the international level. This is understandable to some extent as the international community is not a political body in the same way as the EC is. However, there may be a role for some body, the WTO being an obvious candidate, to try to develop some of these functions as a safeguard for consumers against the dangers which might arise if trade was liberalised without there being any institutional arrangements to safeguard consumer safety.

4 United States

1. INTRODUCTION

In 1972 The United States Congress enacted the Consumer Product Safety Act (hereafter CPSA).[1] This established the Consumer Product Safety Commission (CPSC) which, *inter alia*, collects data on consumer product related accidents (see section 2C), promotes product standards (and now increasingly voluntary standards) or bans hazardous products (see section 2D), imposes reporting obligations in relation to potentially unsafe products (see section 2E), takes action against products which pose substantial product hazards (see section 2F) and imminent hazards (see section 2G) and promotes awareness of consumer safety.

The CPSA resulted from the findings and proposals of the National Commission on Product Safety.[2] The National Commission found an extraordinary high number of injuries and deaths resulting from products. For instance, it found that each year 20 million Americans were injured in the home from consumer products; this figure is particularly startling as the Commission's definition of consumer products excluded food, drugs, cosmetics, cars, insecticides, firearms, cigarettes, radiological hazards and certain flammable fabrics. Out of these 20 million injured persons, 30,000 were killed and 11,000 were permanently disabled. The national cost of product related accidents was stated to exceed $5.5 billion per annum (and that was nearly four decades ago).[3] Some commentators point out that these figures were misleading as they exceeded the amount that could be reduced by a regulatory scheme which aimed at preventing unreasonably hazardous

---

1   For a comprehensive overview of the original Act see R. Rosen, 'The Consumer Product Safety Act: A Federal Commitment to Product Safety' (1973) 48 *St. John's L.R.* 126; care should however be exercised when reading earlier material for as we shall see the Act was subject to major revisions in the Consumer Product Amendments Act of 1981 and the Consumer Product Safety Improvement Act of 1990. For the sake of simplicity references to the Act refer to sections of the United States Code (1977) (U.S.C.).

2   *Final Report*, June 1970.

3   *Ibid.*, at 1. Currently the CPSC estimate annual losses associated with consumer products at 21,400 deaths; 29,400,000 injuries (requiring hospital emergency room visits) and $200,000,000 in societal costs (mentioned by CPSC officials in correspondence with author).

products reaching consumers.[4] The clear implication being that headline grabbing figures were generated to create a climate in which the chance of legislation being enacted was increased. Others, however, have described the figures as 'conservative'.[5]

Looking at specific products the Commission discovered that, *inter alia*, (a) each year 100,000 Americans walked through glass doors, probably because they believed the space to be open,[6] (b) in 1969 10,000 television sets, mostly colour ones, caught fire,[7] (c) bicycles were estimated to be associated with one million injuries a year,[8] (d) 125,000 DIY enthusiasts were injured by power tools every year,[9] (e) power lawnmowers injured 140,000 gardeners every year,[10] and (f) each year 700,000 children were injured by toys, 500,000 by swings and 200,000 by slides.[11]

The National Commission's report was critical of existing regulatory controls. The Report damned the existing system of industry self–regulation which was described as 'chronically inadequate, both in scope and permissible levels of risk'.[12] The existing standards were said usually to fail to address themselves to all significant foreseeable hazards; gave insufficient consideration to human factors such as predictable risk, taking into account juvenile behaviour, illiteracy or inexperience; and allowed levels of exposure to electrical, thermal and mechanical exchanges which were frequently too high. Of the 44 products which were estimated as being responsible for the highest annual number of injuries, 26 were not covered by any industry wide voluntary safety standard. Consumers were found not to have any substantial voice in the standard making procedures; safety was not found to be a high priority for many businesses; the need for consensus tended to water down the proposed standard to little more than an affirmation of the status quo; many standards were out of date; the standard setting bodies were too dependent on industry financing and compliance was said to rest on 'an honor system which has proven on occasion to be less than honorable'.[13]

---

4   See, T.M. Schwartz, 'The Consumer Product Safety Commission: A Flawed Product of the Consumer Decade' (1982) 51 *Geo. Wash. L. Rev.* 32 at 36–37.

5   J.A. Brodsky and M.N. Cohen, '"Uncle Sam", the Product Safety Man: Consumer Product Safety Standards in the Marketplace and in the Courts' (1974) 2 *Hofstra L. Rev.* 619 at 633.

6   *Final Report, op. cit.*, at 12.

7   *Ibid.*, at 13.

8   *Ibid.*, at 18.

9   *Ibid.*, at 26.

10   *Ibid.*, at 29.

11   *Ibid.*, at 30.

12   *Ibid.*, at 48.

13   *Ibid.*, at 62.

The Report was equally critical of state and local regulation of products which it said:

> '– with only a few exceptions – offer consumers little or no protection from hazardous household products. In many instances, consumer product legislation may be worse than none; laws that provide only an illusion rather than the reality of protection destroy confidence in Government and in the legislative process.'[14]

State and local regulation was hampered by 'narrow scope, diffuse jurisdiction, minuscule budgets, absence of enforcement, mild sanctions and casual administration'. At the time of the Report there was only limited federal activity in the area of products outside the automobile and food, drugs and cosmetics sectors. These products were regulated under specific legislation administered by specialist agencies.

The primary motive for reforming the law was therefore to increase consumer protection, but a subsidiary goal was the 'common market' goal of ensuring product regulation does not impede inter–state trade.[15] This contrasts with Europe where creating the internal market was the prime engine for reform and product safety laws were treated as a secondary condition for securing confidence in the products circulating in the single market.

Since 1972 the CPSA has been subject to various amendments. The most significant were in 1981, when at the same time as severe budget cuts the procedures for consumer product safety rule–making were overhauled and the powers of the CPSC to enact rules were reduced in favour of an increased role for voluntary standards.[16] On the other hand the 1990

---

14   *Ibid.*, at 81.

15   This is evident from the Congress's findings which are included in the Act. After citing the goal of protecting the public from the unacceptable number of products which pose unreasonable risks because of the complexity and diversity of products and inadequate State, local and federal regulation it states 'regulation of consumer products the distribution or use of which affects interstate or foreign commerce is necessary to carry out this Act': 15 U.S.C. 2051(a).

16   It has been commented that it was unfortunate that the CPSC was one of the first agencies to face re–authorisation under the Reagan administration, see E. Klayman, 'Standard Setting Under the Consumer Product Safety Amendments of 1981 – A Shift in Regulatory Philosophy' (1982) 51 *Geo. Wash. L. Rev.* 96 at 103. This article also provides a good overview of these reforms.

Consumer Product Safety Improvement Act strengthened requirements on businesses to report potentially dangerous products to the CPSC.[17]

2.   CONSUMER PRODUCT SAFETY COMMISSION

A.   Introduction

The policy of the CPSC is formed by its Commissioners. These are persons appointed by the President with the approval of the Senate. They are political appointees, but the agency does not have a high enough profile for much controversy to be aroused when the Commissioners are announced. In fact it has been suggested that the CPSC may attract some of the less able political appointees because the agency does not have a dominant role in regulation and any weak link can be covered by policies being governed by the chairman and majority of Commissioners.[18] The CPSA provides for five Commissioners, but due to budgetary cuts this has been reduced to three. There can only be a majority of one in the political suasion of the Commissioners. Commissioners are appointed for seven year terms and the President chooses one of their number to act as Chairman of the CPSC.

The choice of a Commission rather than an executive agency was in order to give it a large degree of political independence. The choice of a Commission was adopted in the face of the Ash Report of the President's Advisory Council on Executive Organisation which favoured a single administrator to the collegial decision–making of a Commission. It reasoned that: (i) policy–making was ineffective in Commissions because of the need for agreement and that this tended to result in decisions being put off until a case forced the issue; (ii) there was a lack of accountability as responsibility was diffused between co–equal members and as the Commissioners serve for fixed terms they are insulated from Congressional and Presidential control; and (iii) Commissions lack effective management and are unable to attract and retain able personnel. However, a spirited defence of the CPSC in its early years was made by one of its Commissioners and two of his special

---

17   See, C. D. Erhardt III, 'Manufacturers of Consumer Products, Beware!' [1992] *Prod. Liab. Int.* 66 and 86.

18   K. Viscusi, *Regulating Consumer Product Safety*, (American Enterprise Institute, 1984) at 39. Viscusi is generally hostile to Commissions, but a less than complimentary description of some of the early leaders of the CPSC is also provided by D. Bollier and J. Claybrook, *Freedom from Harm*, (Public Citizen, 1986) at 171–173.

assistants.[19] They pointed to the practice of developing policy outside the boundaries of individual cases; stressed that policy initiatives could result from a wide range of sources; that there was ample room for public participation and that whilst reaching a collegiate decision may give rise to some disagreement all the public can expect is that the final policy statement reflects the majority's view of the public interest. On the question of accountability they contended that the *Ash Report* overemphasised the need for accountability to the President and pointed to various layers of accountability within the legislation and the CPSC's policy of not insulating itself from the public. They believe the issue of effective management is addressed by having a Chairman with the same broad managerial powers which an administrator would have.

Although as an independent agency reporting to Congress the CPSC is not formally subject to direct review by the Office of Management and Budget (hereafter OMB); the OMB remains responsible for its funding and has in practice shown a willingness to influence its operations – witness for instance the policy switch to favour voluntary standards (section 2D). In any event American administrative law provides significant controls over the CPSC through the courts. If anything the point could be taken that the history of CPSC is that of a new agency given novel powers to regulate a heterogeneous set of sometimes complex products and that rather than be given the freedom to learn by its mistakes (of which there were certainly some) the politicians and courts have been persuaded by lobbyists unduly to restrict its ability to protect consumers.

In practice the CPSC is divided into three functional units. One part of the agency is essentially concerned with technical matters such as identifying hazards and proposing strategies for dealing with them. It is mainly staffed by scientists, engineers, human factor specialists, statisticians and psychologists.[20] The compliance and enforcement section employs about a third of the agency's staff. Their task is to enforce standards and to identify and take steps to remedy products which present imminent or substantial product hazards. The consumer information wing of the agency is responsible for running campaigns to raise consumer awareness and for

---

19   C. Newman, J. Hermanson and J. Brodsky, 'The Consumer Product Safety Commission: Does it Can the Ash Report?' (1975) 43 *Geo. Wash. L. Rev.* 1001.

20   The Commission can appoint a Chronic Hazard Advisory Panel, consisting of seven independent experts, to advise it respecting the chronic hazards of cancer, birth defects and gene mutations associated with consumer products: 15 U.S.C. 2077. This replaced the fifteen strong Product Safety Advisory Council, which had been essentially a means of keeping the Commission appraised of industry and consumer views, but could propose product safety rules and had to be consulted before action was taken against imminently hazardous products.

publicising product recalls. The CPSC places great emphasis on the use of national television, both to inform consumers and to act as a deterrent to manufacturers. These non–legal instruments may be some of the most effective tactics of the agency.

The headquarters of the CPSC are in Bethesda, Maryland just outside Washington DC. It has three regional centres in New York (Eastern), Chicago (Central) and San Francisco (Western) and staff in 35 other cities and approximately 135 employees in the field. Each state has a designee whose job it is to liaise with the CPSC: he will usually be based in the state Attorney General's Office, the state's Health Department, or the Office of Consumer Affairs depending on the state structure. The Commission's 1997 budget provides for a staff of 480 FTEs and a total budget of $42.5 M. This of course represents very meagre resources to regulate and monitor the products in circulation in a country the size of the United States. Indeed the agency's budget was halved by the savage cuts Reagan imposed on the public administration in the early 1980's. However, when I visited the CPSC I could not help but be struck by the commitment of the highly motivated staff at the Commission. Many of the senior staff were founder members of the CPSC in 1973 and have stayed with the CPSC through good times and bad and seem genuinely to believe they are performing a worthwhile and rewarding function. Of course one may have fears that it will be difficult to recruit such well motivated staff in the future if the CPSC comes to be seen as an under–funded lame duck.

The National Commission on Product Safety had proposed there be a Consumer Safety Advocate. This was an attempt to strengthen the influence of the consumer movement on the agency. It recognised that whilst public agencies can be expected to defend the public interest, frequently in practice this involves seeking a compromise in which the stronger party (business) normally dominates the weaker party (the consumer movement). The Consumer Safety Advocate would have been able to take up complaints against the CPSC, evaluate safety standards and rules, suggest the need for new standards, issue public statements and take issue with the actions or inaction of the CPSC. Industry was duly outraged at this proposal and one industrialist described the proposed officer as 'a high–level back seat driver'.[21] The consumer activist Ralph Nader retorted that the denunciation by representatives of the industry world of the proposed officer as a 'troublemaker' and 'administrative freak' only underlined the importance of the office, which he argued should be strengthened by giving him independent

---

21   J. Edward Day of the Electronic Industries Association during the House Hearings on the proposed legislation: 92d Congress, 1st Sess., pt 3 at 858, 860 quoted in Rosen *op. cit.,* at 156.

funding and the power to conduct field investigations.[22] The proposal was eventually defeated by the combined weight of the industry lobby and the administration, who did not like to concede that it did not adequately represent the public interest. This is unfortunate for this idea promised to provide an interesting experiment at trying to improve the hitherto lamentable impact of the consumer movement on the regulatory process.

B. Jurisdiction

The CPSA gave the CPSC jurisdiction over 'consumer products' which were defined as 'any article, or component part thereof, produced or distributed (i) for sale to a consumer for use in or around a permanent or temporary household or residence, a school, in recreation, or otherwise, or (ii) for the personal use, consumption or enjoyment of a consumer in or around a permanent or temporary household or residence, a school, in recreation, or otherwise' (15 USC. 2052(a)). One controversial aspect was whether amusement parks were covered. An amendment in 1981 made it clear that CPSC jurisdiction extended to movable amusement park rides, but not fixed rides.[23]

There are, however, various express exclusions from the jurisdiction covering, *inter alia*, tobacco, motor vehicles, firearms, aircraft, boats, food, drugs and cosmetics. Thus the most dangerous consumer products are outside the CPSC's jurisdiction. This inevitably meant that its budget would be smaller than other safety regulators such as the Food and Drug Administration (FDA), Environmental Protection Agency and National Highway Traffic Safety Administration. However, it also meant it was left to deal with a very heterogeneous set of products so that communication with the relevant parties would be complicated. It was also subject to the well worn comment that its work was of potentially little value as the products it regulated caused relatively few accidents, at least accidents which were due to the products' defectiveness rather than the use to which consumers put them.[24]

Food, drugs and cosmetics are regulated by the FDA. At the time the CPSC was being proposed there was a debate as to whether a new agency should be created or increased powers should be given to the FDA. The FDA had, however, been subject to severe criticisms which included accusations

---

[22] 92d Congress, 1st Sess., pt 3 at 898 quoted in Rosen, *ibid.*

[23] For a discussion of the pre–1981 case law and criticism of the solution adopted see, E. Klayman and L. Goodman, 'CPSA Amendment: Consumers Taken for a Ride?' (1982) 32 *Case West. Res. L. Rev.* 888.

[24] Viscusi, *op. cit.*, at 33–38.

that it dealt too leniently with violators, that responsibility within the agency was too diffuse and, perhaps, most tellingly of all that it had given a low priority to regulating the safety of products other than food and drugs.[25] Thus, although there may have been some advantages from having food, drugs, cosmetics and other consumer goods dealt with by the same agency, it was finally determined to establish a new agency. The CPSC took over some of the non–food, drug and cosmetic responsibilities of the FDA and some powers were transferred from the Federal Trade Commission (FTC).[26] Thus, in addition to its powers under the CPSA it was also given responsibility for the Federal Hazardous Substances Act, the Flammable Fabrics Act, the Poison Prevention Packaging Act and the Refrigerator Safety Act. In 1990 the CPSC was given a specific authorisation under the Fire Safe Cigarette Act to investigate and propose a performance standard so that cigarettes would be less likely to ignite furniture and mattresses.

Some confusion was caused by the differences between the powers and procedures contained in the CPSA and the other Acts which the CPSC inherited. For instance, they had different rule making procedures and some of the earlier Acts had no provision for civil penalties. Many of the differences have been removed, but some remain. The CPSC has some discretion to decide whether to regulate a product under the pre–existing specific rules or to use the powers and procedures of the CPSA (15 U.S.C. 2079(d)). Even when those older acts provide the means to eliminate or reduce the risk to a sufficient extent, the CPSC can make a rule based on the public interest to permit it to regulate the matter under the CPSA; and *a fortiori* this is possible where those Acts are inadequate. Certainly the means are provided for the CPSC to use the legislation which best promotes consumer protection.[27] This is more flexible than the approach adopted in Europe, where general product safety legislation is generally viewed as subsidiary to specific legislation (Chapter 2, section 9C).

---

25   See Rosen, *op. cit.*, at 131.

26   The FTC continues to play a role in product safety by using its powers to deal with unfairness, deception and advertising substantiation to control safety claims and even to require information be provided: for a survey see R. Petty, 'Regulating Product Safety: The Informational Role of the US Federal Trade Commission' (1995) 18 *J.C.P.* 387. Petty suggests that the FTC has concentrated on information provided before purchase, and that whilst this is useful great benefits could also be derived from the FTC expanding its role of providing information during product use. He also suggests that this is an area which the FTC have neglected.

27   At least in the early years it seemed to be using this power to relatively good effect: see Note (by V. Schuman), 'Section 30(d) Determinations: the CPSC's Choice of Law in Product Safety Regulation' (1975) *Geo. Wash. L. Rev.* 1211.

Jurisdiction under the old statutes can also be used as a means of regulating products not covered by the CPSA. For instance the Hazardous Substances Act does not exclude motor vehicles and their equipment: thus whilst the CPSC has no direct power to control infant car seats it might treat the small parts on them as being hazardous substances.

It should be noted that the scope of the CPSC's jurisdiction is limited to products. As the line between products and services is an overlapping and somewhat artificial one to draw, it is a perhaps a pity that the CPSC does not include services within its jurisdiction.

C. Injury Data

The CPSA charges the CPSC with the task of maintaining an *Injury Information Clearing House* to collect, investigate, analyse and disseminate injury data and information relating to the causes and prevention of death, injury and illness associated with consumer products. The amount of statistical and empirical information the CPSC collects on product related accidents is remarkable and can only be held up as a model which other countries or international bodies should strive to emulate. It was the inspiration for the national systems which started to develop within Europe, such as the United Kingdom's HASS system (Chapter 5, section 2). Ideally Europe should develop its own fully integrated system (Chapter 2, section 8) and the data from the two systems be made comparable.[28]

The information generated is invaluable to the CPSC in undertaking its work. The CPSC adopts what is termed 'risk based decision–making' to determine its priorities and the data the agency collects is viewed as an essential pre–requisite to that process of prioritisation. However, the limitations of this data need to be understood. Even in the United States where the systems are best developed the data is collected from a rather small sample base. The data is also rather bland. Knowledge that a product was involved in an accident does not mean that it was to blame for it. Only a limited number of follow up studies can be undertaken to investigate accidents in more detail. Attempts to rank products based on the frequency and severity of the injuries they cause and nature of their victims (eg special concern for children) are bound to be controversial and open to challenge on the basis of their subjectivity. Yet the United States data collection system is

---

28   We have noted that the WHO is attempting to produce a common classification system: (Chapter 2, section 5). Cultural differences will mean that data from one country must be used with care when considering it in the context of another country, although the US/Europe in many respects provides a fairly homogenous consumer market.

a useful regulatory tool, so long as the expectations of what can be done with the data it generates are not set too high (Chapter 1, section 2).

(i)   National Electronic Injury Surveillance System (NEISS)[29]

The centre–piece of the CPSC's injury data collection systems is NEISS. The origin of NEISS lies with the National Commission on Product Safety, which established a Hospital Emergency Room Reporting System (HERIS) in fourteen hospitals. Reporting was accomplished by means of sending pre-coded data by keying touch tone telephones. When the National Commission on Product Safety was terminated in 1970 the HERIS system was transferred to the FDA. The FDA operated it in parallel with its own National Injury Surveillance Scheme (NISS) which drew upon 130 hospital emergency rooms, but had practical drawbacks in that there were delays in receiving the mailed in reports and paper jams in the automatic feeding equipment and it also lacked an investigative and follow–back capability.

The present NEISS system covers 101 hospital emergency rooms. It had originally been intended to cover 130 hospitals, but budgetary limitations meant this figure was never reached. At the height of the cuts in the early 1980s the sample size had been reduced to 62 hospitals, but this rose under an agreed plan to 91 in 1991 and in 1997 was further increased to 101. The sample is intended to be representative of hospitals with emergency departments, drawing on information reflecting type and size of hospitals. The identity of the hospitals in the sample can change over time, but most states are represented. There is no NEISS–contracted hospitals in Kentucky, which actually established its own small scale NEISS–type project.

The NEISS system provides information on all product related injuries seen in hospital emergency rooms on a daily basis. During the 1980s the number of reported instances varied between 147,000–200,000 depending largely upon how many hospitals were in the sample each year. Each hospital has someone designated as a NEISS coder. At the end of each day[30] the coder screens the medical records of the patients who have been treated in the emergency room for 'in scope' cases. The coder abstracts information for up to 14 variables including date of treatment, record number, age, sex, injury diagnosis, body part injured, disposition of case eg if hospitalised, location of accident, whether fire or a motor vehicle involved, whether accident work–related and a brief description of the incident. The coder uses a NEISS

---

29   See, *The National Electronic Injury Surveillance System: A Description of its Role in the US Consumer Product Safety Commission*, document produced by the Division of Hazard and Injury Data Systems of the CPSC (March, 1990) .

30   Weekend cases are dealt with on Mondays.

coding manual, which includes about 900 product codes, to identify the product involved. There is also a verbatim report from the emergency room, which usually describes what the patient was doing when the accident occurred. This information is placed on a coding sheet on a personnel computer at the hospital. The computer checks the codes as the information is entered. The data is collected by the CPSC overnight by telephone hook up. The information is then ready for immediate use, but staff will check illogical codings with the coder.

The CPSC's contract with participating hospitals allows for up to six special studies each year. These studies allow additional cases or additional information to be collected. Examples of such studies have included examinations of fireworks injuries and prescription drug ingestion among young children to identify the type of containers involved.

Less than 1% of NEISS cases are selected for follow–back investigation. Usually this simply involves a trained investigator conducting a telephone interview, in fewer than 10% of such cases are further details required which necessitate on–site follow–back investigations: these might for instance involve the taking of photographs.

Data collected in hospital emergency rooms has the important advantage of timeliness. 90% of all emergency room data is collected within 72 hours and it is therefore possible to speak with the accident victim, parent or witness within a week of the accident at a time when the occurrence is still relatively fresh in their memory. The NEISS data does not, however, represent all product–related injuries. By virtue of the nature of the source of information the data will tend to overemphasise severe cases, as those who are only injured in a minor way by a consumer product will not tend to go to hospital for treatment. Equally the NEISS system will not cover all deaths, for those killed at the scene of an incident will tend to go straight to the morgue by–passing the emergency room. Also many accidents caused by fire will not be reported as they will often cause a lot of economic loss, but not necessarily any personal injury. The CPSC has other systems which attempt to plug these information gaps. These, however, tend to concentrate on more serious consequences and hence under–report minor incidents. Details of other sources of information are maintained on the Injury or Potential Injury Incident Data Base (IPII).[31]

The United States has a system to grade cases generated by the NEISS system by severity.[32] Its Hazard Index tries to rank injuries in terms of their

---

[31] See, *A Description of the Injury or Potential Injury Incident Data Base (IPII)*, produced by the Division of Hazard and Injury Data Systems of the CPSC (December, 1989).

[32] See, OECD, *Severity Weighting of Data on Accidents Involving Consumer Products*, (OECD, 1979) at 11–18 and appendices A–C.

frequency, severity, life threat and the vulnerability of children. It produces a ranking of products which, although based on subjective assumptions, at least gives some guidance as to where attention should be focused. The CPSC has tried to back this up with an Injury Cost Procedure which produces more objective assessments of the costs related to particular injuries.

(ii)   Medical Examiner and Coroners Alert Project (MECAP)[33]

Each state has either a medical examiner or coroner who investigates the cause of death in unusual circumstances. The CPSC recognised these people as being a potential source of good information and in 1976 established a pilot project involving 75 coroner/medical examiners. There are now currently 2,600 coroners and medical examiners on the mailing list of the CPSC. They are requested to notify the CPSC immediately of product related deaths, particularly those involving suspected defective products. In order to encourage awareness of, and participation in, the system the CPSC sends a monthly newsletter to all such officials on their mailing list. Although there is clearly a lot of under–reporting, as the system only generates about 2,000 reports each year, the cases are very useful in terms of what they can tell the CPSC about dangerous products. The cases are in a sense pre–screened since they all involve a product related fatality and the medical examiners/coroners only tend to forward cases which they believe will interest the CPSC. About 15% of these cases merit further investigation and an advantage of this system is that investigators can get to the scene of the accident fairly quickly, often before the product is removed and destroyed.

(iii)   Death Certificates[34]

The CPSC purchases death certificates from 52 health jurisdictions (the 50 states, the District of Columbia and New York City). It only purchases certificates which fall within specified external cause of death (E code) categories. The E codes purchased are those which specify products under the jurisdiction of the CPSC as the cause of death, or those for which consumer product involvement is likely to be described on the certificate, such as deaths resulting from electrocution, burns and falls. The selection of

---

[33]   See, *ibid.*, at 8–9.

[34]   See, *A Description of the Death Certificate Project and its Data Files*, document produced by the Division of Hazard and Injury Data Systems of the CPSC (April, 1990).

E codes in any given year will depend upon the resources available to the agency. Although this system gives good coverage of product related deaths it has some major limitations. There is frequently considerable delay before the states forward the information to the CPSC and the death certificates only include very general information.

(iv) Consumer Complaints[35]

Almost 19,000 consumer complaints were received by the CPSC in 1996. 33% of complaints were received through the CPSC's toll–free Hotline. The Hotline serves both as a means of receiving complaints and providing information on general product safety and product recalls. Other complaints are received through the CPSC's regional offices, or come into the headquarters, particularly via the Congressional Relations Office.

(v) News Clippings

The CPSC's regional offices contract with news clipping services to cover all daily, Sunday and weekly newspapers published in their states. The services collect clippings related to any reported deaths, injuries and 'near misses' which involve products under the CPSC's jurisdiction. The CPSC also receives news clippings from other organisation, such as the voluntary standard setting body, the Underwriters' Laboratories. The CPSC received about 6,000 news clippings in 1996.

(vi) Government Agencies

Information has also been collected on product–related injuries or potential injuries reported to the CPSC from federal, state or local agencies. For instance, in 1987 609 reports came from the National Fire Reporting System and in 1989 42 reports on all–terrain vehicles were received from the National Highway Traffic Administration.

(vii) Follow–back Investigations

It is interesting to note the time–scale in which in–depth follow–back investigations are undertaken. The times are typically longer for non–NEISS

---

35   See, *(IPII), op. cit.*, at 7.

sources, since victims' addresses/telephone numbers are usually easier to retrieve from hospital emergency room records than from newspapers and other such sources. For non–on–site investigations the time lag between assignment and final completion is 22 days for NEISS and 54 days for non–NEISS investigations. For on–site investigations, the average time lag is 52 days for non–NEISS investigations directly assigned as on–site visits. For NEISS investigations re–assigned for an on–site visit, following a telephone interview, the time lag averaged 65 days. These long time lags reflect the difficulty of regional office personnel scheduling their time and co–ordinating this with the schedule of the family of the victim and the time it takes to travel to the site, write up reports, evaluate the material and enter it on the computer.[36]

D.   Standards

(i)   Mandatory Standards

We shall see that the role of mandatory standards has been much less significant than was initially anticipated. This has been the result of a combination of both the CPSC realising that rule–making is a more complex process than had been imagined – possibly difficulties were accentuated by the procedures the CPSC had to adopt, which in their original form were over complex – and a change in regulatory emphasis in favour of deregulation and an enthusiasm for voluntary self–regulation. We will set out the current powers of the CPSC, but just as importantly comment on some of the novel features which have been abandoned. In essence the conclusion must be that whilst some of the original features ought to have been modified or abandoned the nature of the reforms amount to throwing the baby out with the bath water and not enough time was given for the CPSC to learn from its experiences.

(a)   Powers

The CPSC uses a risk based decision–making approach. This essentially means using information collected through the NEISS and IPII data bases to determine priorities, for, *inter alia*, creating and amending standards. In addition interested persons are permitted to petition for the issuance, amendment or repeal of a rule (5 U.S.C. 553(e)).

---

[36]   See, *A Description of the Indepth Investigation Data Base*, document produced by the Division of Hazard and Injury Data Systems (January, 1992) at 12–13.

The CPSC can promulgate consumer product safety standards which relate either to performance requirements or requirements that consumer products be marked with or accompanied by clear and adequate warnings or instructions or requirements respecting the form of warnings or instructions (15 U.S.C. 2056(a)). Any such requirement must be reasonably necessary to prevent or reduce an unreasonable risk of injury (15 U.S.C. 2056(a)). Risk of injury means risk of death, personal injury or serious or frequent illness (15 U.S.C. 2052(a)(3)). Where no feasible consumer product safety standard issued under the Act can adequately protect the public from unreasonable risk of injury associated with the product, a rule may be promulgated banning such hazardous products (15 U.S.C. 2057).

There is an understandable desire to prefer performance standards to design standards (see Chapter 1, section 3E(ii)). They encourage innovation and diversity, whilst design standards tend to restrict choice and freeze the state of the art. The original Act had sought to promote performance standards by requiring the CPSC to use them wherever feasible. The 1981 amendments removed the possibility of enacting design standards. In fact the CPSC had been cautious in its use of design standards and had included design specifications in only two of the seven mandatory standards it had enacted. Removing the discretion to use design specifications was perhaps therefore both unnecessary and potentially harmful, if it led to the CPSC being forced to use more frequently its powers to ban products or to seek notification and remedial action. It would also be unfortunate if litigation occurred over whether a standard related to performance or design.[37]

(b) Procedures

It is worth considering the procedures for rule making on mandatory standards in some detail. The detailed procedures illustrate the need for the CPSC's impressive data collection systems, which provide data to support the regulations. They provide a further incentive for the agency to go down the voluntary route, so as to avoid these burdensome procedures.[38] It also

---

[37] Klayman, *op. cit.*, at 104–108. Klayman suggests that, in theory, performance standards can be distinguished from design standards, as performance standards need a test to determine compliance, whilst compliance with design standards can be assessed by visual or tactile inspection. However, he demonstrates how this can break down in practice by reference to the standard for swimming pool edges. This requires them to be designed so that they do not cut human tissue. This is a performance standard, but could also be seen as a design standard as it requires the slide to be designed without any protruding or rough edges.

[38] The procedures are laid down in 15 U.S.C. 2058.

explains why, for a time, the agency favoured bans rather than standards. Schwartz comments that bans could be made to resemble standards; for instance she cites a ban on bicycles which did not meet specified safety standards.[39] However, the incentive to adopt this approach was curtailed when the 1981 amendments made the procedures for bans identical to those for standard–setting. This partly explains why the CPSC has switched its attention to its powers requiring notification and providing for remedial action.

It will be noticed that the procedures demonstrate a preference for voluntary rather than mandatory standards and place a significant burden on the CPSC if it is to adopt mandatory standards. This emphasis on the voluntary approach was a result of the Consumer Product Safety Amendments Act 1981. This change in the legislation can be considered as having been unnecessary as the CPSC had shown itself to be reasonably patient with industry attempts at self regulation. It was also dangerous in the sense that industry lost an incentive to produce voluntary standards, was given opportunities to engage in dilatory tactics and 'weakened the agency in image as well as in practice'.[40]

The procedure for promulgating a consumer product safety rule[41] commences by publication in the Federal Register of an *advanced notice of proposed rule–making*. This must:

(1)   identify the product and the nature of the risk associated with the product,
(2)   include a summary of each of the regulatory alternatives under consideration, including voluntary consumer product safety standards,
(3)   provide information on any relevant existing standard, with summary reasons why it is believed not to eliminate or adequately reduce the risk of injury,
(4)   invite comments on the risk of injury, regulatory alternatives being considered and other possible alternatives,
(5)   invite persons to submit an existing standard or portion of a standard as a proposed consumer product safety standard or to state their intention to modify or develop a voluntary consumer product safety standard to address the risk of injury.

---

[39]   Schwartz, *op. cit.*, at 68. The bicycle rule was actually made under the Federal Hazardous Substances Act which requires the CPSC to issue a ban.

[40]   Klayman, *op. cit.*, at 99–103, quote at 103.

[41]   A consumer product safety rule is a consumer safety standard or a rule declaring a consumer product a banned hazardous product: 15 U.S.C. 2052(2).

If the CPSC accepts that the risk of injury can be eliminated or adequately reduced by a voluntary standard proposed under the above procedure and that it is reasonable to assume users will conform to the standard, then it must terminate the procedure for promulgating a consumer product safety rule. Before doing so it must allow interested persons (including manufacturers, consumers and consumer organisations) a reasonable opportunity to submit written comments regarding the standard. The CPSC must devise procedures to monitor compliance with the voluntary standards which it has relied upon or in whose development it has participated or monitored.

Should the CPSC prefer to continue towards promulgating a rule it must publish in the Federal Register, not less than 60 days after the original notice, the text of the proposed rule, any alternatives and a preliminary regulatory analysis. The preliminary regulatory analysis requires:

(1) preliminary cost/benefit analysis, including matters which cannot be expressed in monetary terms, and identification of those who will benefit and those who will bear the costs,
(2) reasons why any standard or voluntary standard proposed following the notice are not acceptable,
(3) description of any reasonable alternatives to the proposed rule together with a summary of their potential costs and benefits and explanation why they should not be promulgated.

This is then sent to the Senate Committee on Commerce, Science and Transportation and the House of Representatives' Committee on Energy and Commerce.

Within 60 days of the preliminary regulatory analysis the CPSC must either promulgate a consumer product safety rule or withdraw the notice of proposed rule–making. Before promulgating the rule the Commission must make findings on the following matters for inclusion in the rule:

(1) the degree and nature of risk of injury the rule is designed to eliminate or reduce,
(2) the approximate number of consumer products, or types or classes of products, subject to the rule,
(3) the public need for the product proposed to be regulated and the nature and effect of the rule on the utility, cost or availability of such products,
(4) any means of achieving the objective whilst minimising adverse effects on competition or disruption or dislocation of manufacturing or other commercial practices consistent with the public health and safety.

The rule must also comply with the Administrative Procedure Act (hereafter APA) (5 U.S.C. 553). This requires a notice to be placed in the Federal Register including a statement of the time, place and nature of public rule–making proceedings; reference to the legal authority under which the rule is proposed and either the terms or substance of the proposed rule or a description of the subjects and issues involved. The APA then provides for the right of interested persons to make written submissions: the CPSA extends this to allow for the oral presentation of data, views or arguments. The CPSC must incorporate into the rule a general concise statement of the basis and purpose of the rule. The rule must be published 30 days before it comes into effect. The CPSA provides that the rule must express the risk it is intended to eliminate or reduce. It also requires that the CPSC considers relevant product data and in particular takes account of the special needs of the elderly and handicapped. It is perhaps strange that the CPSA does not particularly mention the needs of children, given that the CPSC spends a great deal of time on the particular problems consumer products pose for children. The CPSC must publish with the rule a final regulatory analysis, which must again consider the costs/benefits of regulation, describe the alternatives and summarise the public comments made and the CPSC's assessment of them.

As if to emphasis the last resort nature of mandatory rule–making the CPSC must find and include in the rule findings that:

(1) the rule, including its effective date, is reasonably necessary to eliminate or reduce an unreasonable risk of injury associated with the product,
(2) the rule is in the public interest,
(3) where the rule bans the product, that no consumer product safety standard would adequately protect the public,
(4) a voluntary standard was not suitable as it was either unlikely to eliminate or adequately reduce the risk of injury or there was unlikely to be substantial compliance with the voluntary standard,
(5) the benefits bear a reasonable relationship to the cost,
(6) the rule imposes the least burdensome requirement which prevents or adequately reduces the risk of injury.

The rule must be effective not less than 30 days or more than 180 days after promulgation, unless there is good cause for there to be an earlier effective date. The standard is only applicable to products manufactured after the effective date, but there are provisions to prevent stock–piling. The Commission has the power to amend or revoke rules.

Once a consumer product safety rule has been promulgated there are 60 days for any person adversely affected or any consumer or consumer organisation to petition the courts for judicial review of the rule. The standard of review is that based on 'substantial evidence on the record as a whole'.[42]

In a further move to weaken the powers of the CPSC a congressional veto on consumer product safety rules was introduced in 1981 (15 U.S.C. 2083). This requires that rules be transmitted to the Senate and House of Representatives and effectively gives 90 days in which both houses can agree that a rule shall not take effect. This is a perhaps mainly symbolic weakening of the authority of the CPSC. In fact there is some doubt as to its constitutionality and the power has never been used. However, in 1996 Congress passed a law applicable to all federal agencies providing a procedure for Congressional review of regulations.

(c) Conformity Assessment

Manufacturers or private labellers[43] must issue a certificate that the product conforms to relevant consumer product safety standards. The certificate should accompany the product or otherwise be furnished to the distributor or retailer. The certificate must be based on testing, which can be prescribed by the CPSC, who can also prescribe the form and content of labels specifying compliance with safety standards (15 U.S.C. 2063). The testing can be conducted by an independent third party, but this is at the option of the certificator and there is no compulsion. This contrasts with the position in Europe, where although self certification is the preferred option, third party certification is sometimes required. Also the addressee of the certificate differs between the United States and Europe. In Europe the CE marking is aimed at enforcement officers and indirectly the public, whereas in the United States it is for the benefit of the other links in the distribution chain.

In the United States controversy has surrounded the issue of whether each individual product has to be tested or whether sample tests can be used. In 1976 the CPSA had been amended to prohibit sample testing, but this prohibition was repealed in 1981. The CPSA now provides that the certificate should be based on 'a test of each product or upon a reasonable testing programme' and the CPSC may prescribe rules as to what is a reasonable testing programme. The concept of sample tests in itself ought to be relatively uncontroversial with the assessment being made with respect to each particular type of product as to whether it is appropriate or whether individual testing should be required. The complication in the United States context results from how it interacts with the rules on liability under the

---

42   *AquaSlide 'N' Dive Corpn. v Consumer Product Safety Commission* 569 F. 2d 831 (5th Cir 1978) (CA).

43   Ie the owners of brand or trade marks.

CPSA.[44] We shall see in section H that the CPSA renders it unlawful to distribute or manufacture any consumer product not in conformity with a mandatory standard. If a product is in non–conformity but was not discovered because a sample test was used then although it could be argued that the manufacturer knowingly distributed it, it is at least arguable that it conformed to the mandatory standard if this is construed to apply to a product class.[45] One would hope that these arguments could be overcome by judicial interpretation which favours consumer protection, but in any event a party who had received the certificate based on sample testing would have immunity unless he knew that the particular product did not conform (15 U.S.C. 2068(b)).

(d)   Abandoned Features

Petitioning process
A victim of the 1981 overhaul of rule–making procedures was the provision in the original CPSA granting the right to petition the CPSC. This had been a novel and potentially powerful procedure whereby any interested person, including a consumer or consumer organisation, dissatisfied with any action or inaction on the part of the CPSC could petition the CPSC. The agency then had 120 days to respond and if the petition was denied reasons had to be given. The petitioner could then seek a judicial hearing where if it was demonstrated by a preponderance of evidence that the product presented an unreasonable risk of injury and that the CPSC's failure to act unreasonably exposed the petitioner or other consumers to a risk of injury the court had to order the CPSC to take the action requested by the petitioner.

The aim of this provision was clearly to prevent bureaucratic inertia setting in. However, fears that the power to seek judicial review would lead to too much interference in the CPSC explained why the implementation of this provisions was delayed until three years after the enactment of the legislation. In fact this breathing space was, perhaps unwisely, not taken advantage of by the CPSC who actively encouraged petitions. During its first three years it received 203 petitions, 51 under the CPSA. The petitions became a major influence in establishing the CPSC's priorities. This was perhaps unfortunate, for an agency, especially one with a limited budget and broad coverage needs to prioritise its resources with care; yet the initiatives it undertook were not necessarily those revealing the most serious risks on the CPSC's Consumer Product Hazard Index. Schwartz explained the CPSC's over reliance on petitions as due to its belief that it had to grant any petition

---

44   Klayman, *op. cit.*, at 18–19.
45   *Ibid.*, at 19.

presenting an 'unreasonable risk of injury' even if other priorities were more compelling; inexperience in judging what constituted an 'unreasonable risk' and under estimation of the burden involved in the standards–making procedure.[46] It was anticipating initiating forty proceedings a year: on this basis responding to petitions was no big deal. This was a serious under estimation of the complexity of the issues involved in enacting consumer safety regulation.

Neither should it be thought that the petitioning process was solely a means for giving consumers a greater voice. The majority of petitions were from industry seeking exemptions, harmonised standards or to prevent a product ban.

The CPSC was soon finding that there was a back log of petitions which were not being dealt with within the 120 day period. It introduced management procedures to reduce this by screening out letters and enquiries which were not strictly petitions and requiring petitioners to demonstrate the need for a standard or ban.

The petitioning process is now dealt with under the general rules of the Administrative Procedure Act (APA). The 120 day deadline is removed, but the management changes outlined above now mean that this is not a serious problem. Judicial review of petition denials can now only be on the arbitrary and capricious basis. The CPSC had in fact paid less attention to petitions in any event. This is quite right. Petitions are a useful means for informing and influencing CPSC strategy, but they should not dominate it. Indeed petitions remain useful in alerting the Commission to risks earlier than they might otherwise become aware of them, and have been used as evidence to encourage the upgrading of voluntary standards.[47]

Offeror procedure
Prior to 1981 the offeror procedure had been the centre–piece of the CPSA.[48] Under this procedure the CPSC would as a first stage, when it determined that a mandatory standard was required, issue a Notice of Proceedings. The notice sought offers to develop a standard from non–CPSC entities. Offerors could be individuals, consumer groups, state or federal agencies, standards bodies, trade associations, manufacturers, distributors or retailers. If a self–interested offeror was selected the CPSC could simultaneously develop its own standard, but this option was never taken. On receiving the offeror's submission the CPSC had 60 days in which to decide

46   Schwartz, *op. cit.*, at 47.
47   Schwartz, *op. cit.*, at 54.
48   See A. Scalia and F. Goodman, 'Procedural Aspects of the Consumer Product Safety Act' (1973) 20 U.C.L.A. 899.

whether to terminate the procedure or to propose a standard. If the latter course was taken then procedures based on the informal rule–making procedures of the APA applied.

In order to allow consumer groups the chance to be involved in the offeror process the CPSC was allowed to contribute towards the costs of the offeror. In total $666,300 was paid to offerors, the vast majority to consumer organisations. The Consumers Union (CU) received $250,924 for the lawn mower rule and the National Consumers League (NCL) $196,811 for the miniature Christmas tree light standard.[49] CU was still only partially reimbursed for the costs it incurred in developing the standard and indicated that it would probably not be an offeror in the future. Failure of the CPSC to agree to cover more than out of pocket expenses had caused it not to accept NCL's tender to be the offeror with respect to architectural glass.[50] It is difficult to assess how well the consumer groups performed as offerors and it would be wrong to judge the policy on these isolated case studies, especially when the procedures were in their infancy. However, it is noteworthy that the CU's efforts in relation to lawn mowers has been described by an academic observer as 'creditable' (and this in the context of a highly complicated standard in relation to which the CPSC made several mistakes) and the NCL seems to have been widely praised.[51] This is interesting for it suggests that consumers as well as industry are capable of taking the lead in developing standards. The crucial question is of course funding. Whilst it might be unrealistic to expect consumer groups to become the main standards writers it does suggest that they are capable of more than a mere consultative role.

As well as acting as offerors, consumer groups could also be involved in the development of standards by other offerors, as these were required to provide opportunities for the involvement of interested parties. The CPSA was silent on the power of the CPSC to fund such participation, but in the 1970s it had an active programme of funding such initiatives. The post–1981 procedure does allow the CPSC to compensate those who help the agency develop compulsory standards (15 U.S.C. 2056(c)), but apparently budget restraints have prevented it from doing so.[52] In two articles Tobias has considered the role of public funded experts in CPSC procedures, both under

---

49   Schwartz, *op. cit.*, at 64.

50   See, Note, 'Inside the Proposed Standard for Architectural Glass: An Outward Look at Consumer Participation in the CPSA's Offeror Process' (1975) 43 Geo. Was. L. Rev. 1078. The CPSC agreed to pay other costs, such as lost wages, in only one initiative (when the NCL acted as offeror for miniature Christmas tree lights).

51   C. Tobias, 'Early Alternative Dispute Resolution in a Federal Administrative Agency Context: Experimentation with the Offeror Process at the Consumer Product Safety Commission' (1987) 44 *Washington and Lee Law Review* 409 at 433 and 453–458.

52   Tobias, *ibid.*, at 413.

the offeror process and otherwise.[53] His conclusion is that experiences have been mixed, but that citizen involvement has been sufficiently worthwhile to suggest that continued experimentation is desirable. This is certainly correct. Consumers need to be involved in the standardisation process. The formal right to be involved in matters of consumer concern identified by the CPSC is to be welcomed, but will be empty rhetoric if consumer organisations do not have the financial resources to take advantage of that privilege.

However, the CPSC model was one based on the agency deciding when and what type of consumer input was needed into the process. This approach seems to impliedly be approved by Tobias, although he criticised the CPSC for sometimes mismatching their needs with participant competence.[54] However, whilst it might be efficient for the CPSC to direct consumer involvement it should be recognised that consumers should be given the freedom to determine how they conduct and prioritise their involvement in standardisation.

The United States might wish to consider establishing a body equivalent to ANEC (Chapter 2, section 6D). This could be an umbrella group of consumer organisations interested in standardisation which was financed by the CPSC or other Government departments and those standards bodies involved in the development of standards for consumer products. This body could then determine which products it should prioritise and whether influence should be exerted on the standards bodies or the CPSC.

The offeror process was widely considered to be a failure.[55] In large measure this was due to the inexperience of the CPSC and the offerors in handling the procedures.[56] Certainly the process was far longer than anticipated (and mandated) due to the time allowed for public participation and the need for CPSC to develop its own approach to the subject and to negotiate with the offeror. Even when concluded, the standards were frequently subject to appeals to courts, amendments due to subsequent petitions and even in the case of lawn mowers to congressional amendment after the courts had upheld the standard. The process has, however, been held up as a valiant attempt to democratise the rule–making process. In fact,

---

53 Tobias, *ibid.*, and C. Tobias, 'Great Expectations and Mismatched Compensation: Government Sponsored Public Participation in Proceedings of the Consumer Product Safety Commission' (1986) 64 *Washington Univ. L.Q.* 1101.

54 Tobias (1986), *ibid.*, at 1161. He cited lay consumers being reimbursed where technical input was needed.

55 Tobias (1987), *ibid.*, provides case studies of the seven occasions on which it was used.

56 See Schwartz, *op. cit.*, at 62–68, who suggests projects were badly managed, were too ambitious, worked upon against a background of inadequate data and gave rise to extended periods for public participation.

although the CPSC tried to ensure that consumers could take advantage of the public participation requirement, it was in fact business interests who were organised and financially equipped to take advantage of them.[57] In retrospect it may have been wiser to have had the offeror procedure as an option for the CPSC to invoke on suitable occasions rather than as a mandatory procedure, no matter how complex the issue at stake.[58] What is needed is a procedure under which the CPSC allows the conflicting opinions to be aired and a satisfactory solution for consumer protection derived at. At least the offeror process attempted to reach that goal; the present emphasis on voluntary standards is less promising.

One criticism of mandatory rule–making is that they can soon become out of date and are less easy to amend than voluntary standards. This problem is illustrated by the Standard for the Flammability of Clothing Textiles.[59] This mandates the use of a soap which is not readily available and a dry–cleaning solution which has been found to be carcinogenic and is now strictly controlled. Empirical investigation is needed to determine whether such mistakes are more common in mandatory than voluntary standards. They are of course more serious when found in mandatory regulation, since they may prevent manufacturers from developing better practices or expose manufacturers to the theoretical risk of prosecution for a technical breach of regulation it was impossible for them to have complied with.

(ii)   Voluntary Standards

(a)   The Move to Voluntarism

During the 1980s the CPSC became subject to the Reaganite–deregulation tendency and the emphasis switched from mandatory rule–making towards using voluntary standards wherever possible. This preference for voluntary standards is mandated by the CPSA, which as we have noted in its revised post–1981 form only permits a mandatory standard where compliance with any existing voluntary standard is not likely to result in the elimination or adequate reduction of the risk of injury or it is unlikely that there will be substantial compliance with such standard (15 U.S.C. 2058(f)(3)(d)). Also the President's OMB's Circular A–119 (as amended) and the National Technology Transfer and Advancement Act of 1995, s. 12(d) encourage the

---

57   Schwartz, *ibid.*, at 75.
58   Schwartz, *op. cit.*, at 68.
59   16 Code of Federal Regulations §1610.

involvement of agencies in voluntary standard making procedures wherever possible.

(b) The Pros and Cons of Voluntary Standards

Is this switch to favouring voluntary standards desirable? The National Commission on Product Safety had of course found voluntary standards 'chronically inadequate, both in scope and permissible levels of risk' and criticised the lack of consumer input into the standards–making process.[60] Naturally the quality of standards and the associated issue of consumer representation can be improved, although we shall see that this has not been the case to any significant extent at least with respect to consumer representation. In part this is because in the United States standards–making has not been integrated into the legislative framework so that the best features of both can be married together as has at least been attempted in the EC (Chapter 2, section 4C). Where voluntary standards exist in the United States, they are not fleshing out standards which are set by democratically legitimated legislative processes, but instead reflect the outcome of an often industry dominated consensus based standards–making procedure.

The consensus principle is a key feature of standardisation, as it is important that voluntary standards become widely accepted. There are no hard or fast rules as what amounts to consensus but generally it requires between two–thirds or four–fifths approval.[61] One of the first CPSC Commissioners opined that it would be 'very unlikely that an existing voluntary standard would be appropriately made mandatory... if the standard was developed by a consensual method, its principal feature was that it was acceptable to every body, not that it reflected the best that was available, even within the existing state of the art'.[62]

Nevertheless, in truth the legislative and political impetus to move towards voluntary standards did not affect the CPSC's approach greatly as it had already moved in that direction of its own volition. It had discovered that its rule–making procedures were cumbersome and the task of creating standards more complex than it had anticipated. Thus a partnership between the CPSC and the voluntary standards bodies would have been a sensible way forward. The problem with the 1981 reforms was that they provided no mechanisms through which the CPSC or consumers could directly influence the work of the standards bodies. There is also the danger that industry will be less co–operative in adopting voluntary standards given that the CPSC is

---

60   Final Report, *op. cit.*, at Chapter 4.

61   *Ibid.*, at 52.

62   Commissioner **Lawrence Kushner**, quoted in Brodsky and Cohen, *op. cit.*, at 638.

now required to use its rule–making powers as a last resort. However, one also suspects that the CPSC's budget cuts are likely to have been as great a curb on the effectiveness of the CPSC's negotiations with industry.

(c)   CPSC and Voluntary Standards

The CPSC now works on 8–14 mandatory standards per year and 40–50 voluntary standards. In an interesting twist, recently, the cigarette lighter industry, when subjected to the inevitability of standards being imposed for child–resistant cigarette lighters, actually requested a mandatory rather than a voluntary standard. They wanted to ensure the standard would be enforced against all participants in the marketplace and also preferred the uniformity and certainty of federal legislation to state involvement. This could be achieved by federal legislation since it is pre–emptive: states can only impose requirements which are *identical* to the requirement of the federal standard (15 U.S.C. 2075). States may nevertheless want to enact such local legislation so that they can enforce the laws at the local retail level. States or localities can apply to the CPSC for exemption from this identicality requirement if they can show the local standard both provides a significantly higher degree of protection and does not unduly burden inter–state trade.[63] The second limb, which requires a finding that the regulation does not unduly burden inter–state trade, is the most difficult to overcome and when the CPSC was actually faced with such a request from California, concerning a standard relating to children's clothing, it was unable to make the necessary finding to permit the regulation.

Another interesting feature of the activity in this area has been that whilst during the 1980s and early 1990s Republican Presidents favoured the voluntary approach, the Democrat controlled Congress would occasionally consider a matter of such importance that they would legislate directly without going through the rule–making procedure. Examples of this include laws on lawn darts[64] and automatic garage doors.[65] Occasionally Congress has intervened to relax regulations, as happened in relation to lawn mower standards.[66]

---

[63]   The requirement that the standard was introduced to meet a compelling local condition was dropped in 1976: this was sensible since it was hard to see how a product could pose more of a hazard in one area than another.

[64]   Public Law 100–613, 102 Stat 613, 5 November 1989.

[65]   Sec. 203 of Public Law 101–608, 104 Stat 3110, 16 November 1990.

[66]   Lawn Mower Standard Amendment, sec. 1212 of Public Law 97–35, 95 Stat 724, 13 August 1981.

(d) Standards Bodies

There are numerous standards' writing organisations. The three with which the CPSC works most closely are the American National Standards Institute (ANSI), American Society for Testing and Materials (ASTM) and the Underwriters' Laboratories (UL). All the standards bodies have their own procedures, but the Commission insists that all voluntary standards organisations which it works with have open meetings and allow for the involvement of all materially affected parties. The development of standards in the United States is considered in more detail in section 3.

(e) Legal Status of Voluntary Standards

Voluntary standards have no legal effect as such. This does not mean that they have no effect. Industry is eager to develop voluntary standards and to comply with them, not only to stave off any remaining threat of mandatory regulation but also to use compliance as a marketing tool both at home and increasing in the international marketplace.

Furthermore failure to comply with a national consensus standard can be probative evidence for a jury in a product liability suit. Such cases of course are taken very seriously in the United States (because of the potentially high jury awards). Also, if a producer inaccurately claims that his product conforms to a product safety standard when it does not then he will be in breach of the truth and labelling laws administered by the FTC.

(iii) Assessment of the CPSC's Use of Standards

Both mandatory and voluntary standards share the aim of affecting producer behaviour. Even if some producers would have produced products which met these standards in any event, their freedom to choose is restricted and other producers are forced to abandon their preferred design. Mandatory standards achieve this by force of law, voluntary standards because of market forces or the background threat of regulation. Regulation necessarily restricts the freedom of producers and also consumers, who face a restricted choice. It is not surprising that the CPSC's efforts to regulate consumer safety have been subject to criticism by economists and law and economics scholars, who would in principle prefer the market to decide which products are sold through the interplay of producer responses to consumer preferences and product liability suits. Their criticisms can be broken down into one set of concerns about the process through which the CPSC goes about determining whether to regulate and another set of arguments which allege that the resulting standards have had little impact or have even made matters worse.

Peter Asch briefly considers the CPSC's approach to risk with respect to four standards: three mandatory standards in the late 1970s dealing with baby pacifiers, matchbooks and lawn mowers and the voluntary chain saw standard in 1985.[67] He concluded that although in the first three cases the CPSC may have been proposing useful requirements the background analysis by the CPSC did not make their value clear. He was, however, far more complimentary of CPSC's analysis of the 1985 chain saw standard. This fits in with the picture of an agency learning from its early mistakes and suggests that possibly in the deregulatory heydays of the 1980s there was a rush to judgment and that in some respects the baby may have been thrown out with the bath water.

A more detailed and trenchant criticism of the CPSC is provided by Viscusi.[68] He cites the CPSC guidelines for priorities: (a) the frequency and severity of injuries, (b) the causes of injuries and their amenability to policy influence, (c) chronic injuries and future injuries, (d) costs and benefits of CPSC actions, (e) the unforeseen nature of the risk, (f) the vulnerability of the population at large, (g) the probability of exposure to the hazard and (h) the fact the order of the priorities do not dictate their importance. Viscusi is concerned to emphasise the fourth 'cost–benefit' criteria and is suspicious of the CPSC's view that 'analytical uncertainties... complicate matters and militate against reliance on single numerical expressions'.[69]

However, unless one is obsessed with the internal logic of economics the CPSC's approach is entirely sensible. As we noted in Chapter 1, section 3A(ii) economics can do a great deal to assist decision–makers, but in the final analysis consumer product safety regulation is a social policy question which is dictated by far more than pure economics. For instance, Viscusi questions whether in producing the unvented gas–fired space heaters standard sufficient attention was paid to the fact that the lives potentially to be saved would have been of shorter than average longevity because the main users were the elderly and low income.[70] This may affect the economics, but social policy must surely be entitled to override this.

To summarise, Viscusi's main objections to the CPSC approach to risk are: many of the regulations would not pass benefit–cost effectiveness tests and as a result the focus is on accident reduction rather than the value of that reduction; there are no criteria for what is an unreasonable risk; insufficient

---

67   P. Asch, *Consumer Safety Regulation*, (OUP, 1988) at 111–113.
68   Viscusi, *op. cit.*
69   *Ibid.*, at 43.
70   *Ibid.*, at 98, he does however conclude that the standard may nevertheless have been justified even when taking into account the length of the lives saved!

attention is paid to questions of whether the market is failing; the effect on consumers in terms of reduced choice or having to use alternative products (which also carry risks) are not taken into account.[71] Clearly these are issues which regulators should consider and no doubt the practice of the CPSC could be improved. But regulation is not an exact science and the best 'economic' solution may not be politically practical. Viscusi was of course mainly concerned with experience before the 1981 Amendments took hold. These require the CPSC to find a reasonable relationship between costs and benefits. If anything the pendulum might be seen to have swung too much the other way with the CPSC having to furnish too much proof of the need for regulation.

It must be borne in mind that the CPSC has only limited resources to hand. The most that can be expected of it is that it makes a 'good faith' attempt to produce a solution which promotes consumer safety whilst balancing this against other consumer welfare considerations. It must of course be willing to reassess its policies in the light of experience. Judged against this standard it is instructive that even Viscusi is not totally critical of the CPSC's efforts. For instance he describes it as 'a significant improvement over most agencies' behaviour' and comments on the diverse information gathered and the fact that benefit–cost trade–offs are considered, albeit not prominently.[72] He considers as progressive the CPSC's attempts to go beyond valuing benefits in purely financial outlays[73] and praises a former Chairman (Susan King) for her realism in noting that a 'risk–free society is not attainable'.[74]

What impact have the CPSC induced standards produced. There have clearly been some mistakes. The most obvious mistake was the swimming pool slide standard.[75] The history of this standard points to naïveté on the part of the CPSC in its early days. A trade association petitioned for the standard. The CPSC accepted too readily that the slides posed an unreasonable risk. In 1980 the CPSC reviewed the standard and found that it offered few safety benefits and had adversely affected competition with the number of slide manufacturers falling from seven to one. However, the standard could not simply be repealed because the original petitioner – for

---

71   *Ibid.*, at 101–104.
72   *Ibid.*, at 43.
73   *Ibid.*, at 102, but goes on to suggest considering accident costs on the basis of peoples' willingness to pay for accident reduction (for criticism of this approach see Chapter 1, section 3A(ii)). He considers as particularly innovative the fact that it has commissioned research into the value to be placed on life and health (at 43).
74   *Ibid.*, at 43.
75   Schwartz, *op. cit.*, at 49.

whom the standard had served its desired purpose – promised to challenge any revocation. The CPSC had clearly been sold a sucker.

It is possible for some safety rules to produce unexpected adverse consequences. A good example is the use of the chemical Tris to flame–proof sleep–wear in response to improved flammability standards. Unfortunately Tris proved to be carcinogenic.[76] The answer is of course to address the new risk, rather than simply return to the old dangers.

Few standards have been subjected to detailed impact assessments. One exception is Peter Linneman's study of the mattress flammability standard.[77] He found no significant difference in the number of burns caused by mattresses following the introduction of the standard. However, the data was not sufficient for any conclusive findings to be made and the most that can be argued was that the standard did not have a major effect.[78] Viscusi makes similar claims for two of the CPSC's most widely acclaimed successes concerning the standards for cribs[79] and child resistant bottle caps.[80] His point about the cribs can be dealt with in the same fashion as Linneman's point about mattress flammability. The data is inconclusive and, in any event, is it not better to address perceived hazards, if the costs of doing so are not excessive, and prevent some accidents?

His criticism of the child–resistant bottle caps standard raises some more fundamental questions.[81] For instance, he blames the regulation of aspirin bottles for a rise in total poisonings on the basis that it has made parents lax about children's access to all hazardous products, including unregulated products. This argument seems absurd. Whilst there is a possibility that consumers will optimise their risk–taking so that the safer a product is made

---

76   Asch, *op. cit.*, at 20.

77   P. Linneman, 'The Effects of Consumer Safety Standards: the 1973 Mattress Flammability Standard' (1980) 23 *J. Law and Econ.* 461.

78   Viscusi, *op cit.*, at 75.

79   *Ibid.*, at 80–82.

80   *Ibid.*, at 76–80 and K. Viscusi, 'The Lulling Effect: The Impact of Child–Resistant Packaging on Aspirin and Analgesic Ingestions' (1984) *Am. Econ. Rev.* 324. Since that article the CPSC's protocol has been revised to make the new closures easier for many people, especially the elderly, to open. Recent research has shown that child–resistant packaging can have a significant impact on child mortality, see G. Rodgers 'The Safety Effects of Child–Resistant Packaging for Oral Prescription Drugs' (1996) 275 *Journal of the American Medical Association* 1661.

81   Of course it also poses similar problems regarding the methodology of assessing the impact of standards. For instance Asch makes the point that some of the voluntary changes made prior to the standard being issued may have been in contemplation of regulatory changes and so any effects caused thereby could be attributed to the standard: see Asch, *op. cit.*, at 134–136.

the more risks they will take in using it, this is not the same thing as arguing that safety in one product should not be increased because consumers will mistakenly believe that the safety of all similar products has been increased. Surely the answer is to consider whether the safety rules can be extended to cover the other products. He also suggests that the costs to the consumer have not been considered. The standard requires that the cap be designed so that individuals aged between 10–45 can open the container within five minutes. He argues that if such a person took five minutes to open such a container once a day then this would be thirty hours labour per annum (which costed at $10 per hour costs $300). Viscusi is of course right to draw attention to the inconvenience of such safety features, but the costs and benefits of them cannot be compared in purely monetary terms. One would also hope that such a person would become more efficient with practice at opening such containers. Viscusi also argues that consumer choice should be enhanced so that consumers without children can remove the protective cap.[82] Although a nice idea in theory it may not be sound in practice. Do children never go into households where there are no children normally? Would some parents also not prefer to have the safety cap removed, either through ignorance of the risks or the down playing of the risks which their desire for convenience may expose their children to. Viscusi is obviously not a risk adverse consumer, for he describes his practice of removing the foot–probe guard (required by the lawn mower standard) on his 1981 Lawn Boy Supreme so that it is easier for him to cut around trees and bushes.[83] His point is that with the guard removed the area in which he is exposed to danger from the blades is greater than if the mower had not had to be designed to include the guard. The answer should perhaps be to make it impossible (or at least more difficult) for the guard to be removed. Prof. Viscusi would then never know whether he should thank the CPSC for preventing him lopping off his big toe, but he will of course be able to curse it every Sunday when mowing the lawn takes him those few moments longer. This is the problem for regulators. Their successes are invisible; the burdens they impose on producers and consumers are tangible and they are blamed for every avoidable injury even if the cost of avoiding it would be unreasonable.

---

[82]   In fact the Poison Prevention Packaging Act does permit manufacturers to supply one size of their product in non–child–resistant packaging so long as the label states that it is for households without young children. The purpose of this is to ensure that the product is available to elderly or handicapped persons. From what is said below, there should be caution exercised about the availability of such containers.

[83]   Viscusi, *op. cit.* at 95.

E. Reporting

(i) Section 15 (15 U.S.C. 2064)

S. 15 of the CPSA requires manufacturers, distributors and retailers to report potentially unsafe products to the CPSC. This is in effect an early warning system which allows the CPSC to assess the safety of products and work with industry to remedy any problems before death or injury results. The duty to report arises when the person concerned obtains information which reasonably supports the conclusion that the product has one of the following characteristics:

(a) it fails to comply with an applicable consumer product safety rule;
(b) fails to comply with a voluntary consumer product safety standard which has been relied on by the Commission;
(c) contains a defect which could create a substantial product hazard;
(d) creates an unreasonable risk of serious injury or death (15 U.S.C. 2064(b)).

Reporting grounds (b) and (d) were added by the Consumer Safety Improvement Act 1990 in response to concerns that there was an under–reporting of dangerous products.[84] At the same time new provisions required the notification of products involved in law suits (see below) and the civil penalties for a failure to notify were increased.

The first ground – failure to comply with consumer product safety rules – is self explanatory. However, as we have already noted the CPSC has moved away from adopting rules and indeed the legislation now builds in a preference for voluntary standards. There was therefore a need to extend the reporting requirement to situations where there is breach of the voluntary standards the CPSC has chosen to rely upon. This, however, only covers situations where the voluntary standard is relied on under sec. 9 (15 U.S.C. 2058). Thus it only applies once the advance notice of proposed rule–making has been published and would not cover cases where voluntary standards were relied on to justify not proceeding with a staff initiated proposal for a rule or to deny a petition for a rule–making procedure.[85] Although of course failure to comply with these voluntary standards may be grounds for reporting due to any resulting defect or unreasonable risk which is created. The CPSC's rules provide that the reporting notification arises with respect

---

84 For a consideration of the rules after the 1990 amendments see C. D. Erhardt III, 'Manufacturers of Consumer Products, Beware!' [1992] *Prod. Liab. Int.* 66 and 86.

85 It would seem that the CPSC had originally intended that these be included, Erhardt III, *ibid.*, at 88.

to standards when it has terminated a rule–making proceeding or withdrawn an existing consumer product safety rule because it has explicitly determined that an existing voluntary standard was adequate and likely to be complied with.[86] If the voluntary standard is subsequently modified the CPSC will place a notice in the Federal Register as to whether it continues to rely upon it.

The third reporting ground requires the manufacturer to admit to the product containing a defect; this has proved problematic. The reporting obligation only arises when this defect could create a substantial product hazard. It should be noted that there need not be a substantial product hazard for the duty to report to arise, it is sufficient that the product *could* create such a hazard.

The definition of a 'substantial product hazard' is important both to trigger this reporting requirement and as the basis of the CPSC's power to require remedial action. Such a hazard arises either when (a) the product fails to comply with an applicable consumer safety rule which creates a substantial risk of injury to the public, or (b) a product defect (because of the pattern of the defect, the number of defective products distributed in commerce, the severity of the risk, or otherwise) creates a substantial risk of injury to the public (15 U.S.C. 2064(a)). The Commission's recall handbook states that: 'Generally, a product presents a substantial hazard when consumers are exposed to a significant number of units or if the possible injury is serious or likely to occur.'[87]

Defect for the purposes of the CPSA is defined in the interpretative rules,[88] which state that at a minimum 'defect' covers the dictionary or commonly accepted meaning of the word and thus covers 'a fault, flaw, or irregularity that causes weakness, failure, or inadequacy in form or function'. This is rather general, but the rules go on to make it clear that all the traditional categories of defect are covered, namely manufacturing, design and instruction or failure to warn defects. The question of development risks does not of course arise as the regulation is concerned with prospective

---

86   16 Code of Federal Regulations § 1115.5.

87   See, *Recall Handbook* published by the Directorate for Compliance and Administrative Litigation of the US Consumer Product Safety Commission (October, 1988) at 2.

88   16 Code of Federal Regulations § 1115.4. Of course the definition of defect has been much discussed in the United States in the context of product liability litigation: see G. Howells, Comparative Product Liability (Dartmouth, 1993) at pp 209–13. As shall be seen the rules see at least some correlation between the definition of defect in the product liability and the regulatory context. The question of whether the same approach is appropriate in both contexts is considered elsewhere in Chapter 1, section 1B(i).

control of products rather than the retrospective assessment of a product for the purposes of awarding compensation. The CPSC then goes on to state it will take the following factors into account: the utility of the product, nature of the risk, necessity for the product, population exposed to the product and its risk of injury, the CPSC's own experience and expertise, case law interpreting federal and state public health and safety laws, product liability case law and other relevant factors. As the seriousness of a defect is unlikely to be clear when it first comes to light the CPSC urges companies to report if in doubt as to the existence of a substantial product hazard. It considers that all products causing death or grievous bodily injury should be reported.

A finding that the product was defective was therefore essential to the reporting obligation. Manufacturers were understandably reluctant to admit that their products were defective, with the consequences this might have for civil liability in a country where product liability litigation is rife.[89] There was moreover a clear tendency for firms to report relatively minor hazards, rather than the more serious ones.[90] The 1990 reforms attempted to pin down manufacturers by holding them to the more precise obligation to report whenever there is evidence that the product creates an unreasonable risk of serious injury or death.

This is broader than the substantial hazard reporting obligation in several ways.[91] For instance, whilst the substantial hazard reporting obligation is clearly triggered by a product causing 'grievous bodily injury' the CPSC considers the phrase 'serious injury' as being broader and covering any significant injury. This is supported by the fact that in the same 1990 Act the phrase 'grievous bodily injury' was used as part of the reporting obligation with respect to product liability suits; therefore it can be assumed that the legislature meant something else when it talked of 'serious injury'. Furthermore the phrase 'unreasonable risk' is considered to require notification even when no final determination of risk is possible and hence before any defect can be established and certainly before any actual injuries have been suffered. Firms will be expected to consider expert reports, test reports, lawsuits and claims, consumer complaints, reports of injuries, scientific and epidemiological studies and information from other firms or government entities. The CPSC staff had originally wanted the reporting obligation to be triggered by one adverse court decision.[92] However, this would have possibly been seen to be inconsistent with the express reporting obligation which arises where there have been three adverse lawsuits (see section (ii), below). The CPSC therefore contents itself with saying that it

---

89   Erhardt III, *op. cit.*, at 67.
90   See, Federal Register, Vol. 57, No. 150, 4 August 1992.
91   See, 16 Code of Federal Regulations § 1115.6.
92   Erhardt III, *op. cit.*, at 68.

will attach great significance to whether a firm has learned of adverse court or jury decisions. Of course the reporting obligation only arises where the risk is an unreasonable one. In determining what is unreasonable utility has to be balanced against risk and account has to be taken of the state of the art, the availability of alternatives and the feasibility of reducing the risk.

(ii)   Section 37 (15 U.S.C. 2084)

The 1990 amendments also introduced a duty on manufacturers to report to the CPSC if their product is involved in product liability litigation. These are found in a separate section (s. 37) and require the reports to contain less detailed information about the product than is the case with s. 15 notifications (15 U.S.C. 2084). The duty arises if the manufacturer of a particular model of a consumer product is subject to at least three civil actions alleging death or grievous injury filed in a federal or state court within a 24 month period, which result in either a final settlement or judgment for the plaintiff. When reporting the manufacturer can state that the matter is to be appealed and is also free to deny that the product caused death or grievous injury. The report is subject to strict confidentiality rules (15 U.S.C. 2055(e)) and does not constitute an admission by the manufacturer.

The s. 37 report is essentially viewed as a safety net, because it does not require any discretionary assessments of hazards or causal associations.[93] It is, however, not an alternative to the other reporting obligations under s. 15. Even if a product has been reported because, for instance, it may pose a substantial product hazard a further report should be made once three lawsuits have been settled. More importantly manufacturers should not wait for three law suits before reporting their suspicions under s. 15. The first thing CPSC staff will do when they receive a s. 37 report is to check if there has been a s. 15 report. If none was filed searching questions are likely to be asked and potentially heavy civil penalties can result.[94]

In order to bring about the reporting obligation the suit must have alleged death or grievous bodily injury. The Act defines the latter to include mutilation, amputation, dismemberment, disfigurement, loss of important bodily functions, debilitating internal disorder, severe burns, severe electrical shock and injuries likely to require extended hospitalisation. If a case is litigated and there is an express finding that the statutory criteria are not met then there is of course no duty to report. In most cases there will be a duty to report where a case is determined or settled in which a grievous bodily injury

---

93   16 Code of Federal Regulations § 1116.7((h)(3).
94   Erhardt III, *op. cit.*, at 87.

was alleged. This will be the case regardless of the manufacturer's opinion of the validity of the allegation and even where mere conclusory language was used in the claim, at least this is the position unless the manufacturer investigated the underlying facts. This approach is justified because of the right manufacturers are given to deny the product was responsible and because the report is subject to strict confidentiality conditions.[95] However, it can lead to reports having to be made where manufacturers have simply 'bought off' nuisance claims.[96] However, this is probably a price worth paying if it leads to the authorities being alerted to genuine problems.

The reporting obligation only arises with respect of three law suits in relation to a particular model. It is therefore important to determine what amounts to a 'particular model'. The statute provides that this is one which is distinctive in functional design, construction, warnings or instructions related to safety, function, user population, or other characteristics which could affect the products safety related performance. Although the rules make it clear that the difference must be substantial and material, this is clearly a potential loophole. Indeed the rules go on to make it clear that even if the same characteristic gives rise to three or more lawsuits, there will be no reporting obligation so long as different models are involved.[97] However, if the dangerous characteristic is due to a component, then so long as the component manufacturer is joined as a defendant he will be under the reporting obligation. In any event a manufacturer who has several claims about a specific characteristic of his products, albeit in relation to different models, might well be expected to report a substantial product hazard or unreasonable risk under s. 15.

(iii) Conclusions on Reporting Obligations

These reporting obligations are a particularly distinctive feature of product safety regulation in the United States. By making firms reveal information about product safety risks which they discover within their internal operations it requires the firms to show a respect for the social dimensions of their activities. It creates incentives (in the form of avoiding civil penalties for non-reporting) for firms to take product safety and post-market monitoring seriously. The information provided by firms can alert the CPSC both to dangers of a general nature with respect to which consideration should be given to the possibility of developing rules, bans or standards and

---

95   16 Code of Federal Regulations § 1116.7(b).
96   Erhardt III, *op. cit.*, at 87.
97   16 Code of Federal Regulations § 1116.8.

to more immediate and specific concerns which might require the recall of potentially dangerous products or other remedial action.

There is, of course, always the danger that these obligations are ignored by industry, either wilfully, or through ignorance or because of the burden of other pressures. Indeed the need for the 1990 Amendments confirms the risk of under–reporting. One would have suspected that the American product liability system provided a significant incentive for firms to report serious risks. If a consumer was injured by a product defect which a producer had failed to report to the CPSC then the plaintiff could have grounds to press for potentially heavy punitive damages. The 1990 reforms back this up with increased civil penalties for failing to report. These sanctions are an important feature of the United States system. If reporting obligations were introduced into systems where the only practical sanction for ignoring it was a regulatory fine, which was in practice hardly ever invoked, then their effectiveness may be reduced. Naturally some businesses will continue to fail to report potential dangers either through ignorance of their responsibilities or, as indeed the United States pre–1990 experience suggests, because they prefer not to draw attention to any possible problems with their products. However, some useful intelligence is likely to be generated by these reporting obligations and such rules have the symbolic effects of underlining the need for firms to monitor product safety and emphasising the importance of an effective dialogue between industry and the CPSC. The CPSC's prestige is further enhanced by its follow up powers to require remedial action where a substantial product hazard is established.

F.   Remedial Action for Substantial Product Hazard

The CPSA's definition of 'substantial product hazard' was mentioned in the last section. To recap, such a hazard exists where a substantial risk of injury to the public is created by a product which either fails to comply with a consumer product safety rule or contains a defect. The post–market powers have become more significant since the CPSC's pre–market controls have been weakened.

If the CPSC determines that a product presents a substantial product hazard and that notification is required to adequately protect the public, it may order the manufacturer, distributor or retailer of the product to do one or more of the following; namely (i) to give public notice of the defect or failure to comply; (ii) to mail notice to each manufacturer, distributor or retailer of such product, or (iii) to mail notice to every person he knows the product was sold or delivered to. The form and content of the required notice can be specified (15 U.S.C. 2064(c)).

In addition if the CPSC considers it to be in the public interest it can order the manufacturer, distributor or retailer to choose which of the following actions it wishes to take:

−   bring the product into conformity with the requirements of the applicable consumer product safety rule or repair the defect;
−   replace the product with a like or equivalent product which complies with the applicable consumer product safety rule or does not contain the defect;
−   refund the purchase price. A reasonable allowance for use can be made if the product has been in the consumer's possession for more than one year from the earlier of the time public notice of the substantial product hazard was given or the consumer receives actual notice of the defect or non−compliance (15 U.S.C 2064(d)).

Before the CPSC takes any of the above measures in relation to substantial product hazards it must afford interested persons, including consumers and consumer organisations, the opportunity for a hearing.

Generally, however, the Commission will try to agree a voluntary corrective plan with the businesses concerned.[98] The Commission divides products posing a substantial product hazard into three categories: categories A, B and C.[99] Class A hazards exist when a risk of death or grievous injury or illness is likely or very likely, or serious injury or illness is very likely. Class B hazards exist when a risk of death or grievous injury or illness is not likely to occur, but is possible, or when serious injury or illness is likely, or moderate injury or illness is very likely. Class C hazards exist when a risk of serious injury or illness is not likely, but is possible, or when moderate injury or illness is likely, or possible.

The response to substantial product hazards varies according to how the hazard is classified. Class A hazards merit the maximum effort − direct notice should be given to the product distribution network, consumers and to groups who have or use the product. Techniques used to reach consumers include joint news releases issued by the CPSC and the company concerned, 'bill stuffer' enclosures, paid advertising in newspapers and magazines, publicity in product catalogues, marketing newsletters and sales material, '800' toll−free telephones, incentives (such as free gifts) to prompt the return of the defective products, point of purchase posters, purchase of mailing lists

---

[98]   It is suggested that corrective plans are possible in 95% of cases: see, Erhardt III, *op. cit.*, at 67.

[99]   See, *Recall Handbook* published by the Directorate for Compliance and Administrative Litigation of the US Consumer Product Safety Commission (October, 1988).

of suspected product owners, use of warranty cards and other owner information, such as service contract names, to identify owners and notification to groups and trade associations for whom the product recall may have particular concern. The action required is less for class B hazards and less again for class C hazards. Yet even class C hazards merit a news release, point of purchase posters, a '800' toll free number, notice to distributors and retailers of the product recall and, if details are available, direct notice should be sent to consumers.

G. Imminent Hazards[100]

The CPSC also has powers to deal with 'imminently hazardous consumer products', which are defined as consumer products which present imminent and unreasonable risk of death, serious illness, or severe personal injury. These powers can be exercised even if there is a consumer product safety rule applicable to the product or other actions under the CPSA are pending.

An action may be filed in a United States' District Court against (i) the product itself for the purpose of its seizure, and/or (ii) the manufacturer, distributor or retailer of such product. In the latter case the action should be brought in the district court for the District of Columbia or in any judicial district where any of the defendants is an inhabitant or transacts business: where there is more than one possible district the CPSC is to take account of the convenience of the parties.

If the court declares the product to be 'imminently hazardous' in an action against the manufacturer, distributor or retailer the court can grant such temporary or permanent relief as may be necessary to protect the public from such risks. The relief may include a mandatory order requiring the notification of the risk to known purchasers, public notice or the recall, repair, replacement or refund of the product. If the action is against the product then it can be seized and condemned. As soon as possible after the action the CPSC shall take proceedings to promulgate a consumer safety rule.

One weakness in this procedure is the need to go to court without officials having the power to prevent the products being moved in the meantime. Presumably reliance must be had on the civil consequences, including the threat of punitive damages, which could result if damage is caused by the product and the parties have not co–operated with the CPSC.

---

[100]   15 U.S.C. 2061.

H. Penalties[101]

The CPSA makes various acts unlawful (15 U.S.C. 2068). Thus, *inter alia*, it is unlawful to manufacture for sale, offer for sale, distribute in commerce or import any consumer product which is not in conformity with an applicable consumer product safety standard or which has been declared a banned hazardous product. It is also unlawful not to report an unsafe product or to fail to take the follow–up measures demanded by the CPSC. There are also many prohibited acts relating to the failure to furnish information or to assist the authorities.

There are both civil and criminal penalties for undertaking prohibited acts. Civil penalties apply for each knowing violation (15 U.S.C. 2069). 'Knowingly' is said to include either having actual knowledge or presumed knowledge based on the concept of a reasonable man in those circumstances who takes due care to ascertain the truth of representations (15 U.S.C. 2069(d)). The civil penalties do not exceed $5,000, however, for most of the prohibited acts a separate offence is committed with respect to each product involved, subject to a maximum of $1,250,000 for a related series of violations.[102] However, this cumulation of liability does not apply to the offences of failing to comply with a consumer product safety standard or dealing in banned hazardous products if the person concerned is not the manufacturer, private labeller or distributor of the product and he had no actual knowledge or notice from the CPSC that his distribution or sale was a violation.

Where a person knowingly and wilfully commits a violation they can be subject to criminal penalties of a fine of up to $100,000 and/or one year's imprisonment (15 U.S.C. 2070). The criminal penalties can extend to the directors, officers or agents of corporations.

I. Private Enforcement[103]

The CPSC is the federal enforcement authority, but the CPSA gives interested persons,[104] an albeit little used power, to obtain injunctive relief to enforce consumer product safety rules (ie standards and bans, see section D) and orders under 15 U.S.C. 2064 (providing for remedial action to deal with substantial product hazards, see section F). Thirty days prior to the action,

---

101 15 U.S.C. 2069, 2070.

102 The monetary amounts are to rise in line with inflation by 1 Dec. every five years after 1 Dec. 1994.

103 15 U.S.C. 2073.

104 Including individuals, non–profit, business or other entities.

notice must be given to the Commission and the Attorney General. No civil or criminal suit by the United States in respect of the alleged violation shall be pending.

J. Damages[105]

Breach of a consumer product safety standard can be probative evidence to go before a jury in a product liability suit. The CPSA goes further, however, and allows the injured party a right of action for damages if he sustains injury by reason of any knowing (including wilful) violation of a consumer product safety rule, or any other rule or order issued by the CPSC: but note there is no action for violation of the Act itself.[106] The courts have said that Congress intended the right of action to be 'simply another source of liability in addition to the typical claims which arise from injuries caused by defective products: negligence, breach of warranty and strict liability'.[107] The right of action under the CPSA has the advantage that a successful plaintiff can recover his lawyer's fees, but has the limitation that it is only available for claims in excess of $10,000.

In *Swenson v Emerson Elec. Co.*[108] failure to comply with a substantial product hazard reporting requirement was considered to give rise to the right to sue for damages under the Act. However, the majority of cases have doubted this and have held that to allow an action in such circumstances would have gone beyond the intention of Congress. It has been argued that to allow such a claim would mean that most product liability cases could be brought in the federal courts (with the advantage of lawyer costs being awarded) on the basis that the manufacturer ought to have warned the CPSC of the alleged defect. It is suggested that Congress would have at least mentioned this dramatic change in the law if it had been its intention to achieve this result.[109]

Compliance with consumer product safety rules does not affect liability under common law or state statutes law: equally the failure of the Commission to take action against a consumer product is not admissible as evidence.[110]

---

[105] 15 U.S.C. 2072.

[106] See eg *First National Bank of Dwight v Regent Sports Corpn.*, 803 F 2d. 1431 (CA7) (1986).

[107] *Swenson v Emerson Elec., Co.* 374 NW 2d 690 (Supreme Court of Minnesota) (1985).

[108] *Ibid.*

[109] See eg *Kloepfer v Honda Motors Company Ltd*, 898 F 2d 1452 (CA, 10 Cir.) (1990).

[110] 15 U.S.C. 2074.

K.   Imports

. The CPSC is charged with establishing and maintaining a permanent product surveillance programme in co–operation with other federal agencies to prevent the entry of unsafe consumer products into the United States (15 U.S.C. 2066). The Commission can request the Secretary of the Treasury (in fact the Customs) to obtain, without charge, a reasonable number of samples of products offered for import. Products will be refused admission if they fail to comply with applicable consumer product safety rules; are not accompanied by appropriate certificates of compliance with consumer safety standards or do not comply with labelling requirements; have been determined to be imminently hazardous consumer products; have a defect which constitutes a substantial product hazard or have been manufactured by someone about whom the CPSC has informed the Customs concerning violation of the rules on inspection and record–keeping. Unless the owner or consignee of the products, which it is proposed to ban, has been afforded a hearing under the procedures relating to imminently hazardous products, then he shall be granted a hearing by the CPSC.

Products which are not fit to be imported can be allowed to be modified, but if this fails to render them safe then like all products refused entry they must be exported. The Customs can, however, permit their destruction in lieu of export. If the product is not exported within a reasonable time the Customs may destroy it. The costs of destruction and storage, cartage and labour charges related to a product refused entry are payable by the owner or consignee.

These provisions are an improvement over the previous arrangements.[111] Prior to the enactment of the CPSA goods would be released to the importer under a redelivery bond. If the goods proved to be dangerous, then absent fraud, the customs could not compel redelivery of the goods and simply had to rely on the sanction of forfeiture of part of the redelivery bond. Regulatory authorities might have been able to take injunction and seizure action.

Now, the CPSC can refuse to admit non–complying goods and the importer can not demand their release by tendering a redelivery bond. Of course the legislation does foresee the goods being released for modification, but then the CPSC may direct customs to demand redelivery as well as instituting seizure and injunctive proceedings. Although the CPSC is probably able to detain suspicious goods whilst it carries out tests, there may be occasions when dangers only come to light after customs have released goods under a redelivery bond. Then, although the CPSC can request the assistance of customs they may have to rely on their general enforcement

---

[111]   B. Brown, 'Regulation of Importers Under the Consumer Product Safety Act' (1976) 9 *Cornell Int. L. J.* 317.

powers if either customs do not take the same view of the matter or if the trader ignores Customs' request. The only duty on the trader to comply with a request for redelivery is where goods have been released for modification.

L. Exports

Originally the CPSA had not regulated products manufactured, sold or held for export (except for exports to United States installations' overseas) so long as they were labelled as being for export and were not in fact distributed for use in the United States. In 1978 some significant amendments were made in response to concerns that unsafe consumer goods were being dumped in the third world.[112] Of particular note was the case of children's night–wear treated with the fire–retardant chemical TRIS – dibromopropylphosphate. When this was found to be carcinogenic many manufacturers faced bankruptcy and tried to sell their stocks to developing countries. It has been commented that regulating the export of consumer goods is in some ways more necessary than controls on the export of pesticides and drugs. Dangerous consumer goods pose immediate risks and are almost always instances of 'dumping', whereas pesticides and drugs can be developed solely to meet overseas needs.[113] In response the CPSA[114] was amended both to impose notification requirements and to exclude from the exemption from controls export products which are determined by the CPSC to represent an unreasonable risk of injury to consumers within the United States (15 U.S.C. 2067).

The notification requirement requires anyone exporting a product which fails to comply with a consumer product safety standard or which has been declared a banned hazardous substance to file a statement notifying the CPSC of the exportation. This statement will refer to such matters as the date of shipment, country and port of destination and the quantity of the product involved. Normally the statement should be filed thirty days before exportation, but the CPSC can, for good cause, reduce this to ten days. The CPSC will then inform the recipient Government of the proposed exportation and the basis of any safety standard or rule.

---

112 See F. Schulberg, 'United States Export of Products Banned for Domestic Use' (1979) 20 *Harv. Int. Law J.* 331 and D. Bryan, 'Consumer Safety Abroad: Dumping of Dangerous American Products Overseas' (1981) *Texas Tech. Law. Rev.* 435.

113 Schulberg, *ibid.*, at 358.

114 In fact the TRIS incident was handled under the Federal Hazardous Substances Act, but that Act, the CPSA and the Flammable Fabrics Act were all amended in the same way.

There are some weaknesses in this approach from the perspective of consumer protection. Especially now that there is increased reliance on voluntary standards, many products may be unsafe because they fail to comply with voluntary rules and there will be no notification obligation. There is also always the danger that products are simply not identified as being subject to the reporting obligations. However, although the United States does not fulfil the principles set out on the United Nation's resolution on the protection against products harmful to health and the environment (see Chapter 3, section 5) it operates some of the most rigorous controls in developed countries. It is therefore somewhat surprising to find that the United States was the only country to vote against that resolution and is also unenthusiastic about the United Nation's efforts to pool information on dangerous products.

The United States' rules would have been even stronger had an executive order made by President Carter in 1981 come into force.[115] Although basically believing that international responsibilities could be met through notification procedures it would have made them more effective and efficient by increasing procedural uniformity in the notification process and in the content of notices sent to overseas governments. The controversial aspect would have been the requirement that extremely hazardous prohibited and significantly restricted products would need an export licence which would only be granted in limited circumstances where export would not harm US foreign policy interests and when, after consultation, there had been no objection from the importing country. This order was, however, revoked by President Reagan before it came into force.

Notification represents the international political equivalent of information being the cornerstone of one's consumer protection policy. It assumes the recipient can understand and evaluate the messages. Many third world countries lack the political infrastructure to take on this task. Thus, whilst accepting that there may be circumstances where developing countries legitimately assess risks differently from the United States or where the circumstances justify risks which would not be acceptable in the United States (see Chapter 1, section 5), nevertheless the Carter order would have been a welcome recognition of the need for Western countries to include some moral responsibility in their trade policy. Of course there is also a certain degree of self–interest in these matters. Other arguments used by those who favour regulation of exports point to the benefits it brings to US citizens. They point to the long term trade benefits which accrue from the esteem with which goods 'Made in the US' will be held. They also point to the role bans on exports can play in improving the safety of domestically

---

115   See, D. Harland, 'Legal Aspects of the Export of Hazardous Products' (1985) *J.C.P.* 209 at 219–220.

marketed consumer goods. This is because goods exported can sometimes find themselves illegally imported back into the United States.[116] Moreover it is suggested that the possibility of exporting dangerous goods may lead to lax manufacturing standards as producers are aware that if any products are found to be sub–standard they can be easily sold overseas. Restricting the export option will create more incentives to get things right and lead to generally higher standards amongst the producers of consumer products.

Connected to this issue of the ban on exports of dangerous goods acting as a deterrent to the introduction of such products on to the domestic market is the question of whether products which have been marketed domestically and found to be dangerous can then be released for export. This issue has been litigated on several occasions.[117] Two of the most important decisions came to differing conclusions. In *United States v Salem Carpet Mills, Inc.*[118] the United States Court of Appeals for the Fifth Circuit found that the export exemption in the Flammable Fabrics Act applied not withstanding that they had been introduced into domestic commerce without an intention to export. On the other hand the Fourth Circuit, in *United States v Articles of Hazardous Substance*[119] (a case involving TRIS) found that the export exemption under the Federal Hazardous Substances Act was indeed lost once products had been offered in domestic commerce. In 1983 the CPSC reversed its position under the Flammable Fabrics Act to allow the export of goods previously intended for the domestic market.[120] It argued that the 1978 amendments made it less necessary for it to ban the export of goods which had been marketed domestically as they provided for a policy of notification to other governments and the power to regulate export goods which might pose an unreasonable risk to US consumers gave it adequate controls. Contradictorily its policy with regard to the CPSA and Federal Hazardous Substances Act remained that it could prohibit the export of

---

[116] Pesticides are a special case in this respect as they can create harmful properties in food crops which are then imported into the US.

[117] Cases discussed in S. Cohen, 'Exports of Hazardous Products from the United States: An Analysis of Consumer Product Safety Commission Policy' (1985) 19 *Geo. Wash. J. Int'l L. & Econ.* 123 at 144–148.

[118] 632 F. 2d 1259 (5th Cir. 1980).

[119] 588 F. 2d 39 (4th Cir. 1978).

[120] See, Memorandum Decision and Order in *Matter of Imperial Carpet Mills, Inc*, discussed in Cohen, *op. cit.*, at 148–152 and D. Korotkin, 'An Analysis of the Effectiveness of the Consumer Product Safety Commission's Export Policy in Preventing Hazardous Consumer Products from Entering the Foreign Marketplace' (1986) 12 *Brooklyn J. Int'l L.* 389 at 401–404. This was said to be based on a re-interpretation of the wording of the Act rather than on the basis of the decision in *Salem Carpet Mills*.

goods which had been introduced into domestic commerce.[121] Commentators have been rightly critical of the lack of logic in this position which destroys the uniformity between the three Acts which the 1978 amendments had sought to introduce and which runs counter to the spirit of the 1978 amendments which was to enhance the CPSC's powers, not replace one power by another.[122]

3.   VOLUNTARY STANDARDISATION

A.   Background

It has been estimated that there are 400 voluntary standards writing bodies in the United States.[123] It is therefore a very decentralised model. The American National Standards Institute (ANSI) is essentially a 'trade association of standards setters'[124] which approves American National Standards (ANS) and represents the United States within the ISO. However, half of the standards bodies are not members of ANSI – non–members rarely submit standards to ANSI for approval – and even some members choose not to submit all their standards for approval. The system has therefore been described as 'a hodgepodge of sources of standards rather than a neat pyramid with ANSI at the apex'.[125] Government involvement is co–ordinated through the National Institute for Standards and Technology (NIST) and the secretariat of the Interagency Committee on Standards Policy (ICSP).

The largest standards writing body is the American Society for Testing and Materials (ASTM) which publishes more than 9,100 standards in its *Annual Book of ASTMS Standards*. ASTM accounts for over half of ANSI approved standards and it now submits all its standards to ANSI. The National Fire Protection Association (NFPA) is another important source of standards which are compiled in the *National Fire Codes*. The American Society of Mechanical Engineers (ASME) publishes several hundred codes. Underwriters Laboratories (UL) also produces over 700 of their own standards as well as participating in the work of other standards associations.

---

121   16 Code of Federal Regulations § 1010.

122   See, Cohen, *op. cit.*. at 152–163 and Korotkin, *op. cit.*, at 413–414.

123   *Consumers, Product Safety Standards and International Trade*, (OECD, 1991) at 25.

124   R. Hamilton, 'The Role of Non–governmental Standards in the Development of Mandatory Federal Standards Affecting Safety or Health' (1978) 56 *Texas L. Rev.* 1329 at 1341. This article provides a thorough, but now somewhat dated, analysis of US standards procedures.

125   *Ibid.*, at 1343.

UL is also the leading third party certificator in the United States and its UL label is a familiar feature on American products.

Voluntary standards were slated by the National Commission on Product Safety in 1979. We have already noted that the Final Report concluded that 'these standards are chronically inadequate, both in scope and permissible levels of risk'.[126] They were also the subject of a damning report by the Federal Trade Commission's Bureau of Consumer Protection which pointed to a lack of procedural safeguards in the standardisation process and claimed standardisation and certification procedures delayed or deterred market entry of innovative products, unnecessarily increased costs, deceived consumers about product safety or quality and unjustifiably limited consumer choice.[127] However, we have already seen (section 2D) how the initial belief that consumer safety problems could all be resolved by government regulation by the CPSC soon disappeared and there was a realisation that for either practical or political reasons voluntary standards would have to continue to play an important role. Although the CPSC would monitor some standards to ensure that they adequately protected consumers, these standards remain truly voluntary in the sense that manufacturers are not required to use them. This contrast with the position in Europe where manufacturers in areas covered by new approach directives must apply the standards or otherwise satisfy essential safety requirements. We shall also see that 'pure' consumer representation is less well assured in N. America than at the European level or in the European countries we shall study in detail.

B. ANSI[128]

(i) Introduction

ANSI has organisational members (eg ASTM, NFPA, trade associations, non–profit professional societies), company members (eg corporations, testing laboratories) and government members. Each member section has its own Council. There is also a Consumer Interest Council. Standards activity is co–ordinated through its Executive Standards Council. Standards boards

---

[126] *Op. cit.,* at 48.

[127] *Standards and Certification,* (Federal Trade Commission, 1983).

[128] ANSI developed out of the United States of America Standards Institute (USASI) which was founded in 1966 and in turn this arose from the American Engineering Standards Committee (AESC) which was founded in 1918 from the combination of five leading engineering societies: see M. Opala, 'The Anatomy of Private Standards–making Process: the Operating Procedures of the USA Standards Institute' (1969) 22 *Okla. L. Rev.* 45.

look after the day to day management of areas of standards activity. The Board of Standards Review is responsible for deciding whether standards conform to the requirements for an ANS.

ANSI has a programme for accrediting third–party certification and seeks to obtain worldwide acceptance of US product certificates and to promote reciprocal agreements between US accreditors and certifiers. Its most important function is, however, to co–ordinate standards activity and to develop the system of American National Standards (ANS). ANSI also represents the United States within ISO.

(ii)   ANS

In 1995 there were 11,500 approved ANS. Most ANS are developed by ANSI organisational members, who submit them to ANSI for approval. However, about a quarter of ANS are written by American National Standards Committees. ANSI usually establishes such a committee when no suitable organisation is active in an area. These committees are created by ANSI, but are not actually part of ANSI. ANSI usually designates an organisational member to sponsor each committee and to act as its secretariat.

An ANS can only be developed by an Accredited Standards Developer (ASD). The procedures of the ASD must ensure that materially affected and interested parties can participate, either as part of the consensus body or in the public review stage. The consensus body must not be dominated by any single interest category. These shall usually be divided into producer, user and general interest categories, but other more specific categories are possible, eg consumer. Normally this balance will be achieved by ensuring that no single category constitutes the majority of a committee or in the case of safety a third of the committee. ASDs should review any comments or objections and seek to resolve any objections and must have appeal procedures so that matters can be heard by an impartial body.

The consensus principle is at the heart of standardisation, but it is also controversial. Consensus is said to demand the concurrence of more than a simple majority, but not necessarily unanimity.[129] This means that controversial measures are unlikely to be adopted in the face of significant industry opposition as it would be pointless to adopt standards which depend upon industry's voluntary acquiescence if industry is outrightly hostile to their content. It has been said that the votes are often 'weighted rather than

---

129   *ANSI Procedures for the Development and Co–ordination of American National Standards*, approved by ANSI Board of Directors, 22 March 1995 (hereafter *ANSI Procedures*) at 1.3.

counted' in that the objection of a significant interest group might prevent the adoption of a standard.[130] Read positively this could mean that standards would not be adopted in the face of opposition from the consumer movement, but this is far more likely to mean that the objections of significant industry players will be given serious attention.

ANSI provides for three forms of accreditation by standards developers. Each way provides different mechanisms for ensuring due process is adhered to and for arriving at a consensus.[131]

(a) Accredited Organisation Method

A number of organisations have been accredited under the organisational method. Typically they are bodies which have developing standards as one of their activities. This form of accreditation leaves the organisation with a great deal of flexibility with regard to its procedures and structure so long as they comply with the general criteria for accreditation.

(b) Standards Committee Method

Accredited Standards Committees comprise representatives of directly and materially affected interests who come together to develop a standard. They typically arise when a standard affects a broad range of interests or where several organisations have similar interests. Although committees may adopt their own procedures, a model procedure is set out in Annex 1 of the *ANSI Procedures*. This provides that standards should be approved by a majority of the committee's membership and at least two–thirds of those voting, excluding abstentions.

(c) Canvass Method

A third way of establishing consensus is through the canvass method. This method has traditionally been used by professional societies and small trade associations that have documented current industry practices which they wish to have recognised as national standards. ASD's using the canvass method must adopt the procedures set out in Annex B of the *ANSI Procedures*.

---

130 See, D. Hemenway, *Industrywide Voluntary Product Standards*, (Ballinger, 1975) at 89 (quoted in Hamilton, *op. cit.*, at 1364).

131 *ANSI Procedures, op. cit.*, at para. 2.1.

The standards writing organisation draws up a canvass list of interested organisations and conducts a pre–canvass interest survey. If they wish to participate canvassees should indicate their interest category classification. Once the list is submitted to ANSI it is announced in *Standards Action* to elicit additional canvassees and the list is reviewed. Approval of a standard requires approval by a majority of the canvass list and at least two–thirds of those voting, excluding abstentions. Objections and comments must be considered and an effort made to resolve objections. Unresolved objections and substantive changes must be resubmitted to the organisations canvassed. A major problem with this method of assessing consensus is the low response rate. It is said to be particularly difficult for consumer groups to comment on a standard without having been involved in writing it.[132]

Development of an ANS commences with transmission to ANSI of a Project Initiation Notification System (PINS) form. This leads to publication in *Standards Action* for public comment. Once there is a draft ANS the ASD submits a BSR–8 Form to initiate a 60 day review and comment period following publication in *Standards Action* (30 days if the text can be published in full). The consensus ballot then takes place. Of course, where the canvass method is used the public review only takes place during or after the consensus ballot. If it is determined that consensus has been achieved a BSR–9 Form is submitted.

The Board of Standards Review (BSR) considers whether the *ANSI Procedures* have been carried out properly. Standards are approved by a two–thirds majority of those voting in a letter ballot, excluding abstentions, provided the number of members returning ballots, excluding abstentions, is at least a majority of the Board. The BSR will also ensure that standards are not contrary to the public interest, do not contain unfair provisions, are not unsuitable for national use nor conflict with an existing ANS. There is now provision, subject to special auditing requirements, for ASDs which have a 'consistent record of successful voluntary standards development' to request authority to designate its standards as ANS without the need for BSR approval.[133]

BSR members are appointed because of their 'competence and the ability to render impartial judgment'.[134] Hamilton concluded that they took their role seriously and insisted on proof of procedural compliance and the existence of a consensus.[135] The members of BSR tend to be drawn from business, standards bodies and government. There is no express consumer

---

132   See Hamilton, *op. cit.*, at 1348–1349.

133   *ANSI Procedures*, at para. 1.3.2.

134   ANSI, *Operating Procedures of the Board of Standards Review*, approved by ANSI Board of Directors, 22 March 1995, at para. 2.1.

135   Hamilton, *ibid.*, at 1367.

representation on the BSR, but this is balanced by the requirement that consumer product standards be referred to the Standards Screening and Review Committee of the Consumer Interest Council which has the option of reviewing the standard and providing comments to the BSR.

C. Consumer Participation

(i) Within ANSI

ANSI's Consumer Interest Council was established in 1967 as a means of representing the consumer interest within ANSI, but it has no direct influence on the decision–making process. Its Standards Screening and Review Committee does provide for a consumer input into the approval of an ANS, although the standards developer need not agree with the objections put forward by the Council it must respond to them.

However, the present chair of the Council, now called the Consumer Interest Council (CIC), has conceded that the 'consumer participation in US standards policies is minimal at best'.[136] Moreover the notion of consumer representation – at least at this political level – appears to be different in nature from that espoused in Europe. For example, the chair of the CIC talks about the need for representation from not only all consumer organisations, but also all industry sectors and also aspires to high level representation from each ANSI member company. Participation is sold to companies on the basis that they will be involved in decisions which will affect their business.[137] This wide based membership is perhaps indicated by the fact that it is a Consumer *Interest* Council, rather than simply a Consumer Council. Its membership extends beyond consumer groups to include representatives from business, standards bodies, corporations and Government. Indeed one ANSI employee is cited as suggesting that representatives of large purchasing organisations provided a considerable amount of pro–consumer expertise.[138] However it appears that ANSI's CIC is hardly a forum for consumers to organise and develop their own independent approach to standardisation.

In the United States the emphasis seems to be far more on convincing industry that they have something to gain from listening to consumers than on the right of consumers to be involved in the process in order to protect their interest. This is underlined by a recent ANSI initiative to encourage

---

136 'A Conversation with Nancy Harvey Steorts' *ANSI Reporter*, October/November 1996 at 5–6.
137 *Ibid.*
138 Hamilton, *op. cit.*, at 1385.

industry to set up their own Consumer Advisory Boards, comprised of academics, government officials, consumers etc., to look at the needs of their own consumers. To European ears this model of consumer representation may appear more appropriate to the development of internal company policy than to the generation of legal or quasi–legal norms. In part this may be due to the more purely voluntary nature of standards in the United States, whereas in Europe standards increasingly fall within regulatory regimes based on new approach directives. This should not be an excuse for down–playing the role of consumers in standards development. Indeed the CPSC should monitor standards to ensure that it has no need to invoke its rule–making powers. Possibly in the United States product liability actions act as a greater incentive for producers to ensure that standards adequately address safety issues than civil liability rules in Europe.

The ANSI CICs Standards Screening and Review Committee provides for review of standards in their final stages. What is important, however, is to be able to influence how standards are developed, not just to comment on the final draft. Of course some bodies other than consumer organisations will look out for the consumer interest, but this cannot replace the need for direct consumer involvement in the standards writing committees.

(ii)   Within Standards Writing Bodies

There are so many standards writing bodies in the United States that it would be an enormous task to look at the procedures for consumer representation in all of them. Instead a brief description will be made of how two of the most important standards bodies UL and ASTM involve consumers.[139] Of course one might anticipate less consumer involvement where the standards bodies are based more on trade associations. As a general comment one might state that taken as a whole the mechanisms adopted by the United States standards bodies tend to be less formal than the European structures for consumer representation and the role of consumer organisations is less prominent.

When commencing a new standards project UL puts out a public notification inviting interested parties to contact it, but the response from consumers seems to be modest. UL has a Consumer Advisory Council which comments on draft standards, but consumer organisations only form a portion of its 45 members with the others being drawn from retail organisations, academics, government, publishing etc. However, this Council

---

139   In part this section relies both on the Hamilton article, *op. cit.*, and more up to date information gleaned from presentations at the ISO–COPOLCO workshop on *Consumers in Standards*, 12 May 1997, London made by John Drengenberg (UL) and Kenneth Pearson (ASTM).

considers proposed standards and is not involved at the early stages when the standards are being formulated. At an early stage UL has an Industry Advisory Conference which is closed to everybody except industry representatives. The object is to permit them to raise their concerns without having to go public, but there must be a danger of excessive influence by the industry. Steps are being taken to permit other groups to have an input at an earlier stage. It has created 'Technical Advisory Panels' to provide early input to a standard's development by all interested parties and the CPSC has successfully requested such panels be established for selected consumer products associated with death and injuries. UL also has a consumer sounding board which meets monthly to discuss ideas. This is limited to people who live locally to UL headquarters and is dominated by elderly people who have the time to devote to these matters. The idea of using 'Consumer Sounding Boards' to discuss issues with consumers developed first in the United States. These have been described as being little more than 'rap sessions'[140] and although UL and some other bodies continue to use them they are less widely used now than they were in the past. We noted in Chapter 1, section 3D(ii)(e) that the concept was developed to a greater extent in Canada.

ASTM provides somewhere in the region of $50,000 a year to fund consumer representation work on committees; other funding comes from industry sponsorship of specific standards programmes with the funding being held in trust by ASTM. This is usually enough to ensure two consumer representatives sit on selected committees, subject to ASTM approval. It has also in the past contracted for research with the National Consumers League where it has considered more information is needed to assess the consumer interest. More use is likely to be made of this type of funding (which is usually in the region of $15,000–30,000 per project) in the future and the amount ASTM sets aside to support consumer representation will also probably be increased. This is due to ASTM's review of the implication of its non–profit status. One might think this review was overdue for $50,000 for consumer representation was the figure quoted by Hamilton in 1978.[141] It also funds research relevant to consumer standards through the Institute for Standards Research.

The major standards writing organisations permit consumer representatives to participate in their technical committees. Indeed this contributes to the notion of committee balance which is written into the rules of organisations like ASTM. Participation of consumers is eased in theory by deeming them as being sufficiently knowledgeable persons to serve on committees. Consumer representatives are likely to be found on committees

---

140 Hamilton, *op. cit.*, at 1384.
141 *Ibid.*, at 1354.

dealing with consumer products. ASTM has for instance a committee F15 devoted exclusively to consumer products.

Consumer representatives on technical committees may be technical experts or informed lay persons. However, their involvement has been limited. In part this is because of a lack of volunteers and technical expertise within the movement. However, a more fundamental problem is the lack of funds for travel to enable participation. For instance, ASTM's committee FI5 has 578 members several of whom represent consumers, but a good deal of their involvement is through the mail. This is unlikely to be as effective as personal contact.

The consumer movement also has more deep seated objections to the standardisation process. For instance, even if it is involved in a technical committee, lots of the detailed work will be undertaken by working groups where the rules about committee balance will not apply and where consumers may be excluded because the work depends upon having access to laboratory facilities. Certainly in the past consumers have felt that the consensus principle has not adequately protected the consumer interest. In testimony to the National Commission on Product Safety the Technical Director of the Consumers Union stated:

> 'The consensus principle means in practice that the industry people have veto power... Our proposals [as consumer representatives], our negative votes, are given "due deliberation" but are ultimately vetoed or overridden, as without merit. After a while it seems fruitless to spend time and money to go to such meetings ...Volunteerism and token consumer representation have been generally unsuccessful in protecting the consumer interest.'[142]

Similar resentment about the summary rejection of consumer objections was expressed to a subsequent researcher, who however seemed satisfied that the ASTM Committee on Standards did carefully review such objections.[143] It is of course hard to assess the validity of these judgments or to determine at a distance if the position is still the same today. However, it is significant that the consumer representatives held negative opinions about the standardisation process. This may have been because of the lack of an adequate structure to support consumer representation both because of a lack of funding for such representation and because of the peripheral role consumers have in the organisation's decision–making procedures. The fact that, currently, US consumer organisations seem to be less active in the

---

[142]   Cited in Brodsky and Cohen, *op. cit.*, at 632.
[143]   Hamilton, *op. cit.*, at 1358.

standardisation area than their European counterparts suggests that these problems continue to be present in the United States today.

D. Appraisal

Standards–making procedures now adopt due process procedures which attempt to reach a national consensus. This is an improvement on the closed system which prevailed not too long ago.[144] These procedures would appear to provide business interests with adequate access to the standards process and to be sufficient to insulate the standards bodies from challenges under anti–trust law.[145] However, consumers seem to be inadequately represented both at the technical level and within the political structures of the standards organisations. Consumer involvement seems to focus on its advantages to industry rather than stressing the right of consumers to have a voice in the standards–making process.

4. CONCLUSIONS

There is much to recommend in the United States' approach to product safety. Particularly commendable is the centralisation in one Commission of the tasks of data collection, standards development, enforcement, publicity and education. As many of these tasks are inter–related the benefits from this integrated approach are obvious and seem to be taken advantage of by the highly motivated staff of the CPSC. The data collection systems of the CPSC in particular merit emulation elsewhere.

On the other hand the United States is a large country and there is a danger that a centralised bureaucracy based just outside Washington DC can be remote and aloof from the real concerns and problems of consumers. The CPSC does have a field staff spread throughout the country and contacts in each state and yet one wonders whether this is really adequate for the gargantuan task it faces. This, however, is not a reason for criticising the CPSC – given weak field support the need for a strong central administration becomes even more important – but rather points in favour of strengthening the nationwide enforcement network.

---

144 See Opala, *op. cit.*

145 Cf *Hydrolevel Corpn. v ASME*, 456 US 556 (1982) (US Supreme Court held ASME liable for anti–competitive behaviour of industry members) and *Allied Tube and Conduit Corpn. v Indian Head*, 817 F 2d 938 (US Supreme Court confirmed non–governmental standards bodies are subject to challenge as being an unreasonable restraint on trade).

The luggage of American administrative law history determined that the procedure for setting mandatory standards would be a cumbersome one. Thus, there was likely to be every incentive for the CPSC to rely on voluntary rather than mandatory rules. However, the move towards self–regulation, through the development of voluntary standards, has been more inspired by political dogma and cost saving considerations than any principled policy. The saving grace is that the CPSC retains the threat of regulation to use as a spur to industry to promote voluntary standards in a way which allows consumer involvement and has some satisfactory regard for consumer safety. It can also allow the CPSC to act where there is evidence that the voluntary standards will not be adhered to. However, these are very much fall back last resort powers. The European 'new approach' directives which leave to mandatory regulation the task of setting essential safety requirements, with voluntary standards determining how they can best be met, may be considered to provide a more attractive balance between regulation and self–regulation. Europe also seems to have been more successful at involving consumers in the standardisation process.

The United States law lacks the symbolism of a general safety duty. There is no positive duty to market only safe products in the United States. However, the remedial powers of the Commission where products fail to comply with product standards, voluntary standards which the Commission has relied upon, or where the product contains a defect which could create a substantial product hazard or create an unreasonable risk of serious injury and the power to deal with imminent risks go a long way to deal with the practical problems the general duty aims to address.

Although it may not be a practical problem, especially given the fear United States' business has of punitive damages, there must be some concern that there appears to be no power to detain imminently hazardous products prior to the matter being heard in a district court. Also it is to be regretted that the Commission's jurisdiction does not extend to cover consumer services. On the other hand, the formal granting to interested persons (including consumer groups) of the right to seek enforcement of the laws is an interesting attempt to empower the consumer and to allow him to become more involved in the regulatory process. Regrettably this power does not appear to have been widely used.

The United States' approach to export products of merely informing recipient Governments of the status of the goods can, in the context of exports of unsafe products to the developing world, be seen as little more than a salving of the Western conscience and the placing of an intolerable strain on the enforcement authorities of the third world. One indirect effect of the move towards voluntary standards is that there is no obligation to inform recipient countries where the product fails to comply with a merely voluntary standard.

5 United Kingdom

1. INTRODUCTION

Product safety regulation in the United Kingdom is fairly well developed. As we shall see in section 2 it was the first European country to introduce a data collection system (HASS) and although not as sophisticated or extensive as the US NEISS system it functions fairly well. In the regulatory field the United Kingdom was one of the first countries to recognise the need for general legislation to establish the framework for consumer safety regulation when it enacted the Consumer Protection Act 1961. In section 3 we see how, after various amendments and improvements, by the time the Consumer Protection Act 1987 (CPA) was enacted the United Kingdom had a modern scheme of consumer safety regulation, including a general safety obligation. This only needed minor fine tuning to comply with the EC's General Product Safety Directive.

The United Kingdom and France can both claim to have inspired the EC's approach to horizontal product safety. However, we shall note that the United Kingdom still lacks the power to require the recall of dangerous products which have reached the end consumer. This seems to fail to comply with the spirit and probably the letter of the EC's General Product Safety Directive (see Chapter 2, section 9I). Also we shall see that whilst the United Kingdom has the advantage of strong well organised local enforcement the position of consumer safety regulation within central government is less secure. In section 4 the role of standardisation is addressed. The British Standards Institute (BSI) is one of the leading players in standardisation on the global stage. It also has well developed mechanisms for consumer representation. Finally it will be noted that the United Kingdom is fortunate in having a well organised Consumers' Association (CA), which has technical expertise to support the political aspirations of the movement.

2. ACCIDENT DATA COLLECTION

Data has been collected from admissions to hospital accident and emergency units since 1976. In fact there are two systems. The Home Accident Surveillance System (HASS) collects data on home accidents and the Leisure Accident Surveillance System (LASS) is concerned with accidents involving outdoor products. This data is kept on the Home and Leisure Accident

Database. This is supplemented by data on fatalities resulting from home accidents which are kept on the Home Accident Deaths Database (HADD).

HASS/LASS data is based on accident victims attending accident and emergency departments at 18 hospitals.[1] These are selected to produce a representative sample and must have more than 10,000 Accident and Emergency (A & E) attendances per annum, operate a 24 hour service and take ambulance cases. From 1976 to 1987 the hospitals were routinely rotated, but this is no longer the case. Although there is of course a need to ensure the sample remains representative, there are also advantages in terms of the smooth running of procedures and developing expertise which result from maintaining a relationship with specific hospitals. Data from 11 of the hospitals is supplied to the EC for inclusion in the EHLASS system.

The fieldwork is undertaken by HASS/LASS interviewers, who are actually employed and managed by a commercial organisation, the British Market Research Bureau (BMRB). They attend A & E departments at peak times and identify patients who have suffered a home or outdoor accident which is neither an occupational accident nor a road traffic accident. Ideally the patient (or in the case of children the parent or accompanying adult) is interviewed using a standard interviewing questionnaire with information being subsequently extracted from the hospital's medical records. In about half of the cases an interview is not possible and a record is created from the medical records alone.

Completed interviews are entered on a computer and transferred to the Department of Trade and Industry's (DTI) Consumer Safety Unit (CSU) through a formal 'computer handshake' procedure. Fully electronic means of transferring data to the CSU are currently being evaluated. At each stage the data is screened.

The questionnaire has more than 50 fields, 30 of which relate to the occurrence of the accident. One provides space for a short text description, whilst other data permits statistical tables of up to three variables to be produced. These are found in the annual reports. The data is also made available to businesses, safety professionals and health authorities. Searches on subsets of statistics can be carried out or case listings with the text description can be supplied (although the individuals involved are not identified). The coding system was modified in 1993 when advances in technology permitted a greater number of products to be listed. In making these changes an effort was made to keep in line with changes in the EHLASS codes on which work also started in 1991 (see Chapter 2, section 8) and the current efforts by the World Health Organisation to introduce

---

[1]   Due to budgetary constraints data on leisure accidents was only collected every other day from 1992, but 100% data collection was reinstated on 1 January 1996, *Home Accident Surveillance System, 1994 Report*, (DTI, 1996).

standardisation of injury classifications (see Chapter 3, section 5). The 1994 Annual Report on HASS comments that most developments at the European and International level seem to have been foreseen, but that some detailed changes to codes and classifications may be necessary. However, it notes that the special needs to ensure long term compatibility in order to enable time series and trends analysis will be fully taken into account.[2]

The annual reports produce statistical tables from the HASS/LASS and HADD data. They also contains details of the CSU's other research work. These include short reports which may go on to provide the basis for further research work. The research can be into particular products (eg step ladders), population groups (eg children) or locations (eg bathrooms). Many of these are concerned with looking at ways in which standards can be improved or information campaigns targeted and made more effective. Others are, however, of a more general nature; for instance the 1994 Annual Report cites research into the data quality of statistics on fatal accidents, policy modelling for the CSU and a review of the market and safety of selected second–hand goods.

3. LEGAL REGULATION

A. Background

In 1960 the Molony Committee on Consumer Protection issued an interim report relating to dangerous goods.[3] It concluded that while there was no widespread marketing of dangerous consumer goods, the actual and potential risks from such products favoured the adoption of a general statutory power to prohibit the sale of such products. This recommendation led to the enactment of the Consumer Protection Act 1961.

Prior to 1961 there had only been regulation of specific product sectors such as food, medicines and fireworks. The 1961 Act had in theory a broad scope for it empowered the Secretary of State to make regulations concerning the composition or contents, design, construction, finish or packing for any particular class of goods where he considered this expedient to prevent or reduce the risk of death or personal injury. He could also require that goods

---

2   *Ibid.*, at 22–23. This comment was made in the context of describing the HASS/LASS systems as the 'world's longest running accident surveillance systems'. The United States may quibble at this description (Chapter 4, section 2C). Nevertheless permitting such long term analysis is no doubt a worthy objective in so far as it can be accomplished at the same time as complying with European and international obligations.

3   *Interim Report of the Committee on Consumer Protection*, Cmnd. 1011 (1960).

of that class or component parts were marked with or accompanied by a warning or instructions. Breach of such a regulation would be a criminal offence. Thus the principle of safety regulation of consumer products through delegated legislation was incorporated. Secondary regulations can be adopted far quicker than primary laws.

A major review of consumer safety legislation was undertaken following the consultation document on *Consumer Safety*[4] issued by the Secretary of State for Prices and Consumer Protection.[5] This pointed out certain deficiencies in the existing system which led to three new instruments being added to the Secretary of State's arsenal by the Consumer Safety Act 1978.[6] In addition to passing regulations he was also enabled to issue a prohibition order imposing a general ban on the supply of a particular product for up to 12 months. This was needed to permit the Secretary of State to act quickly when a product caused concern. It had an emergency procedure which avoided the cumbersome procedures required to enact regulations. The prohibition order was made redundant by the subsequent introduction in 1987 of an emergency procedure for adopting safety regulations. The two other measures introduced by the 1978 Act – the prohibition notice and the notice to warn – are still to be found in the CPA. Prohibition notices are served on individual traders to prevent the supply of a particular product. Notices to warn can require suppliers to publish a warning about unsafe goods.

Consumer safety legislation was once again thoroughly reviewed in the 1984 *White Paper on the Safety of Consumer Goods*.[7] This led to the Consumer Safety (Amendment) Act 1986[8] being enacted. This was

---

4   Cmnd. 6398 (1976). Barrett suggests that the reform proposals failed to arouse the same excitement as suggestions to reform the principles of compensation for personal injuries. She regrets this both because accident prevention is better than compensation and because greater public debate might have led to consumer safety and occupational safety being treated as facets of the same subject: see B. Barrett, 'Consumer Safety Act 1978' (1978) *M.L.R.* 707. However, as the German experience suggests (see Chapter 7) there may be some benefits in keeping consumer legislation distinct from health and safety legislation, this is not to say that action in the two areas should not be co–ordinated.

5   This Office no longer exists and as we shall see in section 3B, these matters are now dealt with by the Secretary of State for Trade and Industry.

6   For discussion see, Barrett, *op. cit.*, and S. Weatherill, 'Consumer Safety Legislation in the United Kingdom' [1987] *E. Consum. L.J.* 81. He also considers the Consumer Safety (Amendment) Act 1986 and looks forward to the then imminent CPA 1987.

7   Cmnd. 9302 (1984).

8   See, Weatherill, *op. cit.*, and K. Cardwell, 'The Consumer Protection Act 1987: Enforcement of Provisions Governing the Safety of Consumer Goods' (1987) 50

concerned primarily with improving enforcement. The powers mentioned so far (prohibition orders, prohibition notices and notices to warn) are all exercised by the Secretary of State, yet it is local trading standards officers who are responsible for detecting and prosecuting breaches of safety regulations. The 1986 Act gave them powers to issue suspension notices prohibiting the addressees from supplying the specified goods for up to six months. They were also given the power to seize goods and subsequently to apply for a forfeiture order.

Part II of the CPA 1987 consolidated the existing laws and also introduced a general requirement only to supply safe consumer goods. Some other reforms were included which aimed at improving enforcement.[9] S. 42 requires the Secretary of State to produce a report every five years on the operation of Part II of the CPA. One such report has been published.[10] Part II of the CPA was seen as a complement to part I which introduced strict products liability following the adoption of the European Product Liability Directive.[11] Subsequently, in order to comply with the EC's General Product Safety Directive[12] the UK enacted the General Product Safety Regulations 1994.[13] However, complying with the Directive did not require alterations to the basic structure which had been put in place.[14]

Finally, it is perhaps worth mentioning certain other pieces of legislation which may be relevant to matters of consumer safety. Part III of the Fair Trading Act 1973 permits the Director General of Fair Trading to take action against rogue traders who persist in a course of conduct which is detrimental to consumers' interests, including their interest in health or safety. The Director General can seek assurances from such traders or in the

---

M.L.R. 622 who considers the provisions as incorporated and modified in the 1987 Act.

9 See, Cardwell, *op cit.,* R. Merkin, *A Guide to the Consumer Protection Act 1987,* (Financial Training, 1987) and P. Fairest, *Guide to the Consumer Protection Act 1987,* (CCH, 1988).

10 *Report of the Secretary of State for Trade and Industry on Consumer Safety, 1 April 1988 to 31 March 1993,* H.C. 55 (1993–94) (hereafter, DTI report).

11 OJ 1985 L 210/29.

12 OJ 1992 L 228/24.

13 S.I. 1994/2328, see G. Howells, 'The General Duty to Market Safe Products in United Kingdom Law' [1994] *L.M.C.L.Q.* 479–486 and G. Howells, *Consumer Contract Legislation,* (Blackstone, 1995), Chapter 5 and P. Cartwright, 'Product Safety and Consumer Protection' (1995) 58 *M.L.R.* 222.

14 For a general overview of United Kingdom law following the implementation of the EC General Product Safety Directive, see G. Howells and S. Weatherill, *Consumer Protection Law,* (Dartmouth, 1995), Chapter 12 and C. Hodges, M. Tyler and H. Abbott, *Product Safety,* (Sweet & Maxwell, 1996), especially Chapter 5.

last resort seek an order from the Restrictive Practices Court requiring him to refrain from the unfair conduct. These provisions are not very easy for the Director General to invoke[15] and have tended to be used to protect consumers' economic interests rather that to deal with safety matters. However, some instances of the powers being used to ensure consumer safety can be found. A number of assurances have been provided in relation to the supply of defective motor vehicles and in 1992 two company directors gave assurances that they would refrain from contravening safety regulation relating to electrical goods.[16]

Hodges, Tyler and Abbott suggest that the Attorney General, or more likely local authority trading standards departments, using their power under s. 222 of the Local Government Act 1972, may seek an injunction in the civil courts to restrain the commission of a crime.[17] However, such an approach is unlikely to be used as enforcement officers have adequate powers at their disposal to deal with most situations involving unsafe products. Seeking an injunction might be attractive to officers in one respect, namely they would not be exposed to compensation claims as they are when using their enforcement powers (see, section I). However, the civil courts have shown themselves understandably reluctant to grant injunctions in situations where the criminal matter has not yet been determined, unless there has been a deliberate and flagrant flouting of the law[18] or at least they believe that nothing short of an injunction will restrain the defendants' unlawful activities.[19] Except in exceptional circumstances, the enforcement officers' powers in the CPA are likely to be seen as adequate.

B.   Enforcement Authorities

In the United Kingdom enforcement functions are divided between central and local Government. At the central Government level the Director General of Fair Trading has, under the Fair Trading Act 1973, some responsibilities for collecting information about practices which adversely affect the interests of consumers and can make recommendations to the Secretary of State. In addition, we have already noted his power to take action against traders who persist in a course of conduct detrimental to consumers' interests. Although

---

[15]   For a critique of the provisions see Howells and Weatherill, *op. cit.*, at 511–524.

[16]   Cited in Hodges, Tyler and Abbott, *op. cit.*, at 162.

[17]   *Ibid.*, at 163–165.

[18]   *Stafford Borough Council v Elkenford Ltd*, [1977] 2 All ER 519.

[19]   *City of London Corporation v Bovis Construction Ltd*, [1992] 3 All ER 697, see Bingham LJ at 714.

these powers extend to safety matters, in practice the CSU of the DTI is the main player in the field of consumer safety.

In 1976 the Government came out against the establishment of a Consumer Safety Commission analogous to the US Consumer Product Safety Commission or the transferring of the functions to the Office of Fair Trading.[20] At that time the CSU was housed in the Department of Prices and Consumer Protection. Now that it is within the DTI there may be more concerns about the interests of consumers being considered secondary to industrial and commercial development, which is of course the prime focus of the DTI. There must be doubts about the status of the Consumer Affairs section within the DTI and of the influence which the CSU can assert. A separate agency might provide a surer guarantee that the consumer interest was fully considered. However the downside would be that – as the experience of the Office of Fair Trading perhaps illustrates – when one is not part of a central Government department it is harder to get one's views heard and accepted by ministers and more difficult for the reforms you propose to be given the priority required to secure the necessary legislative time. Nevertheless there are enough policy arguments in favour of having a central agency to support such a development regardless of the political downside, especially as the existing agencies do not seem to have a particularly high profile within Government. Significant benefits can be derived from having one agency which collects data, supervises regulation and standards–making, co–ordinates information campaigns and publicity and, at least, supervises enforcement. The need for centralised support to local enforcement officers is becoming more important because of developments in the trading standards administration, which are discussed below.

The main functions of the DTI's CSU are operating the HASS system (see section 2) and in the regulation and standards–making process. It does have some enforcement powers, but as we shall see it is reluctant to use them and prefers to leave enforcement to the local level. It is also the United Kingdom's contact point for the RAPEX system (Chapter 2, section 9J(b)) and undertakes information and publicity campaigns, notably a firework safety campaign every year in the run up to Guy Fawkes Night.

Enforcement in the United Kingdom is mainly carried out at the local level by weights and measures authorities, ie trading standards officers.[21] This local enforcement is a great strength of the United Kingdom system.

---

20   Cmnd. 6398 (1976), *op. cit.*, at 28–9.

21   A duty to enforce consumer safety legislation was imposed on weights and measures authorities by the Consumer Safety Act 1978 and is now found in s. 27, Consumer Protection Act 1987. The Secretary of State has power to transfer responsibilities to other authorities, but this has not been exercised. The Consumer Protection Act 1961 had been silent on the matter of enforcement obligations.

Local officers develop a good knowledge of their patch and can be quick to react to problem products. However, the system is under strain. Resources devoted to consumer protection services are being squeezed under budgetary pressure and authorities must of course give priority to those services which they are under a statutory obligation to provide. This means that less time can be devoted to actively monitoring the market for dangerous products. Equally there are less funds for the sometimes expensive tests which have to be carried out to assess whether products pose unacceptable dangers. These factors, when combined with the trend to move to smaller unitary authorities, mean that there are less large authorities with the resources to handle complex product safety issues. A national consumer protection agency which could deal with the more serious product safety problems might ensure that local enforcement could continue to provide an effective service, whilst reducing the risk that some serious problems may not be adequately addressed due to local factors. Another solution might be for authorities to co–operate on a regional basis and some see the Labour Party's idea of regional assemblies as a possible model to build upon. The point has been made that enforcement officers may be tempted to use their resources against 'soft targets' such as shoddy children's toys and not take on large manufacturers who can call on large resources and experienced legal advisers to defend any allegations.[22]

There are two obvious problems which might arise from the emphasis on local enforcement: the lack of communication between authorities and the danger of businesses which operate in more than one authority being faced with conflicting interpretations. However, both problems have been largely resolved.

A computer data base TS LINK (operated by the Institute for Trading Standards Administration – ITSA) connects local trading standards officers and allows them to inform other authorities of any developments which might be of interest. The CSU also uses this system. There is also an Enforcement Bulletin which can be used for less urgent communications. ITSA co–ordinates policy approaches and also operates the HAZPROD data base, designed to spread information about hazardous products to enforcement authorities. However, this now seems to be less widely used than TS–Link.

The Local Authorities Co–ordinating Body on Food and Trading Standards (LACOTS) performs an important function in seeking to provide a uniform interpretation of laws. Central to this is the home authority

---

22   B. Cotter, 'Product Liability Law in the UK', paper presented at the *Product Liability in the United States and Europe - the New Regimes*, conference organised by Institute for Commercial Law Studies, University of Sheffield and Nottingham Law School, 23 September 1997, Law Society Hall, London.

principle.[23] The home authority is the authority in which an enterprise has its decision–making base. It is to its home authority that an enterprise looks for guidance and policy advice. The home authority also liaises with other interested authorities, ie the originating authority (the authority in which an enterprise produces or packages goods or services, assuming this is different from the home authority) and the enforcement authority (which is undertaking inspections, receiving complaints, making enquiries or detecting infringements). LACOTS will try to resolve any differences which arise between the authorities and may in the final instance establish a panel to advise on individual cases. It also issues circulars on specific matters. Enterprises should not therefore be faced with having to deal with conflicting advice from two authorities. Although the home authority principle works well on the whole, it is not binding and occasionally authorities will assert their right of action even in contradiction to the position of a home authority.

C. General Safety Requirement

S. 10 of the CPA introduced the general safety requirement. This was the last link in the enforcement powers which had been gradually expanded since 1961.

The notion of a general safety obligation had been raised in the 1976 consultation document on Consumer Safety.[24] At that time the idea of a general offence of supplying dangerous products was seen as being rather drastic as it would place a trader at risk of criminal prosecution even if he had taken all reasonable care. Even with a due diligence defence (on which see section K) this was thought to be unsatisfactory, as the onus would be placed on the defendant to prove he was not negligent in the face of possibly conflicting expert evidence as to what the criteria for safety are.

The Government preferred to canvass views on whether there should be an offence based on the manufacturer, importer or trader having to exercise due care to satisfy himself that, so far as is reasonably practicable, the goods he supplies are safe when properly used for their intended purpose or that any servicing he carries out on any goods does not render them unsafe. Interestingly this proposal would have therefore extended the rule to cover some aspects of service provision, but only in so far as the danger materialised in the form of an unsafe product. This negligence based proposal was inspired by a similar principle which is found in s. 6 of the Health and Safety at Work, etc. Act 1974. This places a duty on designers,

23 See LACOTS pamphlet, *Home Authority Principle*, (April 1994).
24 Cmnd. 6398 (1976), *op cit.*, at 22–3.

manufacturers, importers and suppliers to ensure that work articles are as safe and without risk to health when properly used as is reasonably practical.

By the time of its 1984 White Paper the Government had changed its tune and now favoured a general safety duty. It was argued that this would both encourage a greater sense of responsibility on the part of suppliers not covered by specific regulations and allow enforcement authorities to take swift remedial action in the face of newly identified dangerous products.[25] The latter is the most likely consequence to result from the introduction of a general safety obligation, for one suspects that businesses respond better to precise rules rather than general exhortations to produce safe products, which they would argue is their natural objective. A general safety duty may have a symbolic value and help to push safety up the policy agenda and to underline the Government's commitment to a safe consumer marketplace.

The White Paper commented that there had been no problems interpreting the level of safety required under s. 6 of the Health and Safety at Work, etc. Act 1974. The policy was to link the general consumer product safety standard expected to the concept of 'sound modern standards of safety'. Indeed under the resulting CPA the Secretary of State could approve standards so that compliance with them satisfied the general safety requirement (s. 10(3)(b)(ii)). Between 1987 and 1993 65 British Standards had been approved under this procedure. This provision has, however, now been repealed[26] and the previous approvals have been cancelled, but the reference to standards approach remains a feature of the CPA. Safety standards are expressly referred to as one of the circumstances to be taken into account when assessing the safety of consumer goods (s. 10(2)(b)). This basic approach is of course that followed by the Directive and hence the 1994 Regulations, although compliance with standards can no longer be an automatic defence. Under the 1994 Regulations they are simply factors to be taken into account when assessing safety (reg. 10(2)).

A similar change can be detected with regard to the relationship between compliance with legislation and the general safety requirement. The CPA provides an automatic defence if it was shown that the breach of the general safety requirement was attributable to compliance with community obligations (s. 10(3)(a))[27] or because of the failure to do more than is required by safety regulations or other legislation designated for this purpose with respect of that matter (s. 10(3)(b)(i) and (iii)). Under the Directive where there is specific Community regulation, then, at least so far as it

---

25   Cmnd. 9302 (1984), *op. cit.*, at 7–10.

26   See Reg. 6, General Product Safety Regulations 1994, S.I. 1994/2328 which revoked the Approval of Standards Regulations 1987, S.I. 1987/1911.

27   This is in fact quite a narrow defence as there must have been no way in which the Community obligation could have been fulfilled and the product made safe.

covers the relevant safety aspect, the general safety requirement does not apply, and this is the approach followed by the 1994 Regulations (reg. 4). However, where there are no specific Community regulations the Directive deems a product to be safe if it conforms to specific national rules (art. 4(1)), but goes on to provide that this should not prevent national authorities from taking steps to restrict its marketing or requiring its withdrawal (art. 4(3)). The 1994 Regulations treat compliance with national rules as simply establishing a *rebuttable* presumption that the product is safe (reg. 10(1)) and thus might be stricter than the Directive in the sense that the general safety requirement can be breached by a product conforming to national rules.

Despite the 1994 Regulations introducing a new general safety requirement (the definition of 'safe product' is almost identical to that found in the Directive, see Chapter 2, section 9D), the general safety requirement in s. 10 of the CPA remains in force. It was not repealed by the 1994 Regulations but simply disapplied to the extent that products are covered by the Regulations. S. 10 was therefore disapplied in situations where the general safety requirement must be complied with; namely where products are to be (i) placed on the market, offered or agreed to be placed on the market or exposed or possessed to be placed on the market by *producers*, or (ii) supplied, offered or agreed to be supplied or exposed or possessed to be supplied by *distributors* (reg. 5) (my emphasis). The CPA's general safety requirement may retain some limited relevance as it premises liability on the concept of 'supply'. For *distributors* 'supply' is also the concept used to disapply s. 10, but for *producers* the relevant concept is 'placing the goods on the market'. Neither term is defined in the 1994 Regulations, but one might assume supply would have the same meaning as in the CPA.[28] As supply is given a very broad meaning in the CPA it is possible that for producers it covers some circumstances which go beyond placing the product on the market. As these will be rare in practice the CPA's version of the general safety requirement will be only discussed briefly. Its main interest is as an historical note.

The CPA's general safety requirement had excluded from its scope several important categories of products, namely growing crops and things

---

[28] S. 46(1) of the Consumer Protection Act 1987 provides that references to supplying goods shall be construed as references to (a) selling, hiring out or lending goods, (b) entering into a hire–purchase agreement to furnish goods, (c) the performance of any contract for work and materials to furnish the goods, (d) providing the goods in exchange for any consideration (including trading stamps) other than money, (e) providing the goods in or in connection with the performance of any statutory function; or (f) giving the goods as a prize or otherwise making a gift of the goods, and (g) providing the service by which gas or water is made available for use.

comprised in land by virtue of being attached to it; water, food, feeding stuff and fertiliser; gas; aircraft (other than hang–gliders); motor vehicles; controlled drugs and licensed medicinal products and tobacco. It also did not apply to second hand goods and goods for export. The Directive/1994 Regulations no longer have a list of excluded products and second–hand products are only excluded if sold as antiques or for repair or reconditioning. There is no express exclusion of goods for export, much will depend upon how the 'market' is defined into which producer should not put unsafe products. This could be construed as simply the United Kingdom or taken to cover the whole world. In practice one suspects the relevant market will be treated as being the internal market of the EC.

The Directive/1994 Regulations may also be a little wider in scope than the CPA for they apply to 'any product intended for consumers or likely to be used by consumers' (reg. 2(1), whereas the CPA talked of goods which are 'ordinarily intended for private use or consumption' (s. 10(7)). It might be easier to bring goods which are sometimes used by consumers, although they are not intended for them, eg chemicals used in craftwork, within the Directive's definition.

The definition of safety in the CPA is broadly similar to the approach found in the General Product Safety Directive and 1994 Regulations. However, in some respects it may be seen as being less protective of consumers. It related safety to the purposes for which the product was being marketed, whereas the Directive talks about safety in relation to both the normal *or* reasonably foreseeable conditions of use. Also there was no explicit mention in the CPA of the need to take into account the categories of consumers at serious risk when using the product, especially children, or the effect on other products which could reasonably be foreseen to be used with it. However, too much should perhaps not be read into subtle semantic differences as the rules tend to be interpreted in a more broad brush impressionistic manner. This is especially true as the matter is rarely considered by the courts, but rather tends to form the basis of discussions between enforcement authorities and traders. There is one interesting case involving the application of s. 10 to a cooker hood where the danger arose from how the cooker hood operated when used in conjunction with certain gas cookers.[29] It was held that goods should not be viewed in isolation, but rather should be considered with regard to the use to which they are to be put, which included in that case use over a gas cooker. Interestingly this is the reverse of the situation to that under the General Product Safety Directive, where the definition of safety requires the effect on other products be take into account. Here the goods were unsafe because of the effect of another product on them.

---

[29]   *Whirlpool (UK) Ltd v Gloucestershire County Council,* (19945 159 *JP* 123.

The White Paper had proposed that breach of the general safety requirement should give rise to civil liability. However, neither the CPA nor the 1994 Regulations follow this approach and civil liability remains only available for breach of safety regulations.

D. Regulation–Making Power

Although some product sectors, such as food and drugs, are regulated by specific primary legislation, most consumer product specific regulation is undertaken by means of secondary legislation. Of course there are some exceptions to this. Thus the Fireworks Act 1951 was no doubt inspired by public concern to control this potentially particularly hazardous product. However, this legislation preceded the Consumer Protection Act 1961 which introduced the enabling power permitting the Secretary of State to make regulations to ensure consumer safety. No doubt nowadays the controls found in the Fireworks Act 1951 would be introduced in secondary rather than primary legislation.

One of the main reasons for favouring secondary over primary legislation is that it can be enacted more expeditiously. Although the Secretary of State has a duty to consult when proposing a regulation (s. 11(5), CPA), there is no need to find parliamentary time as the regulation is enacted subject to any negative resolution by either House of Parliament (s. 11(6), CPA). Of course this means that such laws are not as closely scrutinised as primary legislation. This might be thought to be a particular concern now that the regulations are subject to only the negative resolution procedure. This had been the original position under the 1961 Act, but the 1978 Act had required an affirmative resolution. However, it might be questioned as to whether in practice this greatly altered the attention such matters received. The most important influence on the content of the regulations will be the consultation process.

Although the Health and Safety Commission must be consulted where goods are suitable for use at work, the Secretary of State has otherwise a broad discretion to determine whom should be consulted, either as representatives of interests which are substantially affected or for any other reason (s. 11(5)). This broad discretion has been criticised,[30] but in practice there does not seem to be a problem of groups being excluded. There has been one instance where regulations have been successfully challenged because the Minister did not provide the applicant with the evidence from his advisory Committee on Carcinogenicity of Chemicals in Food, Consumer

---

[30] Barrett, *op. cit.*, at 709.

Products and the Environment.[31] In that case there were special considerations which suggested that the Secretary of State should bend over backwards to allow the affected company to make adequate representations. They had relocated a factory into Scotland with Government support and encouragement. Whilst this could not create a legitimate expectation that the Government would never ban their product (oral snuff), nevertheless it did induce sympathy for their position. Furthermore the Regulations would impinge almost solely on them as the sole manufacturer and packager of oral snuff in the United Kingdom and the effect was likely to be catastrophic on the applicant's business.[32] The principal of transparency in government decision–making which lies behind this decision is to be welcomed and of course similar regulations were eventually enacted after full consultation.[33] Although on this occasion an enterprise seems to have been treated badly in the consultation process, structurally the odds are weighted against the consumer movement. Any industry affected by a particular set of regulations has enormous incentives to invest a great deal in lobbying on that topic. The oral snuff case illustrates that they were prepared to seek judicial review and clearly had the finances to fund such a strategy. By contrast consumer representatives and safety campaigners have to spread their more limited amount of resources across a far broader range of topics.

Regulations allow particular consumer safety concerns to be addressed in a way which is appropriate for the relevant product sector. In theory the introduction of the general safety requirement should render specific regulations almost superfluous as now all products have to be safe and prosecutions can be brought if they are not. However, the educative function of developing a common understanding of what is expected of products means that product specific regulations will continue to be important. Under the influence of the EC's new approach (see Chapter 2, section 4C) recent regulations tend to cover a broad sector rather than specific products and do not specify detailed design characteristics but instead contain broad performance objectives which are fleshed out by standardisation.

The Consumer Protection Act 1961 was the first enabling legislation in this area, but the regulation–making powers in that Act were rather

---

31   *R v Secretary of State, ex p US Tobacco*, [1992] 1 All ER 212.
32   *Ibid.*, at 223–4.
33   See Tobacco for Oral Use (Safety) Regulations 1992, S.I. 1992/3134. B. Schwer and P. Brown, 'Legitimate Expectations – Snuffed Out' [1991] *Public Law* 163, criticise the decision not for the result – that the duty of consultation under the Consumer Protection Act 1987 required the applicants to be provided with the evidence on which the decision was made – but for the legal analysis which might suggest the rules of natural justice should apply when legislative functions are being carried out.

restricted.[34] The Consumer Safety Act 1978 contained a far more detailed regime. S. 11 of the CPA now provides the Secretary of State with the power to enact regulations for all goods, except growing crops and things comprised in land by virtue of being attached to it; water, food, feeding stuff and fertiliser; gas and controlled drugs and licensed medicinal products (s. 11(7)).[35] This regulation–making power is therefore broader in scope than many provisions of the CPA as it is not restricted to consumer goods. It also covers some products (aircraft, motor vehicles and tobacco) which had been excluded from s. 10 (the general safety requirement).

Regulations can be enacted to secure that:

- goods are safe;
- unsafe goods are not made available to persons generally;
- goods which would be unsafe in the hands of persons of a particular description are not available to those persons;
- appropriate information is, and inappropriate information is not, provided (s. 11(1)).

The argument that this only permitted regulations to protect consumers from defective goods and did not permit the prohibition of goods which are intrinsically unsafe has been rejected by the courts.[36]

The 1961 and 1978 Acts had specified a restricted list of provisions which such regulations could contain, with the 1978 Act being considerably more extensive than its predecessor. However, such an approach might be objected to on the basis that it simply encouraged litigation attacking regulations on the ground that they were *ultra vires.*[37] The CPA does not place any limits on the provisions which can be invoked to achieve the objectives in s. 11(1). Nevertheless s. 11(2) does contain a non–exhaustive list of provisions which such regulations may contain. These relate, *inter alia*, to:

- the composition, content, design, construction, finish, packing of goods, standards for goods and other matters relating to them;
- matters relating to the approval of goods or descriptions or standards for such goods;

---

34 For criticism see Cmnd. 6398 (1976), *op. cit.*, at para. 44.
35 The DTI. has used this power to enact some 33 sets of Regulations. Other departments may also have used the power, but these Regulations cover the type of products with which we are primarily concerned.
36 *R v Secretary of State, ex p US Tobacco*, [1992] 1 All ER 212 at 219.
37 Barrett, *op. cit.*, at 709. To the best of my knowledge no such challenge was made.

- requiring conformity to regulations or to descriptions or standards specified in or approved by or under regulations;
- the testing or inspection of goods;
- marks, warnings, instructions or other information relating to goods (and for securing that inappropriate information is not provided);
- prohibiting the supply of goods and acts preparatory to supply;
- the provision of information to officials and other matters relating to the prosecution of offences.

It may be questioned whether primary legislation needs to be cluttered with these provisions given that they impose no substantive controls. Two reasons for having this amplification might be suggested. First, if there were not an extensive list of possible provisions, industry could use the political argument that proposed regulations covered too many aspects. For instance, there was reluctance at one time for regulations to cover testing and certification.[38] Second, specifying the range of considerations may cause officials to consider whether each is required in a particular context. On balance this form of legislative drafting probably does little harm, but also little good, and might be simplified.

The regulations cannot themselves provide that contravention is an offence (s. 11(4)). S. 12 provides for five ways in which an offence can be committed by breaching a safety regulation. These are where a person (i) breaches a prohibition to supply etc. goods (s. 12(1)); (ii) fails to carry out a test or procedure (s. 12(2)(a)); (iii) does not deal appropriately with goods, the whole or part of which have not satisfied a test or standards connected with such a procedure (s. 12(2)(b)); (iv) contravenes rules relating to the provision or prohibition of information (by means of a mark or otherwise) (s. 12(3)); (v) fails without reasonable cause to provide information as required to enable others to carry out their functions or in giving the information makes a statement which he knows to be false in a material particular or is reckless in that respect (s. 12(4)). Persons guilty of an offence are liable on summary conviction for up to six months imprisonment and/or a fine not exceeding £5,000.

The Consumer Protection Act 1961 had contained a defence to a charge that regulations had been breached, if the defendant reasonably believed that the goods were not to be used in Great Britain. This provision is not found in subsequent Acts. Therefore the scope of the regulations depends upon how they are worded. For instance, the Furniture and Furnishings (Fire) (Safety) Regulations 1988 are disapplied where the supplier knows or has reasonable cause to believe that the goods will not be used in the United Kingdom.[39]

---

[38]   Cmnd. 1011, (1960), *op. cit.*, at para. 48.

[39]   Reg. 4(c), S.I. 1988/1324 as amended.

Where there is no express statement it is moot whether they should be applied to exports. This is a matter which could be usefully clarified.

The Secretary of State has extensive powers to obtain information for the purpose of deciding whether to make, vary or revoke any safety regulation (s. 18).[40] The same powers are available when he is deciding to serve, vary or revoke a prohibition notice or serve or revoke a notice to warn (see sections F and G). A notice can be served on any person requiring them to furnish specified information or to produce records or permit them to be copied. An offence is committed if the notice is not complied with or if information is supplied which is known to be false in a material particular or where the person is reckless as to its veracity. Such disclosure rules do have the potential to reveal trade secrets, but these are in principal protected by s. 38 which makes it an offence for persons receiving this information to make further disclosures. Nevertheless a trader can be forced to reveal information which may form the basis of civil or criminal proceedings against him (s. 38(2)). Such powers are, however, necessary if efficient enforcement is to be achieved and traders are not to be permitted to hide behind a veil of secrecy.

E. Emergency Regulation–Making Power

The Consumer Safety Act 1978 introduced the 'prohibition order'. This allowed the Secretary of State to prohibit the supply (also the preparatory acts of offering to, agreeing to, exposing for and possessing for supply) of goods of a particular description (s. 3(1)). Under the standard procedure this notice would have been preceded by a 28 day notice period during which representations could be heard. This notice period could, and usually was,[41] dispensed with if the measure contained a statement from the Secretary of State that in his opinion the risk of danger was such that the order should come into force without delay. Indeed it was this power to act without delay which was the key innovation of the prohibition order, as otherwise much the same result could have been achieved by regulation. Prohibition orders could only remain in force for 12 months, the idea being to give the Government time to assess whether any more permanent measure was needed.

---

40 It has not been found necessary to use these powers as information has been volunteered by the trade or enforcement authorities: see, *DTI Report, op. cit.*, at para. 8.

41 Writing in 1987 Weatherill notes that of the eight orders made only one had given 28 days notice and the remainder had followed the emergency procedure: Weatherill, *op. cit.*, at 89.

The prohibition order was repealed by the CPA. However, this was because the regulation–making procedure had been reformed so that the same effect as a prohibition order could be achieved. The duty to consult (s. 11(5)) no longer applies if the regulations are to cease to have effect no more that twelve months after coming into force and contain a statement from the Secretary of State that the need to protect the public requires that regulations should be made without delay. It is perhaps surprising that there is not even an obligation to consult after the making of an emergency regulation (cf the procedure with respect to prohibition notices). Three sets of Regulations have been adopted under the emergency procedure.[42]

F. Prohibition Notice

The Consumer Safety Act 1978 also introduced the 'prohibition notice' and the 'notice to warn'. Whereas the (now defunct) prohibition order allowed the Secretary of State to act to prohibit the supply of goods of a particular by description by any person, a prohibition notice is served on a specified individual and it only prevents that person from supplying (except with the Secretary of State's consent) the goods described in the notice which are considered to be unsafe. The prohibition notice is therefore most useful when the danger can be isolated to a limited number of products and their whereabouts can be established. It is not usually concerned with the general safety features of a particular type of product (although it might be used to deal with a supply of products not usually found on our market), but rather is most often used against rogue products which fall below general standards. If such products reach the market there is no need to disturb general practice, the rogue products simply need to be removed from the market. Prohibition notices have been issued on three occasions with respect to Mercury Soap (1988), Crazy Hand and Mini Snappers (plastic sweet like toys) (1988) and Jelly Balls (1992).

The provisions on prohibition notices are now found in s. 13, CPA. Part 1 of schedule 2 of the Act contains provisions concerning the content of the notice and how affected parties can make representations. The notice should state that the Secretary of State believes the goods are unsafe and set out his reasons. The date on which the notice comes into force should be stated together with information on the trader's right to make representations to the Secretary of State for the purpose of establishing that the goods are safe. Contravention of the notice is an offence.

---

[42] Three–Wheeled All–Terrain Motor Vehicles (Safety) Regulations 1988, S.I. 1988/2122; Imitation Dummies (Safety) Regulations 1992, S.I. 1992/3189 and the Firework (Safety) Regulations 1996, S.I. 1996/3200.

It is important to note that the consultation period occurs after and not before the prohibition notice is made. Consumer protection is seen as the priority. Where representations are made then the Secretary of State must notify the trader within a month of whether he is to revoke or vary the notice or else he must specify a place and time (within 21 days) at which oral representation and the examination of witnesses can take place before a person appointed by the Secretary of State. The Secretary of State has a duty to consider any representation and any report by a person appointed by him. In the Jelly Balls case, cited above, 2 of the 14 traders who had a prohibition notice served on them appealed, but on receiving the appointed person's report the notices were confirmed.[43] However, there is no right of appeal to the courts, except of course by way of judicial review of the Secretary of State's decision. In this way a prohibition order made by the Secretary of State is more draconian than the enforcement officer's power to issue a suspension notice which, as we shall see, has to be confirmed by the courts (see below, section I). Another contrast between the powers of central and local government is that the Secretary of State is not liable to pay any compensation if the representations show that a notice was not justified or not justified in the form it was made. We shall see that the liability of enforcement officers may be an inhibiting factor preventing them from using their powers to the full extent they might wish to.

G. Notice to Warn

A notice to warn requires a person who supplies, or has supplied goods, which the Secretary of State considers to be unsafe to publish a warning about them at his own expense and in the form and manner and on the occasions specified in the notice (s. 13(2)). Contravention of the notice is an offence.

Unlike the prohibition notice the notice to warn does not have immediate effect. Instead, part II of schedule 2 provides for a procedure under which a draft of the proposed notice has to be served on the trader. No action can be taken until 14 days have passed without any representations being made. If the trader indicates that he wishes to make representations a further 28 days must be allowed. If any representations are made then the Secretary of State must consider a report by a person he has appointed to look into the matter. These procedures are very cumbersome and quite inappropriate for situations in which consumer safety is at risk; a 42 day delay can be incurred without the trader even having made a representation!

---

43   *DTI. Report, op. cit.*, at para. 5.

In fact no notice to warn has ever been issued. A recent textbook on product safety has suggested the breadth of these powers and the embarrassment which any required publicity could cause make them a 'particularly potent threat'.[44] Given the procedural hurdles and the practice of the DTI this might seem rather to overstate the utility of this regulatory tool. In fact in most cases the power to issue a notice to warn would be superfluous. There are enough incentives to encourage traders to co–operate with the DTI. One significant incentive is the desire to restrict civil claims for damages should the product injure a consumer. Also many traders will wish to preserve and promote their consumer image by being seen to respond responsibly to product dangers. There is also every reason for businesses to avoid confrontation and be reasonably amenable to realistic suggestions put forward by their regulators. This is especially so as the DTI has on occasions issued press releases about dangerous products. Given the considerable appetite of the media for consumer safety stories, press releases can be a more effective and less burdensome means of achieving the same end as a notice to warn.[45]

The notice to warn is theoretically more intrusive into the trader's business affairs than are regulations or prohibition notices. Whilst the latter may restrict the trader's freedom to produce or supply goods they do not affect his relationship with his customers. Notices to warn can impose requirements which may undermine the trader's image in the mind of his customers and the general public. However, it is still non–interventionist in the sense that, whilst it can require the public to be warned of dangers and the ways to avoid them, it cannot impose an obligation on the trader to recall products or to take steps to rectify the danger. We have argued that the EC's General Product Safety Directive requires authorities to have such a power (Chapter 2, section 2I) and will note that one of the biggest disappointments with the United Kingdom's implementing legislation is that it does not include any recall procedures (see section L).

H. Enforcement Powers

The powers considered so far have all been exercisable by central government, in practice by the CSU of the DTI. Yet we commented in section 3B that the prime responsibility for consumer safety enforcement lies with local government trading standards officers. Indeed even where the DTI has power to act against particular problems, by for instance serving a prohibition notice, it tends to prefer to inform trading standards officers and

---

44   Hodges, Tyler and Abbott, *Product Safety, op. cit.,* at 152.
45   This is the opinion of the DTI, see *DTI Report, op. cit.,* at para. 7.

let them deal with the matter. It is to the powers these officers have to enforce consumer safety regulation that we now turn.

The thrust of the 1984 White Paper had been to make enforcement more effective by improving the powers enforcement officers have to supervise first suppliers, improving communications between customs officials and the enforcement authorities and giving more effective enforcement powers. These changes were enacted by the Consumer Safety (Amendment) Act 1986 and are consolidated into Part II of the CPA.[46]

S. 28, CPA allows enforcement officers to purchase goods and to have them tested. This is a rather traditional power which had, along with the power to inspect goods, been found in the original Consumer Protection Act 1961. The Consumer Safety Act 1978 included the power to enter premises, other than those used only as a dwelling house; to examine whether any test or procedure had been carried out; to seize and detain goods (but only if there was reasonable grounds to believe relevant provisions had been contravened) and also documents which might be required as evidence. On the face of it the 1978 Act provided significant enforcement powers, but these have been described as having been more 'apparent that real'.[47]

One criticism was that the powers were not extensive enough to provide for routine inspection of the first supplier, as enforcement officers had to have reasonable cause to believe there had been breach of a safety provision before they could require the production of documents or seize and detain goods for testing.[48] This has been remedied by giving officers powers to act against manufacturers and importers before goods are supplied for the purpose of ascertaining whether there have been any contraventions (s. 29(4)). Cardwell also noted that a major impediment to mass seizure of goods was the requirement eventually to prove that a regulation had been breached in respect of every item. The cost of testing each item would make this impracticable.[49] The position seems to have improved somewhat as courts can now infer that all goods are in contravention if representative goods are shown to have been in contravention (s. 16(4)). However, this provision may not be as water–tight as it seems. S. 16(4) only permits this inference for the purposes of s. 16 (which deals with forfeiture orders, see section J). As we shall see the threat of a compensation claim remains a significant impediment to effective enforcement practice and in theory, at least, the authorities will have to show a contravention for every product to avoid exposure to compensation claims based on inappropriate seizure of goods or the serving of a suspension notice. Furthermore the inference of

---

[46] See Cardwell, *op. cit.*
[47] *Ibid.*, at 625.
[48] Cmnd. 9302 (1984), *op. cit.*, at para. 21.
[49] Cardwell, *op. cit.*, at 625.

contravention on the basis of a representative sample is at the court's discretion and there may be circumstances when the court is convinced that the sample was not representative, or at least that a considerable number of products were not in contravention. For the avoidance of doubt it would have been better to give a complete defence to compensation claims where a sample, constructed in accordance with current guidelines, was shown to be in contravention.

The CPA provides that customs officers are able to seize and detain goods for two working days for the purpose of facilitating the exercise by the authority of the exercise of its functions (s. 31). They can also disclose information about the goods to enforcement officials (s. 37). These provisions have the advantage that there are no compensation provisions for goods wrongly seized, but on the other hand two days does not give a very long time for ascertaining whether the goods are unsafe. Also these powers are discretionary and it is unlikely that the importation of dangerous consumer products will be a priority for customs officials. This regime is in fact overridden by EC Regulation 339/93 (Chapter 2, section 10). This allows three days within which to assess goods, but on the other hand it prevents s. 31 being applied at all to goods which are already circulating within the EC. However, customs officers and enforcement officials have agreed to continue to liaise closely where they have intelligence that imports may not satisfy safety requirements.[50]

The various powers listed above are now to be found in part IV, ss 27–35, CPA. They are concerned with the powers enforcement officers have to detect unsafe goods and can generally be considered satisfactory. Of course the real problem is funding the officers to be able to make use of these powers. In the next two sections we look at the powers officers have once unsafe consumer goods are detected.

I.   Suspension Notices

S. 14, CPA provides enforcement officers with the power to serve suspension notices when they have reasonable grounds for suspecting that goods contravene any safety provision. Safety provisions include the general safety requirement, any provision of safety regulations, a prohibition notice, suspension notice (s. 45) and the requirements of the General Product Safety Regulations (by virtue of reg. 11(b)). A suspension notice can prohibit a person from, without the authority's consent, supplying, offering to supply, agreeing to supply or exposing goods for supply. The notice should identify the goods, set out the authority's grounds for suspecting contravention of the

---

50   *DTI Report, op. cit.*, at para. 42.

safety provision and provide information on the right of appeal. It can last for up to six months. Contravention of a suspension notice is an offence. Within the first five years of the CPA's operation 1702 suspension notices were served.[51]

The suspension notice was first introduced by the 1986 Act, along with the forfeiture provisions (see section J). They marked an important development in the arsenal of weapons at the disposal of local enforcement officers who are responsible for the day to day administration of product safety regulation. The suspension notice allows them to halt the supply of goods which they suspect to be dangerous either with a view to seizing them or pending prosecution or forfeiture proceedings. One thing that a suspension notice does not do is prevent goods being moved. In the original provision there was a potential danger that enforcement authorities might lose track of goods subject to a suspension notice, this is now remedied in the CPA by a provision which can require a person with an interest in goods to keep the authority informed of their whereabouts (s. 14(3)). The prohibition on supply etc. would also seem to extend to the exporting of goods, although in practice it is understood enforcement authorities will usually allow goods to be re-exported to the country from which they had been imported.

The omission of a power to revoke a suspension notice is perhaps surprising, although the same result can be achieved through the authority using its power to consent to the supply of the goods. If a trader wishes to challenge a suspension order an application can be made to a magistrates' court for an order setting aside the notice. Such an order can only be made if the court is satisfied that there has been no contravention of any safety provision. There is a further right of appeal from the magistrates' court to the Crown Court (s. 15). It is important to note that this right of appeal concerns the factual question of whether or not a safety provision has been breached. The behaviour of the authority is irrelevant. Protection of the consumer is more important than any harm which might have been caused to a trader by the authority mishandling the problem. This was the important conclusion of the Court of Appeal in *R v Birmingham City Council, ex p Ferrero Ltd*,[52] which held that the existence of a statutory right of appeal precluded an action for judicial review. An exception might be possible if it could be shown that an authority had acted out of malice, but this was unlikely to be the case where a safety provision had been breached and in such a circumstance one would hardly want to quash the notice and expose the public to dangerous goods.

The *Ferrero* case went on to discuss, *obiter*, two other aspects of considerable practical importance. First, it held that there was no duty to

---

51   *DTI Report, op. cit.*, at para. 11.

52   [1993] 1 All ER 530.

consult before issuing a suspension notice. The Court recognised that the CPA provided for various consultation procedures either before (in the case of regulations and notices to warn) or after (for prohibition notices). The fact that it provided for none in this instance must indicate that a premium had been placed on swift action. Although in non–urgent cases consultation would be advisable, it would not be right to place a burden on officials to have to consider whether consultation was required. It was noted that the possibility of having to pay compensation (should it be shown that no safety provision had been breached) would in itself be an incentive for enforcement officers to consult where this was practicable.

The Court also held that an authority could legitimately serve the suspension notice despite being offered an undertaking in the same terms by the trader. This is despite the undertaking having the practical advantage that it would be of unlimited duration whereas the notice expired after six months. A trader might wish to take on this more onerous obligation to avoid the stigma of having a suspension notice served on him. It is arguable whether the trader should have the freedom to avoid this stigmatisation. In the event the Court found sound practical reasons why the trader's undertaking need not be accepted by the authority. The authority should not have the burden placed on it of deciding whether a trader can be trusted to honour the undertaking. Moreover, if a notice were withdrawn following the granting of an undertaking, no further notice could be served on the same person even if the undertaking was breached (unless court proceedings were pending). There would also be no sanction for breach of the undertaking, at best an injunction could be sought. Furthermore the court was sensitive to the problems which might arise in enforcing the law in other enforcement authorities once one authority had accepted an undertaking.

We have mentioned on several occasions that enforcement authorities risk having to pay compensation if a suspension notice turns out not to have been justified. This may be payable to any person having an interest in the goods if there has been no contravention of any safety provision and the exercise of the power is not attributable to any neglect or default by that person (s. 17(7)). It is interesting that these compensation powers are not matched by similar penalties on the Secretary of State should he exercise his own powers unwisely. This distinction seems all the more unfair because trading standards authorities issuing suspension notices are typically responding to emergency situations.

There is clearly unease on the part of the business community about giving greater powers to local enforcement officers. It is disturbing to see this attitude was shared by the Minster responsible for introducing the powers. Michael Howard (the responsible minister) stated that 'we are not in the business of creating a new and potentially considerable burden on business by allowing local authorities to obstruct free trade without bearing the consequences of their action.'[53]

This leaves trading standards officers in an unenviable position. They know they will be blamed if they err on the side of caution and permit products to continue to be marketed which turn out to be dangerous and cause injuries. Yet if they act too precipitively they risk having to pay compensation. Exposure to compensation claims does seem to be a real restraint on the freedom of officers to act as they see best.[54] This is despite the fact that officers are not likely to be held personally liable. Some authorities insure against such claims, others (possibly an increasing number) self insure. Of course even if costs are met by insurance cover the occurrence of such claims will inevitably have to be reflected in future premiums. However, even if there is no direct financial consequence for the officer or his authority the desire to avoid the stigma and complications of a compensation claim will weigh heavily on an officer's mind. Individual officers may be mindful of blotting their promotion prospects, whilst senior officers will have to report to elected officials who will in any event most likely be concerned about the impact on local businesses of over zealous enforcement.

Of course one sympathises with traders who suffer losses due to what turns out to be unwarranted concerns of enforcement authorities. However, it might be thought that the present grounds for compensation are flawed in at least two respects. First, compensation turns upon whether a safety provision has been contravened. Yet the loss flows from the issuing of the suspension notice. Such a notice has to be based on the enforcement authority having reasonable grounds for suspecting that any safety provision has been contravened. Should compensation not depend upon whether there were such grounds? If there were then surely public safety outweighs the commercial concerns of the trader. To the extent that these grounds were based upon the neglect or default of the person concerned compensation is in fact already limited, but the defence to a compensation claim should be on a broader basis wherever reasonable grounds for suspicion existed. Second, the amount of compensation should be restricted. Presently the authority is liable for 'any loss or damage caused by reason of the service of the notice'. Thus the authority would be liable not only for any deterioration in the quality of the goods, but also for any lost profit. A fairer approach might be one which models itself on s. 9(7), Food Safety Act 1990 which limits compensation to any depreciation in the value of food which has been wrongly seized or

---

53 Comment to Standing Committee C. cited in Weatherill, *op.cit.*, at 94.
54 This is certainly the view of one practitioner who specialises in this area, Cotter, *op. cit.*

inappropriately subjected to a notice restricting its movement.[55] Most consumer goods, apart from food,[56] would not deteriorate in value if held for a short time; although some products such as computer equipment or fashionware may do so. 'Full' compensation may be appropriate if the rule is changed so that compensation depends upon the authority not having had reasonable grounds for suspecting a contravention, although one might wish to qualify this by requiring a finding of malice or (gross) negligence.

J.   Seizure and Forfeiture Order

We noted that a suspension notice left the goods with the trader. This is not a problem if the enforcement authority trusts a trader and may be very desirable where the goods are bulky and/or would be difficult for the authority to store. Nevertheless it can be a drawback in some situations, particularly if the authority feels the trader cannot be trusted. Therefore s. 29(6)(b), CPA gives enforcement officers the power to seize and detain goods they have reasonable grounds for suspecting may be liable to be forfeited. Use of this power, however, once again exposes the officer to compensation claims should no contravention be established (s. 34). Any person with an interest in the goods may appeal against their detention to a magistrates' court and from there to the Crown Court (s. 33).

S. 16 of the CPA allows an enforcement authority to apply to a magistrates' court for an order for the forfeiture of the goods on the grounds that there has been a contravention of a safety provision. This will usually take place an the same time as an offence is being prosecuted or a trader is challenging a suspension notice or the seizure and detention of his goods. To make the order the court must be satisfied that there has been a contravention of a safety provision, however, it is important to remember that there is no need for there to have been an actual conviction. Thus goods can be subject to a forfeiture order even if the trader would be able to rely on a due diligence defence.

Cardwell suggests that it also means that the trader need not have done a prohibited act in relation to the goods and cites the example of the powers being used against an owner of goods who claimed that he intended to render

---

55   Under that Act full compensation remains payable for inappropriate use of an emergency prohibition notice: s. 12(10), Food Safety Act 1990.

56   Food was not covered by the 1987 Act, although the regulation–making powers could potentially apply to it, but suspension notices do now cover food by virtue of the General Product Safety Regulations 1994, reg. 11(b). In practice the specific food safety legislation is likely to be preferred.

the goods safe before placing them on the market.[57] With respect the trader must have done some kind of prohibited act for the forfeiture order is premised on contravention of a safety provision, the point surely is that under the general safety requirement (s. 10) possessing goods for supply is a prohibited act in its own right. It might be argued that such a trader did not possess the goods *for* supply at that time; the intention to supply would not arise until the goods were rendered safe.[58] In such circumstances the court might be mindful of the need to ensure surveillance of the goods and prefer to make a forfeiture order, but use its powers to allow the goods to be repaired and reconditioned (see below).

Where a contravention of a safety provision can be shown, then a forfeiture order must be made, the court has no discretion. We have already noted that the task of the enforcement authorities (and courts) has been made easier by s. 16(4), CPA which permits the court to infer for the purpose of making the forfeiture order that all the goods contravene the safety provision if a representative sample does.

Usually any goods forfeited will be destroyed under the court's direction. However the court may choose to order that the goods be released to a person on condition that they are only supplied to someone who carries on a business of buying goods of the same description and repairing and reconditioning them. The Act expresses this as two cumulative conditions. The trader to whom the goods are eventually supplied (note not the person to whom they are released) must be in the business of buying that type of goods *and* he must also be in the business of repairing/reconditioning them. It is unclear how closely the court will scrutinise the business to determine whether the buying of goods subject to the forfeiture order are the precise type of goods the trader has bought in the past and whether repairing/reconditioning is a typical part of his business. One suspects the court will be more interested in the general reputation and character of the trader than with these semantic questions, but may find them useful grounds for justifying refusing a request to release the goods. Alternatively the goods can be released on condition that they are only supplied as scrap.

The person to whom the goods are released, who may or may not be the defendant, must also meet any order for costs or expenses made against the person subject to the forfeiture order. S. 35 specifically permits the courts to make an order (in addition to any other order) to reimburse expenditure in connection with the seizure or detention of goods or which has been incurred in compliance with directions in a forfeiture order.

---

57 Cardwell, *op. cit.*, at 633.
58 A similar point arises under the General Product Safety Regulations 1994, S.I. 1994/2328, reg. 13.

It is noteworthy that the court cannot permit goods subject to a forfeiture order to be released for export. Of course if goods were only ever intended to be exported there may be no breach of a safety provision. However, traders seem to be prevented from switching goods to new markets once national authorities have been alerted to their dangers. In practice traders would have to negotiate with trading standards authorities to seek a variation of the suspension notice to permit the exportation of the goods. As commented earlier this is most likely to be granted where goods are being re–exported back to the country of origin and should not ethically be permitted where they are being supplied to a third country, at least without prior approval from an importing state which is able to assess the safety of the goods (Chapter 1, section 5).

During the first five years of the CPA's operation 299 forfeiture orders were made.[59] Goods being withdrawn voluntarily on a further 1237 occasions.

K.   Strict Liability and the Due Diligence Defence

The offences listed above are ones of strict liability, by which is meant that there is no *mens rea*. Doing the act amounts to an offence whether or not the defendant is blameworthy. The rationale for imposing strict liability is two–fold.[60] First, there is a view that such offences are not truly criminal; they often do not have a direct victim and conviction rarely leads to serious penalties involving the loss of liberty. They are often even termed 'regulatory offences' rather than crimes. Thus it is argued there is no need to require *mens rea* as these rules serve the purpose of promoting standards rather than controlling inappropriate behaviour. It might be thought that this argument suggested not that these matters should be strict liability criminal offences, but rather that they be taken out of the criminal law altogether. Indeed arguments for decriminalisation have been put forward.[61] It is argued that removing the threat of the stigma of criminal conviction would make traders more willing to co–operate once the resentment at being criminalised for an act they did not commit either intentionally or due to a lack of care is removed. Equally once such matters are taken out of the realm of the criminal law and procedure it should be possible to remove certain elements, such as the high burden of proof and strict rules of interpretation, which are

---

[59]   *DTI Report, op. cit.*, at para. 13.

[60]   Howells and Weatherill, *op. cit.*, at 415–417. See also B. Wootton, *Crime and the Criminal Law – Reflections of a Magistrate and Social Scientist*, (2 ed.) (Stevens, 1963) Ch. 2.

[61]   D. Tench, *Towards a Middle System of Law*, (Consumers' Association, 1981).

essential to safeguard liberty in the 'true' criminal context, but which can be seen as irrelevant and unnecessary impediments to the enforcement of trading standards laws.

On the other hand the characterisation of offences as criminal does underpin the seriousness with which society treats these matters and there is certainly evidence (from cases such as the *Ferrero* case discussed above and the due diligence cases considered in this section) that companies do not like their behaviour being stigmatised as criminal and will go to great lengths to avoid conviction.[62]

Borrie has suggested a two tier system with practices involving moral turpitude remaining crimes and others being classified as contraventions and being enforced by administrative agencies.[63] Although theoretically appealing this distinction in fact would introduce unnecessary complications. Most traders and enforcement officers currently recognise that regulatory offences differ from typical crimes. Enforcement practice rests largely on negotiation and actual prosecution usually only occurs when a serious contravention has occurred and officers feel public condemnation is appropriate or where the trader has been obstructive. If traders fear public trial in such instances then this is probably no bad thing. What also needs to happen is for the courts to appreciate that they are dealing with a special genre of criminal offences and to adapt their approach to regulatory offences accordingly.

A second justification for imposing strict liability is the role it can play in ensuring effective enforcement of consumer safety laws. It would place enormous costs on trading standards departments if they had to prove that the trader had acted in a culpable manner. Offences would not be prosecuted because authorities could not find evidence of culpable behaviour or could not do so without committing a disproportionate amount of their resources. Moreover it should be reiterated that introducing a *mens rea* requirement would not be entirely consistent with the objectives of the legislation. True one goal of product safety laws is to encourage traders to behave more responsibly, but more importantly it is to ensure that consumers are not exposed to dangerous products.

In the light of the above justifications for strict liability it might be considered slightly strange that, whilst professing to create offences of strict liability, the CPA actually provides an 'escape route' for the non–blameworthy defendant by virtue of the 'due diligence defence'. The legislator

---

[62] For support for the use of criminal law, although possibly with some modifications see G. Borrie, *The Development of Consumer Law and Policy*, (Stevens, 1984), Chapter III.

[63] *Ibid.*, at 53–4.

seems to have baulked at the implications of seeing the strict liability principle through.

In practice the due diligence defence can be a major restraint on the ability of enforcement officers to bring prosecutions. Even though the burden is on the trader to establish the defence (and thus strict liability plus the due diligence defence is still preferable to a *mens rea* requirement), the mere fact that an authority knows such a defence is likely to be raised will force it to consider whether it can justify allocating resources out of its limited budget to challenge the defence. Suspension notices are effective and forfeiture orders can be made on the basis of a contravention of a safety provision regardless of whether an offence was committed, so a due diligence defence could be pleaded. Enforcement officers may therefore be tempted to conclude that as the dangerous goods can be dealt with there is little to be gained from testing a due diligence defence, unless the trader is seen as a particularly bad rogue which the trading standards officers want to make an example of.

The due diligence defence is seen as an attempt to strike a balance between a strict liability rule which focuses on the need to have safe consumer goods and the feeling that honest traders who have done the best they can should not be subject to criminal sanctions. Formally the standard demanded by traders for such immunity is, as we shall see, quite high, but in reality any trader who can show any sort of *prima facie* reasonable quality system is going to have a good chance of avoiding prosecution. Given that the offending goods can still be removed from the market it might be questioned whether this is a real problem. The problems lie in the fact that the possibility of invoking the defence weakens the enforcement authority's ability to negotiate specific improvements in the trader's future behaviour (it may also incidentally reduce the respect in which trading standards' departments are held once it is appreciated that their ability to prosecute is in fact quite restricted) and also reduces the visibility of regulatory misdemeanours. Trading offences are already relatively hidden from the public because of the dominant strategy of negotiation adopted by enforcement officers. Selective prosecution of rogue defenders of serious cases serves an important educative function. Not only is the general public alerted to particular problem products or traders, but perhaps more importantly decision–makers, in the form of local and national politicians and senior policy advisers, are reminded that serious problems do exist and consumer safety cannot be marginalised or ignored when setting priorities.

Various versions of the due diligence defence appear in different consumer protection statutes. The wording to be found in the CPA is rather more concise than many. It provides a defence to a person who shows 'that he took all reasonable steps and exercised all due diligence to avoid committing the defence' (s. 39(1)).[64] This would seem to require evidence of both adequate procedures to try to avoid contravening safety regulations and proper surveillance to ensure those procedures are being complied with.

It has been commented that in determining whether the defence has been established much depends upon fact situations and precedent plays little formal role.[65] Indeed this is one of the reasons why it is difficult for enforcement authorities to justify using resources to challenge a defence the merits of which can only be fully assessed after an exhaustive analysis of a defendant company's internal procedures. Some guidance can however be ascertained from the case law. For instance, less will be expected of village shops than large retailers.[66] Significantly that comment was made in the context of imposing obligations on a large retailer, rather than as an excuse for the behaviour of a corner shopkeeper.

Emphasis has been placed on the need to take *all* reasonable steps with the burden being on the defendant to establish the defence. It has not been held to be sufficient to rely on a contract condition requiring compliance with safety regulations,[67] nor to test to compliance with British Standards rather than Regulations.[68] It will not usually be sufficient to rely on tests carried out by the supplier[69] or an overseas agent.[70] Usually the importer of overseas goods will be expected to carry out his own checks and the sample size must be appropriate. In one case it was found to be inadequate to test just one packet from a batch of 10,800 dozen packets of crayons.[71] One suspects that lying behind some of these decisions is a suspicion of the value which should be placed on assurances provided by distant producers and even testing houses, especially those in the Far East. One might consider this to run counter to the policy of the EC and WTO of promoting mutual recognition. However, whilst EC law imposes some controls on which test results have to be recognised, international economic law has not yet reached this level. Moreover the EC rules govern only conformity assessment procedures for products covered by new approach directives. There may be

---

64   For consideration of the defence in more detail see Howells and Weatherill, *op. cit.*, at 417–431.

65   Howells and Weatherill, *op. cit.*, at 421.

66   *Garrett v Boots the Chemist Ltd*, 16 July 1980 unreported, cited in C.J. Miller and B.W. Harvey, *Consumer and Trading Law Cases and Materials*, (Butterworths, 1985) at 561.

67   *Riley v Webb*, [1987] BTLC 65, [1987] CCLR 65.

68   *Balding v Lew–Ways Ltd*, [1995] *Crim. L.R.* 878.

69   *Taylor v Lawrence Fraser (Bristol) Ltd*, (1977) 121 *Sol. Jo.* 157.

70   *Rotherham MBC. v Raysun*, [1988] BTLC 292, [1989] CCLR 1.

71   *Ibid.* See also *P & M Supplies (Essex) Ltd v Devon County Council*, (1991) *Crim. L.R.* 832.

instances where it will be found to be reasonable, especially for small businesses, to rely on assurances from reputable (particularly European suppliers), but one reported instance of such a successful defence seemed to have had more to do with an exaggerated respect for 'teutonic thoroughness' than the establishment of any general principle.[72]

It is also important that producers and wholesalers take responsibility for the condition in which goods are sold. In one case it was not found to be sufficient that retailers be merely 'recommended' to attach a warning to goods.[73]

Much of the opprobrium which consumerists invoke against the due diligence defence can be attributed to the fact that it allows companies to escape liability by blaming others, particularly their employees. This criticism was particularly heated after the House of Lords decision, in *Tesco Supermarkets Ltd v Nattrass*,[74] that even the store manger was distinct from the company, which could therefore avoid liability by blaming him. This decision seems to be misguided and in particular demonstrates an undue reluctance to impose criminal liability on an 'innocent' employer.[75] Fortunately its application seems to have been marked by a judicial awareness of the need to keep its consequences under wraps so that firms cannot simply blame their employees for any breach of regulations. In *McGuire v Sittingbourne Co–operative Society Ltd*[76] it was made clear that there was still a need to establish how the breach occurred. Moreover there is still an obligation on the company to put effective procedures in place and to monitor them. The case law on this point has mainly arisen in relation to economic consumer protection regulations and one can expect the defence to be even more closely circumscribed in the safety context.

The CPA imposes some further limits on the ability of companies to blame others. If the act or default of another or reliance on information supplied by another is to be pleaded then leave of the court will be needed, unless seven days' notice of such a defence has been provided to the prosecution (s. 39(2)). Furthermore in order to rely on information supplied by another it must be shown that it was reasonable in all the circumstances for the defendant to have relied on the information, having regard in particular to the steps which he took, and those which he might reasonably

72   *Hurley v Martinez and Co,* [1990] TLR 189.
73   *Coventry City Council v Ackerman,* [1995] *Crim. L.R.* 140.
74   [1971] 2 All ER 128.
75   This point is made by Borrie, *op. cit.,* who cites Lord Reid's objection to 'making an employer *criminally* responsible, even when he has done all that he could to prevent an offence'. (Borrie's emphasis) and contrasts this with the courts' willingness to impose civil liability on employers for the action of their employees.
76   [1976] *Crim LR* 268.

have taken, to verify the information, and whether he had any reason to disbelieve the information (s. 39(4)).

Where a company is guilty of an offence then its directors, managers, secretary or other similar officer can also be prosecuted if can be shown that it was attributable to their consent, connivance or was attributable to their neglect (s. 40(2)). On the other hand where the company successfully established that the offence was due to the act or default of another then that person may be prosecuted if he was acting 'in the course of any business of his' (s. 40(1)).[77]

L. Implementation of the EC Directive

The three EC member states studied in detail in this work have implemented the EC General Product Safety Directive in very distinct ways. Germany after a great deal of prevarication has implemented the Directive in a law which builds upon existing laws and seeks to affect them in a minimal way (Chapter 7, section 5). France has done nothing, claiming that its existing law already fulfilled the requirements (for a criticism of this position, see Chapter 6, section 9). The United Kingdom had almost as good a case as France for doing very little to implement the Directive, save for removing the exclusion of certain goods from its existing general safety requirement. However, rather than extend the scope of the general safety requirement the United Kingdom preferred to play safe and not expose itself to any infringement proceedings by introducing regulations which effectively 'copy–out' the general safety requirement obligation established by the EC Directive.

Given that the General Product Safety Regulations 1994[78] largely replicate the Directive it is not proposed to discuss the general features of the general safety requirement again (Chapter 2, sections 9D and E). Furthermore we have already noted the way in which the new general safety requirement differs from that found in the CPA, which is not repealed, but

---

[77] Under earlier consumer protection statutes this 'by–pass' provision had been used to convict private individuals even though they could not be guilty of the primary offence: see *Olgeirsson v Kitching*, [1986] 1 WLR 304 (private individual convicted under s. 23 of the Trade Descriptions Act 1968). The addition in the present statute of the phrase 'in the course of any business *of his*' (emphasis added) would seem to prevent this possibility and indeed the emphasised words also exclude most employees from this provision which seems only to include those who own or hold a controlling interest in the business: *Warwickshire CC v Johnson*, [1993] 1 All ER 299.

[78] S.I. 1994/2328.

merely disapplied in situations covered by the Regulations (section 3C). An overview of the Regulations will be provided with attention being focused on ways in which they differ from or possibly illuminate the meaning of the Directive.

Two interesting points can be made about the scope of the Regulations. The first concerns the relationship between the general safety requirement and specific Community rules (Chapter 2, section 9C). The United Kingdom seems to have adopted the sensible approach (assuming one rules out my preferred option of the general safety obligation applying alongside any specific rules) of retaining the controls afforded by the general safety requirement whenever the specialist legislation does not cover a specific aspect of safety. This seems to be the effect of the Regulations for although reg. 3(c) excludes any product for which there are specific Community rules, this exclusion only applies where the specific provisions govern all safety aspects of the product. Furthermore reg. 4 makes it clear that the Regulations do apply where the product is subject to Community law provisions in so far as those provisions do not make specific provision governing an aspect of the safety of the product. The matter is not entirely free of ambiguity, however, and it may be suggested that this does not properly interpret the Directive (see Chapter 2, section 9C).

The Regulation's exclusions seem to go too far in one respect. Reg. 2(1) provides that:

> 'a product which is used exclusively in the context of a commercial activity even if it is used for or by a consumer shall not be regarded as a product for the purposes of these Regulations.'

Even though it goes on to provide that 'for the avoidance of doubt this exception shall not extend to the supply of such a product to a consumer', this exclusion seems to go too far. It is based on the fifth recital to the Directive which states:

> 'Whereas production equipment, capital goods and other products used exclusively in the context of a trade or business are not covered by this Directive.'

The purpose behind this recital seems to have been to exclude the infrastructure of businesses (such as escalators, ski–lifts and railway carriages). The United Kingdom, at whose insistence the recital was included, seems to have gone further than this and has even excluded products which come into individualised contact with consumers. Thus one might question whether the shampoo used by a hairdresser should be excluded, but this is the effect of the United Kingdom Regulations. This seems wrong in policy terms and can be criticised by applying the *ejusdem generis* rule to recital 5 so that the reference to 'other products' should be given a meaning in accordance with the goods previously cited, ie production equipment and capital goods. Furthermore the rider that the exclusion still applies 'even if the product is used for or by a consumer' is not found in the Directive and such a use could be seen as incompatible with it being used 'exclusively in the context of a trade or business'.

The Regulations impose the same duties as the Directive. Thus producers have a general safety requirement not to market unsafe products (reg. 7) and this is backed up by duties to provide information to consumers (reg. 8(1)(a) and to be informed of product risks (reg. 8(1)(b))). Whereas the liability of the producer is strict, distributors have only to act with due care to ensure compliance with the general safety requirement; in particular they should not supply products they know or should have presumed, on the basis of information in their possession or as a professional, to be dangerous (reg. 9(a)) and should participate in the monitoring of products (reg. 9(b)).

To support enforcement, the Regulations' requirements are treated as safety provisions for the purpose of suspension notices and forfeiture orders under the CPA (reg. 11(a)). Furthermore prohibition notices and notices to warn can be used against products as defined by the Regulations (reg. 11(b)). Reg. 12 also makes it an offence to breach regs 7 or 9(a), that is for producers to market unsafe products or for distributors to supply products they know or should have presumed to be dangerous. Reg. 13 also makes it an offence for producers or distributors to undertake certain preparatory acts, namely offering or agreeing to place on the market or to supply any dangerous product or exposing or possessing any such product for that purpose. Herein lies an inconsistency. Reg. 13 imposes strict liability for these preparatory offences. This is consistent with the general position concerning producers, but creates inconsistencies with respect to distributors, since reg. 9(a) premises the principal offence on the distributors having at least constructive knowledge that the product was dangerous.

We have already noted that the CPA does not contain a power requiring traders to recall dangerous products. It is surprising that the 1994 Regulations do not add this power as it seems to be required by the General Product Safety Directive (Chapter 2, section 9I). The United Kingdom seems to be giving a very narrow interpretation to art. 6(1)(h) of the Directive which requires it to have the necessary powers to organise the effective and immediate withdrawal/destruction of a dangerous product or product batch already on the market. It seems to have read this as requiring it to provide powers to deal with products which are on the market in the sense of being marketed, but not products in the market, ie in the hands of consumers. Such a reading seems to be inconsistent with the spirit, and arguably the letter, of the Directive.

Reg. 14 contains a due diligence defence and reg. 15 provisions on liability of persons other than the principal offender which are in similar terms to the CPA. One interesting point of note is that it is expressly stated that a distributor cannot rely on the due diligence defence if he has breached his obligation under reg. 9(b) to monitor the products within the limits of his activities (reg. 14(5)). Failure to undertake appropriate monitoring steps – and it is relevant to note that reg. 9(b) only requires the distributor to act within the limits of his activities – may well have defeated a due diligence defence in any event. However, the emphasis in the case law to date has been on suppliers checking the quality of their supply and so it is useful to underline that product quality also involves appropriate post–marketing monitoring.

It might be questioned whether providing a due diligence defence is an appropriate way of implementing the General Product Safety Directive as the Directive contains no such excuse on its face. Does the due diligence defence conflict with the obligation on member states to guarantee the effective application of EC law? Probably it is best to view the defence as 'a permissible subtlety within a domestic enforcement regime which generally permits effective control of suspect traders and suspect goods'.[79] Other regimes may achieve similar results by rules of legal interpretation or enforcement policy. Certainly the Commission has not seen fit to challenge, at least in public, the defence in any implementing legislation.

4.   STANDARDISATION

A.   Introduction

The British Standards Institution (BSI) is one of the world's oldest standards organisations. It was founded in 1901 and incorporated by Royal Charter in 1929. It now operates as a non–profit distributing organisation which is formally independent of Government, industry or trade associations. Of course, in practice, as its membership is comprised of businesses and the majority of its committees are manned predominantly by industry representatives, it naturally has close links with industry. Equally Government is interested in and supportive of BSI's work and is involved in the preparation of standards and as we shall see the DTI finances consumer participation in standardisation.

Although it has commercial testing activities, the major function of BSI with which we shall be concerned is its role in developing British Standards. Increasingly, of course, this means being involved in the development of

---

[79]   Howells and Weatherill, *op. cit.*, at 431.

European and international standards which are then adopted as British Standards. It has been estimated that 90% of new standards are based on European and international standards.[80] BSI has a kite mark which demonstrates compliance with standards. However, BSI's own research has shown that in most cases the mark is a weak influence on purchasing decisions.[81] The same research found that consumers saw the kitemark as a safety symbol. The dangers of consumers confusing conformity marks with safety marks has already been alluded to (Chapter 1, section 3E(v), Chapter 2, section 7D). BSI does in fact have its own safety mark specifically indicating compliance with BSI standards concerned with safety or to safety requirements of a BSI standard which also covers other characteristics. This is, however, being played down in favour of the kitemark which is more widely recognised. This runs counter to the consumer's need to be informed of safety characteristics of products.

B. Organisation of BSI

BSI is run by a board, but it essentially has two wings – one dealing with its standardisation function, the other with its commercial activities. Its Standards Board is responsible for standardisation policy and underneath it there are seven Sector Boards to which the numerous technical committees report. Unfortunately it is impossible to be more specific on the number of committees or the scope of the Sector Boards as BSI does not provide this information. The reason given was lack of resources, but it would seem a basic requirement to have this information easily available about a system to which has been delegated a major role in the economy.

BSI also has important commercial testing and certification operations. In order to avoid a potential conflict of interest responsibility for accrediting testing organisation has been handed over to a separate body, the United Kingdom Accreditation Society (UKAS) since 1995. This is a limited company separate from both Government and the BSI. This replaced both the National Measurement Accreditation Service (NAMAS) and the National Accreditation Council for Certification Bodies (NACCB, which BSI had

---

80   *Speaking Up For Consumers*, (BSI, 1997) at 4.

81   See summary report of BSI Standards Stakeholder research project which is annex B to M. Healy and N. Pope, *Consumer Representation in Standards Making*, paper presented at European Academy of Standardisation Conference, *Standards and Society*, Stockholm, 3–5 May 1996.

operated since 1985).[82] UKAS awards the national accreditation of measurement and sampling (NAMAS) to test houses who work to appropriate methods and standards and the national accreditation of certification bodies (NACS) which assures the standard of third party certification. BSI still houses the National Forum for Conformity Assessment and Quality Policy which performs a consultation and information role as well as being the United Kingdom's representative to the EOTC (Chapter 2, section 7C(ii)). However, it might be questioned whether in the long term this would not be better housed within the DTI – who provide most of its funding so as it avoid any suspicion that the commercial and regulatory functions of BSI are being confused.

C. Government and Standards

The Government's commitment to standardisation strengthened following its White Paper, *Standards, Quality and International Competitiveness*,[83] in 1982. It is perhaps no coincidence that this was in the same period as the EC was being converted to its new approach to technical harmonisation. The Government's approach to increasing the role of standards was two fold. On the one hand the quality of the standards themselves had to be improved. Whilst some BSI standards were recognised as world leaders, other were obsolete or not always clear and specific enough for regulatory use.[84] BS 0 – the standard for standards – was recognised as forming a good basis for the drafting of standards, but more industry involvement in the preparation of standards was seen as essential. On the other hand increased Government use of standards was recognised as also being necessary. It was suggested that this could be achieved both through emphasising the need to comply with standards in public purchasing contracts and through the use of standards in regulations.

It was recognised that there were four ways in which standards could be treated in the regulatory regime: regulations could make their use mandatory, they could be deemed to satisfy the requirements of regulations, they could serve as a source of guidance or be treated as an example of *prima facie* compliance.[85] There are some examples of standards being incorporated directly or indirectly into regulations. For example, the Pushchair (Safety)

---

82   NAMAS was itself a combination of the British Calibration Service (BCS, founded in 1961) and the National Testing Laboratory Accreditation Scheme (NATLASS founded in 1981).

83   Cmnd. 8621 (1982).

84   *Ibid.*, at 3.

85   *Ibid.*, at 6.

Regulations 1985[86] make it an offence not to comply with the appropriate British Standard and the Nightwear (Safety) Regulations 1985[87] set flammability performance requirements based on British Standards which are incorporated by reference. It was, however, the second model – the deemed to satisfy requirement – that the Government saw as playing the biggest role in strengthening the status of standards. It previewed possible reforms to the Consumer Safety Act 1976, by suggesting that a general safety duty could be linked to the concept of 'sound modern practice'. Although we have seen that this was not the final form of the general safety requirement in the CPA, the concept of approved standards (see section 3C) was derived from this approach.

D. Consumers and the BSI

It is estimated that at least one third of the over 15,000 standards in the current BSI catalogue relate directly to consumer products.[88] There is a Sector Board concerned with Consumer Products and Services, although consumers also have interests in products covered by other Sector Boards. Although we shall make some criticisms of consumer representation within BSI, it must be acknowledged that it is fairly well developed and reasonably funded in relation to international comparators.

Consumer representation in standardisation is organised by its Consumer Policy Committee (CPC). The origin and history of the CPC is illuminating and illustrates that the problem of the representivity of consumer representatives has been a persistent problem.[89] In 1950 the Cunliffe Committee into the *Organisation and Constitution of the British Standards Institution*[90] reported that one of the most persistent criticisms was the insufficient weight given to consumer and user interests. In response to this report, a Women's Advisory Committee (WAC) was established in 1951 whose members were drawn mainly from the ranks of Women's Institutes. Also in 1955 the Advisory Council on Standards for Consumer Goods (known as the Consumer Advisory Council) was established. This was rather novel in that it ranged beyond standardisation to look at the need for consumers to have a voice on a wide range of issues. It even produced a Shopper's Guide which was a forerunner in style to *Which?* magazine.

---

[86] S.I. 1985/2047.

[87] S.I. 1985/2043.

[88] *Speaking Up For Consumers, op. cit.*, at 2.

[89] See, generally, Healy and Pope, *op. cit.*, at 4.

[90] This was a report to the President of the Board of Trade.

However, the fact that it was housed within BSI caused it to suffer from the perception that it might not be wholly independent.

The Final Report of the Molony Committee on Consumer Protection found that these bodies 'had fought well and hard' and stated that it did not see 'how else or better [the Institution] could have approached the problem'.[91] However, Healy and Pope go too far when they suggest that Molony endorsed this approach.[92] Instead the report was rather critical of both bodies which by 'the manner of their appointment or sponsorship has made it possible for manufacturers' representatives to dispute – whether openly or by implication – that theirs was the authoritative voice of the consumer'.[93] It could too easily be argued that these bodies were not truly representative of consumers as a whole and that they had failed to communicate the value of standards to consumers. Molony's approach was to propose the establishment of a Consumer Council which would fulfil many of these functions.[94] No body of the exact nature envisaged by Molony was established, but in 1963 a Consumer Council was set up which essentially took over the work of the Consumer Advisory Council. This role is today performed by the National Consumer Council.

The WAC continued until 1973 when it became the Consumer Standards Advisory Council, which brought in consumer groups, government representatives and members of the trading standards, consumer advisory and retail communities. In 1987 the title Consumer Policy Committee was adopted. Its greater autonomy within BSI and the fact that its membership embraces a wide range of interested parties, permit it to speak with a greater authority on behalf of consumers. However, as we shall see, there remains a distinction between the CPC itself and the consumer representatives who man the technical committees. It is not so clear that the consumer representatives are, by anything more than a matter of degree, any more representative of ordinary consumers than the members of WAC were. This point is discussed in more detail below.

BSI funds the costs of the CPC's secretariat and administration costs, the costs of holding meetings and some of the expenses of consumer representatives (usually their hotel expenses when attending CEN/ISO meetings). In 1993–4 this amounted to £169,980. In the same year the DTI made £100,000 available to meet the travel expenses of consumer representatives through its Consumer Travel Expenses Fund. This is

---

91   *Final Report of the Committee on Consumer Protection*, Cmnd. 1781 (1962) at 84.
92   *Op. cit.*, at 4.
93   Cmnd. 1781 (1962), *op. cit.*, at 84.
94   *Ibid.*, Chapter 20.

particularly important given the need for consumers to attend European and international meetings.[95]

The CPC operates on both the political and the practical level.[96] At the political level there is the CPC itself. This is made up of the 'great and the good', ie representatives from various consumer and accident prevention organisations, as well as from central government, enforcement officials and consumer advisers. Perhaps somewhat surprisingly, the British Retail Consortium and the co–operative movement also find places reserved for them on this committee. The reasoning seems to have been that these bodies were in touch with consumers as they sold to them. Although the contribution of these bodies is no doubt constructive, it may be seen as inappropriate for these business concerns to be represented on a consumer committee. The chairman and deputy chairman of the CPC's various co–ordinating committees as well as the chairman of the construction user group are also members of the CPC.

The Chairman of the CPC sits on the BSI Standards Board and members sit on most Sector Boards and BSI technical committees addressing quality policy, conformity assessment and product certification. Its role is essentially concerned with the broad politics of the consumer interest in standardisation. It is consulted by BSI on these matters and conveys the consumer interest on standardisation matters to the Standards Board or the BSI Board. It reviews the BSI standards programme and can recommend to Sector Boards the preparation of new standards or the revision or amendment of existing standards.

Perhaps the more important function of the CPC is, however, to represent the consumer interest in the work of the technical committees developing standards and conformity assessment systems, both at the national, European and international levels. The CPC manages this work through four co–ordination committees, the chairman and deputy chairman of which, as we have already seen, are members of CPC. The co–ordination committees deal with broad subject areas covering:

- *Electrical, electronic and fuel using equipment* which deals with household electrical appliances, electrical installation, powered tools, DIY equipment, garden machinery, lamps and lighting, gas appliances, solid–fuel appliances and barbecues, solar heating, road transport, informatics and metering.
- *Household products, furniture and textiles* covering cooking and table utensils, furniture, child care articles and nursery goods, paper and

---

95   These figures are taken from *Consumer Policy Committee Strategy Statement*, March 1994.

96   See document *Speaking up for Consumers, op. cit.*

packaging, floor coverings, wall coverings, clothing and footwear, bedding and toys.

- *Mechanical engineering, construction and health care* including caravans, machinery safety and ergonomics, tools, sanitary appliances, stairs, doors and windows, building products, fire safety, contraceptives, aids for disabled people, spectacles and contact lenses.
- *Personal protection and chemical* which encompasses car safety and security, alarm systems, protective clothing, sport and leisure equipment, graphical symbols and signs, fireworks, matches and lighters, environmental issues, banking, smart cards and information technology and quality management.

Clearly some of the groupings are very broad and all the products they cover are not necessarily related. Equally some of the topics seem to have been forced into not very suitable holes. However, this is probably explained by the need to keep a limit on the number of co–ordinating committees so as not to make the administrative structure too complex or burdensome.

The work on the technical committees is carried out by unpaid volunteer consumer representatives. There are usually 55–70 active representatives each year who manage to contribute to between 250–300 active technical committees.[97] They are recruited on the basis they can attend at least 8 committee meetings a year, but the average representative attends 13 meetings. This has been equated to 6 man–weeks per representative when account is taken of preparation and reporting on meetings. This level of commitment obviously restricts the range of consumers who can participate. There is also a difference in character between them and the representatives of the Consumers' Association who sit on technical committees in their own right. The CPC representatives do not necessarily have any technical experience – they do, however, have limited training provided, have access to some BSI resources and the CPC secretariat maintains a register of expert advisers who can be consulted. By contrast the Consumers' Association representatives are usually technical experts. The Consumers' Association also works to its own policy agenda, whilst the CPC consumer representatives simply bring their own perception of what is in the general consumer interest, although no doubt they are influenced by the contacts they have with the CPC and its secretariat. Therefore they may be some tension between the technically knowledgeable consumer professionals, working to a particular agenda and the well intentioned amateur consumer representatives with no particular political agenda. Of course these two elements could be seen as useful complements (Chapter 1, section 3D(ii)(e)).

---

[97]   *Strategy Statement, op. cit.*, at 4.

Some further thought might be give to the selection process of consumer representatives. It currently works on an invitation basis, mainly because the secretariat cannot afford the resources for a more sophisticated selection procedure.[98] However, this may leave the system open to criticism from industry that the representatives do not represent the bulk of consumers and from consumer groups that they are not radical or professional enough. The BSI has produced a new brochure, *Speaking Up For Consumers*, which as one of its objectives seeks to encourage individuals to volunteer their services as consumer representatives. Hopefully this can be used to both broaden the type of person appointed and as part of a process which makes appointments more transparent. Otherwise criticisms such as we heard of the WAC system may re–emerge. This question is particularly important as the CPC structure is relatively well financed and one might question whether the money could not be more effectively employed by giving funding to the professional consumer lobbyists.

5. CONSUMER MOVEMENT

The Consumers' Association (CA) is the United Kingdom's most important consumer organisation. It has 739,000 members (as of January 1997), the bulk of whom subscribe to its monthly magazine *Which?* It plays a particularly important role in relation to product safety. This is because not only does it speak up for the consumer interest, but thanks to its testing facility at Milton Keynes it has the technical expertise to back this up. It is a member of BSI's CPC and also attends BSI's technical committees in its own right. It is a major source of consumer representation at the CEN and ISO level where it benefits from the DTI travel fund administered by the BSI's CPC and, in the case of CEN, support from ANEC. The technical expertise it brings with it is highly valued.

CA undertakes tests on around 70 products each year. Safety is one of the key aspects it tests for and it has devised a Safety Alert Procedure which ranks products on a scale in which 1 = very low risk; 2 = low risk; 3 = moderate risk; 4 = high risk; and 5 = very high risk. To obtain this guide rating hazards are identified; the limitations on how and by whom the product can be expected to be used are identified and an estimate of risk is made based on the severity of injury, frequency and duration of exposure, the probability of the occurrence of the event and the possibility of avoiding the

---

[98]   A radio appeal for new representatives overwhelmed the secretariat.

risk. Products rated 3 and above are subject a full review procedure to identify what steps need to be taken.[99]

Often CA will deal directly with a manufacturer relying on the evidence from their tests, moral suasion and possibly the threat of adverse publicity. Sometimes it tries to involve the regulatory authorities; when it does so it generally finds trading standards officers to be more receptive than the DTI. This would fit in with the finding that the DTI was reluctant to become involved in the direct enforcement of the laws.

CA believes that its experience can help increase the effectiveness of recall campaigns. For instance, in one case a washing machine manufacturer recalled a dangerous model. It achieved only a 16% success rate. Following an inquest into a death caused by the machine and a CA investigation a 79% response rate was achieved.[100] CA also uses the noticeboard page in its *Which?* magazine to publicise safety warnings and product recalls.

6.   CONCLUSIONS

During the last four decades – from the Consumer Protection Act 1961 through to the General Product Safety Regulations 1994 – the United Kingdom has learned the need for its regulatory and enforcement authorities to have a wide variety of tools to ensure consumer safety. Although there are a few minor quibbles, on the whole the United Kingdom regulatory authorities have an impressive array of powers to seek to ensure that only safe products are marketed and that any dangerous products can be removed from the marketplace.

The present weakness in the regulatory regime lies in its lack of effective means to deal with dangerous products which have left the commercial chain and are in the hands of private consumers. We have seen that the notice to warn procedure is redundant, mainly because the consultation period renders it inappropriate for dealing with emergencies, but also one suspects there is a reluctance on the part of the DTI to mandate how producers and distributors should behave towards their customers. Moreover it may be doubted whether the notice to warn would in fact be any more effective than DTI press releases. What is needed is a power to require not merely the warning of dangers, but also in appropriate cases the recall of dangerous products. Just as important is the need for procedures to exist which can make such recall campaigns effective. The distributor's obligations, under the General Product

---

[99]   K. Biswell, 'Assessing the Risk of Unsafe Consumer Products' (1997) 7 *Consumer Policy Review* 96.

[100]   T. Watt, 'Improving Recalls as Unsafe Products' (1993) 3 *Consumer Policy Review* 204.

Safety Directive, to engage in post–market monitoring seem to open up possibilities for improving the chance of reaching the affected consumers. Whether the United Kingdom is within its rights to refuse to introduce a recall power has already been discussed (see section 3K). The fact that it has not done so signals an unwillingness to intervene directly in the relations between trader and consumer. Cajolery and the threat of private law redress should not be relied upon as the exclusive means to protect consumers. Although most traders will respond to these incentives or be motivated by their own sense of responsibility, a formal recall power would be useful to control unscrupulous traders. It would also be symbolic in strengthening the esteem in which enforcement authorities are held by traders and in underlining to businesses the lengths to which the state expects them to go to safeguard the health and safety of consumers.

The performance of the DTI and local trading standards officers have not been subjected to the same scrutiny as their United States counterparts. Impressionistically one would consider that they use their regulatory and enforcement powers with caution. Particularly since the introduction of rules on cost–compliance it is very hard for regulations to be enacted unless a compelling case can be made out. In fact the procedure is prone to produce too few rather than too many regulations. The costs of regulations tend to be derived from industry estimates and there seems to be few controls on the accuracy or veracity of the figures generated. These rather concrete costs are then weighed against benefits which may be more ephemeral in nature and harder to reduce to precise figures. Moreover there is a less well organised consumer lobby to maximise the presentation of the benefits of safety measures.

The United Kingdom central authorities have not been as strident in their use of those enforcement powers directed towards particular batches of products or producers as has the United States' Consumer Product Safety Commission. The DTI has never used its notice to warn powers and has only served a handful of prohibition notices. The CSU prefers to concentrate on its fairly effective data collection systems and its role in developing general policy and considering the need for regulations and standards. Enforcement is largely left in the hands of trading standards officers where we have seen that a combination of lack of resources, legal uncertainty (particularly surrounding the due diligence defence), exposure to compensation claims and the light enforcement culture tend to militate in favour of officers negotiating rather than prosecuting every contravention.

The strong network of local enforcement officers is an important strength of the United Kingdom system, which other countries might learn from. However, there are signs that it is under stress as local government bears the brunt of financial cuts. There may be a need for some reorganisation on a regional basis to ensure that all areas are able to deal effectively with major product safety emergencies. Local enforcement could of course give rise to problems resulting from different applications of the law in different areas. These problems are largely overcome by the LACOTS home authority system and TS–LINK seems to be an effective means of communicating between authorities. It is true, however, that the chances of prosecution may vary from one area to another depending upon the priority each gives to prosecution as part of its enforcement strategy.[101] There is some evidence to suggest that trading standards officers are more likely to prosecute safety related offences than other matters.[102] However, other factors are also likely to influence the decision to prosecute and these will often be decisive in particular cases: these include matters such as the seriousness of the offence, the trader's past record and how co–operative they have been with the authorities.[103] In the first five years of the CPA there were 1,931 successful convictions and 136 prosecutions were dismissed.[104]

The United Kingdom can be seen as a flexible model for how central and local government can work together, dividing tasks up on a sensible pragmatic basis. Certainly when we contrast the position with the difficulties which can arise under federal systems because of squabbles over competencies (cf the position in Germany Chapter 7, section 3) the position

---

[101]   Woodroffe and Weatherill found 'clear differences in the readiness to prosecute displayed in different areas': see G. Woodroffe and S. Weatherill, 'Postmarket Control of Technical Goods: Consumer Safety in the U.K.' in H.–W. Micklitz (ed.), *Post Market Control of Consumer Goods*, (Nomos, 1990) at 290.

[102]   In a study of four trading standards departments Cardwell found that in three of the four 'the prosecution of a prima facie offence under the safety legislation is the rule rather than the exception': K. Cardwell, 'The Role of Discretion in the Enforcement of Consumer Protection Legislation' (LLM dissertation, University of Manchester, 1984) at 277. Whilst accepting that officers are more likely to prosecute to protect safety than economic interests, one must be hesitant to assume that prosecution is as commonplace as this result from a small sample suggests. Cranston's study of enforcement practice certainly suggests a major role for officers' discretion; see R. Cranston, *Regulating Business*, (Macmillan, 1979). Admittedly that somewhat dated project focused on trade descriptions offences, but perhaps one comment he made should be borne in mind when reading Cardwell's evidence, for he found that 'As with the majority of consumer agencies, however, prosecution–minded consumer agencies settle numerous matters informally' (at 100). Thus stated policy may not always coincide with practice when confronted with real life cases.

[103]   See, Hodges, Tyler and Abbott, *op. cit.*, at 153.

[104]   *DTI Report, op. cit.*, at para. 15. Tables in that report show that 699 cases involved the use of s. 10 (the general safety requirement).

in the United Kingdom does look rather healthy.[105] There are obviously some tensions and jealousies which result from the interplay of two levels of administration. These are most obvious in relation to the fact that the DTI keeps to itself the role of national contact with the EC. To some extent this is a natural role for it to play, but there was a distinct feeling by many enforcement officers that they were not directly enough involved in the development of policy and practice at the European level. The establishment of PROSAFE was in part a response to this feeling (Chapter 2, section 9J). One might also suggest that the DTI is too reluctant to use its regulatory powers and too willing to leave enforcement in the hands of trading standards officers. More judicious use of prohibition notices might relieve enforcement officers of some burdens, especially where exposure to compensation claims may be a real deterrent to action. Many enforcement officers may, however, prefer the existing arrangement rather than have excessive interference from central government. More impressionistically one may suspect some tensions between local trading standards officers who see the promotion of trading standards as their main objective and DTI officials who, whilst desiring a safe consumer marketplace, are also working closely with a Government which for the last two decades was suspicion about the need to regulate and scornful of interventionist tendencies. The CSU of the DTI gives the impression of being an efficient cautious bureaucracy, rather than being an evangelist champion of consumer rights.

Like everywhere else standardisation is playing an increasingly important role in safeguarding consumer safety in the United Kingdom. The BSI is a well established body which provides sophisticated mechanisms for consumer representation. Consumer participation in standardisation is relatively well developed within the United Kingdom, partly because of the commitment of the BSI, but also because of significant Government funding and the technical expertise possessed by CA. However, it remains to be seen to what extent consumer protection is affected by the regionalisation and internationalisation of standardisation. The impact will be most obvious when comparing the content of new CEN or ISO standards to the former BS standards, but a more serious threat may result from British testing houses having to relax their testing requirements in order to keep business which might otherwise be attracted to other EC countries or countries with which the United Kingdom has mutual recognition agreements or whose CE marking has to be accepted under the new approach directives.

---

105   In similar vein see H.–W. Micklitz and T. Roethe, 'Federalism in Process' in H.–W. Micklitz, T. Roethe and S. Weatherill (eds), *Federalism and Responsibility*, (Graham & Trotman, Martinus Nijhoff, 1994).

6 France[1]

1. INTRODUCTION

Specific consumer safety laws were first introduced in France in 1978, but the Law of 21 July 1983 represented a major landmark in the development of French consumer safety regulation for it strengthened the laws, introduced a general safety concept and established a Consumer Safety Commission. The provisions are now to be found in a Consumer Code.[2] Thus, by the time the EC adopted the General Product Safety Directive, France already had a fairly sophisticated consumer safety regime which covered both products and services. Indeed France has taken the position that it need do nothing to implement the Directive, although this position will be criticised (see section 9).

This chapter will first give a brief historical overview of the development of consumer safety law in France. The role and function of the main actors in this field will then be briefly described, before the legal provisions and French approach to standardisation are outlined.

---

1   I gained much assistance in writing this chapter from J. Calais–Auloy and F. Steinmetz, *Droit de la consommation*, (4th ed.) (Dalloz, 1996); the essays in J. Ghestin (ed.), *Sécurité des consommateurs et responsabilité du fait des produits défecteux*, (LGDJ, 1987) and the excellent treatment of the law with specific reference to services (but of general value) produced by I. Marcessaux and attached as an annex to a report entitled *Les lignes d'action possible d'une politique communautaire en matiere de sécurité des services*. This was produced by a team of researchers, of which I was pleased to be a member, under the co–ordination of Prof. Thierry Bourgoignie of the Centre de droit de la Consommation, Louvain–la–Neuve. Other useful texts include Ch. Joerges J. Falke, H.–W. Micklitz, G. Brüggermeier, *Die Sicherheit von Konsumgütern und die Entwicklung der Europäischen Gemeinschaft*, (Nomos, 1988), Ch. 2, section 2 and M.–C. Heloire, 'Le Contrôle de la Consommation des Produits Industriels en France au Regard de la Securité' in H.–W. Micklitz (ed.), *Post Market Control of Consumer Goods*, (Nomos, 1990).

2   Law of 26 July 1993. References to articles will be to articles of the Code rather than the original legislation.

2. HISTORY

The Law of 1 August 1905 was essentially concerned to prevent fraud and unfair competition. It was in fact originally promoted by businessmen to protect their interests against unfair competition, but since the 1970s consumer protection has become its main objective. It provides for penalties where there has been fraud or attempted fraud and permits regulations (décrets) to be passed, breaches of which are also punishable. This Law places a responsibility on the first person to market products to ensure they conform to all regulations in force. This last provision was added by the Law of 21 July 1983.

At about the same time as business was pressing for laws against unfair competition, there was also at the turn of the century the development of industry originated standards. These were first aimed at ensuring the compatibility of standards, but over time came to determine standards of quality and safety. The public interest in standards was recognised by placing the French standardisation body (AFNOR) on a statutory footing in the Law of 24 May 1941. This Law was subsequently replaced by the Law of 26 January 1984, which for the first time recognised the right of consumers to participate in the process of promulgating standards.

In the (Scrivener) Law of 10 January 1978 consumer safety was viewed for the first time as the object of legislation in its own right. However, the 1978 Law was little used and was considered to be defective in some respects. With the absence of a Consumer Safety Commission to prompt it, there was little reason for Government to make use of the powers the Law gave it. In any event those powers were restricted, for instance, there was no right to require that products be recalled, that consumers be informed of dangers or that they be reimbursed for dangerous products. The Scrivener Law only required that products be safe in their normal method of use.

A Commission was established under Prof. Jean Calais–Auloy to review French consumer law. In January 1983 it published an interim report and by the time the final report was published[3] the recommendations on consumer safety had largely found their way on to the statute book in the form of the Act of 21 July 1983. The Calais–Auloy Commission had seen consumer safety as involving three aspects – prevention, repression and reparation –

---

[3]   J. Calais–Auloy, *Vers un nouveau droit de la consommation*, (La documentation française, 1984). In English see J. Calais–Auloy, 'Towards New Laws for Consumer Protection : Proposals of the French Reform Commission' (1985) 8 *J.C.P.* 53.

the last of these still awaits reform as the French Government has not yet implemented the product liability directive.[4]

The Law of 21 July 1983 established the Consumer Safety Commission and provided increased powers to regulate dangerous products and services and deal with emergencies. When another Commission, again chaired by Prof. Calais–Auloy, on the codification of consumer law reported the only major reforms suggested were that consumer organisations should be given the right to petition the court directly in the case of serious or immediate risks[5] and a new penalty be provided for those who marketed goods or services which caused illness or injury amounting to ten days total incapacity from work.[6] However, the Consumer Code has now been enacted without altering the existing state of consumer safety regulation.[7]

3. INSTITUTIONS

A. Consumer Safety Commission

A common criticism of French bureaucracy is that it is very vertically oriented with Government departments and agencies having their, sometimes complementary, sometimes overlapping, areas of competence, but with little co–ordination between them. The problem is accentuated in the area of consumer product safety because responsibility for consumer safety regulation is prone in all countries to be dissipated amongst a number of bodies, because of the range of activities and goods consumers use and because the topic impinges on economic, health and social interests.[8] One

---

4 France already has very protective consumer laws in the field of product liability. For discussion of these and the reform debate see G. Howells, *Comparative Product Liability*, Ch. 7 (Dartmouth, 1993).

5 J. Calais–Auloy, *Propositions pour un code de la consommation*, (La documentation française, 1990) at 75.

6 *Ibid.*, at pp 77–78. This would have lead to penalties of imprisonment between 6 months and 5 years and/or a fine of between 30,000 and 250,000 francs. In the case of the product or service causing death the maximum period of imprisonment would have risen to 7 years and the fines have ranged from 100,000 to 500,000 francs.

7 Law of 26 July 1993.

8 There are of course some means of achieving a co–ordinated approach, see Heloire, *op. cit.*, at 234–5, who describes, *inter alia*, a network of officials in different ministries to deal with emergencies, the Inter–ministerial Group for Consumption and the National Council on Consumption. Note the phrase consumption is used as these bodies are concerned with the process of consumption rather than simply protecting

advantage of the United States' approach of creating a Consumer Product Safety Commission is that it mitigates this problem to some extent by establishing an integrated and focused bureaucracy to deal with consumer safety issues.[9] The French followed this model to a certain extent by establishing a *Commission de la securité des consommateurs* (Consumer Safety Commission). The Commission recognises the need for an integrated approach and indeed tries to act as a catalyst for closer horizontal co–operation between departments. However, for historical reasons, and because the French generally seek to avoid a concentration of power in any one agency, the Commission does not have the same jurisdiction as its United States' counterpart. Notably, whilst the Commission is in many ways the lynch–pin of the Law of 21 July 1983 – collecting information, proposing regulations and educating the public about consumer safety – the enforcement of the laws is carried out by the DGCCRF (see section B).

The Consumer Safety Commission was proposed by the Calais–Auloy Commission on Consumer Law Reform and was established by the Law of 21 July 1983.[10] Its composition is fixed by the décret of 11 April 1984 and comprises three High Court judges; three members nominated by consumer organisations, three members nominated by trade associations, four technical experts and a Government representative (Commisaire du Gouvernement) as well as a President who is appointed for five years. The Commission's secretariat is based in Paris. The Commission is fairly small given the large scale and complex nature of the consumer products and services it seeks to regulate.

The functions of the Commission are (i) to act as a centre for the collection of information on consumer accidents; (ii) to investigate alleged unsafe products and services and, where appropriate, to propose regulations and (iii) to inform and educate the public in matters of consumer safety. The Commission has a pivotal position in the consumer safety regulatory regime established by the Law of 21 July 1983.

---

consumers. Hence business interests are also taken into account or represented on these bodies.

9   There is still the problem of other agencies dealing with specific consumer products such as food, drugs and motor vehicles.

10   See now art. 224 of the Consumer Code. See generally Calais–Auloy and Steinmetz, *op. cit.*, at 246 and R. Loosi, 'La fonctionnement de la commission de la sécurité des consommateurs' in Ghestin (ed.) *op. cit.*

B. DGCCRF[11]

The Law of 1 August 1905 necessitated the establishment of a service to detect fraudulent traders. Such a service was established in 1907. In 1945 another agency was established to enforce laws relating to competition and price regulation. These two agencies were combined to form the Direction générale de la concurrence, de la consommation et de la répression des fraudes (DGCCRF) in 1985. Thus the DGCCRF is an agency with two arms – one is economic dealing with matters of competition policy and marketing practices, the other, with which we are concerned, deals with the technical issues relating to the conformity of goods and services with quality and safety requirements.

The DGCCRF has its headquarters in Paris and training and information headquarters in Montpellier. It has 22 regional centres with 100 branch offices based in the administrative centres of departments (some with a second office in other important towns in the department). As of 1 January 1993 it employed 4,053 officers (514 in central administration, 335 in its 8 laboratories and 3,204 in the departments, its two national investigation units and its own colleges).

The DGCCRF's role is to seek out infractions of the law. When they discover them, and if attempts at informal enforcement are unsuccessful, they can send a report to the public prosecutor who can then decide to bring the matter before the courts. The Regulation of 22 January 1919, as amended in 1972, sets out the detailed enforcement powers under the Law of 1 August 1905. The Law of 21 July 1983 provided that the same powers were enjoyed when enforcing that Law (see now art. 222.3). The DGCCRF are not the only authority empowered to enforce the Laws of 1 August 1905 and 21 July 1983. Enforcement powers are also possessed by a range of specialised officials such as customs officials, veterinary and medical officers. The police also have this power, but rarely use it, because they lack the expertise and have more pressing priorities.

In seeking out infractions of the law officers are given wide ranging powers. These include the powers (i) during the day, to enter factories, stores, sale outlets, transport vehicles and places where animals are kept or slaughtered; (ii) to enter the same places by night, if they are open to the public or business activities are being carried on there, unless the premises are also used as a private dwelling; (iii) to demand information or seize any documents; (iv) to demand to be provided with anything needed by them to complete their investigations; (v) to consult documents held by public authorities; (vi) to require an explanation of the checks carried out by

---

11   See Calais–Auloy and Steinmetz, *op. cit.*, at 463–469.

producers before they put their goods on the market; (vii) to perform tests on the goods; and (viii) to take samples away for laboratory analysis.

One limit on the powers under discussion is that they are only available in order to detect infractions of the criminal law. Under the Law of 1 August 1905 there was no power to investigate products or services which appeared dangerous if they were not actually breaking any law. The Law of 21 July 1983 did however introduce such powers which are now contained in art. 222–2 of the Consumer Code. These powers can be used to detect or confirm dangers and propose remedial action. Art. 222–2 gives officers the right to enter, during the day, the same places as listed in the last paragraph,[12] to take samples and to demand from the business all information needed to determine whether the product is dangerous or not. The results of the investigations and any recommendations are then sent to the préfet (Government representative) in the department, who should, as soon as possible and in any event no later than 15 days after receiving the documentation, send the file to the relevant minister and to the Consumer Affairs Minister together with his opinion (art. 221–6).[13]

To take one year at random, in 1992 the DGCCRF undertook 119,830 investigations relating to the security of products and services.[14] We shall see that the DGCCRF have only limited powers to detain goods on their own initiative. Mostly they refer matters to the local or national governments or the public prosecutor. However, it is worth mentioning that one constraint on all the enforcement agencies is the potential liability for damages they face if their actions are found to be unjustified. France provides no immunity in such circumstances and damages are not even limited to the value of goods concerned, but can also cover lost profit.

The division of responsibility between the enforcement authorities and the Consumer Safety Commission is not clear cut. A glance at the DGCCRF's annual reports show that they are also involved in attempts to prevent accidents, as well as the enforcement of laws and regulations. The DGCCRF involves itself in activities concerned with educating the public and commerce on consumer safety matters and is also involved in the development of regulations. In 1992, again a year selected at random, the DGCCRF ran a campaign on safety in the home, issued press releases, had 22 television slots and sent out reminders to businesses emphasising their obligations under regulations. The DGCCRF have also encouraged the development of codes of practice (for example, in relation to food law); the improvement of voluntary standards (for example, in matters as diverse as

---

12   Similar powers are enjoyed on the public highway.

13   He also has emergency powers he can invoke where the danger is serious or immediate: see section 5D.

14   See DGCCRF, *Rapport d'activité 1992*, (Economic Ministry) at 84.

batteries in children's toys and retractable dog's leads) and have played a role in initiating regulation (for example, the décret of 10 September 1992 prohibiting kits which increased the power of 'cyclo–moteurs') and on monitoring other proposals for regulation.

These overlaps with the function of the Consumer Safety Commission need not be a cause for concern. The publicity efforts of both can be complementary and it is unlikely that there is too much consumer safety education. Equally the DGCCRF's role in regulation fits into the legislative scheme for it alerts the Consumer Safety Commission to the danger and they then go through the process of investigation and consideration of the problem, in a process which may eventually result in legislation. However, the system could arguably be more efficient if the safety enforcement functions of the DGCCRF and the information gathering, educative and advisory functions of Consumer Safety Commission were the responsibility of one properly integrated institution. One point perhaps highlights this issue. The European Commission only sends information under the rapid exchange of information system (Chapter 2, section 9J(b)) to the DGCCRF,[15] but this information would also be valuable to the Consumer Safety Commission who are charged with the collection of information on dangerous products.

C. AFNOR[16]

In France standardisation work is carried out by the Association Française de Normalisation (AFNOR) and by the Union Technique de l'Electricité (UTE). As in most countries, electrical products are dealt with under separate procedures from the mass of products and services. In France, the UTE covers electrical products, whilst AFNOR deals with everything else. We shall concentrate our attention on AFNOR.

Obviously the most important role of AFNOR is to produce standards. However, mention should also be made of the *documents technique unifiés* (DTU). These documents are not strictly standards, but rather codes of good practice drawn up by the business community. However, these statements of

---

15 Because the European Commission sends the information only to enforcement authorities.

16 See Calais–Auloy and Steinmetz, *op. cit.*, at 194–202 and 241–242; J.–C. Fourgoux and J. Mihailov, 'La normalisation en tant qu'instrument de la sécurité des consommateurs' in Ghestin (ed.) *op. cit.*; A. Penneau, *Regles de l'art et normes techniques*, (LGDJ, 1989) at 37–42 and 82–93 and A. Durand and H. Brunet, 'Normalisation' in *Encyclopaedia Universalis*, (Typescript kindly provided by AFNOR).

common practice have a particular significance due to the participation of AFNOR in the discussions leading to their preparation.

AFNOR was founded as a private institution in 1926. Although formed as a private association it was given a semi–public character by the Law of 24 May 1941 and the regulation of the same year, made under that Law, which set out the procedures by which standards were created. The significant aspect of the Law of 1941 was the close relationship which Government forged with AFNOR. Government largely controlled its operations. This Law has now been replaced by the décret of 26 January 1984 in which AFNOR is given more independence, but we shall see that Government still maintains a supervisory role and also has some veto powers. AFNOR is under the general supervision of the Industry Ministry, who in practice delegates this power to an inter–ministerial officer for standards who acts as Commissaire du Gouvernement for AFNOR and who is assisted by an inter–ministerial group responsible for developing standards policy.

AFNOR participates in the work of CEN at the European level and ISO at the international level. Co–operation with EOTC is undertaken by EOTC France which is an organisation of French organisations involved in testing and certification matters. The French member of the European organisations responsible for co–ordinating nationally recognised accreditation bodies (EAC) and laboratories (EAL) is COFRAC (Comité Français d'Accréditation).

D. Consumer Organisations

The Institut National de la Consommation (INC) is a government funded consumer·research organisation. We shall see that it helps to represent the consumer interest in the standardisation process (section 8E). It also has a test centre and informs the public of test results through, *inter alia*, its monthly magazine *60 million des consommateurs*. As a public body the INC is subject to some legal controls, notably it is advised on its testing practices by an Autorité des essais comparatifs (ADEC) made up of 14 members including six consumer and six business representatives. Another of INC's roles is to provide technical assistance to other consumer organisations. One of these – the Union fédérale des consommateurs – publishes its own magazine *Que Choisir?* Both magazines regularly include comparative test results. AFNOR has produced an optional standard on comparative testing.

In France there are 20 state approved consumer associations.[17] These consumer associations (but not the INC) have the right to take actions to protect the collective interest for breach of the criminal law. This could of course be a potentially very effective means for them to act against products which do not meet legal requirements. This right of action was introduced by the Roger Law in 1973, but was not at first effective because the courts found that the description 'civil action' in the provisions required that there be damage caused by the infraction. The Law of 5 January 1988 remedied this problem and the provisions are now to be found in arts 411–1, 422–3 of the Consumer Code.[18]

Such actions can now be brought by approved consumer associations if there has been a breach of the criminal law[19] which is prejudicial, directly or indirectly, to the collective consumer interest. The breach must affect a group of consumers. Such an action would not therefore lie where an individual product was flawed, but would be available where a batch of products was unsafe or their design was inherently dangerous. The problem is that such a product must also breach the criminal law. Thus the action is available where a particular regulation can be shown to have been breached, but is not available where products simply fail to meet standards (unless these have been rendered mandatory). Also the French general safety obligation does not have any sanction directly attached to its breach and so it would not seem to be possible to use breach of the general safety obligation as the basis for such an action. Equally we shall see that the emergency powers are under the control of the public authorities and, despite reform proposals to this effect, consumer organisations cannot ask the court to invoke the emergency powers.

When bringing such an action consumer groups can seek (i) damages for the injury to the general consumer interest, (ii) an injunction against the illegal behaviour, and (iii) an order that the public be informed of the decision at the defendant's expense.

---

17 These associations must have been in existence for at least one year, have effective public activities protecting consumers and be of reasonable size (10,000 members in the case of national associations: see regulation of 6 May 1988).

18 Calais–Auloy and Steinmetz, *op. cit.*, at 473–480.

19 There are separate powers for associations to intervene against unfair terms and they can become involved in individual cases.

4.   LAW OF 1 AUGUST 1905[20]

The Law of 1 August 1905 was introduced to deal with the problems of
unfair competition caused by the use of deceptive practices and the need to
control the quality of foodstuffs.[21] However, over time it has evolved into a
consumer protection measure and has been used in the area of consumer
safety as well as its more obvious role as a means of ensuring the conformity
of products and preventing deception. The major techniques for doing this
are (a) a system of regulations and (b) a general prohibition on fraud. These
are regulated by the enforcement authorities[22] and (c) the 'auto–control'
system whereby the first person to market a product is made responsible for
ensuring it complies with the regulations which are in force. This last
principle was added to the Law of 1 August 1905 by the Law of 21 July
1983.

A.   Regulations [23]

Art. 214–1 of the Consumer Code gives the Conseil d'Etat the power to issue
regulations (décrets) to ensure observance of the objectives of what had
previously been the Law of 1 August 1905; namely, that products comply
with legal obligations and that fraud and adulteration are prevented. In
particular regulations can be made concerning:

–   the production, importing, sale, offering for sale, exposing for sale,
    possession and free distribution of goods;
–   the presentation of goods and descriptions of all kinds (but particularly
    those concerning the nature, 'substantial qualities', composition, content,
    type, origin, identity, quantity, uses, methods of use, as well as the
    marks placed on goods which are to be exported) on the goods, the
    packaging, invoices, commercial documents and promotional material;
–   the definition, composition and denomination of goods, the processes
    they can be subjected to and the characteristics which render them unfit
    for consumers;

---

20   The relevant provisions are now to be found in arts 212–216 of the Consumer Code.
21   See the special provisions on foodstuffs contained in arts 213–3 and 213–4 of the
     Consumer Code.
22   Principally the DGCCRF but other authorities are listed in art. 215–1. Art. 222–1
     lists the authorities which can enforce the safety laws considered below.
23   See Calais–Auloy and Steinmetz, *op. cit.*, at 188–194 and 240–241 and B. Bouloc,
     'La loi de 1905 en tant qu'instrument de la sécurité des consommateurs' in Ghestin
     (ed.), *op. cit.*

- the definition and control of terms and expressions used in publicity, in order to avoid confusion;
- the hygiene of establishments where food is prepared, preserved or sold, and of those employed in such establishments;
- the conditions in which the microbiological and hygienic conditions of human food is determined; and
- the way in which indications of the contents of drinks should be brought to the buyer's attention.

In 1978 the scope of the Law of 1 August 1905 was extended to include services (art. 216–1). European regulations were also treated as if they were regulations made under that Law for the purpose of enforcement and punishment of infringements (art. 214(3)).

It will be obvious that the scope of the regulation–making powers extends beyond issues of mere security to cover matters of quality and truthfulness. However, a significant number of regulations have been passed which concern consumer safety. Among the regulations concerned with consumer safety are many dealing with foodstuffs and the Regulation of 5 March 1985 which subjected cars which are more than five years old to a test requirement.

One of the circumstances when the enforcement authorities can detain goods without the need for authorisation from the court is when a product, object or equipment does not comply with laws and regulations and presents a risk to the health or safety of consumers (art. 215–5). They can also prohibit the movement of goods whilst they await test results if they suspect them of failing to comply with laws and regulations and presenting a risk to the health or safety of consumers (art. 215–7). In the latter case the goods can only be held for 15 days, unless the public prosecutor authorises an extension.

The officers of the DGCCRF, who detect an infringement will send a report to the public prosecutor, who decides whether to take the matter before the courts.[24] The examining magistrate (juge d'instruction) or the court can suspend the marketing of the goods. Such an order continues in force whilst any appeal is being heard.

The type and level of fines under the Law of 1 August 1905 depend upon whether the defendant is considered to have been fraudulent. The position where the defendant is fraudulent is considered below. The fines for mere infractions of a regulation range between 600 and 1300 francs. This may appear negligible, but can in fact be quite severe for each product which infringes the regulation constitutes a separate infraction and the fine can be

---

24   Although of course many matters can be dealt with on an informal basis between the enforcement authorities and the business concerned.

multiplied by the number of infractions. Bouloc has pointed to the iniquitous results which this can cause – the fine for a mere infraction of a regulation can end up, by reason of the multiplication of infringements, being larger than that which would have been awarded were the infringements deemed to have been fraudulent.[25]

Any infraction of a regulation passed under the Law of 1 August 1905 allows contravening goods to be confiscated (art. 216–2) and the defendant to be forced to publish the judgment or an extract of it in a newspaper and to post it at specified places, such as his home, shop, factory or workshop (art. 216–3). In addition where the infractions threatened the safety of the consumer three further complementary penalties can be imposed, namely:

- the issuing of one or several messages informing the public of the decision;
- recall or destruction of the products or prohibition on supplying the service;
- confiscation of all or part of the profit from sales of the products (art. 216–8).

B.   Fraud

Art. 213–1 of the Consumer Code punishes fraud or attempted fraud so long as it concerns one of the elements listed in the article: those of particular relevance in the context of consumer safety include the nature, composition, content and 'substantial qualities' of the goods or services. However, it has been recognised that the element 'substantial qualities' subsumes the others and is the one most frequently referred to in the cases.[26] Where a regulation has been passed under what was the Law of 1 August 1905, the task of finding fraud will be eased for the judge as it can be based on non–conformity with the regulation. However, the scope of this provision is broader than the fields in which regulations have been enacted and in the absence of a regulation the court will itself decide whether there has been any fraud. The case law provides that the court will make its assessment according to business practice,[27] but Prof. Calais–Auloy argues that in the consumer context the only acceptable standard would be the legitimate expectations of consumers.[28] Instances of breach of this general test include

---

[25]   Bouloc, *op. cit.*, at p. 21.
[26]   *Ibid.* at p. 22.
[27]   Crim., 10 March 1987 (D. 1990. S. 361 obs. Roujou de Boubée).
[28]   Calais–Auloy and Steinmetz, *op. cit.*, at 205.

onions containing prohibited pesticides,[29] food which has passed its use by date[30] and the selling of a car, when the fact that the car has been involved in a serious accident was disguised and a high price was charged so as encourage the buyer in the belief that the car could not have been in a crash which would have diminished its value.[31]

However, the Cour de Cassation has confirmed that infraction of this general fraud provision requires intention and that there is no presumption of bad faith.[32] Yet, whilst the judges in the lower courts must find a basis for establishing bad faith, they are given a large leeway in what they use as evidence to prove bad faith and indeed it has been established that it is sufficient to show the defendant failed adequately to test the product before marketing it.[33] Thus the offence can be committed in practice by reckless or negligent behaviour. Calais–Auloy welcomes this extension of liability for he argues that consumers are just as threatened by producers who negligently fail to test their products as by those who set out to expose them to dangers and he points out that similar tests have been invoked in the context of misleading advertising and the civil law relating to the legal guarantee that products do not contain hidden defects, which treats a professional seller of a defective product as a seller in bad faith.[34] On the other hand these developments are objected to by Fourgoux who wants to reserve the most serious penalties for those who have fraudulent intent and impose lesser penalties on those who merely acted rashly or negligently.[35]

The normal fine for breach of art. 213–1 of the Consumer Code is three months to two years' imprisonment and/or a fine of between 1,000 and 250,000 francs. Where however the infractions, *inter alia*, threaten consumer safety the penalties are doubled so that a breach is punishable by a prison sentence of between six months and four years and/or a fine of between 2,000 and 500,000 francs.

---

29 Crim., 8 January 1985, Bull. Crim., No. 15.
30 Crim., 13 October 1981, Bull. Crim., No. 272.
31 Crim., 16 January 1978, Bull. Crim., No. 16. No fraud was found in a later case where the car was sold at a normal price and the repairs had been properly performed: see Crim., 4 January 1986, Bull Crim., No. 5.
32 Crim., 4 January 1977 (D. 1977.336 note Fourgoux).
33 Crim., 12 April 1976, (D. 1977.239 note Fourgoux).
34 Calais–Auloy and Steinmetz, *op. cit.*, 208.
35 J.–C. Fourgoux, D. 1965, Chron. 233.

C.   First Placing a Product or Service on the Market

The Law of 21 July 1983 introduced into the Law of 1 August 1905 a provision aimed at improving the controls on products and services. This makes it the responsibility of the person who first puts a product or service[36] into circulation to check that it conforms to legal requirements relating, *inter alia*, to safety. This person can also be required to show enforcement officers proof of the checks and controls he has carried out. This provision is now found in art. 212–1 of the Consumer Code.

This measure seeks to place the obligation for checking the product on those who have the first opportunity to prevent dangerous products entering the national market. Thus the person responsible will be the producer or in the case of an imported product the importer into France. This obligation to check compliance with regulations has been held to be compatible with the free movement of goods provisions contained in art. 30 of the Treaty of Rome, so long as it is made no more demanding than is necessary to achieve the desired objective, taking into account the general interest and the means of verification normally available to an importer.[37] The intention is not to reduce the obligations of other distributors, but rather to increase the responsibilities on the 'first–marketer'.[38]

The primary role of this obligation is to produce an internal effect on the 'first–marketer' so that he feels obliged to take on responsibility for making the necessary checks on the products and services he markets. There is, however, no specific sanction if he fails to check its conformity with the relevant legal requirements. However, there are indirect sanctions. It has already been noted that failure to perform adequate checks is sufficient for the courts to establish a breach of art. 213–1 of the Consumer Code, which requires a finding of fraud. This idea has also influenced civil liability which has required producers to check the conformity of their products before marketing them.[39]

---

[36]   The section is clearly extended to cover services by art. 216–1 of the Consumer Code. Equally clearly a service is not put into circulation in the same manner as a product, but the provisions would seem capable of being adapted to services so that before providing a new service or adopting a new technique the provider should check that it conforms to the relevant legal requirement: see Marcessaux, *op. cit.*

[37]   *Criminal Proceedings v Bouchara and Norlaine SA*, Case 25/88 [1989] ECR 1105.

[38]   See Calais–Auloy and Steinmetz, *op. cit.*, 191.

[39]   See Civ. 1, 8 January, 1985, Bull Civ. I, No. 11.

5.   LAW OF 21 JULY 1983[40]

We have already noted that the Law of 21 July 1983 was passed to fill
lacunas in the existing law and was based on the proposals of the Consumer
Law Reform Committee chaired by Prof. Calais–Auloy. The relevant
provisions are now to be found in arts 221–225 of the Consumer Code. The
general obligation to market safe products is stated without any sanction
being provided for breach of it. A Consumer Safety Commission was also
established. Various powers to regulate products and to take action against
unsafe products are also specified: these should only be used in proportion to
the danger presented by the product (art. 221–9).

A.   General Safety Obligation

Art. 221–1 provides that products and services must, in their normal
conditions of use or in other conditions which are reasonably foreseeable by
the producer/supplier concerned, offer the safety which one can legitimately
expect and not pose any threat to human health. It is described in art. 221–2
as a *general* safety obligation, presumably to contrast it with the specific
obligations contained in regulations and standards.

This general principle carries no direct sanction for non–compliance.
One might have thought that such a sanction would have to be included in
order for France to comply with the General Product Safety Directive.
However, the French authorities do not accept this. For them a general safety
requirement is the operational concept around which the other powers are
based. It serves to define the scope of the other powers. Regulations can be
made and action taken against products which fail to meet this standard, but
no offence is committed simply by marketing a product which fails to satisfy
the general safety obligation. So long as it provides the mechanisms to ensure
that only safe products are on the market there is no need in their opinion for
a specific sanction for marketing unsafe products. This would not, however,
appear to be effective implementation of the General Product Safety

40   There are several texts discussing this law. Those generally favourable include
Calais–Auloy and Steinmetz, *op. cit.*, at 242–249; L. Bihl, 'Une reforme nécessaire, la
loi du 21 juillet 1983' *Gaz. Pal.* 1983, II doctr. 525 and L. Bihl, 'La loi du 21 juillet
1983 sur la sécurité des consommateurs' in Ghestin (ed.), *op. cit.* Those generally
hostile include J.–C. Fourgoux, 'Le projet de loi sur la securite des consommateurs,
un projet dangereux pour les citoyens?' *Gaz. Pal.* 1983, I, doctr. 525 and by the same
author 'La loi du 21 juillet 1983: La securité des consommateurs et le reste' *Gaz. Pal.*
1983, II, doctr. 395 and M. Peisse, 'La loi du 21 juillet 1983 sur la securité des
consommateurs: une reforme decevante' *Gaz. Pal.* 1986, II, doctr. 785.

Directive as it does not in a legal sense oblige producers to only place safe products on the market. If a producer markets an unsafe product then it can only be removed if it also breaches a regulation or falls within the emergency powers, which require more than that the product is merely unsafe (see section D). This is clearly one example of conflicts in legal culture leading to different results flowing at the national level from a harmonised European legal norm.

The general safety obligation is very broad both in scope and content. The obligation applies to all products and services. However, products and services covered by specific legislation or European legislation are not subject to this Law, except for the emergency procedures. Some authors are concerned that there may be some overlap, and consequent confusion, between these emergency procedures and the controls in specific laws. As we have noted on several occasions any such overlap is likely to be a more theoretical than real problem; both procedures should be working towards the same goal. A more poignant criticism might be as to why products, just because they are regulated by specific regulations, cannot also be subjected to the general controls. If the specific controls work there should be no need to rely on the general powers, if they do not it would be outrageous that products and services which have been considered worthy of special treatment – presumably as they carry a high risk – should not also be caught be the general protective provisions.[41]

Several points can usefully be made concerning the content of the safety obligation. It talks about the safety which one can legitimately expect. One is a translation of the French word 'on' and would seem to indicate that what is legitimate to expect is to be judged by objective standards based on the general expectations of the public, rather than a businessman's view of what is acceptable. The idea of legitimate expectations is a vague expression which masks two competing conceptions of safety (Chapter 1, section 3E(iv)). On the one hand a product or service can be considered to be as safe as can legitimately be expected if it has been produced to the best standards which could reasonably be demanded (this clearly has the danger that business practice can be imported by the backdoor). Alternatively the product or service can be required to meet legitimate objective standards of safety which are created independent of the product or service itself. In this latter scenario the product or service would be held to be unsafe if it failed to meet that standard, even if the reasons for that failure are understandable. Thus the concept of legitimate expectations is to some extent uncertain, and can therefore be subject to different interpretations. Perhaps by oversight, the

---

[41] Any conflict between the two systems could be overcome by making the powers under the general law subject to the failure of other authorities to take more specific measures.

general safety obligation when prohibiting any threat to health does not qualify this by a legitimate expectations test.

The legitimate expectations criterion does, however, cause one to conclude that some dangers are acceptable. Bihl gives the examples of a knife which is inherently capable of injuring the user and of a rope which is harmless in its own right but can be used to hang oneself.[42]

There will, however, be breach of the safety obligation where the danger results from some forms of improper conduct by the user in relation to the product or service. This is because art. 221-1 refers to the use of the product, not only in normal conditions, but also in other conditions which are reasonably foreseeable. The aim is clearly to catch, for example, objects such as rubber erasers made to smell and look like fruit. It is clearly reasonably foreseeable that small children may eat them, even though this is not their normal or even appropriate use. For such instances the definition is perfectly adequate. However, it would seem to be broader than that and be capable of covering other events which are reasonably foreseeable, but are unreasonable uses of the product. The definition might have been better drafted if it had referred to 'other reasonable uses of the product which are reasonably foreseeable' (taking all the circumstances into account, so as to deal with special problems, such as children). To prevent such results occurring the reasonable foreseeability test will have to be used as a constraining device so unreasonable uses are deemed not foreseeable, unless of course there are special reasons, such as the age of the user, which the producer/supplier should have taken into account.

The general clause does not make any use of the reference to standards approach. Indeed the Consumer Safety Commission has expressly said that the general safety obligation may be more demanding than AFNOR Standards.[43] The fact that the French general clause is left so open is a possible explanation for why there is no direct sanction for its breach.

B. Consumer Safety Commission[44]

As noted above, the French Consumer Safety Commission was inspired by the United States' Consumer Product Safety Commission, but does not have

---

42 Bihl in Ghestin (ed.), *op. cit.*, at 54.

43 Commission de la Sécurité des Consommateurs, *1er Rapport au President de la République et au Parlement*, (Direction des Journaux Officiels, 1985, at 15, cited in Joerges *et al*, *op. cit.*

44 See, in addition to the texts which deal with the Law of 21 July 1983 generally, R. Loosli, 'La fonctionnement de la commission de la sécurité des consommateurs' in Ghestin (ed.), *op. cit.*

as wide ranging a jurisdiction as its United States' counterpart. It was also modelled on the French Commission on Unfair Terms (Commission des clauses abusives), although it has been more successful in influencing Government than that Commission.

The Commission is comprised of a President, three High Court judges, three representatives each from national consumer and trade associations, four technical experts and a Government representative (Commisaire du Gouvernement). The Commission has three principal functions: (i) the collection of information on consumer safety; (ii) the consideration of consumer safety issues and proposing measures to improve consumer safety; and (iii) informing the public on consumer safety matters.

(i)   *Information*

The Commission collects information from several sources: death certificates, INSERM (the national institute for health and medical research), CNAM (medical insurers) and the French part of the EHLASS system. The French EHLASS system comprises 8 hospitals. Although not as well developed as the United Kingdom, Dutch or Danish systems which preceded the EHLASS system, France can, of the other member states, be viewed as one of the countries which has made a serious effort to establish a data collection system and use the data generated as a result of EHLASS. The Commission is also the French recipient of information under the OECD alert system. One suspects that it is a matter of some annoyance that the European Commission insists on dealing with the DGCCRF under its rapid exchange of information system. The Commission would in fact be an ideal recipient of this information as it has established a computer network to distribute urgent information. This is one example of the need for flexible channels of communication between different level of product safety regulators (see Chapter 1, section 4A).

(ii)   *Consideration of Consumer Safety Problems*

Before a consumer safety regulation is enacted the Commission must first be asked to deliver at opinion. The Commission can also investigate a consumer safety problem on its own initiative or be requested to investigate a consumer safety problem by the courts or by any member of the public. This direct access by the public could prove to be a potentially onerous burden on the Commission, but is eased somewhat by the fact that the Commission is allowed to decline to consider requests which do not appear to be well founded.

The Commission's investigations are confidential until its opinion has been delivered or its decision to decline to investigate has been announced. However, the Commission remains free to bring to the public's attention matters which cause it concern, for example by issuing warnings where a product poses an imminent danger.

The Commission has wide ranging powers to access documents, interview witnesses and obtain scientific and technical opinions. In non–emergency cases the Commission has the duty to listen to the opinions of those affected by the enquiry. To ensure that trade secrets are respected members of the Commission and its officers are subject to a duty of confidentiality and where production secrets are concerned a reporter is appointed from within the Commission, who then releases to the Commission only such information as is relevant to the dangerous character of the product or service. Art. 141 of the Calais–Auloy Reform Commission project, which led to the Law of 21 July 1983, had proposed that an obligation be imposed on business people to inform the Consumer Safety Commission of dangers which they became aware of during their professional activities. This was included in the draft Bill (art. 2.1), but was not included in the final Act. The original proposal may have been drafted too broadly, for it would have caught employees and contractors working for the company concerned and have placed them is a difficult position.[45] However, it is regrettable that there is no equivalent of the reporting requirement which exists in the United States, which requires businesses to report to the Consumer Product Safety Commission when their products or services might pose a danger to the safety of consumers (Chapter 4, section 2E). Whilst responsible businesses might be expected to consult the Commission in any event, if only to limit their exposure to civil liability, it would have been useful if ethical standards could have been underpinned by legal requirements.

The Commission has produced a very useful folder outlining all the opinions which it has delivered.[46] This shows the Commission has recommended a range of measures concerning the giving of warnings, product recall, suspending the marketing of products or services and the development or modification of standards or regulations. Frequently the Commission has been able to agree voluntary procedures with businesses without having to resort to requesting that the authorities use their legal powers. One of the functions of the Commission is to bring business and consumer groups into dialogue with one another and the success of the

---

45 See criticisms of Fourgoux, *op. cit.*, *Gaz. Pal.* 1983, I, doctr. 142 at 144 who perhaps goes too far when he seems to equate it to the actions of governments in undemocratic countries.

46 Commission de la sécurité des consommateurs, *Sécurité des consommateurs: Fiches pratiques et avis de la commission*, (Direction des Journaux Officiels).

Commission in seeking voluntary compliance, as well as in establishing consensus for law reform, can be seen as linked to the 'contradictory' procedure which it adopts. This allows businesses to be fully integrated into the decision–making process. Significantly this is done in a context where the businesses understand that if a satisfactory resolution cannot be achieved then the Commission may be able to exert pressure for legal action to be taken against them.

The Consumer Safety Commission seems to have been more successful than the Commission on Unfair Terms in persuading Government to act upon their recommendations. One can only speculate as to the reasons for this, but one might suspect that warnings about safety are more compelling than concerns about protecting consumers economic interests. Cynically, one might suggest that Governments may fear being blamed for accidents which occurred if they did not follow the advice of their Consumer Safety Commission.

(iii) Publicity

The Commission is clearly reliant on the media to a great extent to inform the public of consumer safety issues. It has already been noted that the Commission can issue warnings to the public, even if this breaches the general rule of confidentiality during the investigatory process. The media are of course expected to help in getting the message over to consumers.

The Commission also publishes advice sheets on consumer risks. These are collected together in the same folder that contains all of the Commission's opinions.[47] These are very practical, but perhaps too detailed to be read by the general public. However, they are distributed to the media, who pick up on them and produce articles and news items which do reach the general public. Since 1992 the Commission has also produced a newsletter on safety issues.

The Commission also takes part in safety campaigns to alert consumers to dangers, for instance there have been campaigns to make skiers aware of the risks involved in skiing. Also safety information is included on minitel (3614 **SECURITAM**) and this receives between 600 and 1,000 calls per month.[48]

The actual opinions of the Commission only have to be sent to the person who requested the investigation, the businesses concerned and the relevant ministers, including the Consumer Affairs Minister. Although they are

---

[47]   *Ibid.*

[48]   Commission de la sécurité, *8e rapport au president de la republique et au parlement*, (Direction des journaux officiels, 1992) at 46.

published as an annex to the Annual Report of the Commission, the Secretary General of the Commission has expressed the regret that they do not have to be published in the Official Journal within a period of one or two months of their being decided upon.[49]

C. Regulations

Art. 221–3 permits regulations to be made governing products so long as they are not subject to specific regulatory provisions or community law regulation. These regulations can deal with:

- the prohibition or regulation of the production, importing, exporting, offering for sale, selling, giving, possessing or circulating of goods or services;
- regulating their labelling, condition and method of use;
- regulating the hygiene and cleanliness required of those whose work involves the production, distribution and selling of goods and services;
- withdrawing products and services from the market or their recall to be modified or exchanged
- imposing an obligation to provide a total or partial reimbursement of the price;
- destruction of the product where this is the only means to avoid the danger.

This, rather than art. 214–1 (see section 4A) is now the primary means by which consumer safety objectives are secured. It will be noted that the last three matters in the above list are more concerned with regulating the consequences of marketing an unsafe product rather than determining the safety standard and there would appear to be some overlap between these powers and the sanctions for breach of the regulations (see below). The regulations must have as their sole objective the prevention or removal of a danger and the securing of the safety that can be legitimately expected and must also be proportionate to the danger presented by the goods or service. The measures must also take into account France's international obligations, which is intended to refer to the supremacy of Community law and in particular the rules on free movement of goods and services.

Breach of a regulation passed under art. 221 of the Consumer Code gives rise to the fines specified in the regulation. This can however be multiplied by the number of infractions and if the element of fraud can be established then breach of such a regulation can be the basis for a

---

[49] Loosli, *op. cit.*, at p. 47.

prosecution under article 213–1 of the Consumer Code (see section 4B). However the comment has been made that in practice the sanction for breach of health and safety rules are rather low.[50]

Where a tribunal finds that a regulation has been breached it may, in addition to any other penalty, order:

–   the guilty party to publish the decision and to issue one or several messages informing the public of the decision,
–   the recall or destruction of the products or prohibition on supplying the service;
–   the confiscation of all or part of the profit from sales of the products.

These powers are contained in art. 223–1 of the Consumer Code and it will be noticed that they are similar to the powers given to the courts under art. 216–8 of the Code which relate to breaches of what previously had been the Law of 1 August 1905. The court can also order the temporary suspension of sale of a product or service.

D.   Emergency Measures

The emergency provisions introduced by the Law of 21 July 1983 cover all products and services, even those governed by specific French regulations or Community regulations. Emergency measures can be taken either at a local level by the préfet (the state's representative in a department) or at the national level by the Consumer Affairs Minister or other relevant ministers (arts 221–6 and 221–5 respectively). These emergency orders (arrêtés) can be invoked in cases where the products or services pose a serious or immediate danger.

The grounds of intervention in emergencies are very broad for serious and immediate are seen as alternative grounds for intervention. This can be contrasted with the European General Product Safety Directive, where the obligation to inform the Commission only arises where member states have taken measures in respect of a serious *and* immediate risk presented by a product. The French approach is to be preferred for it covers both products where the danger is immediate (and although the risk may not be serious, it may nevertheless not be negligible) and serious (where even if the risk is not immediate it may be continuing to pose a significant threat to safety during the time taken to regulate the matter or produce standards). However, it is perhaps not worth spending too long debating the intricate legal wording of the emergency powers, for one suspects that decision–making in emergencies

---

50   Heloire, *op. cit.*, at 237.

depends as much on instinct as anything else and in practice the difference between the EC and French standards is unlikely to affect most decisions. In advocating these broad powers of intervention it should be noted that the provisions do not require action to be taken, but simply give a discretion to take such action: a discretion which is in the final instance always subject to Ministerial review. In any event the measures taken must be proportionate to the dangers concerned.

The préfet's role is pivotal. It is to him that the enforcement authorities report the results of their investigations when they believe a product or service to be dangerous or have serious doubts about the safety of a product or service. He must then, within 15 days, forward the file together with his opinion on the matter to the Consumer Affairs Minister and other relevant ministers. However, the préfet also has important powers of intervention where products or services pose serious or immediate dangers. The scope of these powers is very wide, for he is allowed to take whatever emergency measures appear necessary to him; often this will involve detaining the suspicious objects. He must, however, refer the matter to ministers, who must make a decision on the matter within 15 days. So while he has very wide powers, they are of short duration. Whilst awaiting the Ministerial decision the préfet can prohibit the goods from being moved. They are, however, left with the person in whose possession they are being held, after an inventory has first been taken.

The Consumer Affairs Minister and other relevant ministers can issue emergency orders in cases of serious or immediate dangers. These orders can remain in force for a maximum of one year. One of their purposes is to provide a breathing space in which the procedure for formulating regulations or standards can take place. They are also available to deal with a short term crisis. Between 1984 and 1995 more than sixty orders were made: some were aimed at categories of products, but others were targeted at individual brands. Unlike the préfets, who are given a free hand in deciding the measures they should take, the ministers have a finite range of measure they can include in the emergency orders; but the list of powers is very broad and broadly approximates to the measures which can be included in regulations. The ministers may suspend the production, importing, exporting and marketing of a product or require its recall or even destruction if that is the only means of removing the danger. It is also possible for ministers to require the issuing of a warning, or instructions on how to use the products as well as requiring recall for the purpose of modification. A partial or total reimbursement of the price can also be ordered. The businesses concerned and other interested parties, such as employees of the business concerned and consumer associations must be consulted within 15 days of an emergency measure being taken. This seems to strike a sensible balance between the need to act expeditiously in the case of an emergency and the right of the people affected to make representations. Of course one can always argue about whether 15 days is too long or too short a period for the subsequent consultation period. What is quite surprising however is that the minister(s) are under no duty to consult the Consumer Safety Commission.[51]

Art. 221–5 of the Consumer Code states that products or services can be put back on to the market once they are confirmed as conforming to the regulations in force. This seems rather curious for one of the innovations of the provisions is to allow the enforcement authorities to investigate not merely products which breach regulations, but also those where danger is suspected even though no regulations are being breached either because there are no regulations or because the regulations may be found to be deficient. It highlights the gap created by not making breach of the general safety obligation an offence in its own right.

E.   Notices

In contrast to the regulations (and to a lesser extent the emergency orders just considered), which typically apply to all products or services of the type concerned, notices are directed at particular producers, importers, distributors or service providers. There are two types of such notices which can be issued by the Consumer Affairs Minister or other relevant ministers (art. 221–7). One type is concerned with products which are already regulated and serves as a warning, requiring the product or service to be put in to conformity with the regulations. This seeks to ensure enforcement of the law without having to seek the assistance of the courts.

The other type of notice concerns products and service, which are not regulated, but with respect to which concerns are held about their safety. The notice can order that the product or service be subjected to safety controls by a recognised centre. The aim here is to see whether regulation is necessary and this power can be invoked to assist the Consumer Safety Commission in the course of its enquiries.

Failure to comply with a request to submit a product or service to inspection leads to a presumption that the product does not satisfy art. 221–1 of the Consumer Code, ie it does not offer the security which can legitimately be expected. However, the effect of this are unclear for there is no express sanction for breach of this general safety principle and whilst this would seem to justify preventative measures being taken it might be countered that the authorities should first establish that there is a danger. There may be civil law implications, but as the provision allows the person in default to prove

---

[51]   See Bihl in Ghestin (ed.), *op. cit.,* at 60.

that his product is safe, the most that will be achieved by the presumption in the civil law is a reversal of the burden of proof.

6. GENERAL CRIMINAL LAW

Arts 319–320 and R. 40–4 of the Penal Code punish those who cause death or personal injury through their lack of skill, negligence or failure to observe regulations. Art. 319 applies where this leads to death and provides for imprisonment of between 15 days and two years and/or a fine of between 1,000 and 30,000 francs. Art. 320 provides for imprisonment of between 15 days and a year and a fine of between 500 and 20,000 francs where the injuries cause more than three months incapacity and for lesser injuries R. 40–4 provides for imprisonment for between ten days and a month and fines of between 1,200 and 3,000 francs.

The penalties can be considered inadequate, especially as the court has no additional powers to order that warnings be issued or to confiscate any profit. Reliance on these general provisions can also be criticised from a consumer protection perspective as the enforcement authorities do not have the same powers to search and require verification as they have under consumer protection statutes. Also the Penal Code only intervenes once damage has been caused. This contrasts with the position under art. 213–1 of the Consumer Code where the law can intervene with severe penalties before damage is caused, but only where there has been fraud.

7. REFORM

The authorities have in theory an impressive array of powers to combat any threat to consumer safety. However, it will be noted that the powers are almost exclusively under the control of public authorities. Consumer organisations have some powers to act where there has been a breach of the criminal law, but this does not extend to a general power to intervene where the consumer's health and safety is threatened. Whilst some commentators fear administrators may be overtaken by a missionary–like zeal to remove all products and services which have a sniff of danger about them,[52] this

---

[52] Peisse, *op. cit.* Whilst this may once have been a genuine concern, it would not appear to be as great a problem in the present climate where the global accent is on deregulation and lifting the burden on businesses so that they can compete in the global economy. If anything the danger is that regulators may be too light handed and more concerned with economic prerogatives than consumer safety. Bihl in Ghestin (ed.), *op. cit.*, at p. 60, explained his support for giving the judges some control of

concentration of powers within administrations also poses potential threats to consumer safety. There may be fears that too much is being entrusted to bureaucrats, who, even if well intentioned, can sometimes be slow to react, if only because of resource constraints. For these reasons the original Consumer Law Reform Commission[53] and the Consumer Reform Commission, which preceded the creation of a Consumer Code,[54] both recommended that consumer organisations should be given the right to bring an action before a judge where a product or service posed a serious or immediate danger. The judge would be able to order that the product be recalled or that provision of the service be prohibited for up to one year. In addition he would have been able to order the distribution, at the defendant's expense, of a text warning the public of the dangers. The consumer organisation would then have had to inform the Consumer Safety Commission of this order straightaway. Unfortunately this proposal was not included in the Consumer Code.

8.   STANDARDS

A.   Background

We have already noted the central role AFNOR plays in the development of standards.[55] In the first place it is responsible, after consulting interested parties, for the drawing up of an annual programme for standardisation activities. This is submitted to the Standardisation Council (Conseil Superieur de la Normalisation). This council comprises 52 members, namely the President of AFNOR and representatives of the state (15), industry, agriculture and commerce (15), local collectives (4), trade unions (5), consumer organisations (3), standardisation boards (3), laboratory and technical centres (3) and scientists and academics (3).[56] To ensure

---

dangerous products and services by reference to their greater independence and less likelihood of being influenced by political and economic affairs.

53   Calais–Auloy (1984), *op. cit.*, at p. 81. Under these proposals the emergency powers were restricted to situations of immediate danger and did not include serious but non–immediate dangers.

54   Calais–Auloy (1990), *op. cit.*, at p. 75.

55   It should also be noted that AFNOR also helps produce 'fasicules' which set out good practice, but have not been subjected to the approval procedures in the same way as standards.

56   Penneau, *op. cit.*, at 84, comments that changes in 1984 to the Council's constitution resulted in an increase in representatives of the business community to a third from a

standardisation work is properly organised AFNOR has established standardisation programmes looking at sectors or horizontal issues at the national, European and international level. This work is overseen by strategic orientation committees (COS) who work out priorities and strategies for achieving them.

B. Standards Development

The process by which a standard is developed starts with the inclusion of the topic in the annual programme or a request from the government representative (Commissaire du Gouvernement) to AFNOR. AFNOR will then determine within which standardisation board (bureau de normalisation) the particular commission established to develop the standard will be based. The standardisation boards are bodies recognised by the Industry Ministry and other relevant ministries as having the technical capacity to develop standards. Where there is no relevant standardisation board, or the existing boards are not able to produce a proposal in the necessary time, AFNOR can establish a standardisation commission of its own.

Once the standardisation commission has produced a draft this is studied by AFNOR and then subjected to a public examination after being published in the Official Journal and Official Standardisation Bulletin. The purpose of the examination is to ensure that it is in the public interest and that there are no objections to its adoption. The commission takes any comments raised during the public examination into account before producing their final proposal. AFNOR can then adopt the standard, although the Government representative can object to its adoption. The power to adopt standards lies with AFNOR's administrative council (Conseil d'administration), although this power can be delegated to its Director General.[57] Each month a list of adopted standards appears in the Official Journal. Since 1966 it has been possible for standards to be simply registered rather than adopted, in which case they do not have the specific legal status described below. This is becoming a popular form of standardisation because it involves a less onerous procedure. It is also possible for AFNOR to issue experimental standards or documents for information.

---

quarter of all members, and a proportional reduction in the influence of consumer members from a seventh to a seventeenth of the total.

[57] Previously there was the need for a Ministerial order.

C.   Legal Status of Standards

A standard which has been adopted must normally be complied with when contracting with the state. In other cases the norms have a non–binding status unless they have been rendered mandatory. The Industry Minister and other relevant ministers can make the observance of a standard mandatory in certain circumstances, including where this is needed, *inter alia*, to protect health and for consumer protection reasons. Only a small proportion of the total number of standards (which is in excess of 10,000) have been rendered mandatory but many of these are standards concerned with safety. Where a mandatory standard has been breached the only sanction, in the absence of fraud, is a fine of between 30 and 250 francs under article R. 26–15 of the Penal Code, although this can be multiplied by the number of infractions. Where there has been fraud however the more severe sanctions for breach of art. 213–1 of the Consumer Code can be invoked (see section 4B) and fraud can be presumed in the case of the first person to market the product who should have checked its conformity with regulations in force, which include mandatory standards (see section 4C). For non–mandatory standards there is no sanction if they are not complied with, although civil courts may take this into account in product liability actions. Even for non–mandatory standards there will be liability under article 213–1 of the Consumer Code if there has been unauthorised use of the 'NF' mark.

D.   NF Mark

AFNOR has the right to grant the 'NF' mark to products and services which comply with all applicable French and European standards. This mark, of which it is claimed 87% of French consumers are aware,[58] can be applied for by any French or foreign business. Once AFNOR receives an application the product or service is subjected to tests to check it conforms to the relevant standards and that there are effective quality control systems in place. Once the right to use the mark has been granted AFNOR retains the power to undertake subsequent tests to ensure the goods or services continue to conform to the standards and that effective control procedures are being maintained. However, whilst the NF mark informs the consumer that all standards have been complied with, it is not necessarily the case that the applicable standards concern safety. France does not have a specific safety

---

58   Figures quoted in AFNOR's document *NF* which seeks to promote the use of the mark by French business.

mark such as exists in Germany[59] and Japan.[60] Some French commentators have argued that the creation of a safety mark may be needed in order to compete at a European level.[61] Although it would be nice of this were so, one suspects that the NF is more in line with the prevalent philosophy behind the CE marking (see Chapter 2, section 7D). We have already noted that the United Kingdom has all but abandoned its safety mark (see Chapter 5, section 4A).

E. Consumer Representation[62]

Of crucial importance is the influence consumers have on the standardisation process. Consumers have been given the express right to be involved in these processes since the Law of 26 January 1984. It has already been noted that they have 3 representatives in the Standardisation Council, but that this is only 3 out of 52 members and when the size of the Council was increased in 1984 their representation was proportionately decreased. Consumers also have two seats on the Administrative Council of AFNOR and another place is reserved for the Institut National de la Consommation (INC), a Government supported body which, *inter alia*, undertakes comparative tests on products.

AFNOR also has a committee to monitor the work of standardisation bodies as they affect consumers, which is known a COSAC (Comité d'Orientation et de Suivi des Activités de Consommation).[63] This is chaired by one of the three consumer representatives on the Administrative Board of AFNOR. There are seven other representatives from consumer associations as well as a representative from the Ministry of Industry, the Secretariat of State for Consumer Affairs, the National Testing Laboratory and the CNPF, (Conseil National du Patronat Français, the French equivalent of the CBI). The chairman of COSAC is also one of the 12 members of the Orienting and

---

59 The voluntary GS mark (Chapter 7, section 4D). The French national laboratory (Laboratoire National d'Essais) does, however, have the right to award the German mark for certain categories of products under a bilateral agreement.

60 There is a voluntary SG mark awarded by the Consumer Product Safety Association and a compulsory S mark for 7 categories of products, which is administered by the Ministry of Industry. The French national laboratory can award these marks for products being exported to Japan.

61 Fourgoux and Mihailov, *op. cit.,* at 40.

62 For a brief description of the structure of consumer participation, in English, see *Consumer Participation,* (ANEC, 1996) at 25–27.

63 This body also defines the French position to be taken at COPOLCO, the consumer representative body of the ISO.

Programming Committee, which is a sub–committee of the Administrative Board responsible for establishing the goals and priorities of the standardisation programme. Consumers can also be represented within the COS structure and have chosen to join 12 out of the 19 COS. Of course the bulk of work carried out at this level is political. A criticism of the French system might be that there is less active involvement by consumers with the relevant expertise at the technical level.

AFNOR has also established a Consumer Bureau to co–ordinate activities concerning consumers and to help consumers be involved in the standard–making process and discussions related to the NF mark. It also co–ordinates consumer input at the European level (through CEN) and at the international level (through ISO–COPOLCO). However, it is important to note that AFNOR's vision of the role of its Consumer Bureau is different from that performed by the United Kingdom and German Consumer Councils and their secretariats. AFNOR does not see it as the function of its bureau to represent the consumer interest. Rather it should have the task of facilitating the possibility of consumer involvement, by informing them of developments and providing the means for them to be involved. In brief it is a communicator rather than an agitator. In practice this leaves the level of consumer representation in France rather weak. One of the major problems is the lack of technical knowledge amongst the consumer activists. A well meaning political consumer activist is unlikely to be effective in the technical discussions which go on within standardisation committees. AFNOR might care to consider whether it should not see it as its responsibility to ensure not merely that consumer input is possible, but also that it actually takes place in an effective manner.

Another problem is the lack of involvement of French consumers at the European level. The work of CEN is becoming increasingly important. We have seen that besides influencing this work through representation in national delegations, consumers can also exert influence through ANEC (see Chapter 2, section 6D). French consumer representatives have, however, been reluctant to become involved with ANEC as it works through the medium of the English language and French representatives are uneasy with this.

9.   CONCLUSIONS

The state plays a central role in French product safety regulation.[64] For instance, official intervention is needed to invoke every one of the post market controls. Symptomatic of this is the fact that the courts are excluded

---

[64]   See Joerges *et al*, *op. cit.*, at 67.

from the development of a safety policy as they have no room to interpret the general safety obligation as it does not of itself form the basis for legal intervention against unsafe products. Although AFNOR is less closely connected to the state than it was before 1984, it still remains under the supervision of the state to a greater degree than the other standards bodies which we study in Germany, the United Kingdom and the United States. It is unfortunate that this state involvement has not led to consumer representation being adequately guaranteed in the standards process. Consumers are formally well represented, but lack the technical expertise to influence the standardisation process.

In many ways France represents a model for a modern scheme of consumer product safety regulation. It has impressive powers to regulate products and to deal with emergencies. Particularly important are the powers of the Consumer Safety Commission to warn the public of dangers and of the courts to order the recall or destruction of dangerous products.

It is encouraging to note that France has established a Consumer Safety Commission. However, its functions are limited and its budget relatively small. An agency which combined the research and information roles of the Consumer Safety Commission and the enforcement role of the DGCCRF would produce a more potent force. This would be more in line with the United States' Consumer Product Safety Commission model.

An interesting development in French law is that the safety rules have been applied to services.[65] Although our study is restricted to product safety it is worthwhile commenting on this modern aspect of French product safety laws. This contrasts markedly with the failure of the EC to address horizontal issues of service safety.[66]

Although French consumer safety law is fairly well developed, nevertheless, some problems remain. Despite the adoption of a Consumer Code the law remains fragmented. For example, in France there is the typical distinction between voluntary standards and legally binding regulations. However, in France standards can be made mandatory and sanctions imposed for their infringement; standards are most frequently made mandatory when the standard is concerned with safety. In addition mandatory regulations affecting product safety have been enacted under both the Law of 1 August 1905 (which is primarily concerned with fraudulent

---

65   Services are covered by the general safety obligation and the enforcement powers apply equally to services. Art. 221–4 provides for services not meeting the general safety obligation to be prohibited or regulated by regulations.

66   See, G. Howells and T. Wilhelmsson, *EC Consumer Law*, (Dartmouth, 1997) at Ch. 2, section 2D. When implementing the General Product Safety Directive some member states did use the occasion to extend its provisions to services (eg Belgium and Finland).

practices) and the more explicitly safety oriented provisions of the Law of 21 July 1983. The recent enactment of a Consumer Code may ease the problem of understanding and locating the law somewhat, but the Code remains a codification of previous consumer laws rather than an attempt to integrate and rationalise consumer law.

It is regrettable that the proposal to permit consumer organisations to take action before the courts where products or services pose a serious or immediate danger has not been adopted. It is not known how widely these organisations have used their powers to bring actions where safety regulations have actually been breached. However, the power to act in such clear instances is not very significant as no doubt the public authorities would also react to such clear breaches. It would be more useful if consumer groups had the power to respond to emergencies which the authorities had failed to deal adequately with or to be more proactive by testing products against the general product safety standard.

Although the Law of 21 July 1983 expounds the general principle that goods and services should be safe, there is no direct sanction if this general aspiration is breached. Indeed the most severe sanctions either require there to have been fraud or adulteration or in the case of the general criminal law actual personal injury.[67] The weakness is that breach of the general safety obligation is not an offence *per se*. The General Product Safety Directive would seem to require that such an offence be created. The French prefer to see the Directive as modelled on their law and not requiring them to do anything to implement it. This contrasts markedly with the United Kingdom approach where regulations have been passed to mirror the general safety requirement in the Directive, although a similar requirement already existed in British law. The different definitions of safety in the Directive and French law would seem to require that implementing legislation be enacted in France. Indeed if breach of the general safety requirement were to be made an offence, a new definition may be needed for the very open French text may seem too vague a standard against which to impose criminal liability. The temptation may be to move towards a 'reference to standards' approach.

---

[67]   Calais–Auloy and Steinmetz, *op cit.*

7 Germany

1. INTRODUCTION

The traditional German approach and philosophy to product safety regulation has several characteristics which caused it difficulties in coming to terms with the European legislation in this sector. This is perhaps surprising given that the new approach to technical harmonisation is largely modelled on German practice. However, Germany is less comfortable with the more general moves to create a broader European consumer safety framework. Thus it has continually been opposed to the EHLASS data collection system and still does not participate in it fully (Chapter 2, section 8). It also opposed the General Product Safety Directive even to the extent of challenging it before the European Court of Justice.[1]

The most notable characteristic of the German regulatory system for the safety of consumer goods is its reliance on self–regulation, supported by a well publicised GS mark which is awarded to goods which comply with safety standards. Given the global trend towards reliance on self regulatory standards the German experience is likely to be highly instructive on the benefits and pitfalls of this manner of regulation. However, the German tradition clashes with the European model because the German approach largely entrusts the self–regulatory authorities with responsibility for ensuring safety levels are achieved, whilst European law requires public authorities to have strong fall back powers to monitor and intervene in the market.

Another key feature of the German system is its preference for sectoral controls. Historically most countries developed controls on specific products; the creation of general obligations has been a modern phenomenon. In Germany regulation of consumer goods has always been something of an afterthought and has been achieved by extending the scope of application of laws aimed primarily at regulating neighbouring sectors, especially laws regulating food and industrial work materials.

The Gesetz zur Neuordnung und Bereinigung des Rechts in Verkehr mit Lebensmittel, Tabakerzeugnissen, kosmetischen Mitteln und Bedarfsgegenstände (Act to Reform and Streamline the Law on Trade in Foodstuffs, Tobacco Products, Cosmetics and Consumer Goods: hereafter

---

1   See *Federal Republic of Germany v Council of the European Union*, Case C–359/92 [1994] ECR I–3681.

LMBG)[2] was extended from being a law regulating food to encompass 'Bedarfsgegenstände'. This extended the scope of the Act quite considerably (it had previously already gone beyond food to cover cosmetics). Fortunately (as 'Bedarfsgegenstände' is a difficult term to translate) the Act enumerates the objects controlled under this heading. In addition to items such as tableware, drinking vessels and kitchen utensils, which had previously been regulated as items which are likely to come into contact with food and therefore affect its safety, the objects listed now also include, *inter alia*, objects which come into contact with the mucous membranes, household cleaning and preservative agents, deodorants and indoor insect controls.

Equally the Gerätesicherheitsgesetz (Machine Safety Act, hereafter GSG)[3] is primarily an Act governing the safety of appliances in the work place. However, its scope has been widely extended to cover other technical consumer goods and toys, but some consumer goods (such as radios and televisions) still seem to slip through its net, and are generally controlled by self–regulatory institutions.[4] In addition there are numerous other specific pieces of legislation covering commodities such as medicines, wine and guns.

As well as a tradition of sectoral regulation, the German regulation of consumer safety is further fragmented by a tradition of decentralised supervisory institutions. Many countries have some form of vertical separation of supervisory functions; but this vertical segmentation is a little more pronounced in Germany than in some other countries. The problem is also exacerbated by the federal structure of Germany, which leads to horizontal divisions on a regional basis in addition to vertical sectoral divisions. Supervision of the GSG and the LMBG is the responsibility of the Länder. This enforcement role for the Länder is enshrined in art. 80H of the Basic Law and the Länder jealously guard their autonomy with the result that it is not easy to co–ordinate activities horizontally between the Länder authorities and there is suspicion of the central authorities even performing co–ordinating functions. These are viewed with caution lest they result in attempts to interfere with the autonomy of the Länder. Whilst national regulation of product safety may have developed to take account of this feature, it has caused some problems when fulfilling the obligations under the General Product Safety Directive in relation to the Rapid Exchange of Information System (RAPEX) which requires a national contact point (Chapter 2, section 9J(b)).

---

2   Act of 15 August 1974 (subsequently amended). For further details see N. Reich and H. Micklitz, *Consumer Legislation in the Federal Republic of Germany*, (Van Nostrand Reinhold, 1981) at 139 *et seq.*

3   Act of 13 August 1979 (subsequently amended).

4   Reich and Micklitz, *op. cit.*, at 132.

In many ways the German federal structure highlights some dangers which may result if care is not taken with the way European and international product safety regulation is developed. Whilst continued local or regional supervision is essential and local traditions should be respected as far as possible, product safety can no longer be viewed as a purely local matter. Trans–national co–operation is essential to cope with the new threats posed by cross–border trade. The layers in the supervisory network should view themselves as part of an integrated team with the same objectives and not seek to maintain rigid spheres of influence.

One of the major criticisms of the German implementation of the General Product Safety Directive is that it treats the general rules it introduces as being very much subsidiary to the existing rules and structures. The intention is clearly to do the minimum to comply with the Directive and to leave business free to continue dealing with the laws and officials they have become acquainted with. Yet product safety regulation requires a focused and co–ordinated framework which can produce an effective and balanced regulatory regime. Implementation of the Directive should have provided Germany with an opportunity to re–group, re–organise and build on its traditions. This has been passed by in order to secure short term stability and continuity, but there may be a longer term price to be paid. The creation of a more focused institutional arrangement should have encouraged a more pro–active role for the authorities in seeking to prevent dangerous products being produced and marketed in the first place. As we shall see the German system is better placed to react to dangers than to head them off. This seems to be a positive (but unfortunate) choice of the German regulators. It is also one which may pose threats to German consumers now that the system has to cope with the far wider range of goods from different origins which are freely circulating within the European single market.

2. DATA COLLECTION

Information about product related accidents is an essential foundation for a product safety regulatory regime. As resources are scarce, data allows priorities to be set: evidence concerning the sources of accidents can lead to resources being directed to improving standards for a particular category of product, concentrating market supervision and targeting information and education campaigns on vulnerable groups of consumers. Collecting information is, however, expensive and shows few immediate direct tangible returns. It also highlights inadequacies in the system and there is a suggestion that the German authorities and vested interests like to paint an over rosy picture of the level of safety of German consumer goods.[5]

There is no systematic system for collecting data on home and leisure accidents in Germany.[6] This is in contrast to the very detailed statistics on workplace, school and road accidents. By deducting fatal accidents in these sectors from the total number of fatal accidents and categorising the remainder as household and leisure accidents, Falke comes to the startling conclusion that whilst by 1986 fatal accidents had fallen to between a third and a quarter of their 1971 level in the other sectors, in the household and leisure sector they still stood at three quarters of their 1971 level. It is tempting to agree with Falke's suggestion that there is a link between the lack of measures to promote consumer safety and the lack of decline in accidents. Comparisons can be made with the safety campaigns in relation to work place and road accidents and the fruits they seem to have borne. It must be implied that the lack of consumer safety campaigns is in part explained by the lack of data highlighting the need for such campaigns and possibly also the lack of a central body charged with the task of promoting consumer safety.

The only systematic survey of household and leisure accidents has been carried out by HUK–Verband (the Association of Liability Insurers, Motor Vehicle and Legal Cost Insurers), which is hardly an independent body.[7] This involved a survey of 89,303 representative households and asked for details on household and leisure accidents which occurred within the previous twelve months. It concluded that there were around 3 million household and leisure accidents which required medical attention or caused longer term impairment, with hospitalisation being required in 15% of cases. In addition there were more than 100 million trivial accidents. However, the study has been criticised because it did not record accidents as they occurred, but rather depended upon the memory of the respondents to the survey. For

---

5   See J. Falke, 'Post Market Control of Technical Consumer Goods in The Federal Republic of Germany' in *Post Market Control of Consumer Goods*, H.-W. Micklitz (ed.) (Nomos, 1990) especially at 355–363 (this section draws heavily on the data included in that chapter); in German see C. Joerges, J. Falke, H.-W. Micklitz, G. Brüggermeier, *Die Sicherheit von Konsumgütern und die Entwicklung der Europäischen Gemeinschaft*, (Nomos, 1988) especially Ch. 3 on 'Die Produktsicherheitspolitik in der Bundesrepublik Deutschland'.

6   Although there are a certain number of equipment specific investigations, carried out by, for instance, the Bundesanstalt für Arbeitsschutz – BAU (Federal Institute for Worker Protection) or Trade Supervisory Offices.

7   See K. Pfundt, *Bedeutung und Charkteristik von Heim– und Freizeitunfällen. Ergebnis von 90.000 Haushaltsbefragen*, Mitteilung Nr. 26 der Beratungsstelle für Schadenverhütung des HUK–Verbandes, (1986).

instance, respondents were 5.3 times more likely to report an accident for the month prior to the survey than for the same period in the previous year; even for hospitalisation cases there was a 'forgetfulness factor' of 2.1. A further telephone survey was carried out involving 3,064 accidents to seek more details on the causes and consequences of the accident and brief studies were made of those accidents caused by an object. In the report the user's behaviour was frequently described as being variously, 'relaxed', 'carefree', 'unattentive', 'paying attention to the T.V. set', 'overloaded with luggage', 'having chosen a bad position' and 'being distracted by children'. However, Falke rightly criticises these studies for concentrating too much on the behaviour of the user as a means of explaining away the accident. Even if consumer behaviour has to be taken into account it seems wrong to do so when relying on the distant memory of the consumer. Also there is a tendency for accident victims to blame themselves. Moreover, it is wrong to expect consumers to know whether improved design or construction could have avoided the accident. The conclusion of the report (as summarised by Falke) are quite alarming:

> 'Technical inadequacies in newly–purchased machines, tools or equipment are of no importance in the causation of household and leisure accidents. The Law on Safety of Equipment has ensured that hardly any inadequately or dangerously operated machines may be sold. Ninety nine percent of household and leisure accidents are the consequence of more or less aggravating misconduct.'[8]

Falke also quotes Mertens who argues that machines and equipment account for less than 0.5% of household and leisure accidents.[9]

This seems unduly complacent given that in 24% of tests carried out by the Gewerbeaufsichtsämtern (Trade Supervisory Offices, see section 3B) equipment was found to be defective and the central testing station in Nordrhein–Westfalen continually disclosed serious and widespread defects. Furthermore, it is hard to classify a cause of the accident as being due to the user without considering the possibility of avoiding foreseeable misuse by redesign, better warnings or instructions for use. The German standards DIN 31000/VDE 10002 'General Guidelines for the Proper Safety Construction of Technical Products' and DIN 820, Part 12 'Standardisation Work, Standards with Technical Safety Designation and Construction', both require standardisation work to take account of the possibility of foreseeable misuse.

Falke suggests that technical design improvements should take account of the empirical evidence on how accidents are actually caused in the real

---

8   Falke (1990), *op. cit.*, at p. 358.
9   A. Mertens, 'Heim und Freizeitunfälle: Aufklärung intensivieren' (1986) *B.Arb.Bl.* 32.

world by human error. Indeed Falke points out that a re–evaluation of the accidents recorded within the framework of the HUK study revealed that in 1.4% of cases a technical alteration appeared necessary, in 4.15% an amendment would help avoid human misconduct and in 7.3% an amendment was conceivable but impracticable. Based on the estimate of 3 million households and leisure accidents, Falke concluded 166,000 accidents involved objects for whom a technical improvement was necessary or recommendable.

Germany has always opposed EHLASS (Chapter 2, section 8). It claims it is too expensive and, at least initially, would have preferred to have studies carried out at irregular periods.[10] It has always had an opt out from the hospital data collection scheme and instead provides figures based on a questionnaire survey.

3. INSTITUTIONS

Before turning to the substantive regulations governing product safety it is useful to explain the structure of the authorities involved. This is complicated by the federal structure, the fact that consumer safety has largely developed out of health and safety at work legislation and by the significant role played by non–governmental bodies.

A. Federal Government

At the federal level the GSG is the responsibility of the Ministry for Labour and Social Affairs. Consumer safety in general falls within the remit of the Economics Ministry and has recently been transferred to a consumer affairs department, which does not, however, have enforcement powers. This latter change in responsible departments perhaps explains why the Government has taken a more positive response and conceded that a general consumer product safety law had to be enacted to comply with the General Product Safety Directive.

The Minister of Labour and Social Affairs has to establish a Committee for Technical Work Materials to advise him on the application of the GSG (§ 8, GSG). This consists of no more that 21 members drawn from the Länder, insurers, employers, trade unions and interested groups. The Federal Institute for Occupational Health and Safety (Bundesanstalt für Arbeitsschutz – BAU) serves as the executive body for the Committee. The BAU also supervises test centres, organises information exchanges between centres,

---

10   See answer to written question no. 2194/84: OJ 1985 C 203/3.

produces a 500 run monthly internal bulletin about the GSG for the Trade Supervisory Offices and works with DIN to determine which standards shall be deemed to fulfil safety requirements.[11] It also operates as the reporting office for the EC RAPEX system.

B. State Level

Enforcement of the GSG is the responsibility of the Länder and is carried out by the Trade Supervisory Offices. In 1986 there were 71 Trade Supervisory Offices and 2,969 officers. Since then the numbers have of course increased as the new Länder have been integrated into Germany. The Trade Supervisory Offices have a wide range of responsibilities, including environmental protection, all forms of health and safety at work and radiation protection. Given the breadth and gravity of their other responsibilities it is perhaps not surprising that consumer safety takes a low priority. A 1979 survey found that only 2.2% of their working time is spent on applying the GSG.[12] This highlights the point that effective consumer safety regulation requires an agency which sees protecting consumers as being its central goal. In Germany the devolution of power does not therefore provide the close supervision of business, which is perhaps achieved by the United Kingdom system of trading standards officers (Chapter 5, section 3B).

The division of power also causes problems relating to the co–ordination of activities. Some Länder try to overcome this by establishing a central headquarters to co–ordinate and support the work of the other offices. The work of the Zentralstelle für Sicherheitstechnik of Nordrhein–Westfalen (Central Office for Safety Technology) was very influential. This had a modern laboratory which was able to test for electrical and mechanical defects. It undertook selective market controls, investigated accidents and fulfilled a supportive and advisory role for the Trade Supervisory Offices (in practice, for the whole of Germany). Its results were drawn upon by national and international standardisation committees and in particular its research highlighting problems with technical medical equipment caused new regulations to be adopted. However, this valuable institution of national (and international) importance has been closed down, presumably because one Land could not justify supporting such an extensive operation.

A further problem with decentralising control is that it can lead to duplication of work if each Land is dealing with the same problem and can expose consumers unnecessarily to dangers if information on risks is not

---

[11] These are listed in an annex to administrative rules: see section 4C(ii).
[12] Quoted in Falke (1990), *op. cit.*, at 369.

passed between the Länder. Amazingly there appears to be no formal system for circulating information between the Länder. Reliance is placed on the monthly bulletin produced by BAU, but this would not be adequate to deal with emergencies. Apparently officials feel that informal exchanges between experts suffices. It may be that there are fears that formal schemes requiring the sharing of information would undermine the independence of the Länder.

C.   RAPEX Co–ordinator

The EC RAPEX system requires a national contact point to notify the Commission of dangerous products and to receive notifications from the Commission (Chapter 2, section 9J(b)). This caused some problems in Germany because of the traditional autonomy of the Länder. A central co–ordinator is now to be found within BAU who collects information and distributes it to Brussels or conveys information received from Brussels to the Länder. There still appears to be no formal method of communicating other matters expeditiously horizontally between the Länder. As the obligation to notify Brussels only arises once the decision has been taken to take action against a product where there are implications for other states, this still means that there is the danger of a slow and unco–ordinated response to a problem within Germany.[13]

D.   DIN and BG

Of central importance is the Deutsches Instituts für Normung – DIN (the German Standardisation Institute). The constitution of DIN and the role of standards will be considered in more detail later (see section 6).

In addition to standards, which are (at least formally) voluntary, Germany also has worker protection and accident prevention rules. These are developed by the Berufsgenossenschaften – BG (Industrial Injuries Insurance Institutes) in expert committees where alongside the experts from the BG are representatives of the trade supervisory authorities, producers and users of technical work goods, trade unions and employers. The emphasis is on worker safety rather than consumer safety and consumers are not involved in this process. Before the regulations, which are legally binding, enter into force they must be approved by the Minister for Labour and Social Affairs. These regulations mainly contain detailed rules on how employees should

---

13   Decisions taken by one Trade Supervisory Office will bind other offices, but as a lot of the work in this area is negotiation rather than formal decision–making there is still a danger that the response will be unco–ordinated.

conduct themselves and the protective equipment which should be worn. When the regulations deal with the safety standards of machines and equipment they tend simply to refer to the 'generally recognised technical standard'.

Indeed in 1982 an agreement was made between DIN and the BGs, which is similar to the new approach to technical harmonisation adopted at the European level (Chapter 2, section 4C). Under this agreement the BGs would set safety objectives in an abstract way without providing technical details on how the goals were to be achieved. DIN standards would then be used to concretise the means of achieving the safety objectives.

E. Test Centres

We will see later that the GS safety symbol plays an important role in the German product safety regime. The awarding of the GS label is performed by test centres recognised by the Minister for Labour and Social Affairs. § 9(2) GSG lists the requirements of testing laboratories or certification bodies, which are:

a)   the persons in charge of the centres and those conducting the tests must be independent from any persons involved in the development, production, distribution or maintenance of the product or who are in any way dependent upon the results of the testing or certification procedure;
b)   the availability of the necessary organisational structure, personnel, means and equipment to ensure the independent fulfilment of appropriate duties;
c)   the personnel must have adequate technical competence, professional integrity, experience and independence;
d)   possession of liability insurance;
e)   protection of trade and professional secrets disclosed during testing and certification procedures; and
f)   observance of testing and certification procedures.

There is a Register of Testing Centres which lists the recognised centres as well as the areas to which their recognition extends. The registration is supervised by BAU which checks the centre has the requisite personnel and practical resources and requires the centre to demonstrate its ability to test in the area it has applied to be registered for. An agreement has been reached whereby French test centres can also be recognised.

F.   Stiftung Warentest

Stiftung Warentest is a private foundation established by the federal Government in 1964. Its purpose is to undertake comparative testing of products and publish the results. The results can affect the behaviour of consumers who may change their purchasing practices, manufacturers who may take Stiftung Warentest's testing criteria into account in their product development, design and quality control and wholesalers and retailers who may alter their purchasing plans in the light of favourable or negative reports. Foundation staff also co–operate with DIN standardisation committees. Stiftung Warentest has helped on occasions to raise safety standards above those preferred by DIN.[14] This is achieved by setting higher standards than the DIN norms. This will cause some producers to comply with the Stiftung Warentest's criteria in order to obtain positive test results. Even if the Stiftung Warentest criteria are not universally adopted by industry they can serve as a point of reference which over time DIN can be persuaded to recognise. The freedom of Stiftung Warentest to adopt different and higher standards than those set out in DIN norms has been recognised by the Bundesgerichtshof (BGH, Federal Court of Justice).[15]

The BGH had earlier protected the activities of the Stiftung Warentest by allowing it to invoke art. 5.1 of the Basic Law concerning freedom to express opinions. Industry can be criticised so long as the investigations are carried out neutrally, expertly and objectively. Stiftung Warentest's procedures meet these criteria. Its directorate proposes projects to a board of trustees. Goods to be tested must be sold nationwide, identify the manufacturer, be of interest to a wide range of consumers and not be newly launched products. About 20 products are usually selected for each sector scrutinised including those with a large share of the market as well as those with a new design or peculiar form of construction. Manufacturers are involved to ensure that the latest models are identified and the goods are anonymously purchased by Foundation staff. An engineer drafts a test programme which is considered by a committee comprising neutral experts and representatives of consumers, manufacturers, traders and testing institutes. The directorate then determines the test programme and circulates it to the manufacturers. A testing institute is chosen to perform the test and produces a detailed written report on each part of the test. The measurements are then passed on to the manufacturers to allow them to object, where, for example, during testing damage occurred which made the results worse than would normally be expected.

---

14   Falke, *op. cit.*, at 381–2 cites the examples of spin dryers and compost choppers where Stiftung Warentest's criteria eventually came to be included within standards.

15   Decision of 10 March 1987; BGH, NJW [1987] 2222–2225.

G. Consumer Associations

In Germany the consumer organisations (Arbeitsgemeinschaft der Verbraucherverbände – AgV) play a major role in enforcing consumer rights. For instance, they have the right to challenge unfair terms in the courts.[16] The suggestion was made that they should have a similar right to seek warning or recall actions.[17] Nothing came of this proposal largely because, until forced to introduce an effective administrative recall duty by the EC General Product Safety Directive, the Government favoured relying on the private law of product liability as a sufficient incentive for industry to institute warning or recall programmes. In any event because of the time delays whilst consumer associations brought legal actions any right of action by consumer organisations should at best only be supplementary to more effective administrative controls.

4. GERÄTESICHERHEITSGESETZ (GSG)

A. Background

The GSG has been the most important German law regulating consumer goods. It is therefore important to study it in detail as it represents the German approach to the regulation of product safety. As the German model provided the inspiration for the EC's Low Voltage Directive and the new approach to technical harmonisation, its philosophy is clearly of interest. However, it is not merely of academic interest, for the GSG retains practical relevance since we shall see the German approach to implementing the General Product Safety Directive was to leave in place the existing laws and structures as far as possible.

The GSG is based on an Act which was originally enacted in 1968. It has the important consequence of making the producers and importers of machinery responsible for its safety in the workplace, but its scope has always been wider than simply ensuring workplace safety and has encompassed the safety of technical goods, wherever used. The original Act has been amended on several occasions, most notably in 1979 and 1992. The 1979 reforms brought suppliers within the scope of the law to a limited extent. Certain sorts of equipment which it was considered needed

---

16   See, s. 13, Law against Unfair Competition and s. 13(2)(1), Law on Standard Business Conditions.

17   W. Löwe, 'Rückrufpflicht des Warenherstellers' (1978) *D.A.R.* 288 and AgV, *Consumer Policy Correspondence No. 6* of 5.2.1985, 2(3), quoted in Falke, *op cit.*, at 347.

supervision and spare parts and accessories were also covered for the first time. Special provision was also made for regulating technical medical machines and equipment. The 1992 reforms were intended mainly to bring the law into line with the new approach to technical harmonisation adopted within the EC (and perhaps were viewed by some as an attempt to forestall calls for more dramatic reforms to implement the EC General Product Safety Directive). Thus the safety standard was varied depending upon whether or not the goods were covered by an EC Directive; the powers of the authorities were extended to ensure only safe goods reached the market and the rules for accrediting testing institutions and awarding the CE mark were brought into line with European law requirements. The 1992 reforms also placed suppliers more firmly within the scope of the law.[18]

B. Scope

The GSG regulates the putting into circulation and exhibiting of technical work materials[19] by professionals or by others in the course of a commercial enterprise (§ 1(1) GSG). Previously the GSG had only regulated the marketing or exhibiting of goods by producers or importers. The 1992 version, however, makes it clear that the obligation also extends to suppliers.[20] The rules only bite when the goods have been put into circulation or exhibited. Goods are put into circulation each time they are handed over to another party or when they are imported into the EC. Exhibiting means exhibiting or displaying goods for the purpose of promoting sales.

Certain products are completely excluded from the reach of the GSG (eg vehicles and military goods); whilst others are excluded to the extent that specific provisions guarantee the safety standard set by § 3 GSG.[21] However, such products remain subject to regulations passed under § 4 GSG

18　See, W. Jeiter, *Das neue Gerätesicherheitsgesetz*, (C.H. Beck, 1993); Sattler, 'Die Novelle zum Gerätesicherheitsgesetz' (1992) 24 *Eu.Z.W.* 764, H. Micklitz, 'Die Richtlinie über die allgemeine Produktsicherheit vom 29.6.1992' (1992) 5 *V.u.R.* 261.

19　As mentioned above the law has been extended to cover certain pieces of equipment, but we will largely leave this complication to one side. Likewise we will not consider the special rules on technical medical devices.

20　However, to make the text more readable we will refer to producers as a shorthand for referring to those placed under a duty by the GSG to market safe products.

21　A toy has been cited as an example of a product governed partly by the GSG and partly by other legislation. Its toxicity may be governed by the LMBG with the mechanical risks being governed by the GSG: see Joerges, Falke, Micklitz, Brüggermeier, *op. cit.*, at p. 144.

(see section CC(i). § 2 defines the work materials covered; of interest to us is the fact that it expressly extends to, *inter alia*, household equipment, sport and leisure, goods and handicrafts as well as toys. It seems that most technical consumer goods are included.[22] However, an important recent safety alert concerned office chairs which had a tendency to explode and these were considered to be outside the scope of the GSG.[23] The rules generally only apply to goods which are in a condition in which they can be used.

C. Safety Concept

§ 3 is the cornerstone of the GSG. It sets down the level of safety which must be achieved. § 3a GSG states that products not complying with the standard should not be sold in retail business and only in the trade when accompanied by a visible notice that they do not comply with the requirements and must first be improved before being sold on. However, there are no direct criminal consequences for failing to comply with this standard. Rather reaching the safety standard is important as a pre–requisite for the awarding of the GS mark and failing to reach it gives grounds for intervention by the supervisory authorities. Since 1992 the GSG distinguishes between products covered by an EC harmonising directive and those products for which there are no harmonised EC rules.

(i) Products Covered by EC Harmonised Rules

§ 4 GSG gives the federal Government the power to make regulations to fulfil, *inter alia*, EC law obligations. Thus if an EC Directive is passed covering a certain sector there is the power to implement this by regulation. Technical work materials can only be marketed if they comply with the technical safety requirements and special conditions (eg information requirements or requirements concerning the CE mark). Even if the goods satisfy these conditions they still cannot be marketed if they pose a danger to the life or health (or other legal interests specified in the regulations) when used in the prescribed manner ('bestimmungsgemässe Verwendung' – this concept also appears in relation to non–harmonised products and is discussed

---

[22] But not (as noted above) apparently radios and televisions which are governed by self–regulatory rules: see Reich and Micklitz, *op. cit.*, at 132.

[23] See J. Falke, 'Foodstuffs Control and the Regulation of Business Practices in Emergency Situations in the Federal Republic of Germany' in *Federalism and Responsibility*, H. Micklitz, T. Roethe and S. Weatherill (eds), (Graham & Trotman/Martinus Nijhoff, 1994) at 319.

below). Significantly this category of products does not have to comply with German worker protection and accident prevention rules. Unless the regulations specify otherwise the product is assessed on the basis of the legal position when it was first marketed in the EC.

(ii)   *Products Without Harmonised Rules*

Products not covered by regulations implementing EC harmonisation directives are becoming steadily fewer in number. However, the remaining areas are covered by the traditional GSG rules, which are interesting because they highlight certain key features of the German approach to product safety regulation.

The GSG requires that before these goods are marketed they are designed according to the generally accepted technical rules as well as complying with any worker protection or accident prevention rules, so that when used in the prescribed manner the user and third parties are protected against all kinds of dangers to their life and health to the extent that this is consistent with the specified use. We noted earlier that, under an agreement worked out between the BGs and DIN, the worker protection and accident prevention rules tend simply to refer to generally accepted technical standards when they deal with safety specifications for products. Thus everything turns on the content of the generally accepted technical standards. In turn this means that DIN norms, although not expressly mentioned in the GSG have a substantial impact as they represent the easiest way of ascertaining what represents the generally accepted technical standards. Presumably in those instances where the Stiftung Warentest's more demanding criteria have become industry standard these should be taken to be the generally accepted technical rules, but such instances are likely to be rare and it would be even rarer for a producer to be condemned for complying with DIN standards,

The General Administrative Regulations (Allgemeine Verwaltungsvorschrift – AVV) to the GSG contains three annexes containing rules of art which according to the Ministry of Labour and Social Affairs if complied with lead to a presumption that the product reaches the required standard. The list is continually revised and updated. By March 1992 Annex A contained 1,486 safety rules mainly DIN and VDE[24] standards. Annex B had 285 accident prevention regulations and Annex C had 116 of the French AFNOR

---

24   VDE = Verband Deutscher Techniker and is the equivalent organisation to DIN dealing with electrical standards.

standards, which are recognised under a bilateral agreement between France and Germany.[25]

The 'generally accepted technical standards' and the worker protection and accident prevention rules can be deviated from so long as the same level of protection is achieved by other means. The product is assessed based on the legal position when first marketed within the jurisdiction of the GSG.

Several criticisms from the consumer perspective have been made of the GSG's safety standard. First, there is the restriction only to preventing damage when the product is used in the prescribed manner. The criticism here is that account should be taken of the possibility of designing the product so as to avoid or minimise the damage caused by foreseeable misuse. Indeed, we have already noted, that DIN committees are required to take the possibility of foreseeable misuse into account in their standardisation work (section 2), but these rules are only internal rules and are not binding on producers and distributors. To the extent that the GSG continues to be the standard applied to consumer products this may constitute a breach of the General Product Safety Directive, which requires that reasonably foreseeable uses be taken into account.[26]

For the purpose of the GSG 'specified use' is defined in § 2(5). The definition contains both (i) a subjective definition based on the directions given by the person who placed the product in circulation (albeit taking into account any advertising) and (ii) an objective definition based on what could typically be expected given its design and type. Of course it is possible that the objective and subjective definitions conflict, where for example the instructions state the goods should not be used for a purpose for which they are typically used. Such a dispute came before the Oberverwaltungsgericht (OVG, Superior Administrative Court) for Münster,[27] which decided in favour of the objective test. A trader could not release himself from responsibility for providing the standard of safety which users had come to expect. Some commentators argue that the subjective opinion of the producer should be dominant as it allows the most recent knowledge of the producer to be taken into account. However, it would be dangerous to allow design to be based on the specialist knowledge of producers rather than the actual habits of users. However, even the decision of the OVG Münster leaves the user unprotected as regards foreseeable misuse.

---

[25] Falke (1994), *op. cit.* at 269 cites the total of such rules as being 1,908 and so there is a minor discrepancy between this figure and the sum of the three annexes (1887), but the figure is clearly very large!

[26] Micklitz, *op. cit.*, at 262–3.

[27] OVG Münster 26.10.1978 – XIII A 881/76, quoted in Joerges, Falke, Micklitz, Brüggermeier, *op. cit.*, at 145 and Jeiter, *op cit.*, at 33.

The guiding standard is that of the 'generally accepted technical standards'. This is not perceived to be very demanding as it condones producers for not being at the forefront of technological development.[28] It is only once a technological development has become generally recognised that it has to be followed. To be generally accepted it seems that a rule does not have to be dominant, but must be sufficiently tested and proven to be effective in commercial practice. A more demanding standard might require products to comply with 'the state of technology' or if one wanted to be even more demanding the 'state of knowledge and technology'.

The very technique of creating a standard by reference to 'generally accepted rules' raises for German jurists interesting juridical questions about the drafting of legislation.[29] In practice this technique means abrogating decisions concerning the content of the safety standard to DIN.[30] The desirability of this will depend upon the quality of DIN standards and the democratic input into the decision–making process (issues which are considered in section 6).

It cannot be objected that producers are having trading standards dictated to them by private actors rather than the state, since the GSG leaves then free to depart from 'generally accepted technical rules' so long as they achieve an equivalent level of safety. This ensures that at least in theory dominant industry interests cannot force competitors out of the market by packing DIN committees and ensuring standards are adopted which favour them over their competitors. In practice, of course, it is important to be able to influence DIN standard drafting committees since life is a lot easier if the DIN standard reflects one's current practice.

A greater danger is faced by consumers since they will tend to have to accept the DIN committee's opinion of what should be the generally accepted technical standards and hence what level of safety is technically possible. In theory it is possible to argue that goods complying with DIN standards do not comply with generally accepted technical standards – for instance where Stiftung Warentest's criteria have become generally accepted – or that notwithstanding compliance with generally accepted standards the goods still do provide satisfactory protection. In practice this is unlikely to happen. Goods complying with DIN standards which are listed in Annex A of the

---

28 Joerges, Falke, Micklitz, Brüggermeier, *op. cit.*, at 137 and 147.

29 See Joerges, Falke, Micklitz, Brüggermeier, *op. cit.*, at 136–141, who also discuss the technique of integrating a reference to a standard in legislation; cf the views of P. Marburger, *Die Regeln der Technik in Recht*, (Heymann, 1979).

30 The same point could be made about BG rules (see section 3D), but these are approved by Ministers. In any event on the relevant point they tend to refer to generally accepted technical rules and so DIN standards will be the focus of our concern.

AVV to the GSG benefit from a presumption that they meet the required standard and will almost automatically receive the GS mark. The supervisory authorities will not be pro–active in supervising the safety of goods carrying the GS mark. A case study of the so–called 'exploding office chairs' shows that as the goods carried the GS mark the risk they posed was not taken seriously until a major incident occurred causing serious personal injuries.[31] The General Product Safety Directive does not give technical norms quite this privileged position and this may be another way in which continued adherence to the GSG standard constitutes a breach of the Directive.[32]

D. GS Mark

The GS mark (geprüfte Sicherheit) was introduced in 1977 by the Minister of Labour after the association of bodies responsible for awarding safety marks had failed, despite seven years of discussions, to agree on a common mark. The GS mark differs from the CE mark in three important respects. It is a voluntary mark, whereas the CE mark is usually mandatory. Also the GS mark is exclusively concerned with the safety aspects of products. The GS mark is awarded after third party assessment, whereas the CE marking is often based on a producer's self declaration of conformity. The GS mark seems to have achieved a wide degree of popular awareness. It provides consumers with some guarantee of safety, whilst producers awarded with the mark can use it as a marketing tool. It is estimated that some 16,000 –17,000 test certificates are issued annually and that by 1985 85,000 types of equipment and machines carried the GS label.[33] As the GS and CE marks serve different functions it is useful to allow them both to be used together. This is allowed so long as there is no risk of confusion or unless it is specifically prohibited in a regulation.

The GS mark can be attached to goods when the producer or their authorised representative within the EC has applied to a recognised centre and been issued with a certificate based on testing of the design. The certificate must state:

(i) that the model tested conformed with the safety requirements described in § 3(1);

(ii) the conditions exist to ensure that goods produced conform to the model;

---

31   See Falke (1994), *op. cit.*, at 310–319.

32   See Micklitz, *op. cit.*, at 262.

33   See Falke (1990), *op. cit.*, at 364–69.

(iii) the notified body has procedures to supervise the production process and application of the GS mark;

(iv) the person responsible for production has accepted responsibility to ensure the conditions remain such that goods can be produced in conformity with the model and has agreed to facilitate supervisory controls;

(v) the certificate will be withdrawn if either the safety requirements change or the conditions are no longer such as to ensure goods are produced in conformity with the model.

The GS mark also serves a useful function for the supervisory authorities, since they may exempt goods bearing the mark from examination unless they believe it is being used illegally.[34] Of course, as noted above, when considering the example of 'exploding office chairs' this may have some dangers for consumers unless both the standard of testing and monitoring by the centres and the standards they are applying are very high. Falke points out that 8% of products referred to trade supervisory authorities with 'uniform defect notices' concerned products bearing the GS mark and the Stiftung Warentest regularly discover dangerous products bearing the label.[35]

Falke is right to conclude that the matter cannot simply be left to self–regulatory authorities; there needs also to be supervision by public authorities and private bodies (such as Stiftung Warentest). This is particularly so because, in light of the thousands of certificates issued each year, supervision of the testing centres is no easy matter. This is the responsibility of the BAU and Falke notes that it has difficulties in determining whether the entire product has been submitted to testing or only parts of it. Supervisory bodies report difficulties when the certificate is held by someone other than the producer or importer.

The GS mark does seem to have produced some benefits in terms of improved product safety standards. Thus Falke cites a 1988 survey showing that between 60 and 95% of goods submitted to testing had to be modified. Presumably, but for the need to apply for the GS mark, these are goods which would otherwise have been marketed with that defect. Generally the centres found the producers or importers willing to co–operate to overcome the fault and in only a very few cases did centres have to report an applicant to the Trade Supervisory Office. The testing centres are also under an obligation to monitor products, including factory inspections, to ensure the safety requirements continue to be met. This is again a positive way of

---

[34]   § 6(1) AVV–GSG (administrative rules to the GSG).
[35]   Falke (1990), *op. cit.*, at 365.

supporting the statutory safety requirements. The testing centre staff also serve a useful function by serving on DIN expert committees.

E. Supervision

Supervision of the market is the responsibility of the Trade Supervisory Offices. There is no obligation for the authorities to inspect each of the estimated 180,000 new technical work materials which are placed on the market each year. Indeed products bearing the CE or GS mark are presumed to fulfil the requirements and are tested only on a random sample basis (§ 5 (2) GSG). Tests must be carried out when a worker protection authority, legal accident insurance agency, the police or other authorities or institutions concerned with ensuring goods comply with the safety requirements of the GSG (such as Stiftung Warentest, testing centres or works councils of firms which use such goods, but significantly not consumer organisations) report a defective product or an accident caused by a defective product.

In order to make the best use of resources most inspections are carried out at trade fairs and exhibitions. This has the advantage that resources can be concentrated to their greatest effect, since these represent a limited number of places at which all new gadgets are brought together and displayed. However, this approach has the drawback that only visual external inspections can be made. To take one example, in 1988 the Trade Supervisory Offices of Nordrhein–Westphalia examined 17,164 technical work tools. 60% of inspections took place at trade fairs and exhibitions with 51.2% concerning tools for the home, leisure, nursery or school. 21.5% of the devices were found to be defective. In only 1.1% of cases was the defect found to be so serious that the product had to be discarded, in other cases the defects could be remedied by additions (35.5%), construction measures (44%) and changes to instruction manuals (19.4%). Falke explains the low level of defects about which nothing could be done as being explainable by the attitude of officials who act cautiously and see their role as an advisory one (rather than it being a testament to the safety of products on the German market).[36]

In carrying out their functions the authorities can require producers, importers and those who market or exhibit technical work materials to co–operate and provide them with information (§ 7(1) GSG). However, it is possible to refuse to answer questions if the answers might be incriminating. Parties can be requested to hand over products to be tested. Agents of the trade supervisory authorities can enter premises to view and test products, to inspect the production process and to take samples away (§ 7(2) GSG).

---

[36]   Falke (1994), *op. cit.*, at 289.

Prior to the revision of the GSG in 1992 the authorities had only one sanction against dangerous goods, namely issuing a prohibition order (Untersagung). In practice agencies used a host of less drastic measures such as cautions and the giving of advice to ensure defects were remedied. § 5(1) GSG now requires the authorities to take all necessary measures to prevent or restrict the marketing of dangerous goods or to withdraw them from the market. If the goods bore a safety mark action can be taken against those who awarded or affixed the mark.[37] The trade supervisory authorities have to investigate whether such measures need to be taken when a worker safety body or legal accident insurance agency notifies them that either (i) a technical work material has a defect which renders it dangerous, or (ii) an accident has occurred which seems to be due to a defect in technical work materials.

Since 1992 the necessary measures can include prohibiting the marketing of goods, ordering their recall (Rückruf) and ensuring this by seizing the goods (§ 6(1) GSG). In fact the number of prohibition orders made has declined dramatically (from a high in 1975 of 779 to a low in 1988 of 19). Falke wonders whether the use is now so infrequent that the threat of action has become so weak that it can hardly be used as a lever to ensure co–operation.

The authorities' powers can be used against the producer, his representative or the importer. Action can only be taken against a supplier if he has failed to exercise a right to return the goods in question; the previous rules had restricted the right of action against a supplier even further by requiring that a prohibition order have been made against the producer and that the supplier had been aware of this and yet had failed to avail himself of the opportunity to return the goods. The authorities cannot take these steps when the persons responsible for the goods have taken their own effective measures to remove the danger.

Before taking such measures the authorities must consult one of the legal accident insurance agencies whose members use goods of that type. This consultation duty does not apply if the danger is immediate, or the defect is obvious or the person against whom the measure will be taken legitimately claims his legitimate interests would be threatened by such a consultation (§ 6(2) GSG).

When measures are taken the BAU is informed. If the goods bore a safety mark issued by an authorised centre then the state authority responsible for authorising the centre is also informed (§ 6(3) GSG). The BAU reports the matter to the technical committee for work materials, the EC and other member states in order to fulfil its information duties.

---

[37]   The exhibition of dangerous goods can also be prohibited: § 5(4) GSG.

The BAU has the power to publish prohibition orders which are indisputable or immediately effective. Between 1981 and September 1987 BAU published 53 such orders in the Federal Labour Gazette (Bundesarbeitsblatt), but it is doubtful whether this form of publication is effective in reaching the necessary broad range of audiences. Its utility is further limited by the fact that publication seems to take around 11 months.[38]

It is possible to issue an official public warning about dangerous goods if other equally effective measures are not possible (§ 6(1) GSG). The efficacy of official public warnings is, however, restricted by the rulings in the *Birkel* case.[39] This concerned a 43M claim for damages by Birkel resulting from a report on the 'fluid eggs scandal' by the Stuttgart administration which cited five samples of Birkel pasta as being 'microbially spoiled products'. This was true, but some supplementary data was required to substantiate the claim and there was no question of the products being harmful. Birkel won the case with damages being decided separately. Birkel argued the case based on its constitutionally protected right to commercial freedom. Although the power to issue warnings in that case derived from a different source than the express provision in the GSG, one can anticipate that similar constraints will be placed on the power under the GSG (and indeed on the use of the powers in the subsequent Prod SG, see section 5E).

The Court decided that the power should only be used when there is a danger to life or a protected interest; unless the danger is immediate the manufacturer should be given a hearing before publication and the warning must be proportionate to the danger posed. Clearly industry has a great deal to fear from publicity about dangers posed by its products and where the company is a responsible one the use of such public warnings should be used as a last resort and handled with care. Public warnings can have far greater economic consequences resulting from lost reputation than orders prohibiting or restricting the supply of goods which can be resolved internally between the company and regulatory authorities. On the other hand where dangerous goods have reached the marketplace the public needs to be informed of the risks. If businesses do not take steps to inform the public, the authorities should have the power to do so and should not be afraid to use their powers for fear of law suits demanding large damages.

---

[38] Falke (1994), *op. cit.*, at 291. Since 1985 the date of the order is no longer reported. Falke also notes that the Trade Supervisory Offices place a great deal of restrictions on when publication is possible.

[39] Landgericht (District Court) Stuttgart, 23 May 1989, NJW [1989] 2257, Oberlandesgericht (Regional Appeal Court) Stuttgart, 21 March 1990, NJW [1990] 2690: see discussion in Falke, *op. cit.*, at 294–297.

5.   IMPLEMENTATION OF THE EC GENERAL PRODUCT SAFETY DIRECTIVE

The 1992 amendments to the GSG were aimed at co-ordinating German product safety regulation with the European new approach to technical harmonisation. However, 1992 also saw the adoption at the European level of a General Product Safety Directive. Germany was not very enthusiastic about this Directive and even took the Council to the European Court arguing that there was no legal basis for arts 9–11 of the Directive which laid down an emergency procedure under which the Commission could require member states to take temporary measures against products which posed a serious and immediate risk (Chapter 2, section 9K). Germany was clearly concerned that the Commission would have more power than its federal Government had over its Länder, but the European Court was unimpressed with its legal arguments.[40]

After the European Court decision Germany conceded that it had to do something to implement the Directive. The Federal Economic Ministry had produced a draft law for a public hearing which took place in December 1993. A draft of the Produktsicherheitgesetz (Product Safety Law) (hereafter Prod SG) (which regulates the safety of products and the protection of the CE mark)[41] was published in May 1995. In September the Bundesrat opposed the law on the basis that a general law complicated matters which should continue to be dealt with in specific legislation. The German Government persisted with its approach and issued another draft in November 1995 together with a response to the Bundesrat and detailed supporting reasoning.[42] Finally a law was passed on 22 April 1997[43] which came into force on 1 August 1997. The Prod SG which was eventually enacted was similar to earlier drafts, save that a provision was added to clarify that the powers of the Länder to issue warnings or recall products under specific regulations was not affected. The late implementation of the Directive of course creates the potential for Francovich type actions to be brought, but none are known to be pending.

The German implementation of the General Product Safety Directive will now be considered. Attention will be paid to peculiarities of the implementation as consideration of the general principles of the Directive can be found in Chapter 2, section 9.

---

[40]   *Federal Republic of Germany v Council of the European Union*, Case C 359/92, [1994] E.C.R. 1–3681.

[41]   The opportunity was taken to also implement the CE Marking Decision. § 14 Prod SG prohibits the misuse of the CE mark.

[42]   Drucksache 13/3130.

[43]   B.G. Bl. (1997) I–934.

A. Subsidiary Nature

The overriding characteristic of the Prod SG is that it is very much subsidiary to existing specific controls. Thus 16 laws regulating specific product sectors are listed to which the provisions on product safety do not apply. However, ten of these laws lacked comprehensive warning and recall powers as required by the General Product Safety Directive and so §§ 8 and 9 of the Prod SG which deal with those matters are to be applied to products covered by those laws.

These new warning and recall powers will perhaps have their greatest impact on the food sector, but they also provide a new basis for such actions for goods covered by the GSG. The powers in §§ 8 and 9 of the Prod SG are wider than the corresponding powers in the GSG since they include the power to destroy products, allow action to be taken against persons other than the producer and distributor and do not include the limitation which exists under the GSG restricting actions against the distributor to situations where the distributor has not handed back dangerous goods.

Even where the new powers derive from the Prod SG the question of whether a product is unsafe will be considered under the special legislation. The idea of making general provisions subject to specific laws is also one which is familiar to European law. However, it has the danger that the philosophy underpinning the specific laws may diverge from the general safety philosophy. In the General Product Safety Directive there is at least the partial safeguard that this subsidiary role does not apply where the specific regulations do not cover certain aspects of safety or categories of risk. The Prod SG seems to have taken the subsidiarity principle to extremes. There seems no reason why the general obligations could not be complementary to specific rules. If the specific rules were adequate the general rule would not have to be invoked, but it could be there to cover any gaps in the specific laws. As noted when considering the GSG, it is possible that German law fails to comply with the General Product Safety Directive when it seeks to rely upon the GSG, for instance, to implement it as the GSG has different safety standards and enforcement procedures to those required by the Directive.[44]

It is obviously sensible that businesses be permitted to deal with the authorities they have become accustomed to working with and that they should be required to liaise with as few authorities as possible. Thus it is understandable that, as well as looking to the pre–existing laws, the Prod SG also provides for the law to be enforced by the existing authorities, albeit that those which did not have a consumer protection function previously should now take dangers to the consumer into account. What is to be regretted,

---

[44] Micklitz, *op. cit.*, at 261–263.

however, is that Germany still fails to have an agency with a clearly focused mission to ensure consumer safety and that there is no central co–ordinating agency. The implementation of the Directive could have provided the opportunity for such institutions to be created. Indeed one must doubt whether agencies who have just been assigned consumer protection as an add–on function will do more than pay lip–service to it.

In fact the half–hearted nature of the implementation is illustrated by the explanatory material which accompanied the draft law which made great play of the fact that there would be few costs attached to the new law since it was not intended to introduce any preventative monitoring obligations and only applied to a limited range of goods not covered by specific legislation.[45]

B. Scope

One area where the Prod SG will have some impact is in relation to second hand goods. These were not fully included within the scope of the specific laws, but are included within the Prod SG unless they are antiques or products in relation to which the person to whom they are supplied is informed that they need to be repaired or reconditioned. Such second hand products are to be judged against the general safety standard in § 6 Prod SG, rather than the criteria laid down for new products in specific legislation.[46]

Like the Directive, the Prod SG only applies to consumer goods which are commercially marketed. However, the implementation appears to be too narrow. Whereas the Directive includes products intended or likely to be used by consumers, the Prod SG only includes products intended for consumers or used by them according to general customs. Goods may be likely to be used by consumers even though this is not their customary use. For instance, some chemicals are not considered to be products intended or customarily used for private purposes, yet it is known that they are likely to find their way into craft shops and be used by consumers.

It is interesting to compare the German implementing legislation with the English concerning the exclusion of certain goods used in trade. It will be remembered that the English text went further than was seemingly permitted by excluding all products exclusively used in a commercial activity even if it is used for or by a consumer (so long as it is not supplied to the consumer) (Chapter 5, section 3L). This seemed to go beyond the exclusion of capital goods which appears to have been what was intended by the relevant preamble to the Directive (Chapter 5, section 9B). It would for instance exclude a shampoo applied by a hairdresser. The explanatory memorandum

---

45 Drucksache 13/3130 at 10.
46 *Ibid.*

to the draft German law seems to adopt a better approach. Production, investment and goods only intended to be used by professionals would be excluded, but goods used in providing services would be covered in so far as they are delivered in an unaltered condition. For example, a hairdresser's equipment (scissors, blow dryers etc.) would not be covered, but the shampoo would be unless the hairdresser had altered its condition in some way, for example, by mixing two preparations. This seems to draw the right line between product and service safety.

C. Safety

The definition of safe product in § 6 Prod SG follows that in the Directive in many respects, but again gives rise to some cause for concern. For instance, the Directive requires there be no or only minimum risk. The Prod SG defines a product as safe unless it gives rise to a considerable risks. Under the Directive the product must be safe under both normal and reasonably foreseeable conditions of use. In contrast the Prod SG talks about appropriate or expected uses, which seems rather narrower. The explanatory notes to the draft law stated that what is to be expected should be judged from the perspective of the producer, but not subjectively, rather on the basis of what a responsible producer could expect given his knowledge of business and everyday life.[47] This comes close to equating what is expected with what is reasonably foreseeable, but still seems capable of possibly being interpreted more narrowly. Similarly, in the list of factors to be taken account of when assessing the safety of a product, the Directive talks of the effect on other products, where it is reasonably foreseeable that it will be used with other products whilst the Prod SG is again drafted more tightly and refers to products it can be expected to be used with.

Perhaps the most startling part of the Prod SG's definition of when a product is safe is that a product is deemed to be safe if the only dangers are such as are unavoidable when applying the generally accepted technical standards. By this slight of hand the German penchant for standardisation is imported into the implementing regulations.[48] Although the Directive makes reference to national standards it merely cites them as one of a list of factors to be taken account of when assessing the conformity of a product with the general safety requirement. The Directive only treats compliance with specific national law rules as being sufficient to deem the product safe. This approach of the German Prod SG appears therefore to illegitimately weaken

---

[47] *Ibid.*, at 12.

[48] It does extend the understanding of generally accepted technical rules to cover standards and provisions of other member states.

the level of safety required. It is probably therefore somewhat tongue in cheek that the explanatory notes explain this reference as a means of putting into practice the Directive's requirement that the safety definition should be consistent with a high level of protection. German standardisation may or may not provide a high level of protection: one thing is sure – consumers are better off with standardisation as being a means to secure a statutory safety level rather than with standards restricting the content of the safety concept.

D. Producer and Supplier

The Prod SG defines producer and supplier in a similar way to the Directive (§ 3(1)(3)). It bases control on the time when goods are put into circulation. It defines (similarly to under the GSG) the time when goods are put into circulation as being each time they are handed over to another party (§ 3(2)).

§ 4 Prod SG outlines the duties of producers and § 5 outlines those of the distributor. As under the Directive the producer should only put safe goods into circulation and has obligations to inform the consumer of any risks and to monitor his products. Distributors have to co–operate to ensure only safe products are marketed and in particular should not market products they know or ought to know are not safe. However, some critical remarks can be made about the scope of the duties placed on producers and suppliers. Firstly, regarding the producer's duties it fails to include reference to the fact that monitoring measures should include marking products to ease identification, sample testing, investigating complaints and keeping distributors informed. Although it could be argued that these are implicit within the general duty and are not always mandatory, only being required where appropriate,[49] it would have been useful (not least to producers) to make express reference to such potential obligations. Perhaps more serious is the limited scope of the distributor's obligations. Not marketing unsafe products is only one specific manifestation of the distributor's duty under the Directive to act with care in order to help ensure compliance with the general safety requirement. In appropriate circumstance the requirements of due care can be quite onerous on distributors and it is unfortunate no reference is made to this obligation in the German implementing legislation. Also the general duty to co–operate to ensure only safe products are marketed, fails to mention the particular obligations to pass on information on product risks and to participate in monitoring which are cited in the Directive. Again they could be said to be implicit in the German law, but it would be better if express reference had been made to them.

---

[49] But where they are appropriate they are required.

E. Supervisory Powers

§ 7 Prod SG sets out the powers of the authorities. The explanatory memorandum again stresses that there is no suggestion of introducing a general preventative monitoring regime.[50] Where there is knowledge that a product is unsafe the authorities can take appropriate measures to prevent a possible danger materialising. Where a product has caused an actual danger the authorities can act against a product even if it complies with the relevant safety provisions, technical standards (technisches Regelwerk) or the state of technology. The explanatory memorandum to the draft points out that the state of technology is actually a higher standard than the generally accepted technical standards which form part of the definition of a safe product.[51]

The thrust of the intervention powers, however, follow the German tradition of being reactive rather than pro–active. Indeed action can only be taken when there is suspicion of a danger and products which comply with rules, standards or the state of the art are only seriously questioned when they have actually caused damage.

Some specific examples of the authorities' powers are cited in § 7(2) Prod SG, namely:

– the right to prohibit unsafe products;
– the right to prohibit the marketing of a product, whilst it is tested, where there is evidence that it is dangerous; and
– the right to order that a product is not marketed until specific steps have been taken to render it safe or suitable warnings are provided.

§ 8 Prod SG introduces into German law a general power to require warnings to be issued about dangerous products which are in circulation. This is seen as being in the first instance a duty of the producer, but the explanatory memorandum makes it clear that the supplier can be required to issue a warning especially where they are better placed to identify those who are in possession of the dangerous products.[52] A public warning from the authorities can be issued when the danger cannot be averted by other equally effective measures, especially warnings by producers. But the *Birkel* case probably remains relevant in this case (see section 4E).

§ 9 Prod SG gives the authorities the power to recall unsafe products, to seize such products and, where the danger to the consumer cannot be

---

[50] Drucksache 13/3130 at 13.
[51] *Ibid.*
[52] *Ibid.*

removed, to destroy the product.[53] Such measures cannot, however, be taken when the producer or distributor takes their own steps to remove the danger.

The authorities are also given powers to seek information which has to be provided, although answers do not have to be provided if they would be incriminating (§ 11(1) Prod SG). Officers can enter premises to view and test products, to inspect how they are produced, to undertake tests and to take samples (with a second similar object being returned to the producer) (§ 11(2) Prod SG). There is no liability for tests undertaken, unless cheaper means of inspection could have been used, in which case the liability is limited to the selling price of the goods.

The measures can be addressed by the authorities to the producer, distributors (especially the party responsible for the first distribution of the goods on the national market) and any other person, so long as in the last case an immediate and considerable danger is not avoidable by other means. This third party can have a claim for compensation, unless an alternative remedy is possible or the person's property was protected by the measure taken.

§ 12 Prod SG makes provision for the authorities and federal and state institutions to communicate to ensure the necessary measures are taken. There are obligations to report infringements and suspected infringements and to co–operate in investigations. When authorities prohibit or restrict the marketing of products falling within RAPEX they have to report the matter to the designated federal agency (the BAU). Whenever information is shared or obtained under the law data protection principles must be respected.

The Prod SG also empowers regulations and administrative rules to be made to achieve the law's objectives and to implement future EC directives falling within the scope of the law (§ 13 Prod SG).

6.   STANDARDISATION[54]

A.   Background

The Deutsches Institut für Normung e.V. (DIN) has its origins in a body established in 1917 to increase standardisation in an effort to improve

---

[53]   The explanatory notes make it clear that if destruction is undertaken then environmental concerns have to be respected: *ibid.*, at 14.

[54]   Many of the rules governing the operation of DIN are brought together·in DIN, *Grundlagen der Normungsarbeit des DIN*, (6th ed.) (Beuth, 1995). For a useful discussion of these arrangements see Joerges, Falke, Micklitz and Brüggermeier, *op. cit.*, at 171–190.

defence production. By 1926 a body with a much broader base was established. In 1975 this was renamed as DIN.

Although there are over 200 bodies in Germany involved with the establishment of technical rules DIN is pre–eminent. It works closely with Government. Germany has a tradition of preferring voluntary standards to regulatory controls. This is evidenced by the use of the reference to standards approach in the GSG. The political practice of favouring standardisation as a means of concretising expectations was formalised by an agreement between the federal Government and DIN in 1975.[55] This recognised DIN as the German national standards organisation and as the representative within non–Governmental international standards organisations. The intention was to consolidate the use of standards within the regulatory framework. To this end, DIN promised to try to ensure its norms could be used within a regulatory context. It also promised that the public interest would be taken into account and that the procedures laid down in DIN 820 would be followed: these ensure a certain degree of transparency and public participation. The Government also agreed to publish new DIN standards in the *Bundesanzeiger* and now pays subventions, for instance, to support a Consumer Council within DIN. In 1984 the agreement was extended so that DIN took on responsibility for furnishing the EC Technical Standard Committee with the information required under the Technical Standards Directive (Chapter 2, section 3).

The importance of DIN also lies in the agreements it has made with other standards organisations for standards to be made within its framework. The most important such agreement was in 1970 with the Verband Deutscher Elektrotechniker (VDE). This provided for standards relating to electrical goods to be integrated into the DIN system.

DIN meets two–thirds of its costs from its publishing subsidiary, Beuth Verlag. The remainder comes in roughly equal amounts from industry, through subscriptions, and from public funds. Industry also subsidises the work of the standards committees.[56] In 1994 there were 5,973 members of DIN; DIN had produced 22,554 standards (8,615 in English) and 7,311 draft DIN standards and it ran 375 certification programmes.[57]

B. Organisation

Overall control and policy formulation for DIN is undertaken by its Presidential Board (Präsidium) of between 30–45 elected members. This is

---

55 The text is found in DIN, *ibid.*, at 43.
56 *A Word About DIN*, (1995) at 10.
57 *Ibid.*, at 2.

headed by a President; whilst a Director oversees the administrative officers of DIN. The Presidential Board has three important standing committees. The Standards Supervisory Board (Normenprüfstelle = NP) comprises up to 21 members as well as up to 7 DIN officials including the heads of various units concerned which the quality of the standards–making process. There is also a DIN Consumer Council (see section 5D). The DIN Council on conformity assessment (DIN KonRat) defines the interface between standardisation and conformity assessment and advises the Presidential Board on matters of conformity assessment. It represents Germany in the EOTC (Chapter 2, section 7C(ii)).

Incidentally, the German member of EAC (Chapter 2, section 7C(ii)) is the Deutscher Akkreditierungsrat (DAR). DAR is also the EAL (Chapter 2, section 7C(ii)) contact point for accreditation of laboratories for testing; calibration matters are handled by the Physikalisch–Techn. Bundesanstalt (PTB) and Deutscher Kalibrierdienst (DKD).

The standards work is carried on by a number of Standards Committees responsible for various sectors (Normenausschüssen). These will usually establish technical Committees (Arbeitsasschüssen) to consider particular proposals, but it is also possible for these working groups to operate outside Standards Committees and report directly to the DIN Presidential Board. In 1994 there were 99 Standards Committees and 4,427 Technical Committees.[58]

C. Procedures

The procedures for developing standards are laid down in DIN 820.[59] Anybody is free to request that DIN produces a standard. If such a request is refused the aggrieved party can appeal to the Presidential Board. It is a general principle that before including a measure in its work programme the relevant organ of DIN must establish that it is, or will be, needed; that the interested parties are willing to participate and the necessary finance is assured. DIN standards must be reviewed every five years.

The normal procedure (this is modified in various instances, such as where CEN or ISO standards are involved) is for the technical committee to work in private before publishing a public draft standard (that has been checked internally within DIN to ensure all regulations and procedures have been complied with) which is open to public scrutiny and comment. Those who commented should be invited to a meeting of the working group. If they are not happy that their point of view has been properly taken into account

---

[58]   *Ibid.*
[59]   This is reproduced in DIN, *op. cit.*, at 331.

they can invoke conciliation and arbitration procedures. Sometimes a second public consultation may be desirable if a number of changes have been made. Within two years of consultation a decision must be made as to whether to adopt the standard. Such decisions are reached on the basis of the consensus principle. Consensus is of course a general principle of standardisation work, because of the need for voluntary standards to be accepted by the business community. However, it is a point of criticism by opponents of self–regulation who suggest that this prevents standardisation imposing rigorous standards. The DIN rules do not specify what amounts to a consensus, but rather talk about the need to reach a common understanding and state a preference for avoiding a formal vote.

D. Consumer Representation[60]

The DIN Consumer Council (Verbraucherrat) was established in 1974. It comprises five members appointed by the President after consulting the Arbeitsgemeinschaft der Verbraucher (Federation of Consumer Associations, hereafter AgV) and the Economics Ministry. It has been commented that this method of appointment is likely to lead to rather moderate consumer representatives being appointed.[61] Presently the members represent the AgV, Stiftung Warentest, Verbraucher Zentrale (the Consumer Advisory Centre Berlin), the Federal Material Research and Testing Institute and the Home Economic Science department of Hamburg University. The Consumer Council is responsible for setting strategic and political guidelines for its secretariat – the Consumer Council Office (Geschäftsstelle des Verbraucherrates). It meets three times a year with all staff members being included in one session. The chairman of the Consumer Council is an associate member of the Presidential Board.

The most important work is probably the representation of the consumer viewpoint in the technical committees. This is undertaken by the staff members of the Consumer Council, of which there are five full time technical experts whose backgrounds include engineering and home economics. They try to establish the consumer interest in consultation with other relevant bodies, eg consumer organisations, scientific experts etc. and even use opinion polls and surveys, but in the final analysis, absent such information on a particular topic, they have to use their own interpretation of the

---

60   For a summary of the arrangements in English see ANEC, *Consumer Participation in Standardisation*, (ANEC, 1996) at 27–30. For an explanation of the value of DIN standards to consumers, written by a DIN official, see H.–W. Bosserhoff, *DIN– Normen – Nutzen für den Verbraucher*, (Beuth, 1984).

61   Joerges. Falke, Micklitz and Brüggermeier, *op. cit.*, at 187.

consumer interest. This means that the consumer interest is being represented by individuals, who, however well intentioned, have no mandate to represent consumers.[62] Also, although the staff of the DIN Consumer Council are granted an autonomous status they nevertheless remain employees of the standards movement. One must wonder whether this inhibits their willingness to suggest radical reforms either because of a, perhaps unconscious, acceptance of certain limits to criticisms or because they develop a similar ethos to the rest of the DIN workforce with whom they rub shoulders every day.

The Consumer Council cannot follow in detail the progress of all technical committees dealing with matters of interest to consumers and so a priority programme of about 100 projects is selected. These are followed in detail, although comments will be made on draft standards outside the priority programme. Each staff member will follow about ten projects himself and be responsible for another ten projects where the consumer viewpoint is represented by 60–80 volunteers. The permanent staff provide the volunteers with support including an annual three day training seminar.

The volunteers come from various sources including consumer organisations, consumer advice centres, child protection associations, comparative testing institutes, independent test institutes and the universities. The range of sources of volunteer indicates that it is possible for the consumer interest to be represented by someone from an institution other than one whose primary objective is consumer protection.[63] Although consumer groups can participate in DIN technical committees in their own right it is generally considered more advantageous if they can co–operate with the DIN Consumer Council so that a co–ordinated position can be adopted which strengthens the consumer position.

In 1994 the Consumer Council had a budget of 1.5 M DM. 80% of this came from Government, with the remainder being provided by DIN itself. This meets the travel expenses of volunteers and the cost of the secretariat. Whilst accepting that there is a role for a Consumer Council to have a political role within the DIN structure itself, one wonders whether the public funds could not be better used to support the work of consumer groups rather than paying for in house consumer technical expertise. Whilst it is useful to have a source of that rare breed – technical experts who advocate the consumer cause – on the other hand these experts might be more effective consumer advocates if based within independent organisations. The limited funds available might be stretched further if support was given to such posts within consumer groups.

---

62   They are of course subject to the overall supervision of the Consumer Council members.

63   Joerges. Falke, Micklitz and Brüggermeier, *op. cit.*, at 188.

In 1994 the Consumer Council staff participated in 44 European and 11 International Standards Committees. They also co–operated with ANEC and participated in ISO–COPOLCO.

E. Certification

In 1971 DIN established a sister organisation, the Deutsche Gesellschaft für Warenkennzeichung Gmbh (DGWK) responsible for certification matters.[64] This provides for the independent testing of products and the award of the DIN mark. A product can either be permitted to be labelled with the DIN number to show that it complies with that particular standard or can use the DIN mark if all relevant standards have been complied with. This is of course in addition to the GS mark (see section 4D).

7. CONCLUSIONS

Germany has placed great faith in the ability of its standards process to assure consumer safety. Regulatory intervention has been viewed as very much a measure of last resort. This philosophy has undoubtedly influenced the EC's approach to technical harmonisation. However, the benefits of this 'new' or 'reference to standards' approach can only be assured if there are effective supervisory controls to ensure consumer safety.

Criticism can be made of the European approach in that it adopts a hands–off supervisory approach to goods bearing the CE mark; these types of criticisms apply with even greater force in Germany where goods carrying the GS mark have been shielded from close supervision. Continued adoption of this style of market supervision is potentially dangerous given that the creation of the single market means that German consumers are likely to be exposed to goods from wider sources of origin than previously.

There is also the danger that German consumers will not trust the CE marking and retreat to preferring goods which bear the GS mark.[65] Thus the functioning of the single market will be threatened and the benefits of the single market will not be enjoyed by German consumers. Less sophisticated consumers or those unable to afford GS marked goods will have to hope that the supervision of goods bearing the CE marking is not too weak.

---

[64]   *Ibid.*, at 189–190.

[65]   Indeed the author was 'amused' that, whilst in Germany researching for this book, he observed a consumer programme giving German consumers just such advice to favour the GS mark.

Enforcement of consumer product safety rules in Germany also suffers from institutional structural problems. The Länder are fiercely protective of their constitutional right to enforce consumer safety laws. However, this does not meet with the needs of consumer safety regulation in the modern world where there is a need for a central focal point to co–ordinate activities, to promote consumer awareness and to act as a liaison point with other states and regional and international organisations in order to deal with cross–border matters. The experience of Germany can be extrapolated to the global scheme of things and be used as a warning that local enforcement is a necessary but not sufficient requirement. There is also a need for central co–ordinating bodies, be this at the national, regional or international level.

Germany has influenced the EC's new approach to technical harmonisation. It is more uneasy about the EC's attempts to fashion a consumer safety policy. This is reflected in its belated and minimalist implementation of the General Product Safety Directive. It is disheartening to observe that the federal government was only able to adopt the measure it did after considerable opposition and debate. Germany may feel that it has a system that has worked well for it in the past. Leaving aside doubts as to whether the system was as effective as its proponents claimed, the important question is to ask whether its laws and procedures will continue to be adequate to protect consumers in the new era of free cross–border trade?

8 Conclusions

This book is longer than was intended, because the subject matter proved far richer and more complex than I had imagined when I naïvely started out to study product safety regulation following the implementation of the EC's General Product Safety Directive. In particular I discovered that the worlds of standardisation and conformity assessment represent largely un–chartered territory to lawyers and consumer policy makers, but are of vital interest for the promotion of consumer safety and other consumer interests. The reader who has read this far will hopefully be aware of my position on most of the key areas. However a brief restatement of some of the main conclusions may serve as an *aide memoire* and may encourage those who tend merely to read conclusions to dip into the text in more detail.

1. INTERNATIONALISATION OF CONSUMER PRODUCT SAFETY

Protectionism will no doubt come back into fashion from time to time when nations are feeling the worst effects of economic recessions. However, the general trend of capitalism since the industrial revolution has been to encourage an apparently inexorable movement towards free trade. This has intensified in the post–war era as institutional arrangements such as GATT, WTO and ISO have been established and strengthened. This can be associated with a diminution in the power of the state and a corresponding growth in the influence of corporations, particularly multi–national corporations.

There are inevitably going to be further efforts to reduce technical barriers to trade between nations. Supervision of technical regulations will become particularly important, for as more obvious barriers to trade are dismantled (eg quotas and tariffs) states may be tempted to use technical regulations as a form of disguised protectionism. The important task will be to differentiate the sham pretences at consumer protection, which are really disguised barriers to trade, from those regulations which represent genuine expressions of concern for consumer safety.

Businesses are also going to press for increased harmonisation. Ultimately there should be harmonised international standards and mutual recognition agreements for conformity assessment procedures for most, if not all, products. Manufacturers would then be able to have free access to global markets by complying with local standards and procedures. However, this process will take time. There are a lot of vested interests in the standards bodies and testing houses who stand to lose income in direct proportion to the extent that burdens are removed from businesses. Moreover, such a system of mutual recognition must be built on a trust in one another's standards and institutions which does not yet exist. States are likely to want to continue to regulate for minimum safety standards.

2.   ROLE OF THE REGIONS

At least regarding pre–market controls, few individual states are likely to be able to act in isolation in the future. With the possible exception of the United States, most national markets are too small to require particular technical specifications which would require producers to alter their design if they are to sell there. Traders will simply be put off trading in those countries. The obvious answer is for countries to group together to form a trading block whose economic importance is sufficient that traders will be eager to meet its requirements. Individual countries will then have to convince fellow members that their concerns are important and should be recognised in the resulting rules and standards, but at least they will benefit from free trade whilst ensuring some minimum standards.

Europe is leading the way in recognising that, in the global trading economy, influence is increasingly best exercised through trading blocks rather than by individual states. Of course the EC is fortunate in that its members include several significant economic powers. However, it has also exploited this by establishing an integrated legal and policy framework which is leading the way in the field of technical harmonisation. Thus new approach directives represent agreed common safety standards (subject to safeguard clauses) which are fleshed out in CEN standards. The EC has co–operation agreements with CEN and CEN in turn works closely with ISO. This close relationship is no doubt helped by ISO's physical proximity to Brussels (it is based in Geneva), but is also due to Europe being quick to spot the increased role of standards and particularly the need to establish a common European policy to influence international debates.

In the future technical standards and consumer safety policy are increasingly going to be determined within the WTO and ISO framework. Europe seems to have appreciated the need for strong regional representation at this level. Other regions have more fledgling regional free trade organisations. One suspects that they will have to become more integrated and produce clearly defined common positions if they are to catch up on the close relationships which European institutions have established with ISO.

3. DEREGULATION – STANDARDS AND BEYOND

Hand in hand with the regionalisation and internationalisation of consumer product safety regulation there has been an emphasis on deregulation. This has evidenced itself in an increasing role for standardisation and flexible methods of establishing conformity. To the extent that these reduce costs and promote flexibility and innovation they should be welcomed. However, care should be taken to ensure that the baby is not thrown out with the bath water and that the self–regulatory structures maintain effective consumer protection. This is particularly so given that the trend away from national standards at least poses the threat of standards being reduced to a lower common denominator than prevails in states with high levels of consumer protection. Mutual recognition agreements may also allow traders to seek out conformity assessors who operate a laxer regime than had previously been applied by their domestic organisations (even if they comply with minimum agreed standards).

Three safeguards would appear necessary if the benefits of free trade and deregulation are not to cause consumer harm. First, the use of self–regulatory standards should take place within a regulatory framework. In this respect the EC's new approach is to be preferred to the position in the United States where voluntary standards are adopted with minimal supervision. Second, consumers must be involved in the decisions made by self–regulatory authorities. Again Europe seems to offer consumers a better – though far from perfect – deal than exists in the United States. Third, there is a need for stronger rather than weaker enforcement agencies. There might appear to be a certain contradiction in advocating strong enforcement of a deregulated regime. But, whilst there is always the danger of re–imposing burdens at the enforcement stage which were lifted from the design stage, it is all a question of balance. If more trust is being placed in industry's ability to set safety standards and even affirm conformity with those safety standards (through a policy of preferring wherever possible manufacturer's self–declaration), then it seems only sensible to have procedures in place for monitoring and reviewing their performance against objective criteria. The hands–off approach to enforcement which lies behind the philosophy of the CE marking suggests that in Europe the balance has swung too far away from the interests of consumer protection.

4. CONSUMER INPUT

The case for effective involvement of consumers in the standardisation process has been made at length elsewhere (Chapter 1, section 3D). To reiterate, this involves political participation in the constitution of standards bodies so that the need for consumer representation is understood and appropriate priority is given to consumer projects in work programmes, which are undertaken in a manner which takes account of the legitimate concerns of consumers. However, the most important work involves representing the consumer viewpoint on technical committees and working groups where the concrete decisions are made. Ensuring consumers have the right to be represented on these bodies is, however, only half the story, for the major problem is finding consumer representatives with the appropriate expertise who can engage in dialogue with the industry sponsored technical experts. Such consumer experts are a scarce commodity and there are limited funds to finance their participation, particularly at the European and international level where the travel and subsistence expenses can be rather high.

The focus of standardisation is increasingly moving to the regional and international level. This poses problems for consumers in trying to influence such large organisations which are heavily industry dominated. Consumers also face additional costs arising from having to co–ordinate their activities across several countries and having to attend foreign venues for technical meetings. In addition there are the problems of reconciling different national viewpoints. Different cultural traditions or national approaches to safety regulation may cause consumers in even a fairly homogeneous trading block such as the EC to have different viewpoints on the level of safety desirable or the most effective means of achieving safety objectives. However, the problem is exacerbated when the needs of consumers in the first and third world are juxtaposed. Although they share many common concerns, sometimes it is better to recognise that there are some legitimate differences of interest between groups of consumers. Unfortunately the ISO does not have effective procedures for differentiating the concerns of consumers in different regions. The suggestion has been made for regional representation of consumers within ISO to replace the existing position whereby Consumers International (CI) is the only body permitted to represent consumers on technical committees.

Consumer organisations also play an important role in testing products and publicising product defects. It would be desirable if they could have increased access to the courts when they detect product dangers, but the enforcement authorities have failed to act. However, these powers would inevitably be subsidiary to the efforts of public enforcement agencies, who should remain the primary guardian of the public's safety.

5. REGULATORS

The role of regulators is pivotal. They have the duty to ensure that the regulatory regime protects consumers, but does not impose unnecessary burdens on industry or create illegitimate barriers to trade. To achieve these objectives with limited budgets they need to target their limited resources effectively. Data collection systems can assist them to focus on the most pressing consumer concerns in order to enable them to produce regulations which address those problems and/or inform and educate the public about such risks. This type of pre–marketing regulation is typically carried out at a fairly centralised level. Traditionally within Europe the nation state has fixed these rules, but as political integration has increased the new approach directives illustrate a shift of competence to the EC. Equally in the United States the federal Government is pre–empting the ability of states to provide for different safety standards.

However, even the most effective pre–marketing controls will not prevent dangerous products reaching the market. Dangerous products may be sub–standard products marketed by irresponsible producers; they may simply be 'lemons' or the risks attached to them may only become known after marketing. To deal with this wide range of situations in which products can be dangerous enforcement authorities need a variety of powers. A general obligation only to market safe consumer products is needed to ensure that all products are subject to regulatory supervision. Ideally this general obligation would be available in addition to any specific regulations, but typically it is made subsidiary to specific rules. In this case the specific laws should contain safeguard clauses which permit action to be taken against dangerous products even if they are deemed to comply with the regulation, for example by virtue of satisfying existing safety standards.

Enforcement authorities need adequate powers to be able to monitor the marketplace. They should have powers to take samples, obtain documents etc. and to seize goods which they suspect are dangerous. Officers should have powers to act against products which are both dangerous in fact and misleading because of false claims that they comply with regulations or standards. These powers should not be emasculated by imposing severe compensation obligations on enforcement officers if their suspicions turn out to be unfounded.

Post–market control is often most effectively carried out at the local level. The United Kingdom system of trading standards officers represents one of the most effective systems of local enforcement, although care needs to be taken that smaller authorities are able to deal with large scale consumer safety problems. However, there is also a need for co–ordination at the national level to ensure consistent application of principles and to enable intelligence to be communicated to other areas. At the regional (and possibly also at the international level) there should be information exchange systems so that products which may cause problems in more than one country can be quickly detected and the danger eradicated. Just as trade and standards–making has become internationalised so too must enforcement.

Enforcement officers need the power to prohibit the marketing of dangerous products (where this applies to a class of products, this objective may be achieved by enacting emergency regulations). They also need to be able to issue warnings or require producers and distributors to warn about products which have already reached the consumer. In the final analysis they must have the power to order the recall of dangerous products. Most traders will voluntarily agree to recalls, but placing this power in the hands of the enforcement authorities gives them a significant lever to ensure traders take comprehensive steps to make the recall campaign a success. Most enforcement involves negotiating in the shadow of the law; therefore it is important to provide enforcement officers with strong clearly worded powers so that the shadow of the law looms large and threateningly over any recalcitrant trader.

6.   EXPORTS

Governments are naturally primarily concerned to ensure the safety of their own citizens, but it is worthwhile noting that there is an ethical demand that dangerous goods are not dumped on other countries, particularly third world countries. Although there are some instances where goods banned or restricted in one country can be legitimately exported to another state, these situations must be controlled and export only permitted when the importing country is both willing to accept the goods and able to assess any risk posed. Moreover the exporting country should be able to exercise its own discretion to control the export of dangerous goods in order to protect its own name as a reputable trading nation and to satisfy its own ethical values. Also there are selfish reasons for countries to be concerned about the export of dangerous products. Their citizens may be exposed to them when they travel overseas, they may be re–imported and possibly the ability to export poor quality dangerous goods may cause manufacturers to be less careful over the quality of goods produced for the home market, if they are secure in the knowledge that they can be diverted elsewhere should the authorities question their safety.

7. FINAL HOPES

It has not been my objective to criticise the principle of promoting free trade or the desire to lift unnecessary burdens on producers. No one likes red tape, nor wants to see consumers subsidise unnecessary bureaucratic structures. However, I hope to have convinced those involved in this process to recognise the need to include legal rules safeguarding consumer safety and encouraging consumer participation within the new (self–) regulatory regime. The goal is to create a framework for the development of a product safety regime which can achieve an equitable balance between free trade and consumer protection.

Consumers should be able to participate in self–regulatory structures. Harmonisation and systems of mutual recognition should not proceed at a pace beyond that justified by the degree of confidence which consumers have in those systems. Moreover it must be understood that less direct control on production actually necessitates more (rather than less) efficient market supervision by enforcement authorities.

One cannot have free trade, deregulation and also guarantee consumer safety without providing the means for consumers to influence the new self–regulatory systems and for authorities to police the marketplace. The rationale behind promoting increased international trade in a deregulatory context must be that the benefits in terms of increased trade, economic growth, lower costs for regulatory compliance, increased competitiveness and consumer choice outweigh the resources which are needed to ensure consumers can be properly represented and protected in this new regime. This policy seems to be set for the foreseeable future so it is to be hoped that it is correct. What is certain, is that no chances should be taken with consumer safety. Guaranteeing consumer safety should a pre–requisite for any system of international trade, but it is sometimes difficult for the consumer's voice to be heard. The law has an important role to play in ensuring that economic considerations cannot sideline concern for consumer health and safety.

Index

Abbott, H. 256
accidents
  CPSC 203–8
  data collection 13–15, 20, 251–3
  EHLASS 117–18
  France 316
  Germany 333–6
  home and leisure 2
  prevention 304
accreditation, organisation method
  243
accreditation bodies 110–14
Accredited Standards Developer
  (ASD) 242
ACCSQ *see* ASEAN Consultative
  Committee for Standardisation
  and Quality Control
activists 35
AECMSA *see* Association
  Européene des Constructeurs
  de Matériel Aérospatial
AFNOR *see* Association Francaise
  de Normalisation
African Regional Organisation for
  Standardisation (ARSO) 180
agency capture 3
Agreement on Technical Barriers to
  Trade (ATBT) 161, 168–76
Agreement on Trade–related
  Aspects of Intellectual Property
  163
AgV *see* Arbeitsgemeinschaft der
  Verbraucherverbände
AIDMO *see* Arab Industrial
  Development and Mining
  Organisation
American National Standards
  Institute (ANSI) 31, 221, 240–

9
American Society of Mechanical
  Engineers (ASME) 240
American Society for Testing and
  Materials (ASTM) 221, 240–9
amusement parks 201
ANEC *see* European Association
  for the Co–ordination of
  Consumer Representation in
  Standardisation
anonymity 19
ANSI *see* American National
  Standards Institute
Arab Industrial Development and
  Mining Organisation (AIDMO)
  180
Arbeitsgemeinschaft der
  Verbraucherverbände (AgV)
  341
architectural glass 216
ARSO *see* African Regional
  Organisation for
  Standardisation
Asch, Peter 222
ASD *see* Accredited Standards
  Developer
ASEAN Consultative Committee
  for Standardisation and Quality
  Control (ACCSQ) 180
Ash Report 198–9
ASME *see* American Society of
  Mechanical Engineers
assistance 176
Association Européene des
  Constructeurs de Matériel
  Aérospatial (AECMSA) 90
Association Française de
  Normalisation (AFNOR) 33,

300, 305–6, 324–5, 329
standards 100
ASTM *see* American Society for
Testing and Materials
ATBT *see* Agreement on Technical
Barriers to Trade
Australia, OECD 187
auto–control system 308
autonomy 9, 17, 68

baby pacifiers 222
bad faith 311
banned products 55–9, 192
BAU *see* Bundesanstalt für
Arbeitsschutz
beef, American 55
*Bernard Keck and Daniel
Mithouard* 63
Bernstein, M. 26
Berufsgenossenschaften (BG) 338–
9
BEUC *see* Bureau Européen des
Union Consummateurs
BG *see* Berufsgenossenschaften
bicycles 196
Bihl, L. 315
Birkel pasta 351
BMRB *see* British Market
Research Bureau
Borrie, G. 279
Bosma, F. 97
Bouloc, B. 310
brand name 12
Bretton Woods System 160
British Market Research Bureau
(BMRB) 252
British Retail Consortium 32
British Standards Institute (BSI)
251, 286–7
Consumer Council 31, 34, 37
lay consumers 36
Broome, J. 23
BSI *see* British Standards Institute

Bundesanstalt für Arbeitsschutz
(BAU) 336–7, 350–1
Bureau Européen des Union
Consummateurs (BEUC) 96

CA *see* Consumers' Association
(CA)
Calais–Auloy, Jean 300–1, 310–11
calibration 112
Canada
consumer input 36
OECD 187
canvass method 243–5
Cardwell, K. 271, 276
Carter, President J. 58, 238
Cassis de Dijon 64, 167
CE mark 45–6, 79, 109, 114–17
Germany 363
self–declaration 9
CEFIC *see* European Chemical
Industry Council
CEN *see* European Committee for
Standardisation
CENELEC *see* European
Committee for Electrotechnical
Standardisation
certification 110–14
chain saw standards 222
child resistant bottle caps 224–5
children 315
see also toys
baby pacifiers 222
clothing 220, 224, 237
nightwear 55, 289
safe product 126
safety 2, 56–7
Christmas tree light standard 216
CI *see* Consumers International
cigarettes 167, 202
civil liability 4
COCON *see* Consumer Council of
the Dutch Standards Institute
Code of Good Practice for the

Preparation, Adoption and Application of Standards 171
Codex Alimentarius Commission 189
Comité d'Orientation et de Suivi des Activités de Consummation (COSAC) 327
Commission de la securité des consummateurs see Consumer Safety Commission (France)
Committee on Consumer Policy (ISO) (COPOLCO) 182–4
Committee on Consumer Policy (OECD) 187
comparative advantage 160
comparative testing 306
compensation 272–6, 358
    objectives 4–5, 7
    traders 49–50
complaints 207
Completing the Internal Market (1985) 64
conditions of use 125
confidentiality 317
conformity, proof of 81–2
conformity assessment 41, 45–6, 100–17, 173–6
    CPSC 213–14
    France 112
    Germany 112
    procedures 8
    UK 112
Conformity Assessment and CE Marking Decision 110
conformity to type 106–7
consensus principle 219, 242
construction products 84
Construction Products Directive 92
consultation duty 30
consumer
    behaviour 2–3, 18–19
    BSI 289–93
    education 23

input 29–39, 181–7, 367–8
organisations
    France 306–7
    Germany 341
    post–market control 54
    resources 3
protection policy 1
representation 31–8, 245–9
    France 327–8
    Germany 361–3
    standardisation 94–9
    US 245–9
safety campaigns 318
third world 38
Consumer Advisory Panels (Canada) 36
Consumer Code (France) 308–12, 330
Consumer Council of the Dutch Standards Institute (COCON) 37
Consumer Council (UK) 31, 34, 37
Consumer Interest Council (US) 31, 245
Consumer Interpol 191
Consumer Policy Committee (CPC) 289
Consumer Product Safety Act (CPSA) 195–7, 24
Consumer Product Safety Amendments Act 1981 (US) 210
Consumer Product Safety Commission (CPSC) 8, 25, 195, 198–240
    corrective action 51–2
    death certificates 206–7
    notification 11, 58
    post–market controls 16
    voluntary standards 8, 9
consumer products, definition 195
Consumer Protection Act 1987 (CPA) (UK) 251, 253

Consumer Safety Act 1978 (UK) 254

Consumer Safety Advocate (US) 200

Consumer Safety Commission (France) 25, 299–302, 315–19, 329

Consumer Safety Improvement Act 1990 (US) 226

Consumer Safety Unit (UK) 33

Consumer Sounding Boards (Canada) 36

Consumer Standards Advisory Council 290

Consumers' Association (CA) (UK) 293

Consumers International (CI) 38, 182, 185–7, 368

Consumers Union (CU) 216

COPANT *see* Pan–American Standards Commission

COPOLCO *see* Committee on Consumer Policy (ISO)

corrective action 51–3

correspondent members, ISO 177

COSAC *see* Comité d'Orientation et de Suivi des Activités de Consummation

cost–benefit analysis 20

cost–effectiveness 20

CPC *see* Consumer Policy Committee

CPSA *see* Consumer Product Safety Act

CPSC *see* Consumer Product Safety Commission

crayons 281

Crazy Hand and Mini Snappers 268–9

cribs 224

criminal law 24
  France 323

CU *see* Consumers Union

damages 304
  CPSA 235

dangerous products 51, 369
  export 54–8
  information 48–9

data collection 2, 13–15, 20, 251–3
  EHLASS 117–18
  France 316
  Germany 15, 333–6
  injury 189

death certificates 206–7, 316

decision–making
  risk based 203
  transparency 264

defect, minimum 227

Department of Trade and Industry (UK) 26

Depo–provera 56

deregulation 8–9, 26, 367

design 209, 227
  alternatives 23
  standards 41–2

destruction 51

detention 51

Deutsches Instituts für Normung (DIN) 335, 338–9, 358–63
  Consumer Council 34
  standards 100

development risks, insurance 6

development risks defence 4

DGCCRF *see* Direction générale de la concurrence, de la consommation et de la répression des fraudes

DIN *see* Deutsches Instituts für Normung

Direction générale de la concurrence, de la consommation et de la répression des fraudes (DGCCRF) 303–5

directives, product safety 84–5

discrimination 165–6

Dispute Settlement Body (DSB) 161, 168
Dispute Settlement Understanding (DSU) 161, 168
distributors
  CPA 261
  obligations 132–4
documents, translations 176
documents technique unifiés (DTU) 305–6
doors
  garage 220
  glass 196
drugs 1, 3, 56–7, 190, 237
DSB *see* Dispute Settlement Body
DSU *see* Dispute Settlement Understanding
DTU *see documents technique unifiés*
due care 132
due diligence defence 278–83, 286
dumping 55, 160, 237
durability 125
duties, enforcement 135–7
duty
  consultation 30
  US 250

EA *see* European Co–operation for Accreditation
EASC *see* Euro–Asian Council for Standardisation, Metrology and Certification
EC *see* European Community
ECISS *see* European Committee for Iron and Steel Standardisation
ECJ *see* European Court of Justice
ECMA *see* European Computer Manufacturers Association
economic integration 63
economic models 18
economic theory, comparative

advantage 160
ECOSA *see* European Consumer Safety Association
'effective equality of opportunities' test 166
EHLASS *see* European Home and Leisure Accident Surveillance System
ejusdem generis rule 85
electrical equipment 2
emergency powers 12, 320–2
emergency procedures, EC 148–54
emergency regulation–making 50
EN *see* European standards
enforcement 369
  duties 135–7
  France 46, 303
  Germany 46
  negotiation 53–4
  private 234–5
  UK 256–9, 270–2, 295
enforcement powers 49
EOTC *see* European Organisation for Testing and Certification
Essential Drug List 191
essential safety requirements 71, 79, 85–6
ETSI *see* European Telecommunications Standards Institute
Euro–Asian Council for Standardisation, Metrology and Certification (EASC) 180
European Association for the Co–ordination of Consumer Representation in Standardisation (ANEC) 90, 96–8, 182
European Chemical Industry Council (CEFIC) 89
European Co–operation for Accreditation (EA) 113
European Committee for

Electrotechnical Standardisation (CENELEC) 87

European Committee for Iron and Steel Standardisation (ECISS) 90

European Committee for Standardisation (CEN) 87–100
  International Standards Organisation 160
  Primary Questionnaire 181
  Unique Acceptance Procedure 181

European Community (EC)
  A New Impetus for Consumer Protection Policy (1986) 61
  Committee on Product Safety Emergencies 143
  Completing the Internal Market 64
  Consumer Consultative Council 96
  consumer protection 70
  consumer representation 97–9
  data collection 15
  Development of European Standardisation: Action for Faster Technological Convergence in Europe (1991) 77
  emergency procedures 148–54
  General Programme for the Elimination of Technical Barriers to Trade Caused by Disparities Among National Legislation (1969) 70
  Global Approach to Certification and Testing (1989) 101
  Global Approach to Conformity Assessment (1989) 76
  harmonisation 343–4
  New Approach to Technical Harmonisation and Standards (1985) 76
  On the Broader Use of Standardisation in Community Policy (1995) 77
  product safety 61–2
  Report on the Progress of European Standardisation (1995) 77
  standardisation 28
  Standardisation in the European Economy (1992) 77
  standards organisations 87–100
  technical harmonisation 77–85
  type–examination 106

European Computer Manufacturers Association (ECMA) 89

European Construction Industry Federation (FIEC) 89

European Consumer Safety Association (ECOSA) 147

European Court of Justice (ECJ) 10, 331, 352
  free movement of goods 61
  harmonisation 67–70
  mutual recognition 64

European Home and Leisure Accident Surveillance System (EHLASS) 15, 117–18
  France 316
  UK 252

European Organisation for Testing and Certification (EOTC) 101, 111–12

European Product Liability Directive 255

European Safety Agency 47

European standards (EN) 99–100

European Telecommunications Standards Institute (ETSI) 87

European Trade Union Technical Bureau for Health and Safety (TUTB) 89

European Workshop for Open Systems (EWOS) 90
EWOS *see* European Workshop for Open Systems
export 370
  banned products 192
  controls 54–59
  CPSA 237–40
exposure, toxic substances 2
externality arguments 17–18

failure to warn 227
fair trading 65
Fair Trading Act 1973 (UK) 255
Falke, J. 103, 334–6, 348, 349
FAO *see* Food and Agriculture Organisation
FDA *see* Food and Drug Administration (FDA)
Federal Institute for Occupational Health and Safety (Germany) 336–7
Federal Trade Commission (FTC) (US) 18–19, 202
FIEC *see* European Construction Industry Federation
fines 309, 323
fireworks 257
Fireworks Act 1951 (UK) 263
first–marketer 312
Flammable Fabrics Act (US) 239
flick–knives 66
follow–back investigations 207–8
Food and Agriculture Organisation (FAO) 189
Food and Drug Administration (FDA) (US) 201–2
food products 1
food standards 189
formal due process 30
Fourgoux, J.–C. 311
France
  accident prevention 304

Association Francaise de Normalisation 33, 300, 305–6, 324–5, 329
conformity assessment 112
Consumer Safety Commission 25, 299–302, 315–19, 329
criminal law 323
Direction générale de la concurrence, de la consommation et de la répression des fraudes 303–5
emergency regulation–making 50
Institut National de la Consommation 306, 327
Law of 1 August 1905 300, 308–12
Law of 21 July 1983 299, 313–23, 330
local enforcement 46, 303
standards 324–8
woodworking machines 66
franchisees 129
fraud, France 308, 310–11, 330
free movement 61, 82–3
free trade 367
  consumer safety 189
  international trade 159
FTC *see* Federal Trade Commission
full quality assurance 109
funding, CEN 91

garage doors 220
garden equipment 2, *see also* lawn mowers
gas burning appliances 85
gas cookers 262
GATT *see* General Agreement on Tariffs and Trade
General Agreement on Tariffs and Trade (GATT) 160, 164–8
General Agreement on Trade in Services 163

General Product Safety Directive
11, 42–4, 119–57
Germany 331–3, 352–8
harmonisation 67–70
minimal directive 69
recalls 52
UK 255, 283–6, 294–5
*General Programme for the
Elimination of Technical
Barriers to Trade Caused by
Disparities* 60
general safety obligation 42–5,
128–9
France 307, 313–15
UK 259–63
Gerätesicherheitsgesetz (GSG) 332,
336–8, 339, 341–51
German Standardisation Institute
see Deutsches Instituts für
Normung (DIN)
Germany
conformity assessment 112
Consumer Council 34
consumer representation 361–3
data collection 15, 333–6
Deutsches Instituts für Normung
335, 338–9, 358–63
federal structure 333
General Product Safety Directive
331–3, 352–8
GS mark 45, 110, 331, 347–9
local enforcement 46
Product Safety Law 352–8
prohibition order 50
Siftung Warentest 33, 340
standards 100
woodworking machines 66
Gesetz zur Neuordnung und
Bereinigung des Rechts in
Verkehr mit Lebensmittel,
Tabakerzeugnissen,
kosmetischen Mitteln un
Bedarfsgegenstände (LMBG)
331–2
Gewerbeaufsichtsämtern 335
glass, architectural 216
glass doors 196
global approach, standardisation
76–7
Good Laboratory Practice
guidelines 112
government intervention 24–7
GS mark 45, 110, 331, 347–9
GSG *see* Gerätesicherheitsgesetz
Guy Fawkes Night 257

HADD *see* Home Accident Deaths
Database
Hamilton, R. 244, 247
Harland, D. 193
harmonisation 365–6
EC 343–4
legislation 67–70
mutual recognition 64
positive 75–85
Harmonisation Documents (HD) 99
HASS *see* Home Accident
Surveillance System
Havana conference 160
Hazard Index (US) 205–6, 214
hazards
foreseeable 196
imminent 233
substantial 227, 231–3
HD *see* Harmonisation Documents
HERIS *see* Hospital Emergency
Room Reporting System
Hodges, C. 256
Home Accident Deaths Database
(HADD) 252–3
Home Accident Surveillance
System (HASS) 251–3
home authority 46–7, 259
horizontal standards 42, 93
hospital admissions 14
Hospital Emergency Room

Reporting System (HERIS) 204
Howard, Michael 274
human error 335–6

IAF *see* International Accreditation
    Forum
IBRD *see* International Bank for
    Reconstruction and
    Development
ICA *see* International Co–operative
    Alliance
Iceland, conformity assessment 112
ICSP *see* Interagency Committee
    on Standards Policy
IEC *see* International
    Electrotechnical Commission;
    International Electrotechnical
    Organisation
ILAC *see* International Laboratory
    Accreditation Conference
IMF *see* International Monetary
    Fund
imports
    CPSA 236–7
    inspection 66
INC *see* Institut National de la
    Consommation
inconvenience 225
independent test houses 33
Industrial Injuries Insurance
    Institutes (Germany) 338–9
information 176, 318
    dangerous products 48–9
    exchange of 137–48
    risks 39–40, 131
information obligations 130
Information Technology Steering
    Committee (ITSTC) 88
injury
    CPSC 203–8
    data collection 189
Injury or Potential Injury Incident
    Data Base (IPII) 205

inspection 112
    importation 66
Institut National de la
    Consommation (INC) 306, 327
Institute for Trading Standards
    Administration (ITSA) (UK)
    258
instructions 40–1, 227
insurance, development risks 6
inter–state trade 197
Interagency Committee on
    Standards Policy (ICSP) (US)
    240
internal production control 103
International Accreditation Forum
    (IAF) 113
International Bank for
    Reconstruction and
    Development (IBRD) 160
International Co–operative Alliance
    (ICA) 182
International Electrotechnical
    Commission (IEC) 37–8, 177
International Laboratory
    Accreditation Conference
    (ILAC) 113
International Monetary Fund (IMF)
    160
International Register of Potentially
    Toxic Chemicals (IRPTC) 190
international rules 28–9
International Standards
    Organisation (ISO) 159, 177–
    87, 366
    guides 184–5
International Telecommunications
    Union (ITU) 177
international trade, free trade 159
International Trade Organisation
    (ITO) 160
internationalisation 10, 365–6
IPII *see* Injury or Potential Injury
    Incident Data Base

IRPTC *see* International Register of Potentially Toxic Chemicals
ISO 9000 8
ISO *see* International Standards Organisation
ISONET 172, 190
Italian Discrimination against Imported Agricultural Machinery (1959) 165
ITO *see* International Trade Organisation
ITSA *see* Institute for Trading Standards Administration
ITSTC *see* Information Technology Steering Committee
ITU *see* International Telecommunications Union

Jackson, J. 169
Japan, OECD 187
Jelly Balls 268–9
Joint Technical Programming Committee (JTPC) 177
JTPC *see* Joint Technical Programming Committee
justice, access to 4

Keymark certification 116–17
King, Susan 19, 223

labels 213
LACOTS *see* Local Authorities Co–ordinating Body on Food and Trading Standards
ladders 2
LASS *see* Leisure Accident Surveillance System
lawn mowers 216, 220, 222, 225
lawnmowers 196
laws
 local 28
 private 4–7
legitimate expectations 43, 314–15

Leisure Accident Surveillance System (LASS) 251–3, 285
liability
 civil 4
 France 311
 standards 3–4
 strict 278–83
licenses 7, 10
Lichenstein, conformity assessment 112
Linneman, Peter 224
Lisbon Agreement (1989) 180
litigation, liability 229
LMBG *see* Gesetz zur Neuordnung und Bereinigung des Rechts in Verkehr mit Lebensmittel, Tabakerzeugnissen, kosmetischen Mitteln un Bedarfsgegenstände (LMBG)
Local Authorities Co–ordinating Body on Food and Trading Standards (LACOTS) 258, 296
local presence 46–7
locality, notification 138
Lomotil 55
Low Voltage Directive 84, 341

McGuire v Sittingbourne Co– operative Society Ltd 282
Machine Safety Act (Germany) 332
machinery 84
Machinery Safety Directive 85
'mandatory requirements' 64–5
 exception 62
mandatory standards, CPSC 208– 18, 221
manufacturer 3, 129
 conformity assessment 104–5
manufacturing 227
 specifications 79
market surveillance 10
matchbooks 222
mattress flammability standard 224

means of attestation of conformity
81–2
MECAP *see* Medical Examiner and
Coroners Alert Project
medical devices 1, 84, 85
Medical Examiner and Coroners
Alert Project (MECAP) 206
member bodies, ISO 177
membership fee, CEN 91
mens rea 278
Mercury Soap 268–9
Mertens, A. 335
MFN *see* most favoured nation
60 million des consummateurs 306
Ministry of Agriculture, Fisheries
and Food (UK) 26
minitel 318
misuse 44
model directive 80–5
Molony Committee on Consumer
Protection (1960) (UK) 253,
290
most favoured nation (MFN)
principle 161, 164–5
motor vehicles 1, 3, 19, 190
mutual recognition 174, 371
agreements 9
principle of 64

NACCB *see* National Accreditation
Council for Certification
Bodies
Nader, Ralph 200
NAMAS *see* National
Measurement Accreditation
Service
National Accreditation Council for
Certification Bodies (NACCB)
287
National Commission on Product
Safety (US) 195, 200
National Commission on Products
Safety (US) 2

National Electronic Injury
Surveillance System (NEISS)
14, 204–6
National Fire Protection
Association (NFPA) 240
National Institute for Standards and
Technology (NIST) 240
National Measurement
Accreditation Service
(NAMAS) 287
national standardisation 74
national treatment provision 161,
165–6
negligence 259, 311, 323
negligence standards 4
negotiation, enforcement 53–4
NEISS *see* National Electronic
Injury Surveillance System
Netherlands, Consumer Council of
the Dutch Standards Institute
(COCON) 37
New Zealand
compensation 5
OECD 187
Newcastle disease 65
news clippings 207
NF mark 326–7
NFPA *see* National Fire Protection
Association
NIST *see* National Institute for
Standards and Technology
Norway, conformity assessment
112
notice to warn 269–70, 295
notices, France 322–3
notification 137–48, 192
hazardous products 232–3, 238
United States 58
nuisance claims 230
nursery equipment 2

obligations, reporting 229–31
OECD *see* Organisation for

Economic Co–operation and
Development
offeror procedure 215–18
office chairs 348
Office of Management and Budget
(OMB) (US) 199
OMB *see* Office of Management
and Budget
optimism 22
oral snuff 264
Organisation for Economic Co–
operation and Development
(OECD) 160, 182, 187–9

Pacific Area Standards Congress
(PASC) 180
Pan–American Standards
Commission (COPANT) 180
PASC *see* Pacific Area Standards
Congress
paternalism 16–18
penalties, CPSA 234
performance standards 41–2, 209
personal injury 4
personal protective equipment 84
pesticides 237
Phare countries, RAPEX 147–8
positive harmonisation 75–85
post–market controls 10–11, 43,
46–53, 369
potential dangers 11
poultry, Newcastle disease 65
power tools 196
PQ *see* Primary Questionnaire
pre–market
controls 10–11, 15–45, 366, 369
safety regulations 63
precautionary principle 12
préfet 321
pressure vessels 84
prevention 300
price 6
Primary Questionnaire (PQ) 181

private enforcement, CPSA 234–5
private labels 213
private law 4–7
Procureur du Roi v Dassonville 62
Prod SG *see*
Produktsicherheitgesetz
producer
CPA 261
definition 129–30, 356
obligations 130–2
technical knowledge 3
product
definition 119–21
design 2
first placement 312
liability 3–6, 22–23
monitoring 11, 131–2
quality assurance 107–8
verification 108–9
Product Liability Directive 68
product risk, information 39–40
Product Safety Enforcement Forum
for Europe (PROSAFE) 147,
297
Product Safety Law (Germany)
352–8
Produktsicherheitgesetz (Prod SG)
352–8
'professional' consumerists 35
prohibition notice 254, 268–9
prohibition order 350
CSA 267
Germany 50
PROSAFE *see* Product Safety
Enforcement Forum for Europe
*Protection against Products
Harmful to Health and the
Environment* (1982) (UN) 192
protectionism 365
psychological research, risk
assessment 21–22
public regulation 5, 7–10
publicity 318–19

pushchairs 289

quality assurance 8, 107–8

*R v Birmingham City Council, ex p
    Ferrero Ltd* 273
RAPEX *see* Rapid Exchange of
    Information Systems on
    Dangers Arising From
    Consumer Products
Rapid Exchange of Information
    Systems on Dangers Arising
    From Consumer Products
    (RAPEX) 48, 139–48
  emergency procedures 149
  Germany 332, 338
  UK 257
rationality 21
Reagan, President Ronald 238
recall 51–3, 350, 357
  order 16
  UK 251
regional rules 28–9
regionalisation 10
regulators 369–70
regulatory offences 278
regulatory strategy 3–10
Reich, N. 65
reparation 300
reporting obligations 229–31
repression 300
resources 3
responsibility 12–13
*Restatement of the Law, Torts:
    Product Liability* (American
    Law Institute, 1997) 22–23
retailer, responsibility 12–13
risk 2
  acceptability 11–12
  acceptable 6
  CPSC 222–3
  horizontal norms 42
  information 131

predictable 196
  tolerance 19
risk assessment, psychological
    research 21–22
risk based decision–making 203
risk of injury 210–11
risk–free society 19, 223

safe product 124–8
  definition 261
safety
  campaigns 318
  definition 314, 330
  norms 43
  obligations 10–11, 15, 42–5
  risks 11–12
Safety Alert Procedure 293–4
safety caps 224–5
safety policy
  paternalism 16–18
  social science research 18–23
sample testing 213
Schulberg, Francine 56
Schwartz, T.M. 210, 214
scientific research, international 65
seat–belts 19
SECO *see* Secretariat Européen de
    Co–ordination pour la
    normalisation
Secretariat Européen de Co–
    ordination pour la
    normalisation (SECO) 96–7
seizure 51
seizure and forfeiture order 271,
    276–8
self–declaration 110
self–regulation 27, 30, 196, 371
Siftung Warentest 33, 340
Simon, Herbert 21
Single European Act, Art. 100a 69
soap 218
social insurance 5
social policy 222

social science research 18–23
sounding boards 36
space heaters 222
specified use 345
sports equipment 2
standardisation 73–4, 368
  consumer input 29–39
  consumer representation 94–9
  France 300
  government intervention 24, 27–8
  UK 286–93
  voluntary 197, 221, 240–9
standards 85–6
  committee method 243
  France 324–8
  horizontal 42, 93
  making 92–4
  mandatory 208–18, 221
  negligence 4
Standards Code 169
standards making, transparency of 172
standards officers 33–5
standards organisations, consumers 38–39
state of the art defence 4
statutory regulations 8
strict liability 4
subscriber members, ISO 177
subsidiarity 68
subsidiarity principle 353
'substantial qualities' 308, 310
supplier
  definition 356
  responsibility 13
suspension notices, UK 272–6
Sutherland Report 137
Swenson v Emerson Elec. Co. (1985) 235

tariffs 161
technical documentation,
  conformity 103
technical expertise 7, 32, 36, 168
  government intervention 25
technical harmonisation 77–85
  UK 288
technical regulations 71, 169–71, 365
technical standards 345–6, 357
Technical Standards Directive 70–5, 169
  emergency procedures 144
television sets 196
Tesco Supermarkets Ltd v Nattrass 282
testing 33, 110–14
  comparative 306
Testing, Inspection, Calibration Certification and Quality Assurance (TICQA) 112
Thailand, cigarettes 167
third party conformity assessment 8–9, *see also* conformity assessment
third world 38, 237
TICQA *see* Testing, Inspection, Calibration Certification and Quality Assurance
Tobias, C. 216
Tokyo Round 161–2, 168
tolerance, risk 19
Toy Safety Directive 85, 88
toys 2, 84, 85, 196, 305
TPRM *see* Trade Policy Review Mechanism
trade
  inter–state 197
  technical barriers 62–70, 77–85, 161, 365
trade associations, technical knowledge 3
trade barriers
  regional rules 28–9
  standardisation 9

Trade Policy Review Mechanism (TPRM) 163
trade secrets 317
Trade Supervisory Offices (Germany) 335, 337, 349
traders, compensation 49–50
trading blocks 155
trading standards officers (UK) 46, 369
translations 176
transparency, decision–making 264
Treaty of Rome, Arts 30–36 62–7
TRIS 55, 224, 237, 239
TUTB *see* European Trade Union Technical Bureau for Health and Safety
Tyler, M. 256
type–examination 106

UAP *see* Unique Acceptance Procedure
UKAS *see* United Kingdom Accreditation Society
UL *see* Underwriters' Laboratories
UN *see* United Nations
Underwriters' Laboratories (UL) 221, 240
UNEP *see* United Nations Environment Program
Union Technique de l'Electricité (UTE) 305
Unique Acceptance Procedure (UAP) 181
unit verification 109
United Kingdom
see also British
accident data collection 251–3
BSI Consumer Council 31, 34, 37
conformity assessment 112
emergency regulation–making 50
enforcement 256–9, 270–2, 295
General Product Safety Directive
255, 283–6, 294–5
general safety requirement 259–63
government intervention 26
standardisation 286–93
suspension notices 272–6
trading standards officers 46
United Kingdom Accreditation Society (UKAS) 287
United Nations Environment Program (UNEP) 190
United Nations (UN) 160, 189–93
export controls 58–9
United States
see also American
Consumer Product Safety Act 195
Consumer Product Safety Commission 195, 198–240, 302
data collection 14
local enforcement 46
National Commission on Products Safety 2
NEISS 14, 204–6
notification 58
OCD 187
personal injury 4
statutory regulations 8
voluntarism 218–21, 240–9
United States – Section 337 of the Tariff Act of 1930 (1990) 165, 167
United States v Articles of Hazardous Substance (1978) 239
United States v Salem Carpet Mills, Inc. (1980) 239
Uruguay Round 159, 161, 163
use
appropriate 355
conditions of 125
UTE *see* Union Technique de

l'Electricité

Velsico 55
verification, product 108–9
vertical norms 42
vertical regulation 121–3
vertical standards 93, 121–2
Vienna Agreement on Technical
    Co–operation (1991) 93, 180
'Villamora' agreement 75
Viscusi, K. 222–5
voluntarism 8, 218–21

warnings 40, 51–3, 254
Which? 289
WHO *see* World Health

Organisation
'willingness to pay' 20
Women's Advisory Council 290
woodworking machines 66
'World Bank' *see* International
    Bank for Reconstruction and
    Development
World Health Organisation (WHO)
    189
    injury classification 15, 252
World Trade Organisation (WTO)
    159, 160–76
    Standards Codes 163
WTO *see* World Trade
    Organisation
Wyndham–White, Eric 162